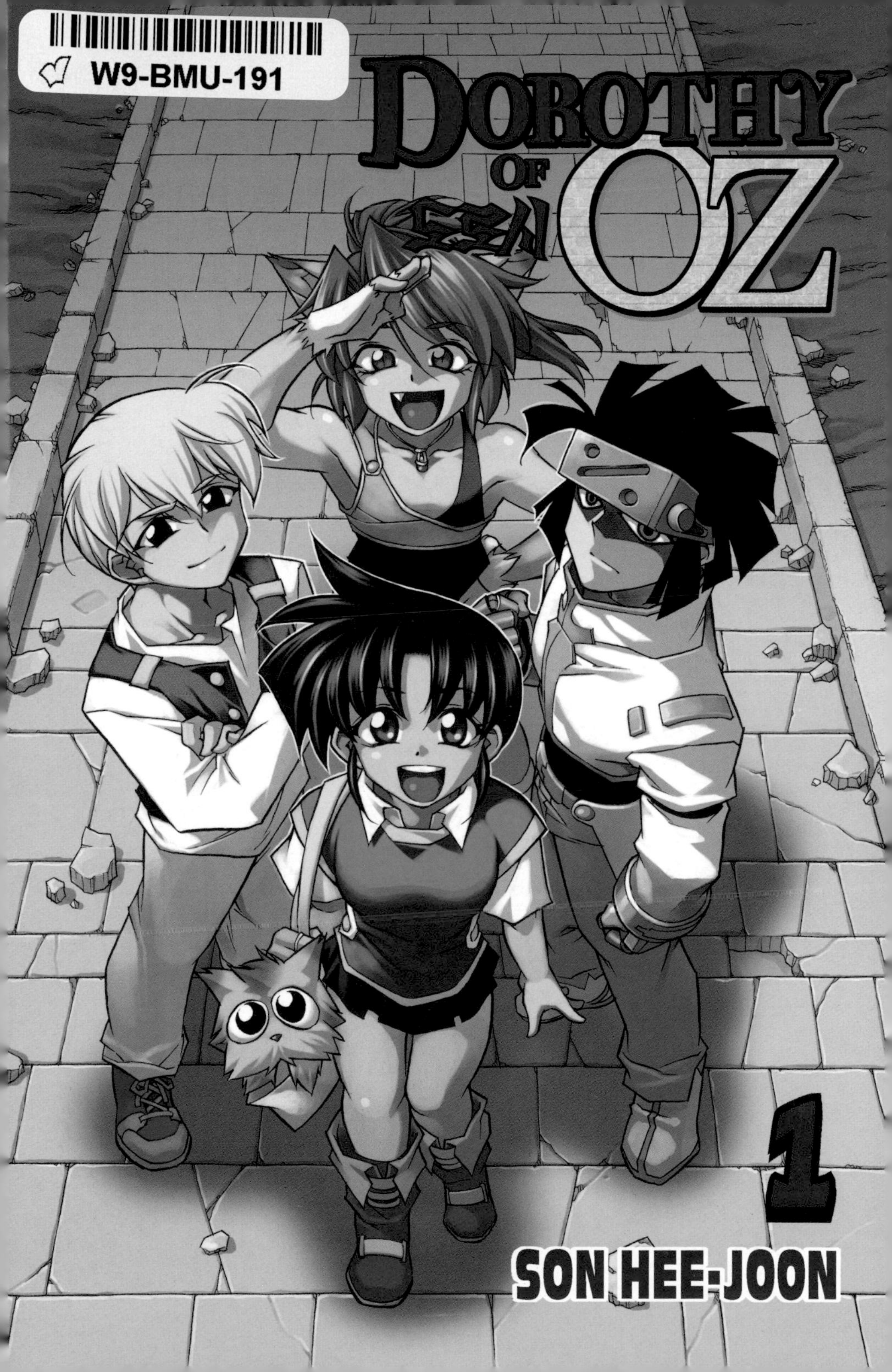
DOROTHY
OF
도로시
OZ
1
SON HEE-JOON

DOROTHY OF OZ 1
CONTENTS

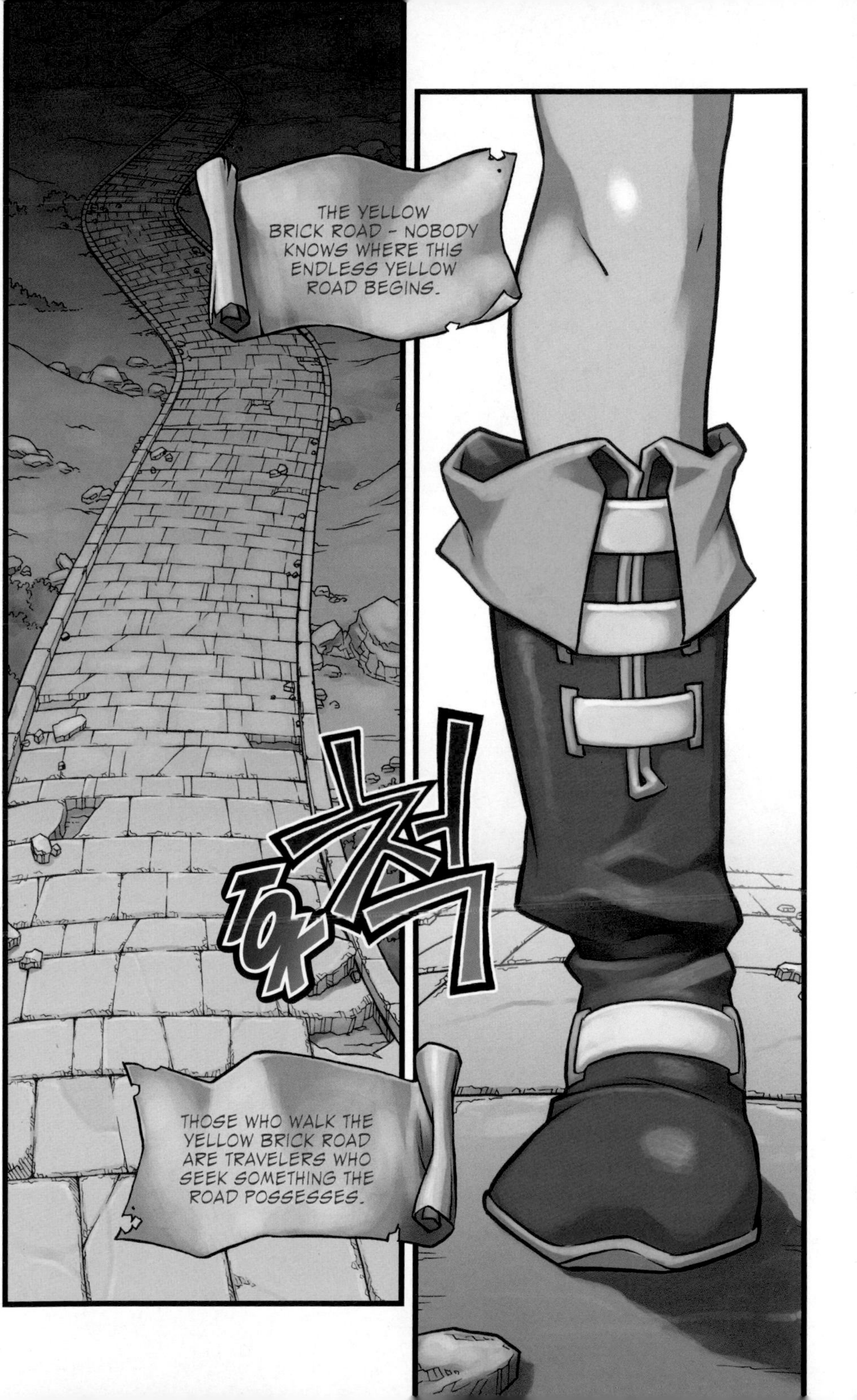
THE YELLOW BRICK ROAD - NOBODY KNOWS WHERE THIS ENDLESS YELLOW ROAD BEGINS.
TOK
THOSE WHO WALK THE YELLOW BRICK ROAD ARE TRAVELERS WHO SEEK SOMETHING THE ROAD POSSESSES.

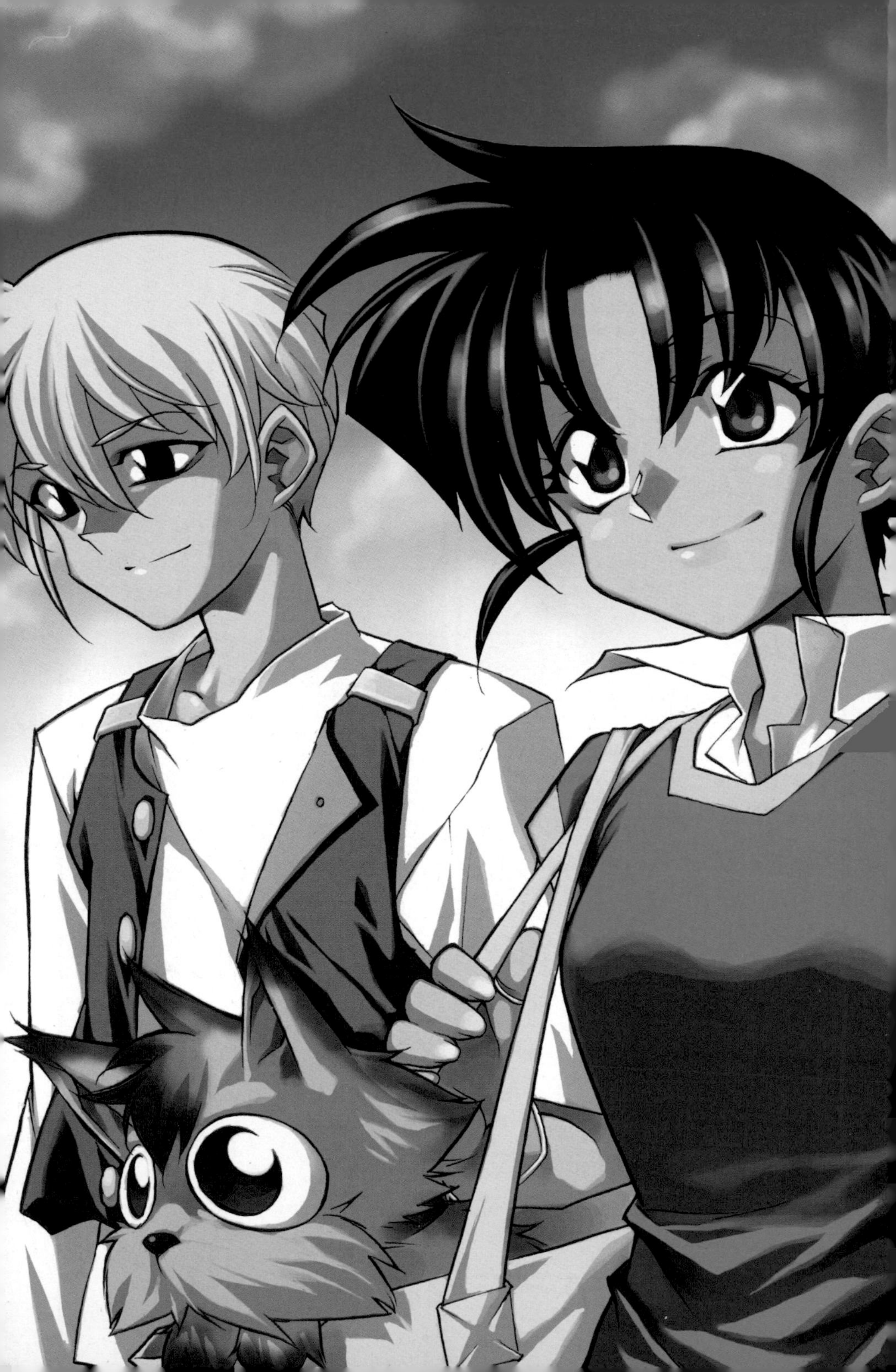

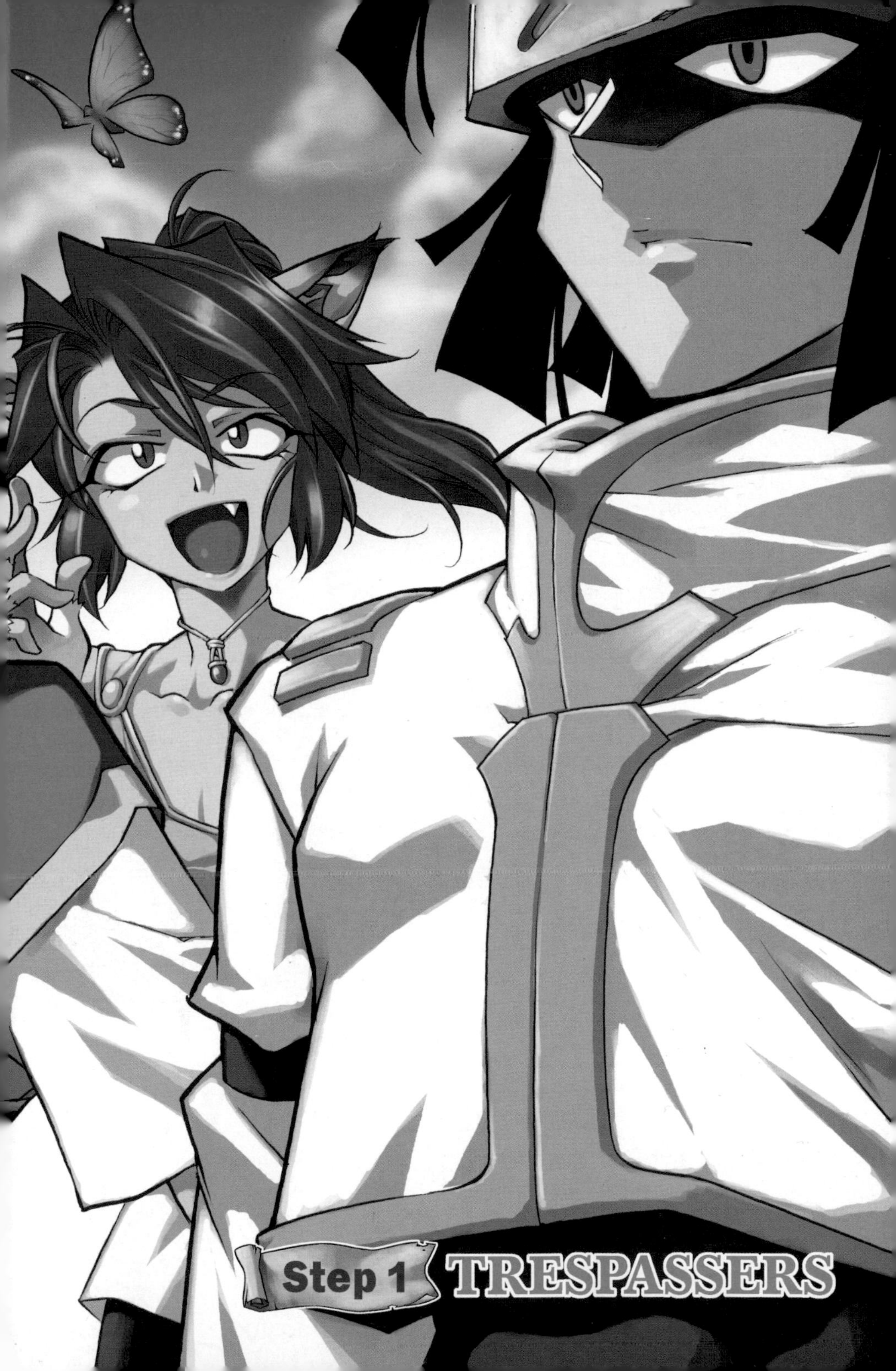
Step 1
TRESPASSERS

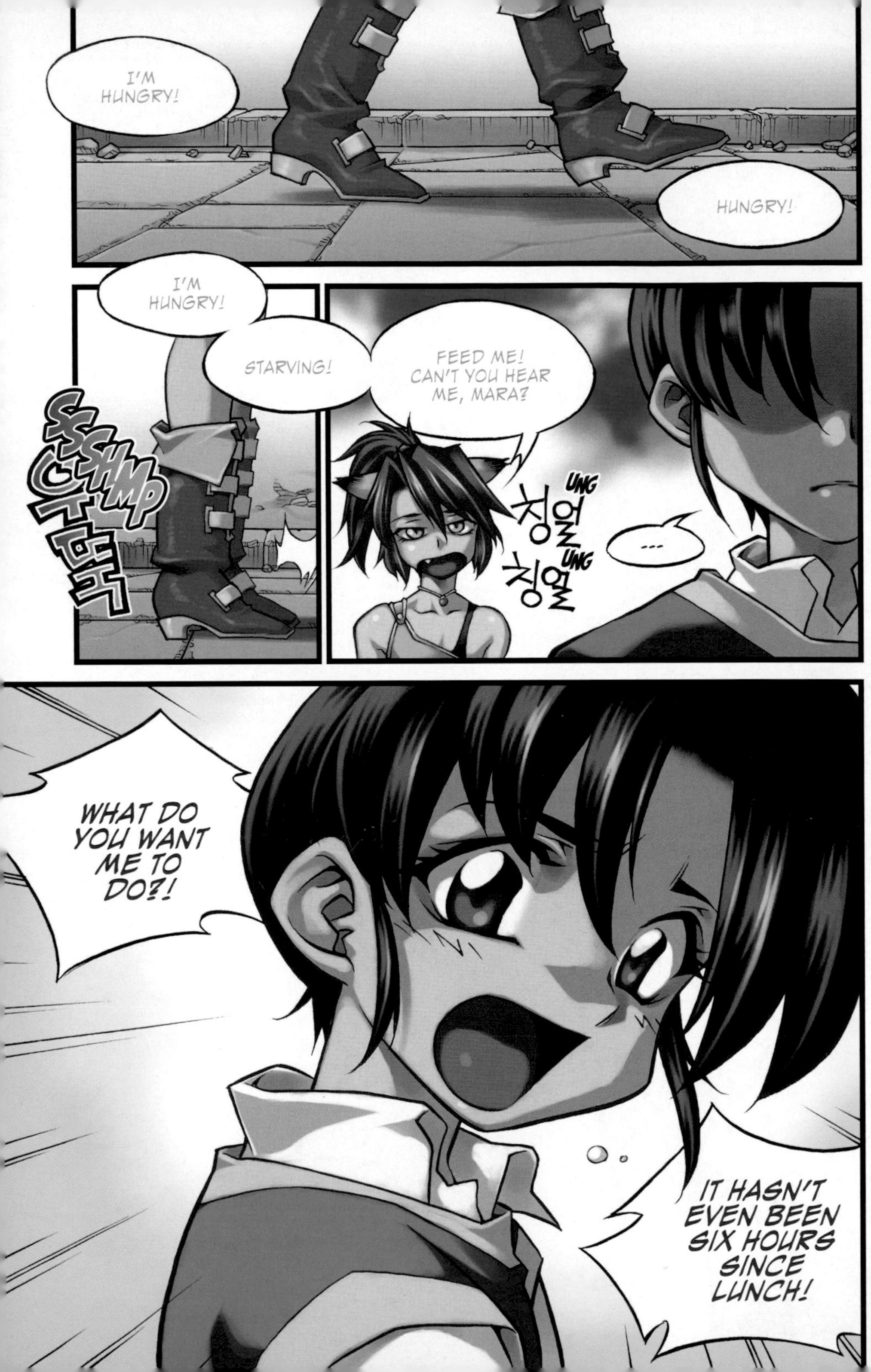
I'M HUNGRY!
HUNGRY!
I'M HUNGRY!
STARVING!
SSSHMP
FEED ME! CAN'T YOU HEAR ME, MARA?
UNG 칭얼
UNG 칭얼
...
WHAT DO YOU WANT ME TO DO?!
IT HASN'T EVEN BEEN SIX HOURS SINCE LUNCH!

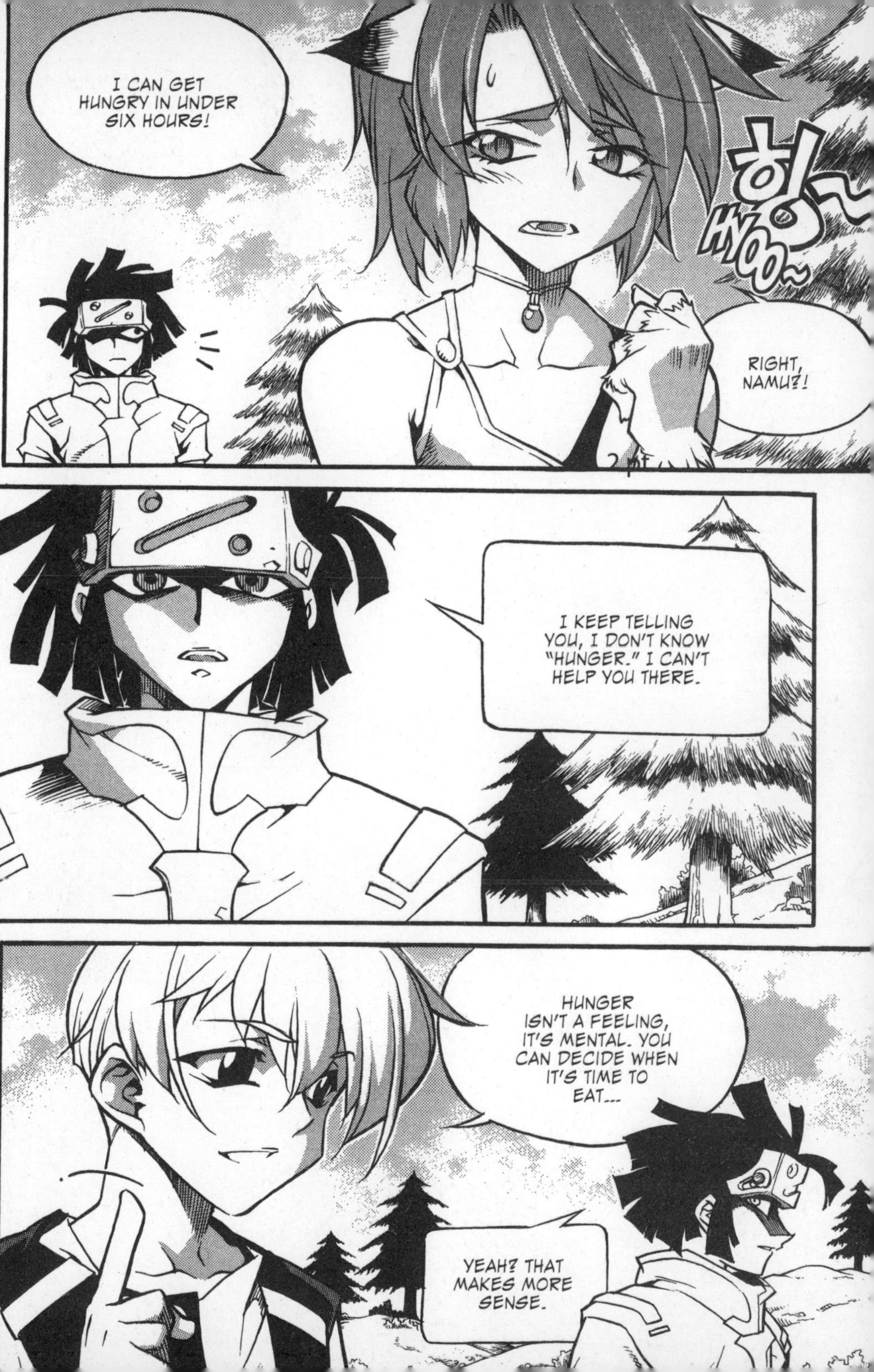
I CAN GET HUNGRY IN UNDER SIX HOURS!
HYOO~
RIGHT, NAMU?!
I KEEP TELLING YOU, I DON'T KNOW "HUNGER." I CAN'T HELP YOU THERE.
HUNGER ISN'T A FEELING, IT'S MENTAL. YOU CAN DECIDE WHEN IT'S TIME TO EAT...
YEAH? THAT MAKES MORE SENSE.

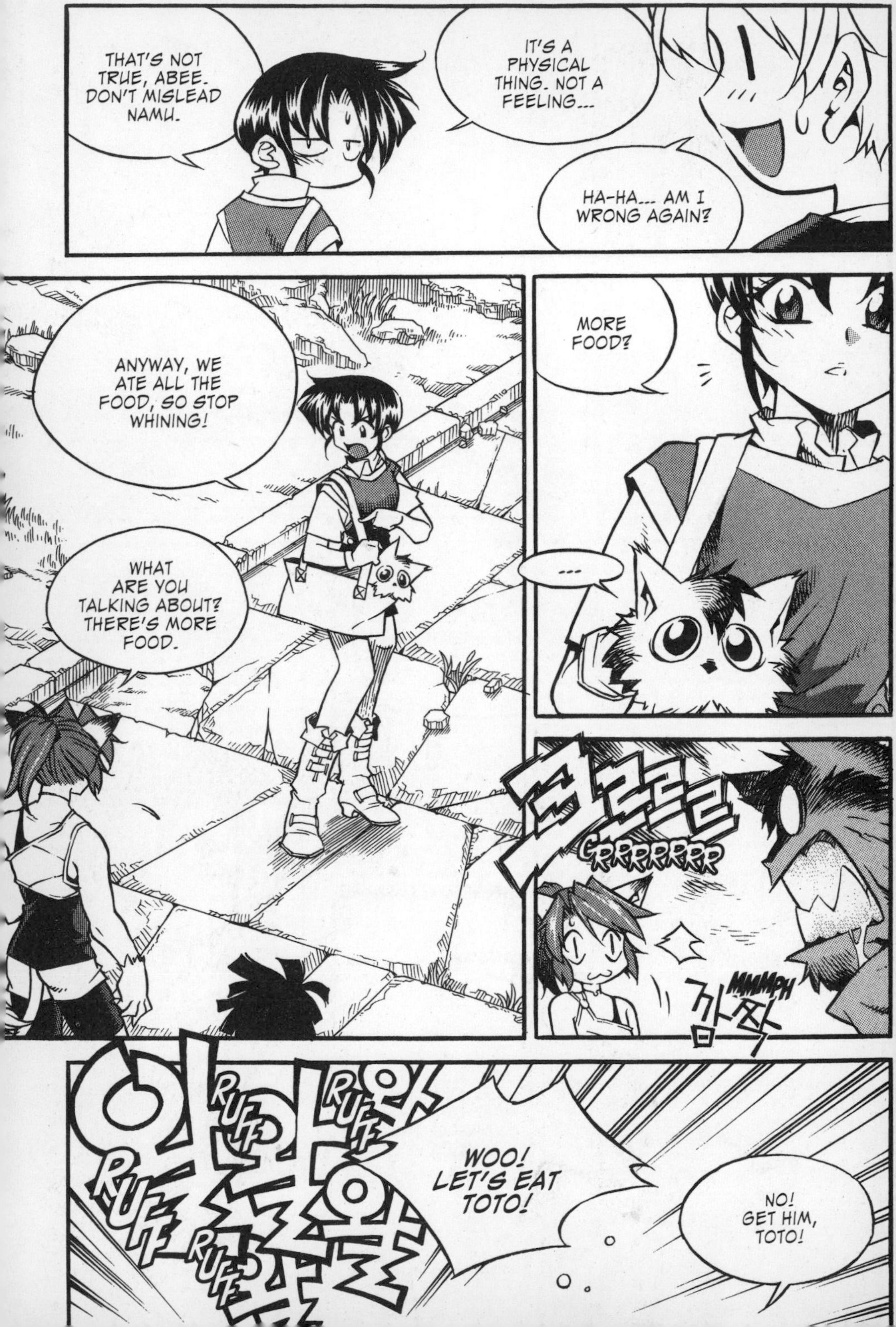
THAT'S NOT TRUE, ABEE. DON'T MISLEAD NAMU.
IT'S A PHYSICAL THING. NOT A FEELING...
HA-HA... AM I WRONG AGAIN?
ANYWAY, WE ATE ALL THE FOOD, SO STOP WHINING!
WHAT ARE YOU TALKING ABOUT? THERE'S MORE FOOD.
MORE FOOD?
...
CRRRRRRR
MMMPH
깜짝
RUFF
RUFF
RUFF
RUFF
WOO! LET'S EAT TOTO!
NO! GET HIM, TOTO!

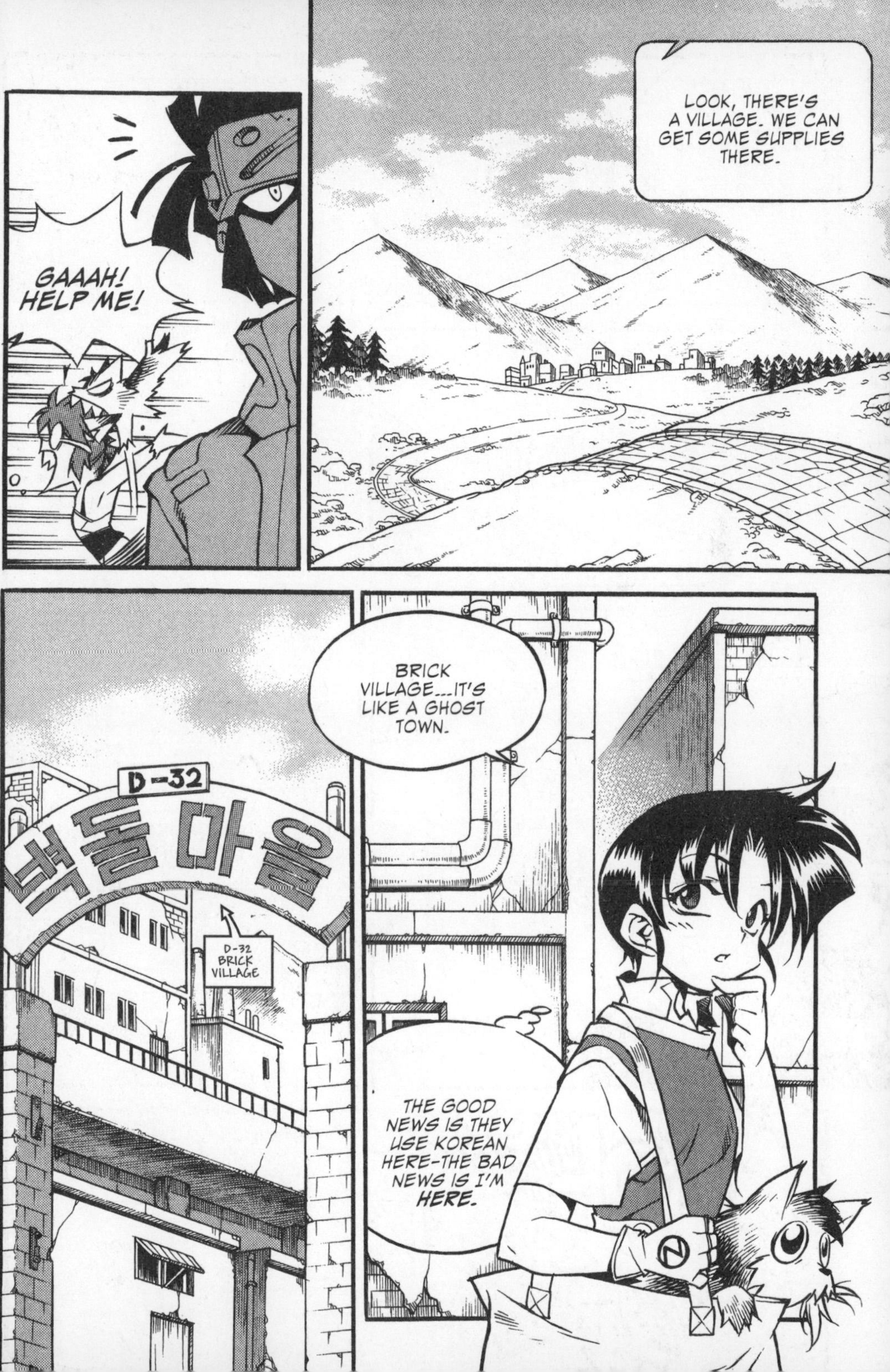
GAAAH! HELP ME!
LOOK, THERE'S A VILLAGE. WE CAN GET SOME SUPPLIES THERE.
D-32
벽돌마을
D-32 BRICK VILLAGE
BRICK VILLAGE...IT'S LIKE A GHOST TOWN.
THE GOOD NEWS IS THEY USE KOREAN HERE–THE BAD NEWS IS I'M *HERE*.

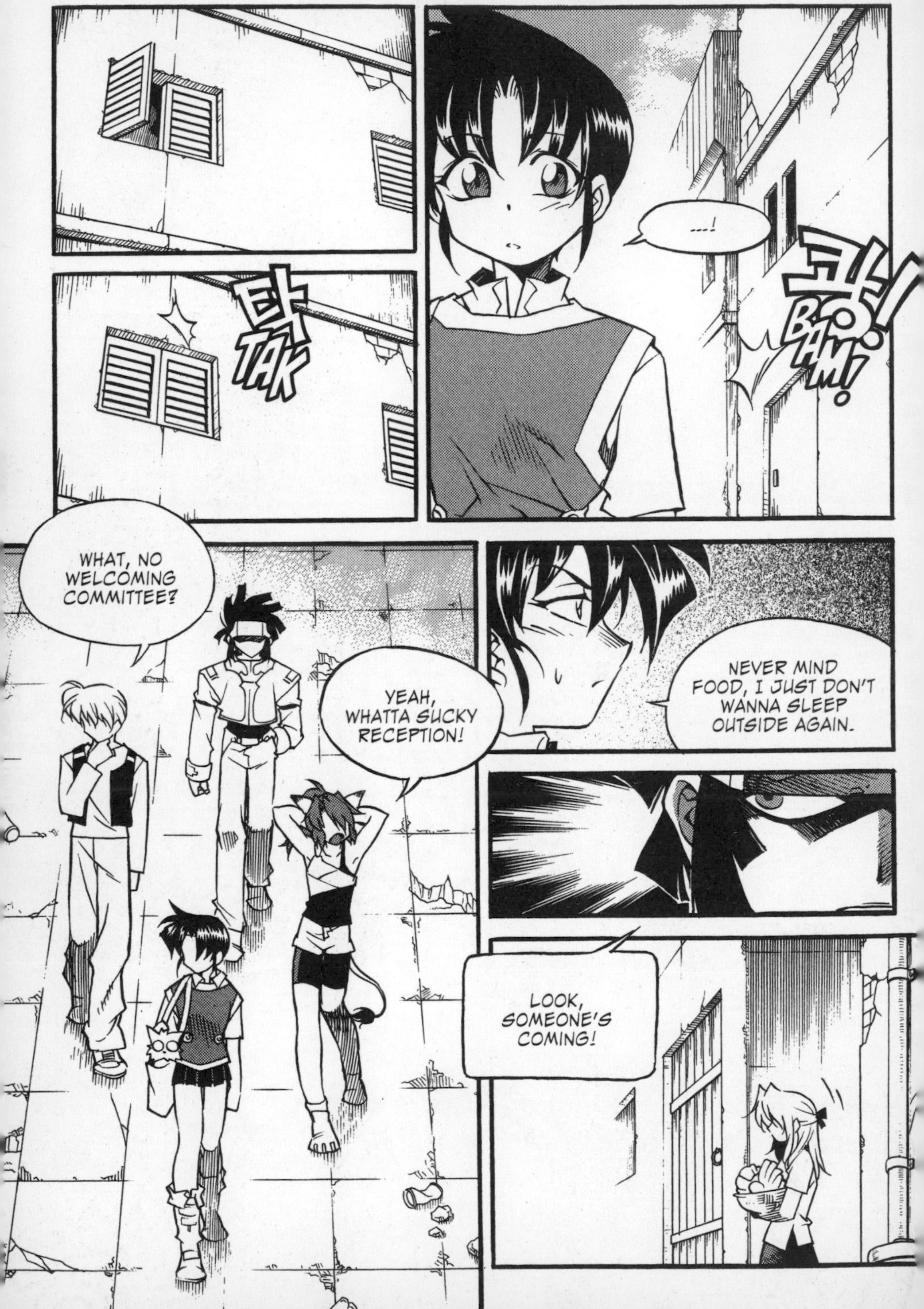
TAK
...!
BAM!
WHAT, NO WELCOMING COMMITTEE?
YEAH, WHATTA SUCKY RECEPTION!
NEVER MIND FOOD, I JUST DON'T WANNA SLEEP OUTSIDE AGAIN.
LOOK, SOMEONE'S COMING!

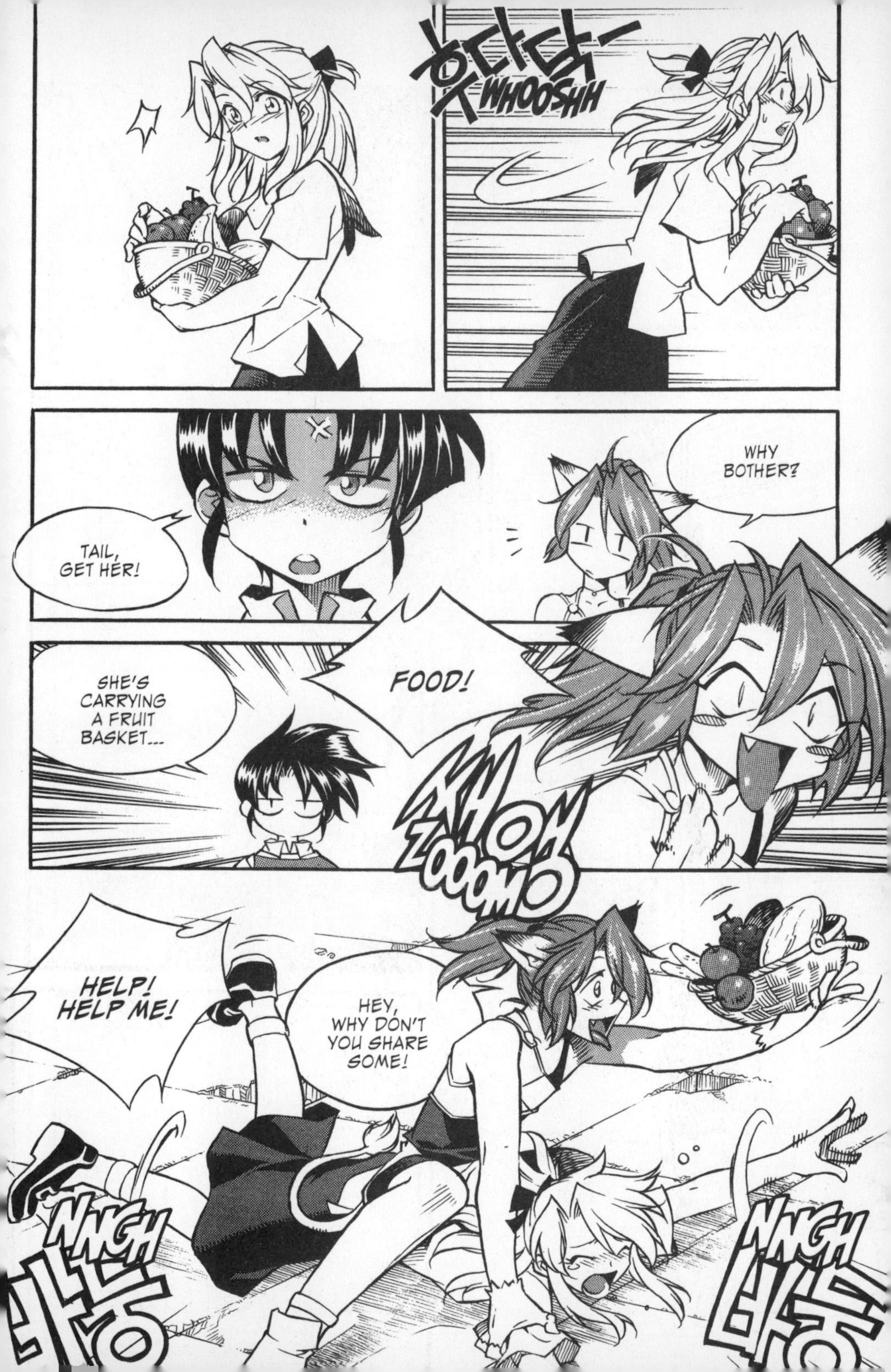
WHOOSHH
TAIL, GET HER!
WHY BOTHER?
SHE'S CARRYING A FRUIT BASKET...
FOOD!
ZOOOM
HELP! HELP ME!
HEY, WHY DON'T YOU SHARE SOME!
NNGH
NNGH

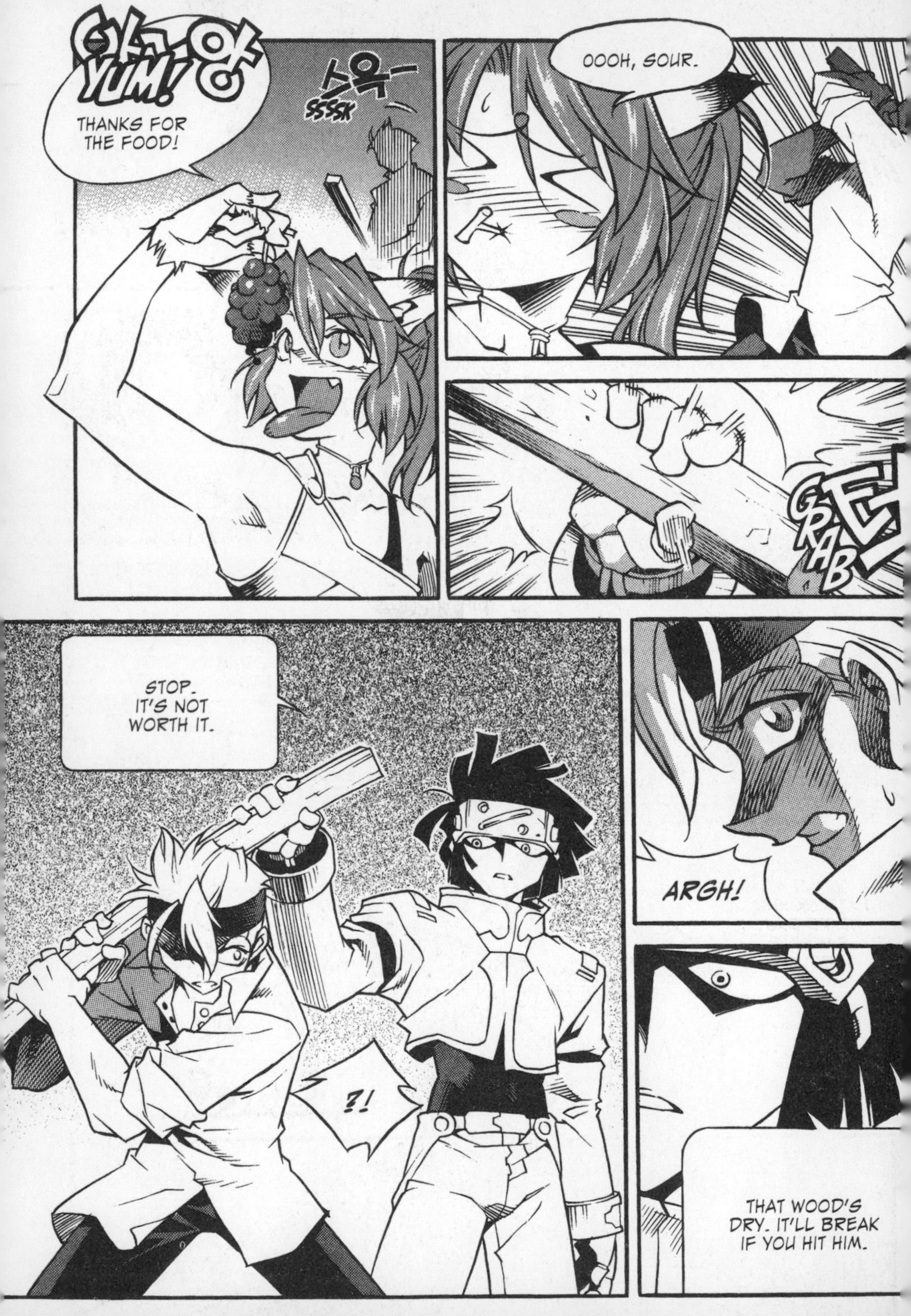
YUM!
THANKS FOR THE FOOD!
SSSSK
OOOH, SOUR.
GRAB
STOP. IT'S NOT WORTH IT.
?!
ARGH!
THAT WOOD'S DRY. IT'LL BREAK IF YOU HIT HIM.

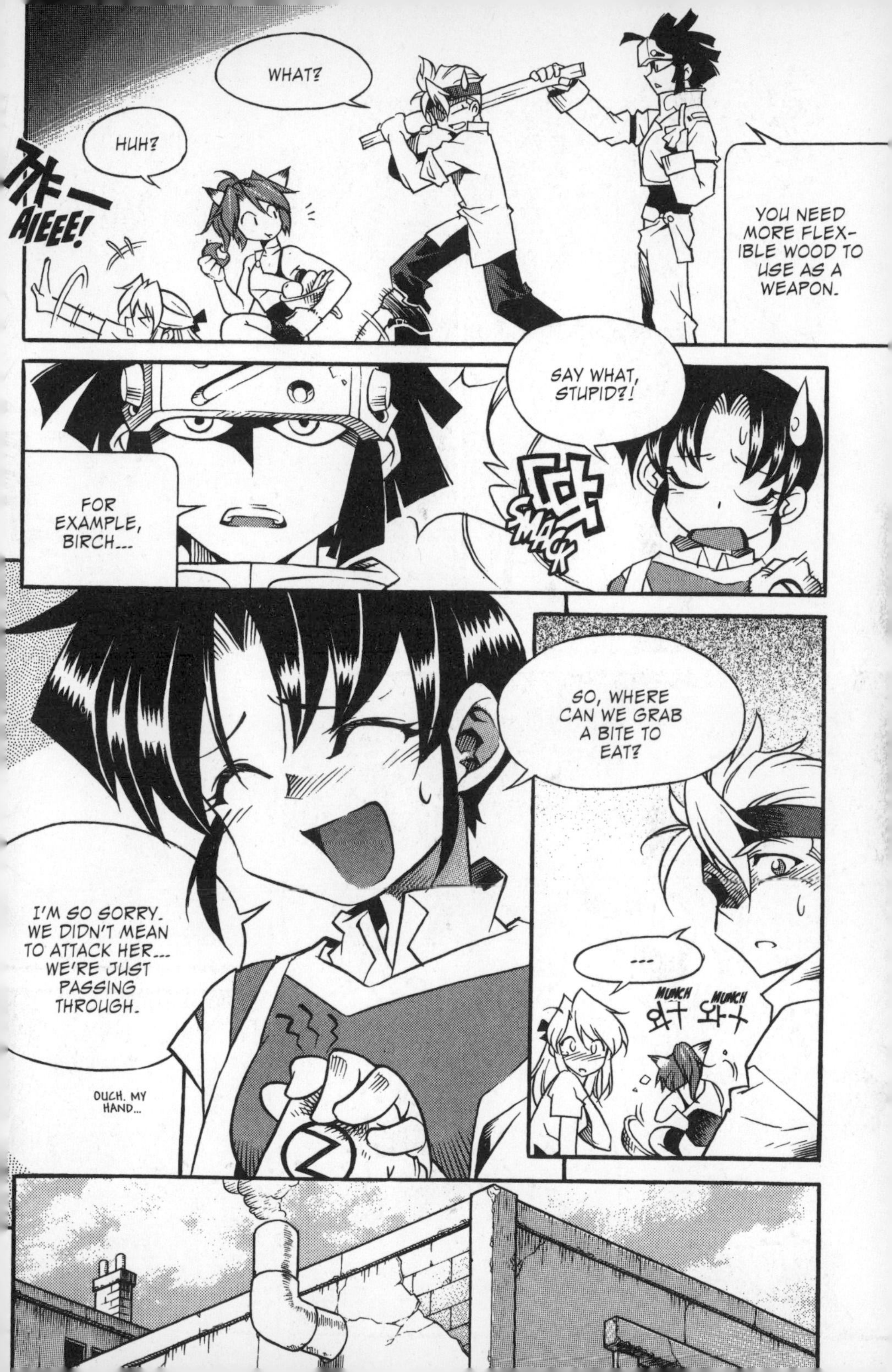
AIEEE!
HUH?
WHAT?
YOU NEED MORE FLEX-IBLE WOOD TO USE AS A WEAPON.
FOR EXAMPLE, BIRCH...
SAY WHAT, STUPID?!
SMACK
I'M SO SORRY. WE DIDN'T MEAN TO ATTACK HER... WE'RE JUST PASSING THROUGH.
OUCH. MY HAND...
SO, WHERE CAN WE GRAB A BITE TO EAT?
...
MUNCH MUNCH

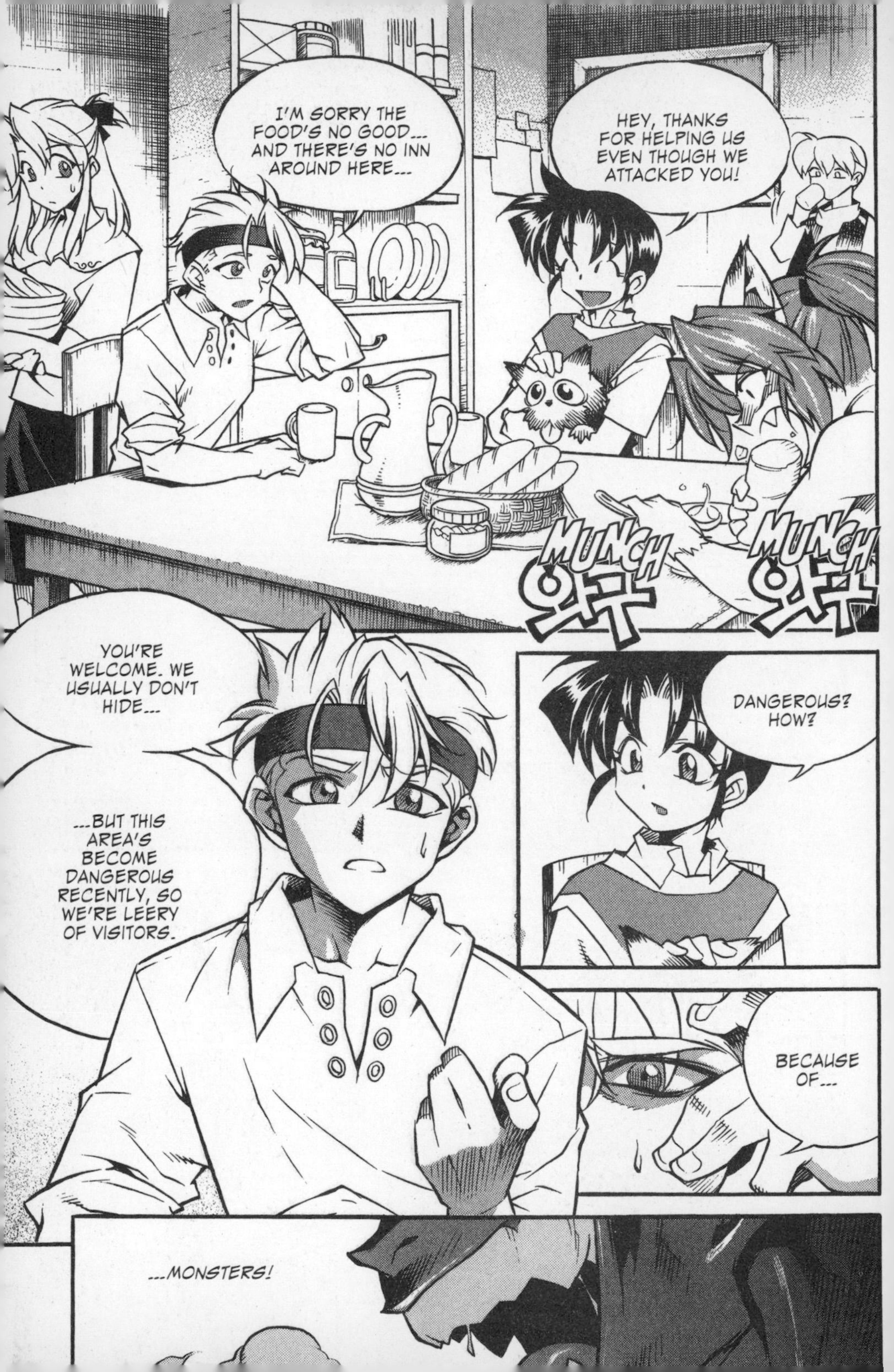
I'M SORRY THE FOOD'S NO GOOD... AND THERE'S NO INN AROUND HERE...
HEY, THANKS FOR HELPING US EVEN THOUGH WE ATTACKED YOU!
MUNCH
와구
MUNCH
와구
YOU'RE WELCOME. WE USUALLY DON'T HIDE...
...BUT THIS AREA'S BECOME DANGEROUS RECENTLY, SO WE'RE LEERY OF VISITORS.
DANGEROUS? HOW?
BECAUSE OF...
...MONSTERS!

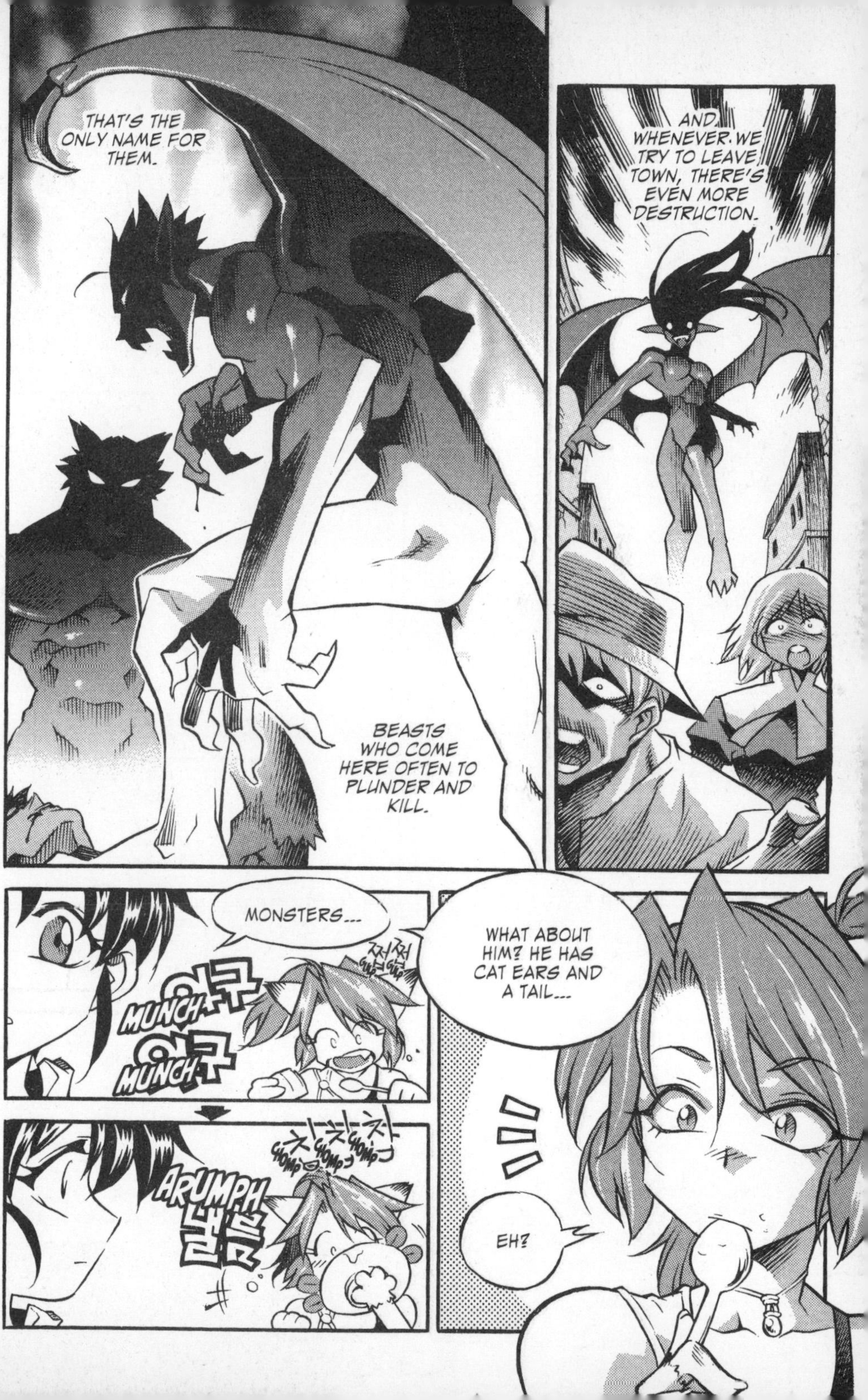
THAT'S THE ONLY NAME FOR THEM.
BEASTS WHO COME HERE OFTEN TO PLUNDER AND KILL.
AND WHENEVER WE TRY TO LEAVE TOWN, THERE'S EVEN MORE DESTRUCTION.
MONSTERS...
GULP GULP
MUNCH
MUNCH
CHOMP CHOMP CHOMP
ARUMPH
널름
WHAT ABOUT HIM? HE HAS CAT EARS AND A TAIL...
EH?

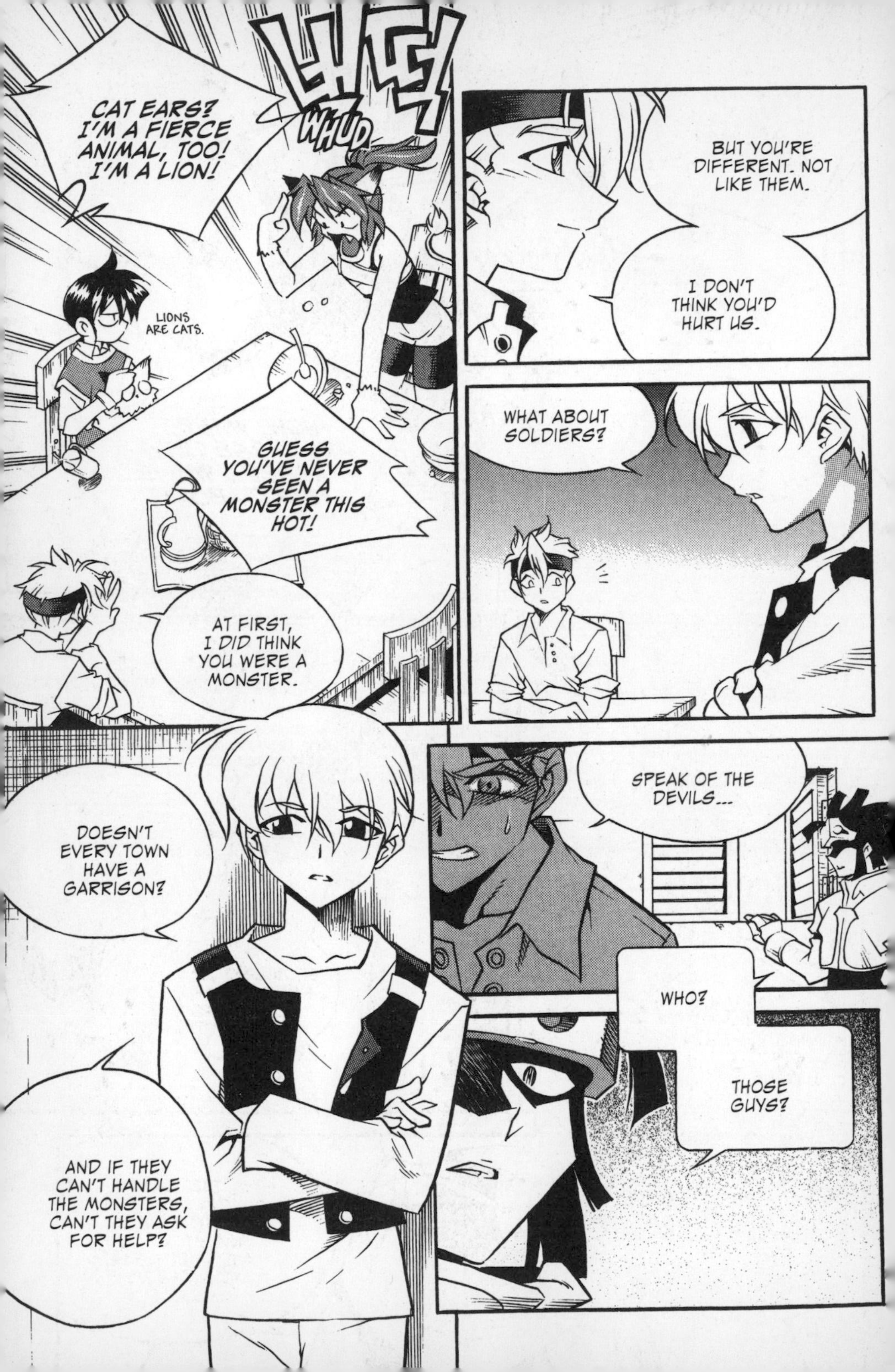
CAT EARS? I'M A FIERCE ANIMAL, TOO! I'M A LION!
WHUD
LIONS ARE CATS.
GUESS YOU'VE NEVER SEEN A MONSTER THIS HOT!
AT FIRST, I DID THINK YOU WERE A MONSTER.
BUT YOU'RE DIFFERENT. NOT LIKE THEM.
I DON'T THINK YOU'D HURT US.
WHAT ABOUT SOLDIERS?
DOESN'T EVERY TOWN HAVE A GARRISON?
AND IF THEY CAN'T HANDLE THE MONSTERS, CAN'T THEY ASK FOR HELP?
SPEAK OF THE DEVILS...
WHO?
THOSE GUYS?

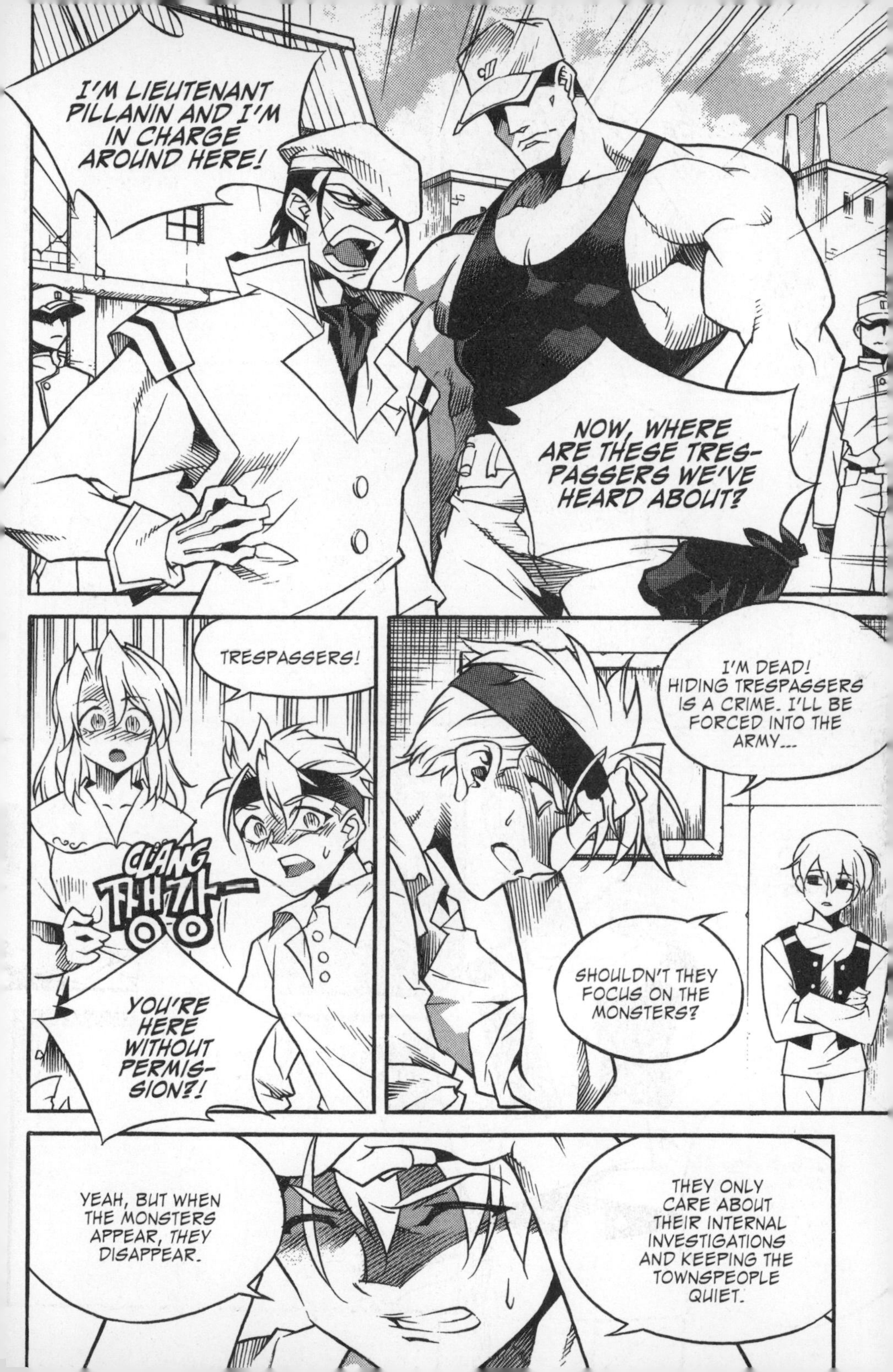
I'M LIEUTENANT PILLANIN AND I'M IN CHARGE AROUND HERE!
NOW, WHERE ARE THESE TRES-PASSERS WE'VE HEARD ABOUT?
TRESPASSERS!
CLANG
YOU'RE HERE WITHOUT PERMIS-SION?!
I'M DEAD! HIDING TRESPASSERS IS A CRIME. I'LL BE FORCED INTO THE ARMY...
SHOULDN'T THEY FOCUS ON THE MONSTERS?
YEAH, BUT WHEN THE MONSTERS APPEAR, THEY DISAPPEAR.
THEY ONLY CARE ABOUT THEIR INTERNAL INVESTIGATIONS AND KEEPING THE TOWNSPEOPLE QUIET.

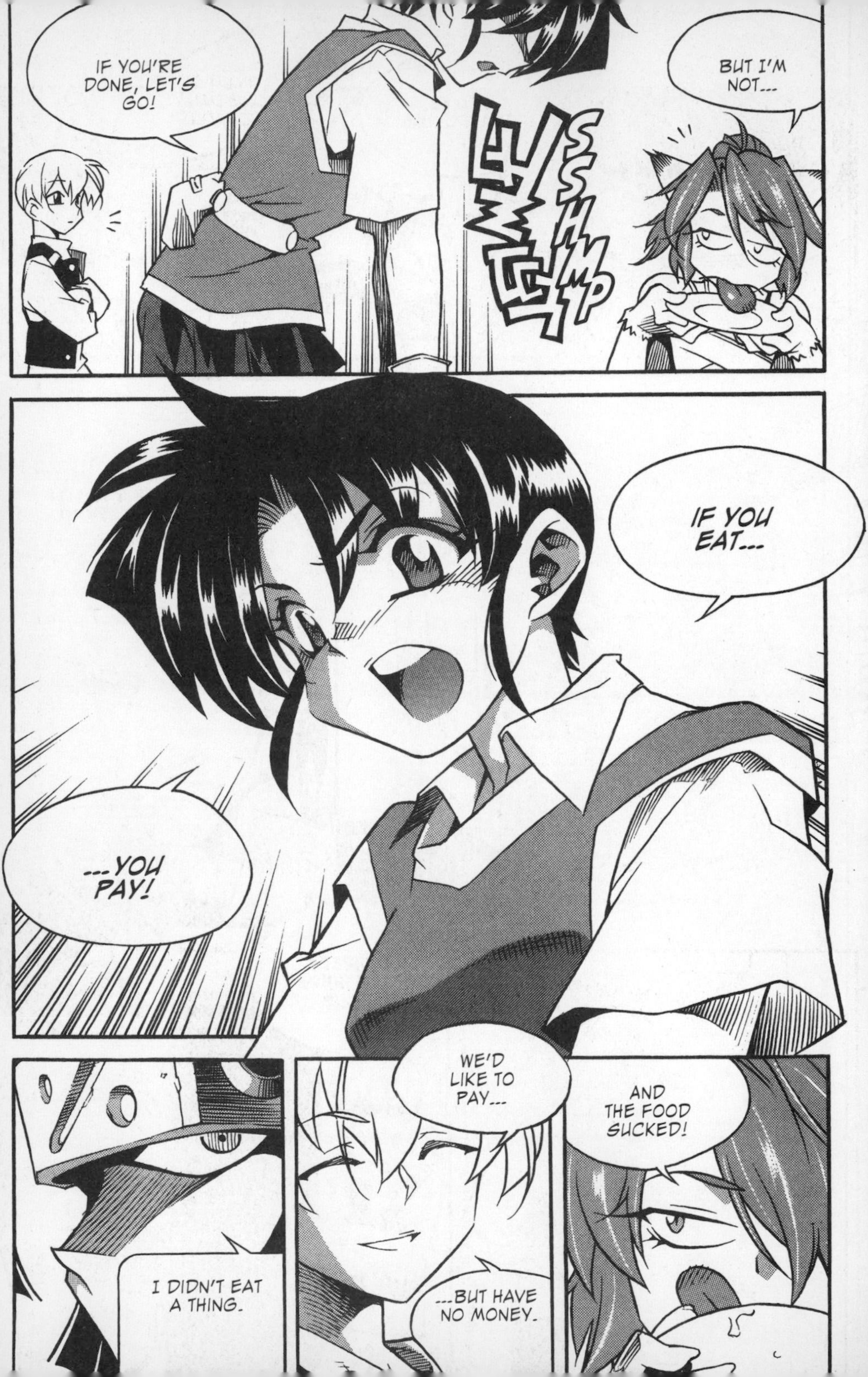
IF YOU'RE DONE, LET'S GO!
BUT I'M NOT...
IF YOU EAT...
...YOU PAY!
I DIDN'T EAT A THING.
WE'D LIKE TO PAY...
AND THE FOOD SUCKED!
...BUT HAVE NO MONEY.

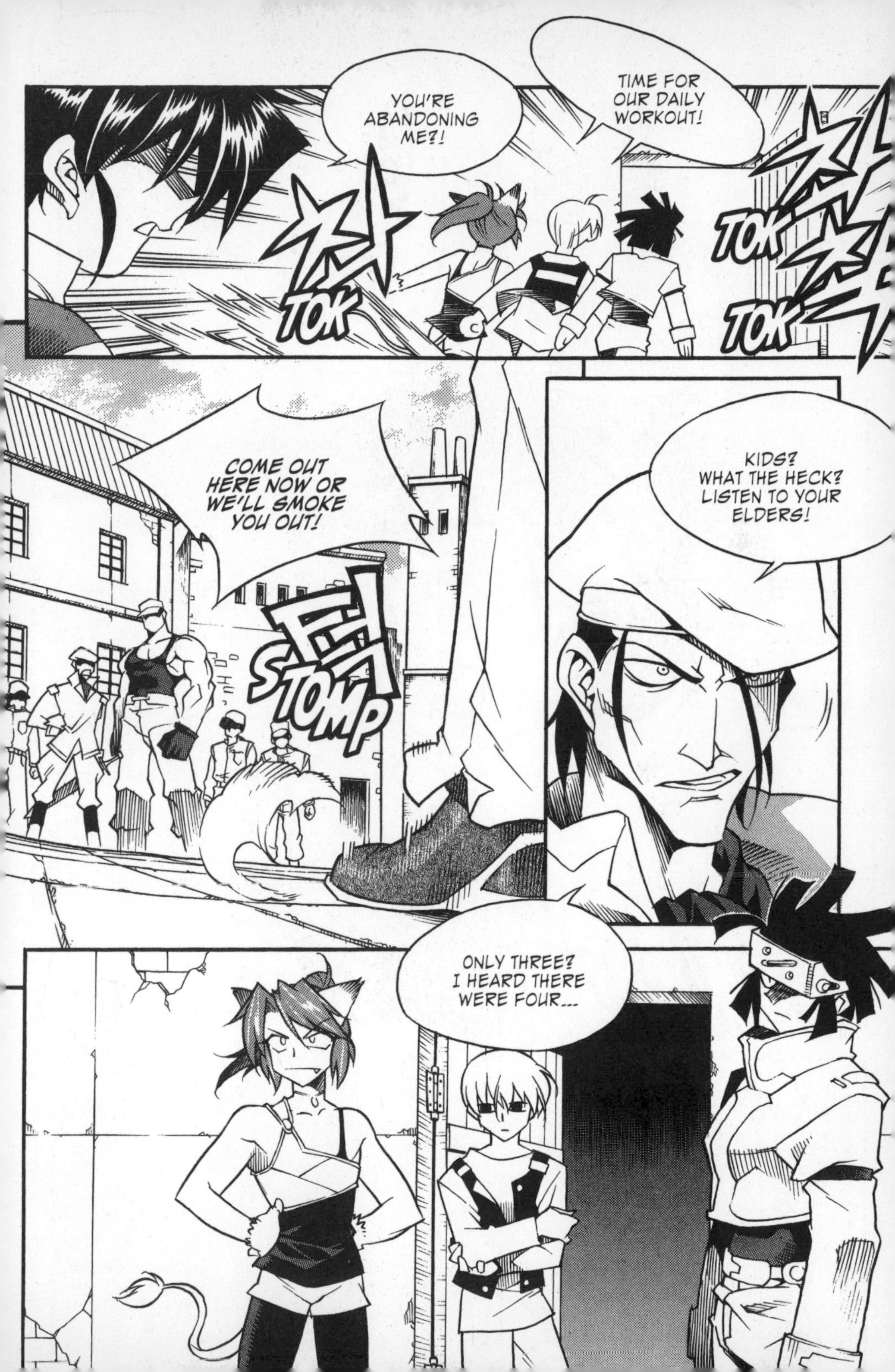
YOU'RE ABANDONING ME?!
TIME FOR OUR DAILY WORKOUT!
TOK
TOK
TOK
COME OUT HERE NOW OR WE'LL SMOKE YOU OUT!
STOMP
KIDS? WHAT THE HECK? LISTEN TO YOUR ELDERS!
ONLY THREE? I HEARD THERE WERE FOUR...

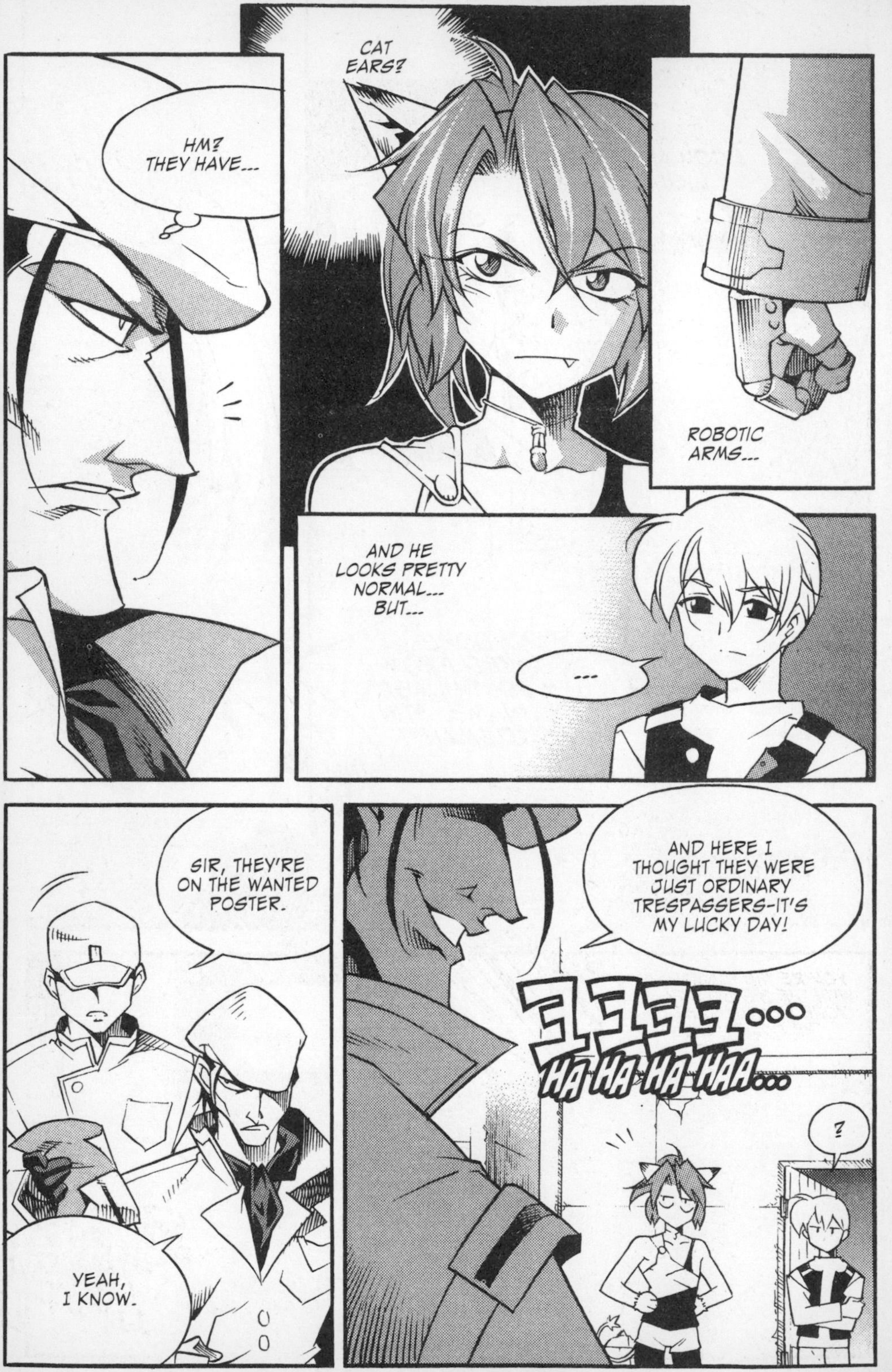
HM? THEY HAVE...
CAT EARS?
ROBOTIC ARMS...
AND HE LOOKS PRETTY NORMAL... BUT...
...
SIR, THEY'RE ON THE WANTED POSTER.
YEAH, I KNOW.
AND HERE I THOUGHT THEY WERE JUST ORDINARY TRESPASSERS-IT'S MY LUCKY DAY!
HA HA HA HAA...
?

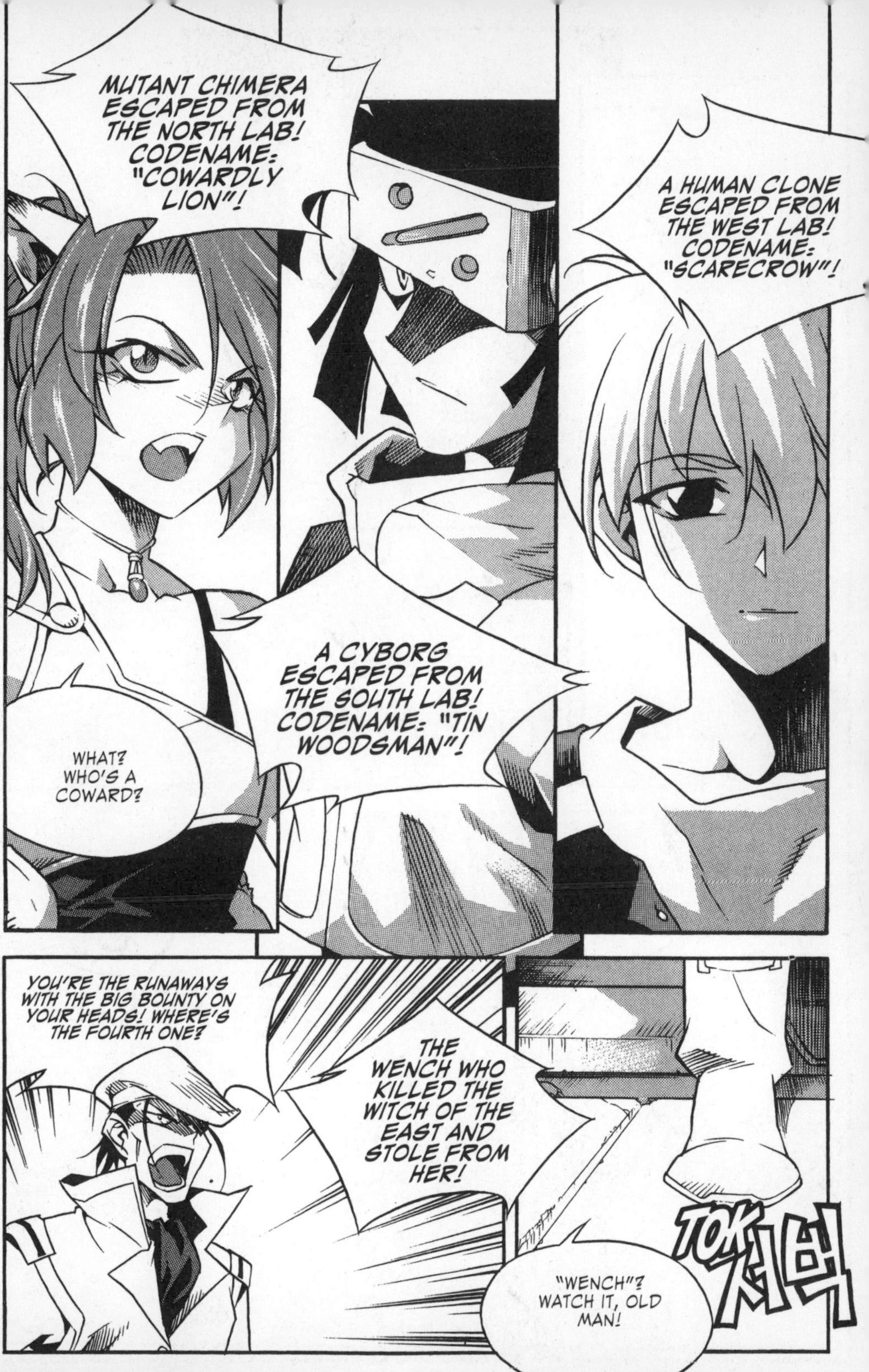
MUTANT CHIMERA ESCAPED FROM THE NORTH LAB! CODENAME: "COWARDLY LION"!
WHAT? WHO'S A COWARD?
A CYBORG ESCAPED FROM THE SOUTH LAB! CODENAME: "TIN WOODSMAN"!
A HUMAN CLONE ESCAPED FROM THE WEST LAB! CODENAME: "SCARECROW"!
YOU'RE THE RUNAWAYS WITH THE BIG BOUNTY ON YOUR HEADS! WHERE'S THE FOURTH ONE?
THE WENCH WHO KILLED THE WITCH OF THE EAST AND STOLE FROM HER!
TOK
"WENCH"? WATCH IT, OLD MAN!

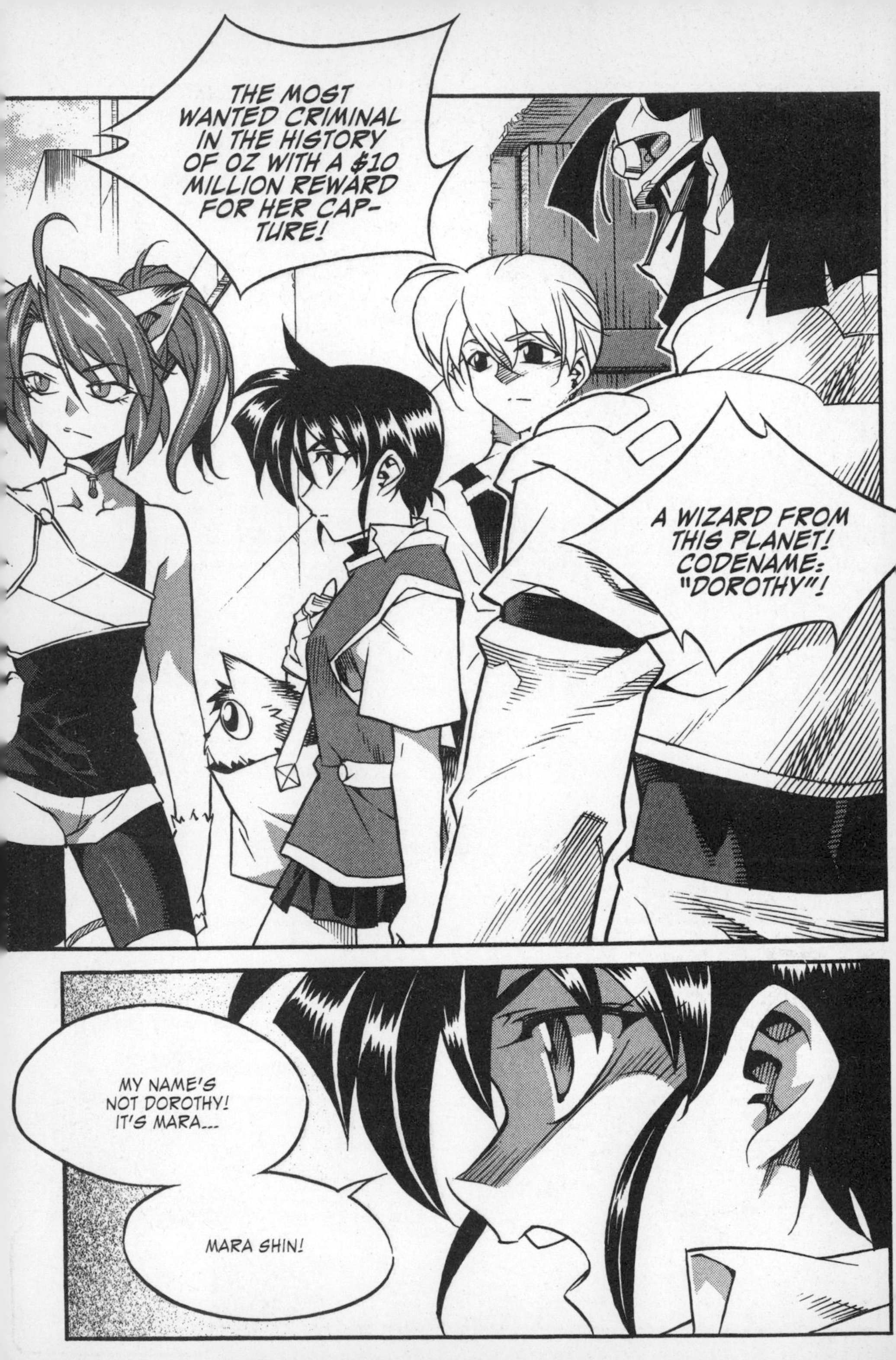
THE MOST WANTED CRIMINAL IN THE HISTORY OF OZ WITH A $10 MILLION REWARD FOR HER CAPTURE!
A WIZARD FROM THIS PLANET! CODENAME: "DOROTHY"!
MY NAME'S NOT DOROTHY! IT'S MARA...
MARA SHIN!

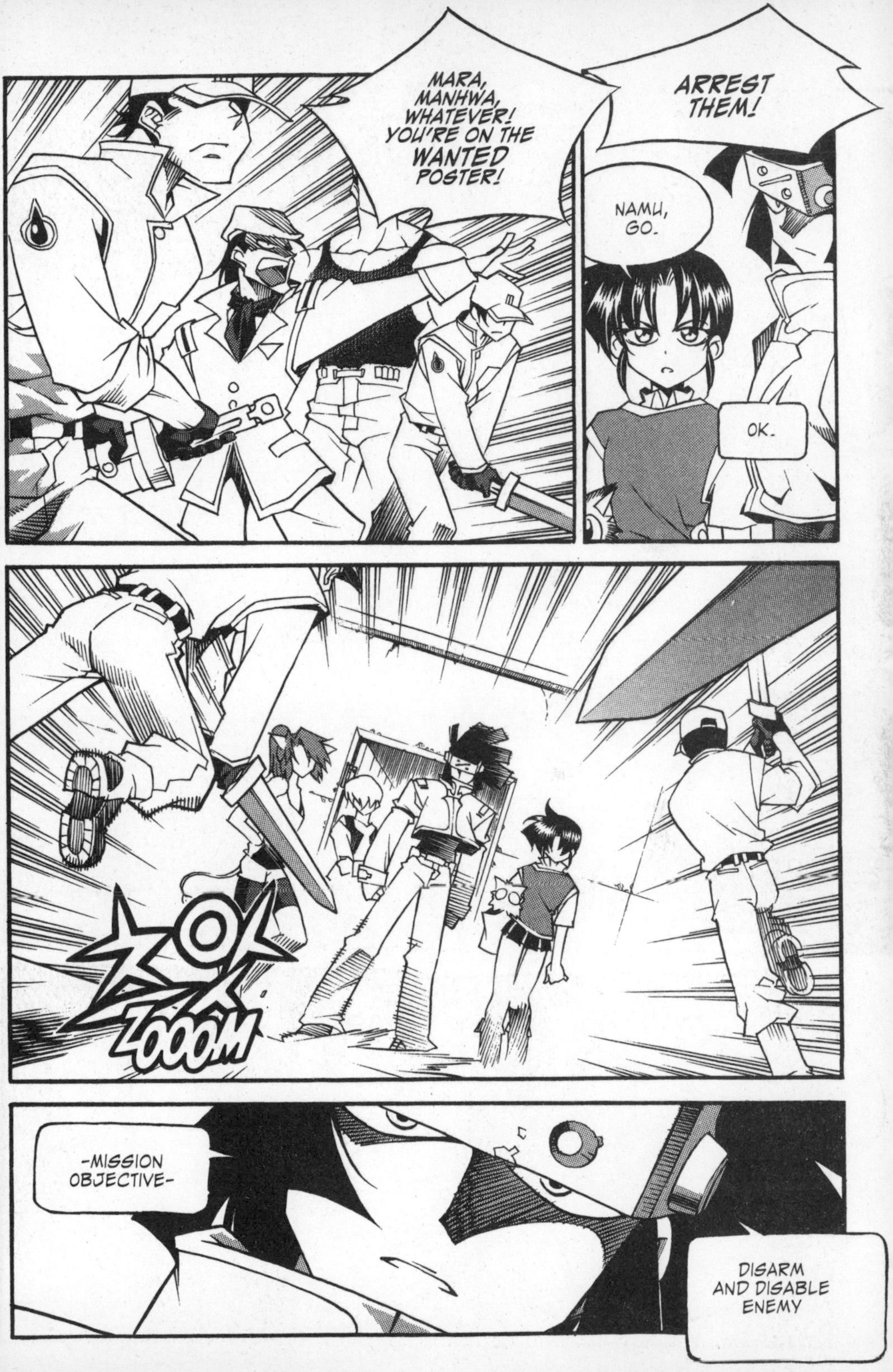
MARA, MANHWA, WHATEVER! YOU'RE ON THE WANTED POSTER!
ARREST THEM!
NAMU, GO.
OK.
ZOOOM
-MISSION OBJECTIVE-
DISARM AND DISABLE ENEMY

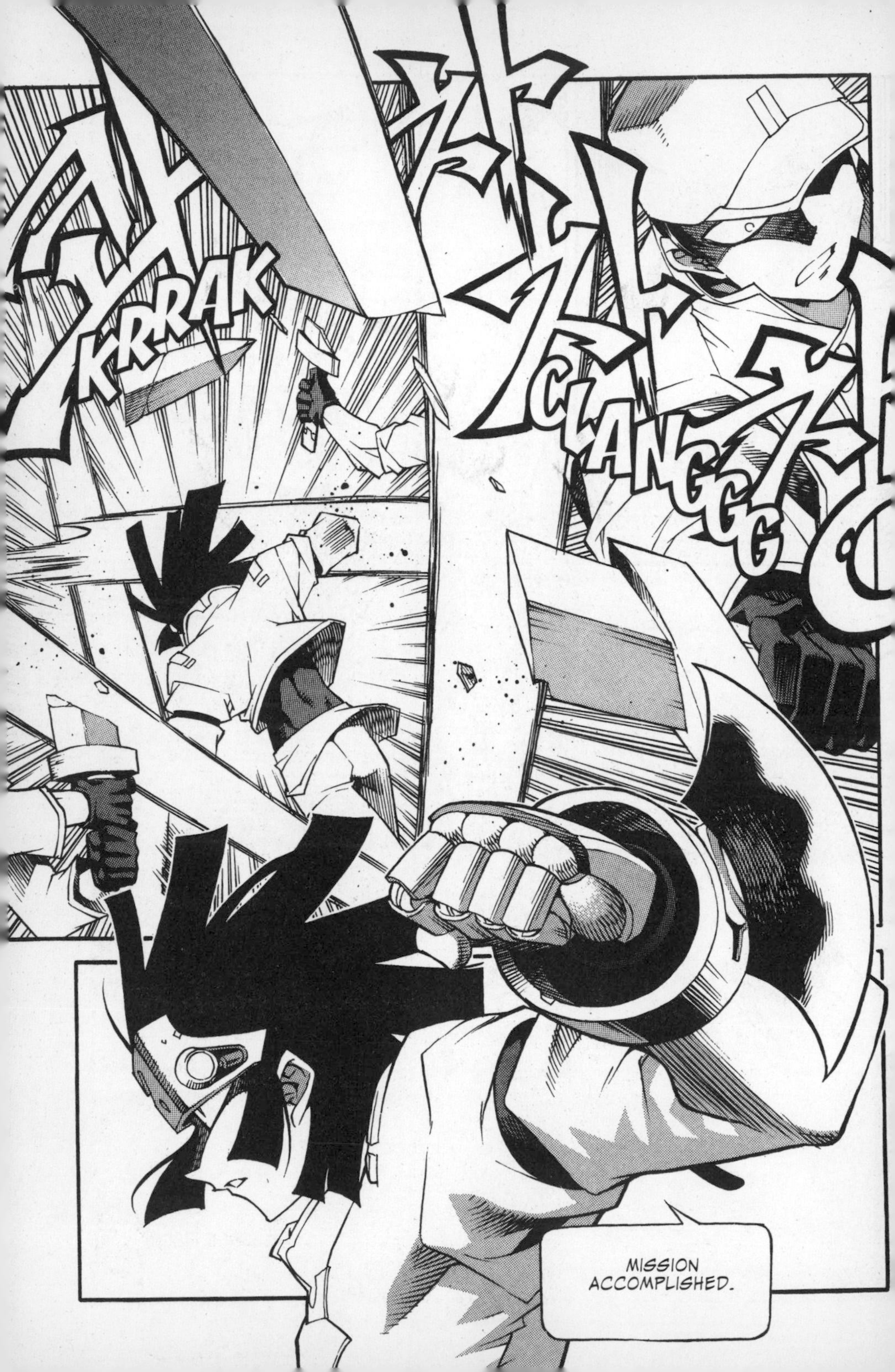
KRRAK
CLANGGG
MISSION ACCOMPLISHED.

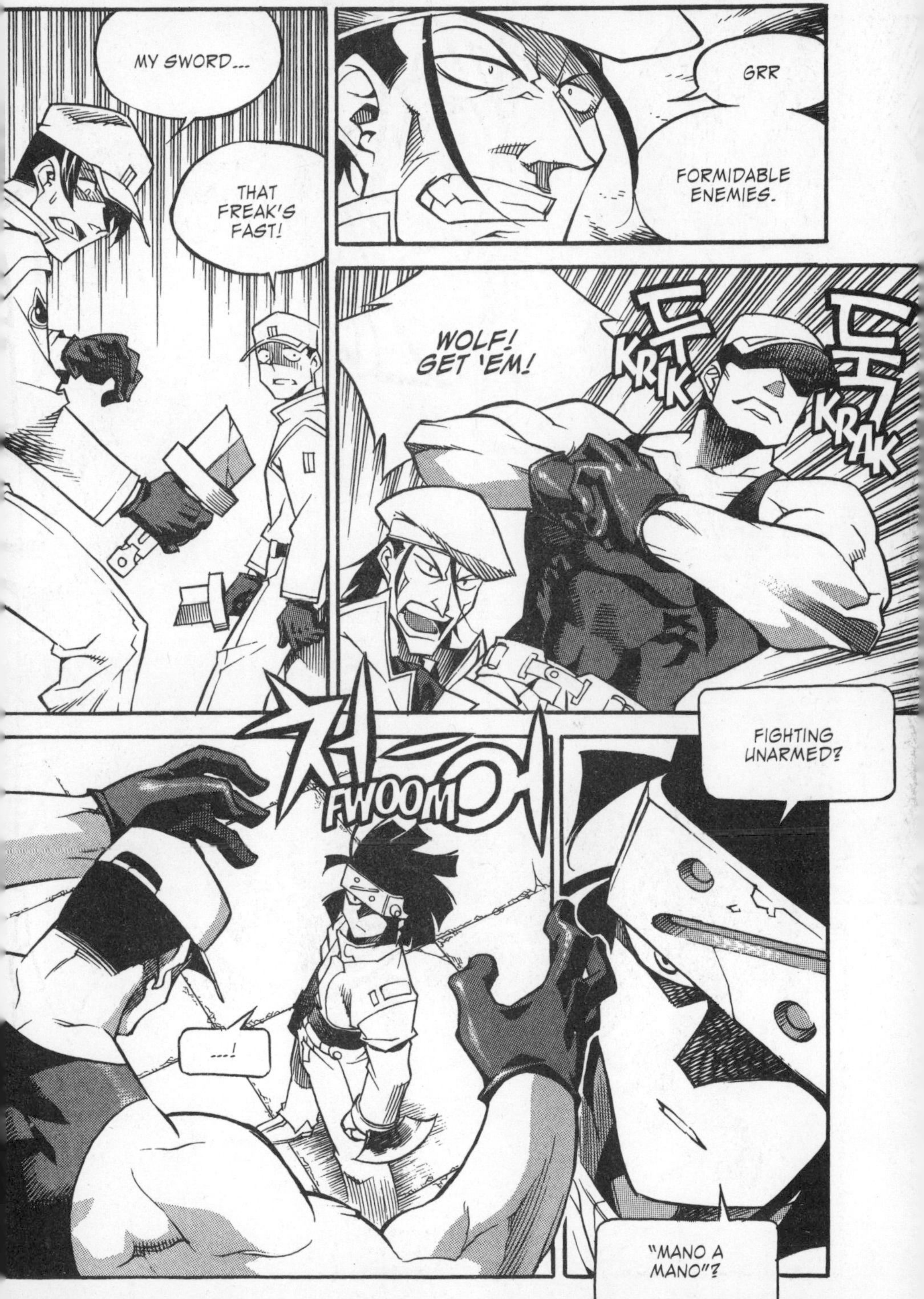
MY SWORD...
THAT FREAK'S FAST!
GRR
FORMIDABLE ENEMIES.
WOLF! GET 'EM!
KRIK
KRAK
FWOOM
...!
FIGHTING UNARMED?
"MANO A MANO"?

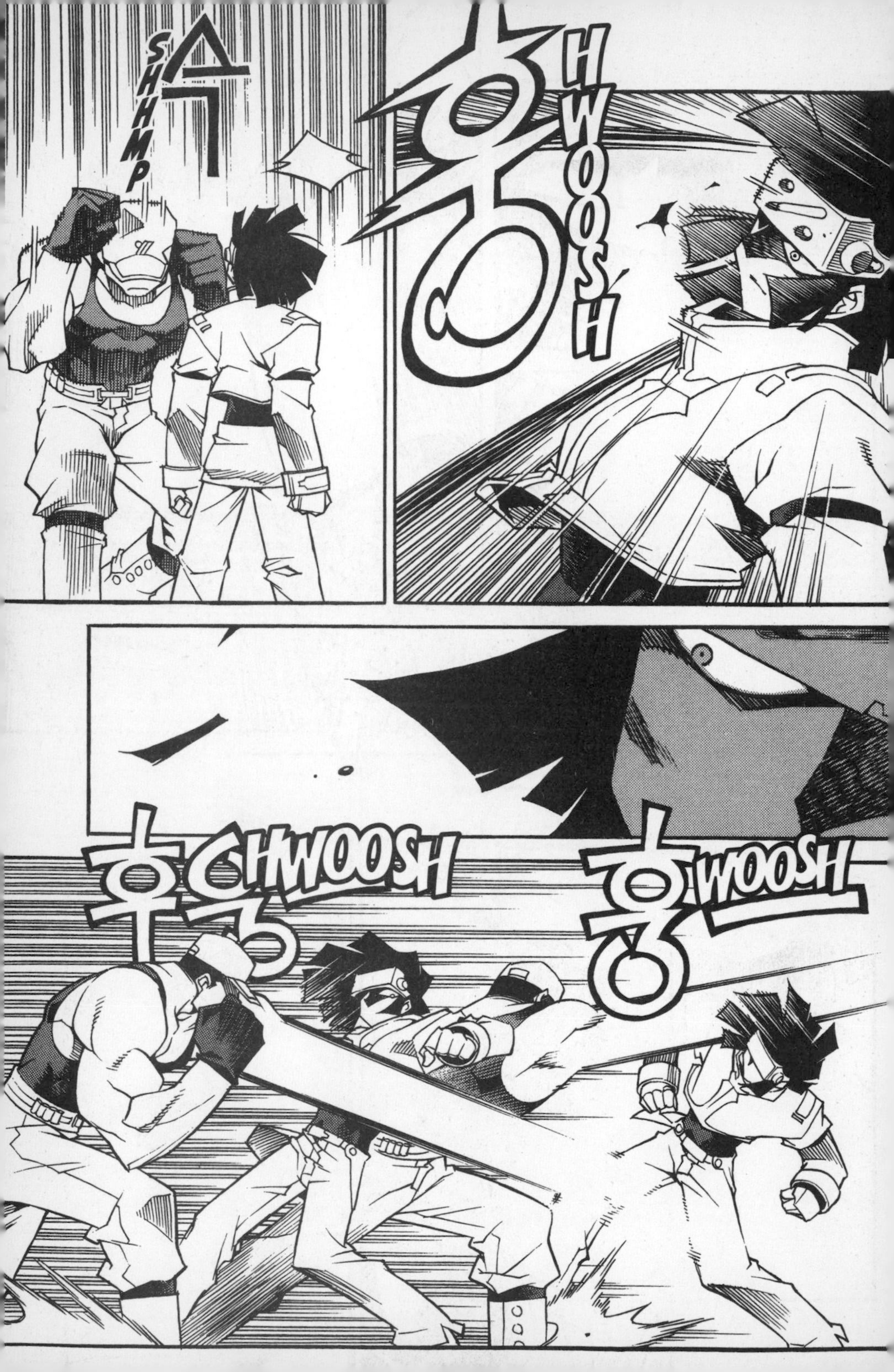
SHHMP
HWOOSH
CHWOOSH
WOOSH

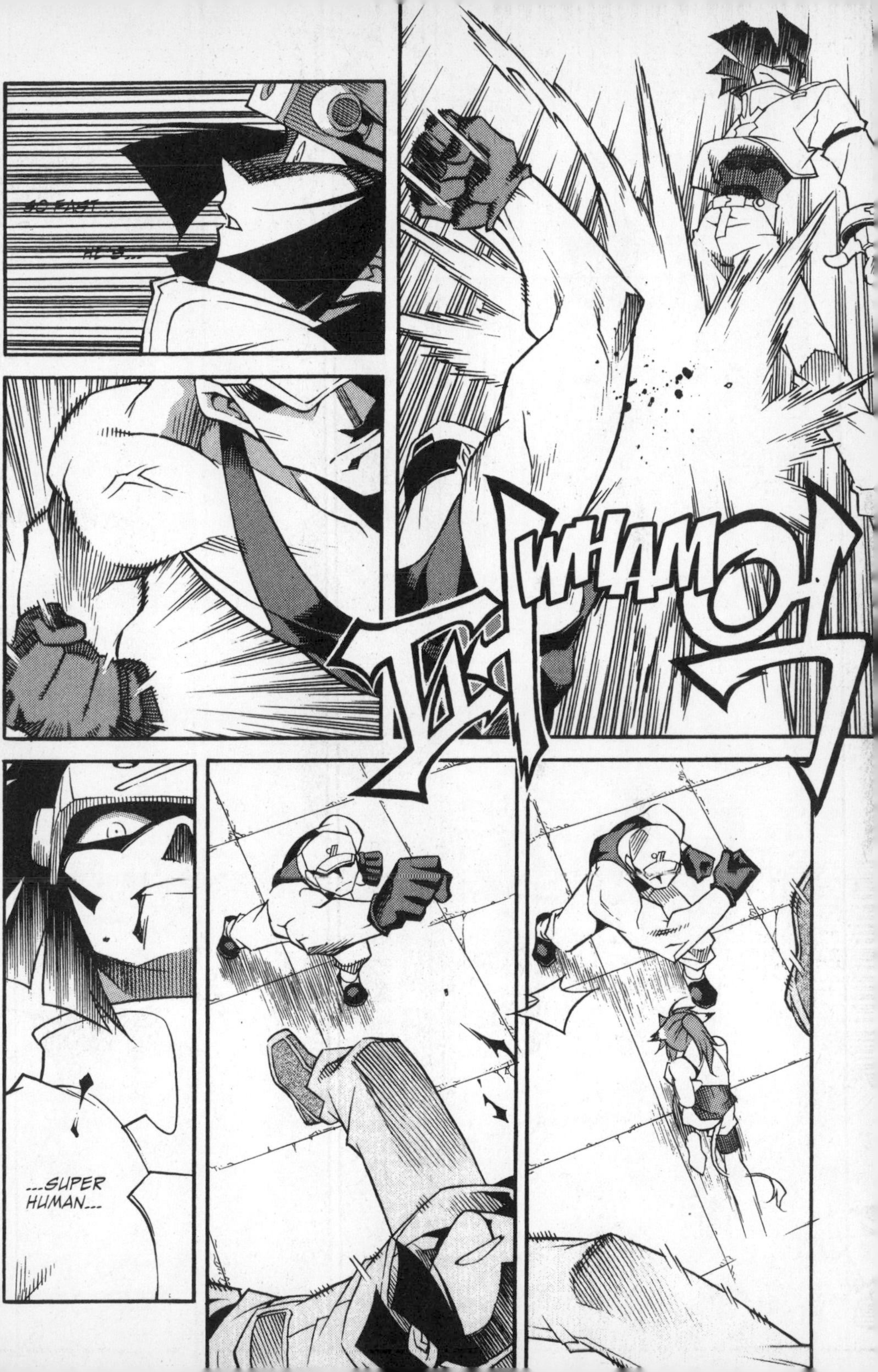
SO FAST...
HE'S...
WHAM
...SUPER HUMAN...

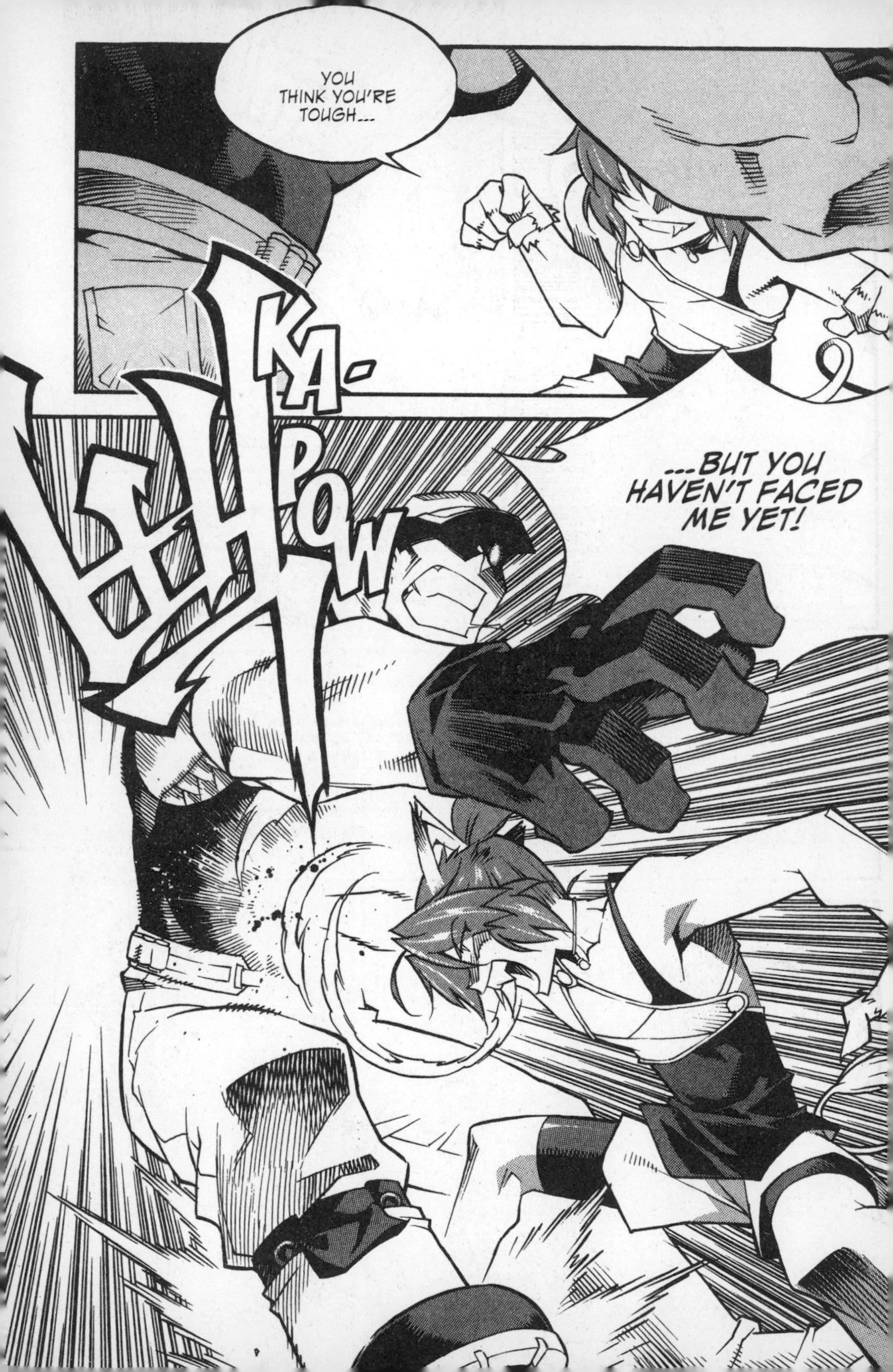
YOU THINK YOU'RE TOUGH...
KA-POW
...BUT YOU HAVEN'T FACED ME YET!

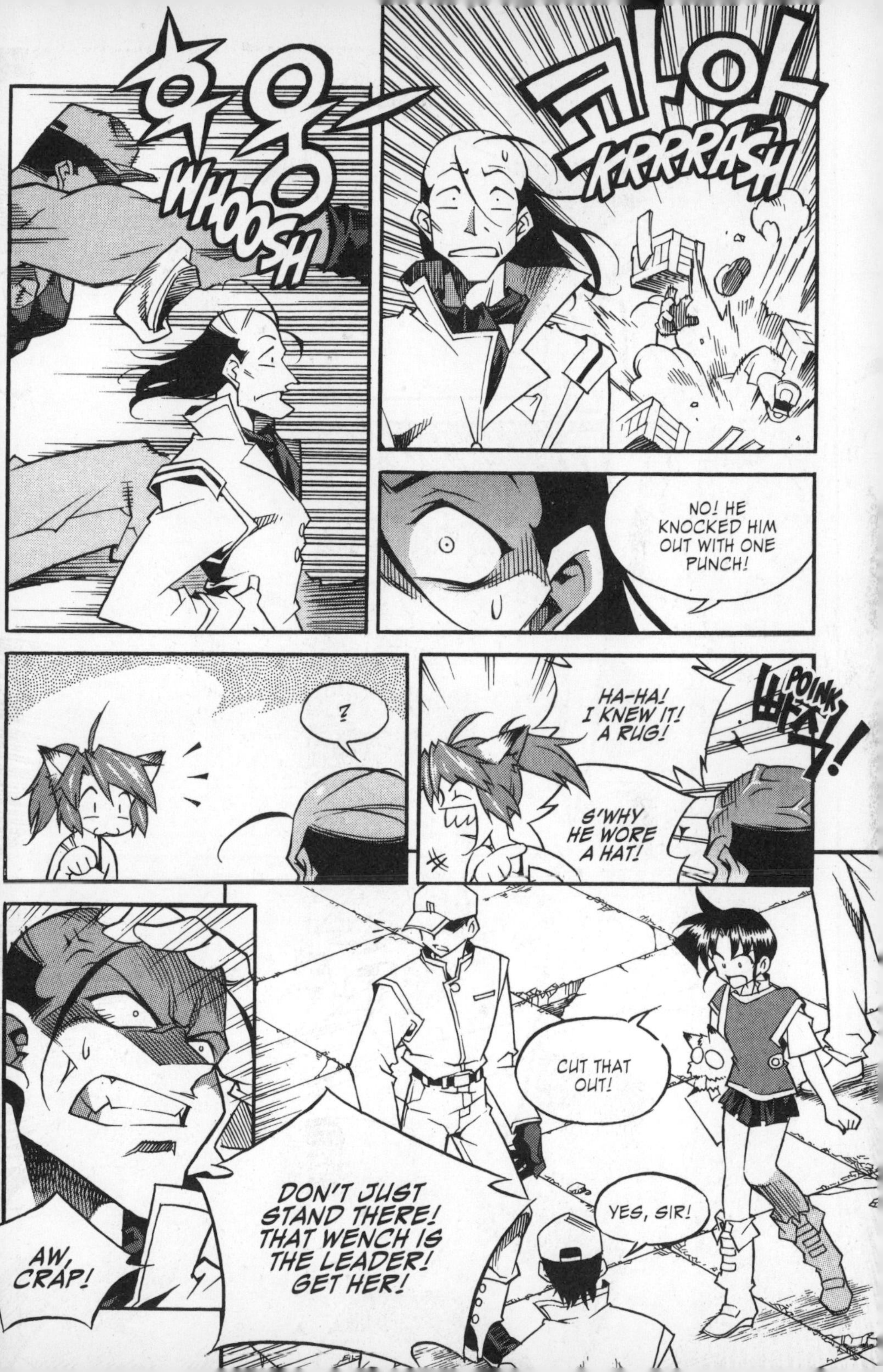
후웅
WHOOSH
KRRRASH
NO! HE KNOCKED HIM OUT WITH ONE PUNCH!
?
HA-HA! I KNEW IT! A RUG!
POINK
S'WHY HE WORE A HAT!
AW, CRAP!
CUT THAT OUT!
DON'T JUST STAND THERE! THAT WENCH IS THE LEADER! GET HER!
YES, SIR!

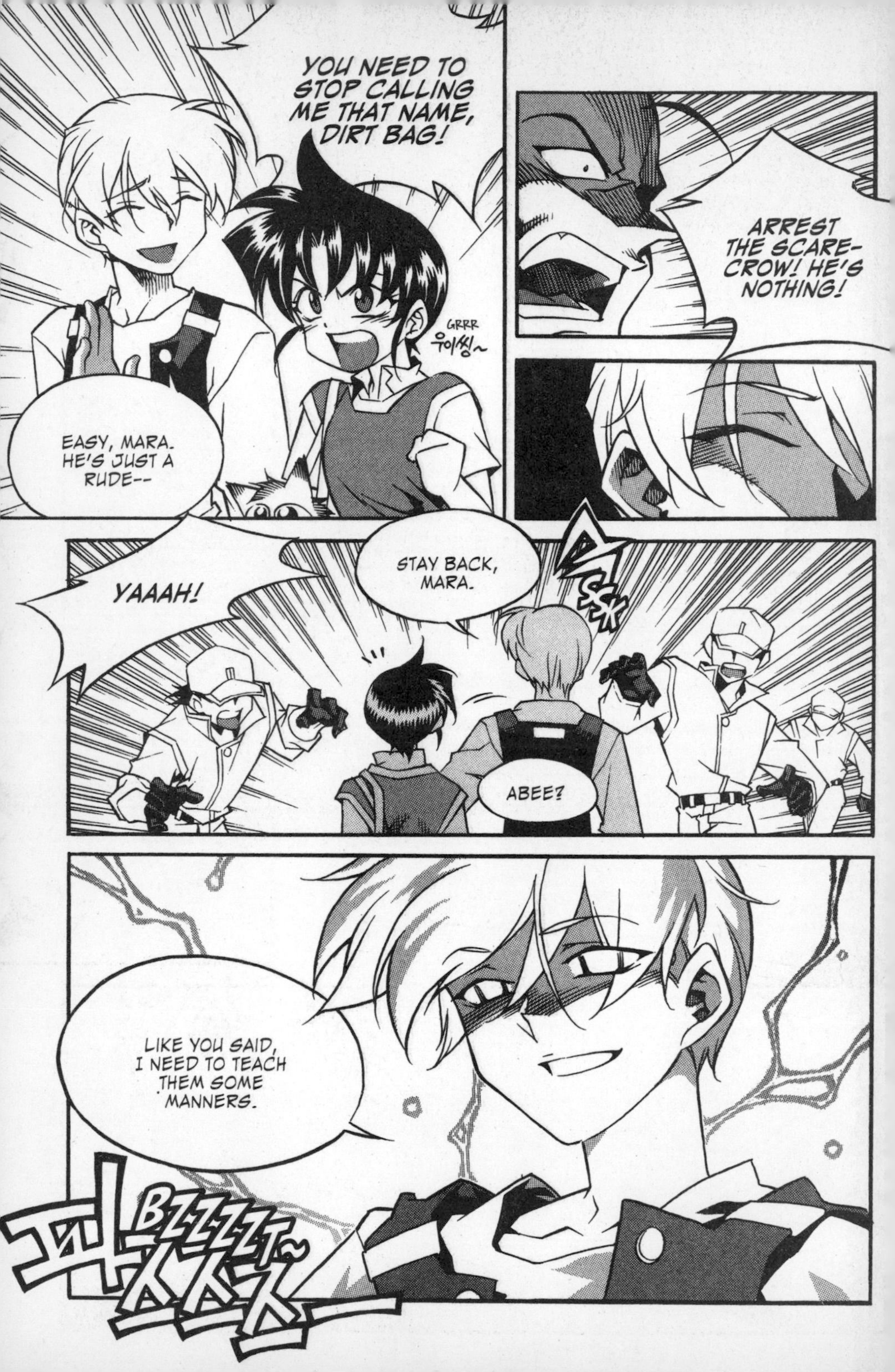
YOU NEED TO STOP CALLING ME THAT NAME, DIRT BAG!
GRRR
우이씽~
EASY, MARA. HE'S JUST A RUDE--
ARREST THE SCARE-CROW! HE'S NOTHING!
YAAAH!
STAY BACK, MARA.
SSK
ABEE?
LIKE YOU SAID, I NEED TO TEACH THEM SOME MANNERS.
BZZZZZT~

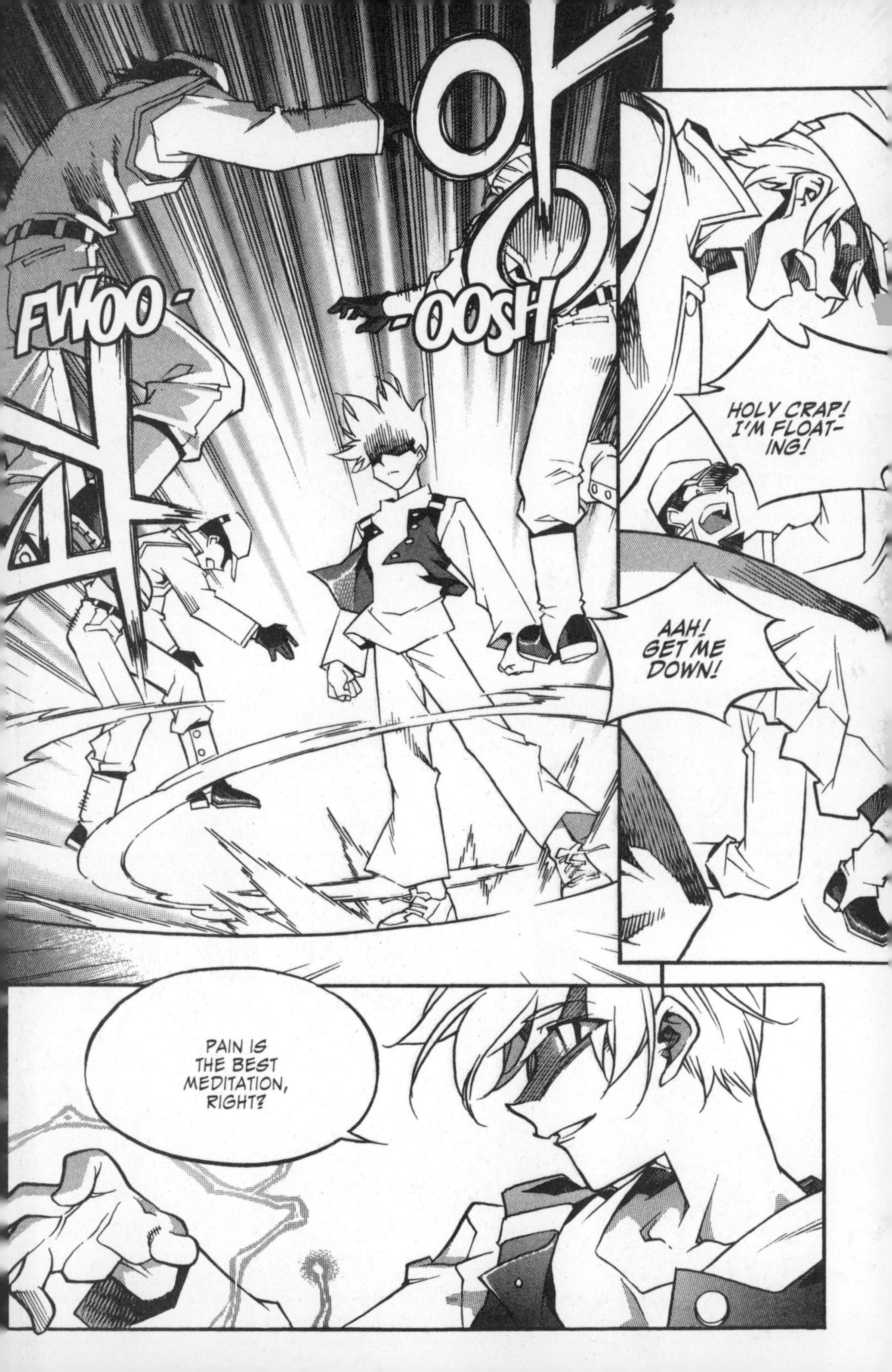
FWOO-
-OOSH
HOLY CRAP! I'M FLOAT-ING!
AAH! GET ME DOWN!
PAIN IS THE BEST MEDITATION, RIGHT?

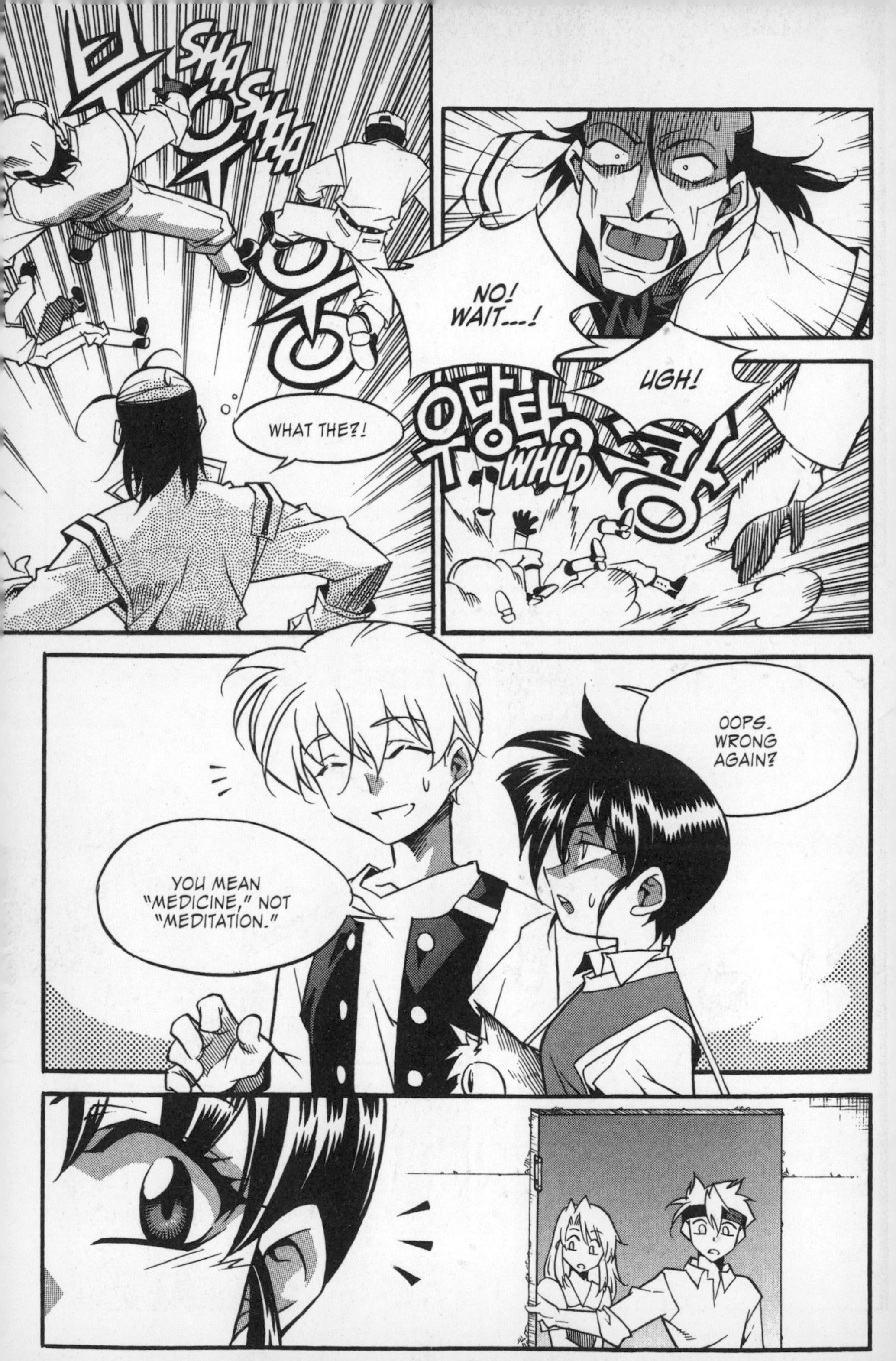
SHA
SHAA
WHAT THE?!
NO! WAIT...!
UGH!
WHUD
OOPS. WRONG AGAIN?
YOU MEAN "MEDICINE," NOT "MEDITATION."

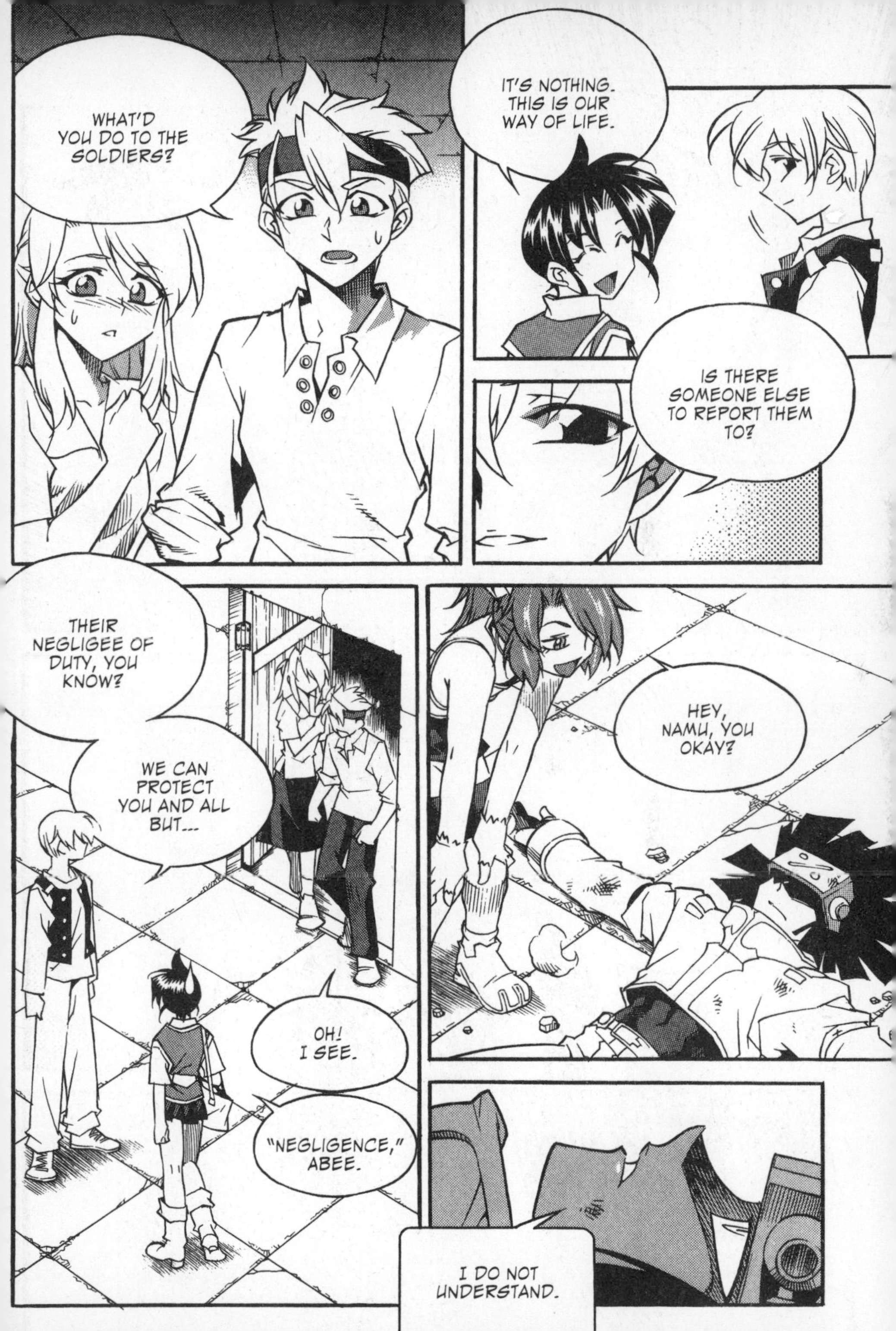
WHAT'D YOU DO TO THE SOLDIERS?
IT'S NOTHING. THIS IS OUR WAY OF LIFE.
IS THERE SOMEONE ELSE TO REPORT THEM TO?
THEIR NEGLIGEE OF DUTY, YOU KNOW?
WE CAN PROTECT YOU AND ALL BUT...
OH! I SEE.
"NEGLIGENCE," ABEE.
HEY, NAMU, YOU OKAY?
I DO NOT UNDERSTAND.

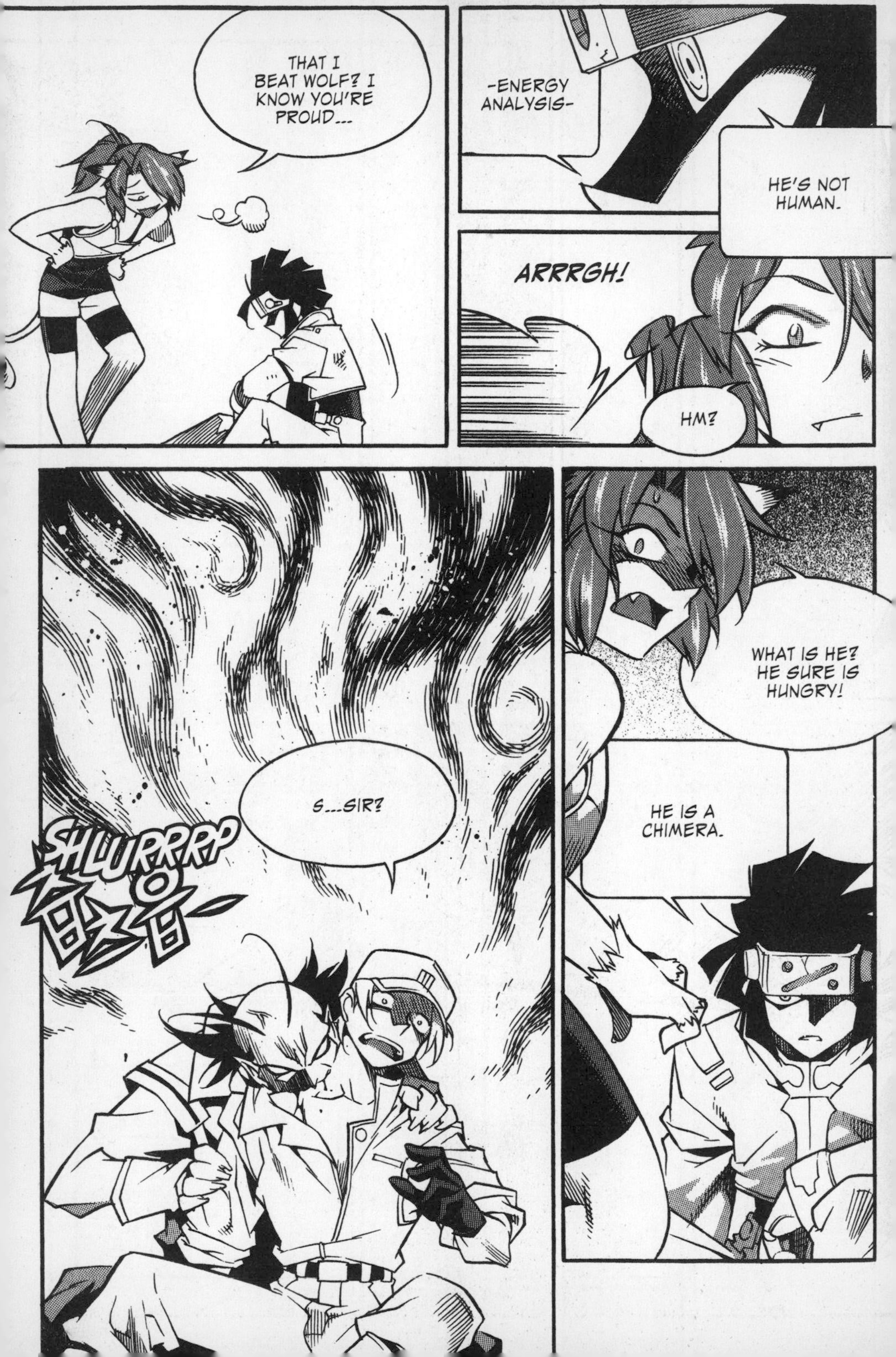
THAT I BEAT WOLF? I KNOW YOU'RE PROUD...
-ENERGY ANALYSIS-
HE'S NOT HUMAN.
ARRRGH!
HM?
S...SIR?
SHLURRRP
WHAT IS HE? HE SURE IS HUNGRY!
HE IS A CHIMERA.

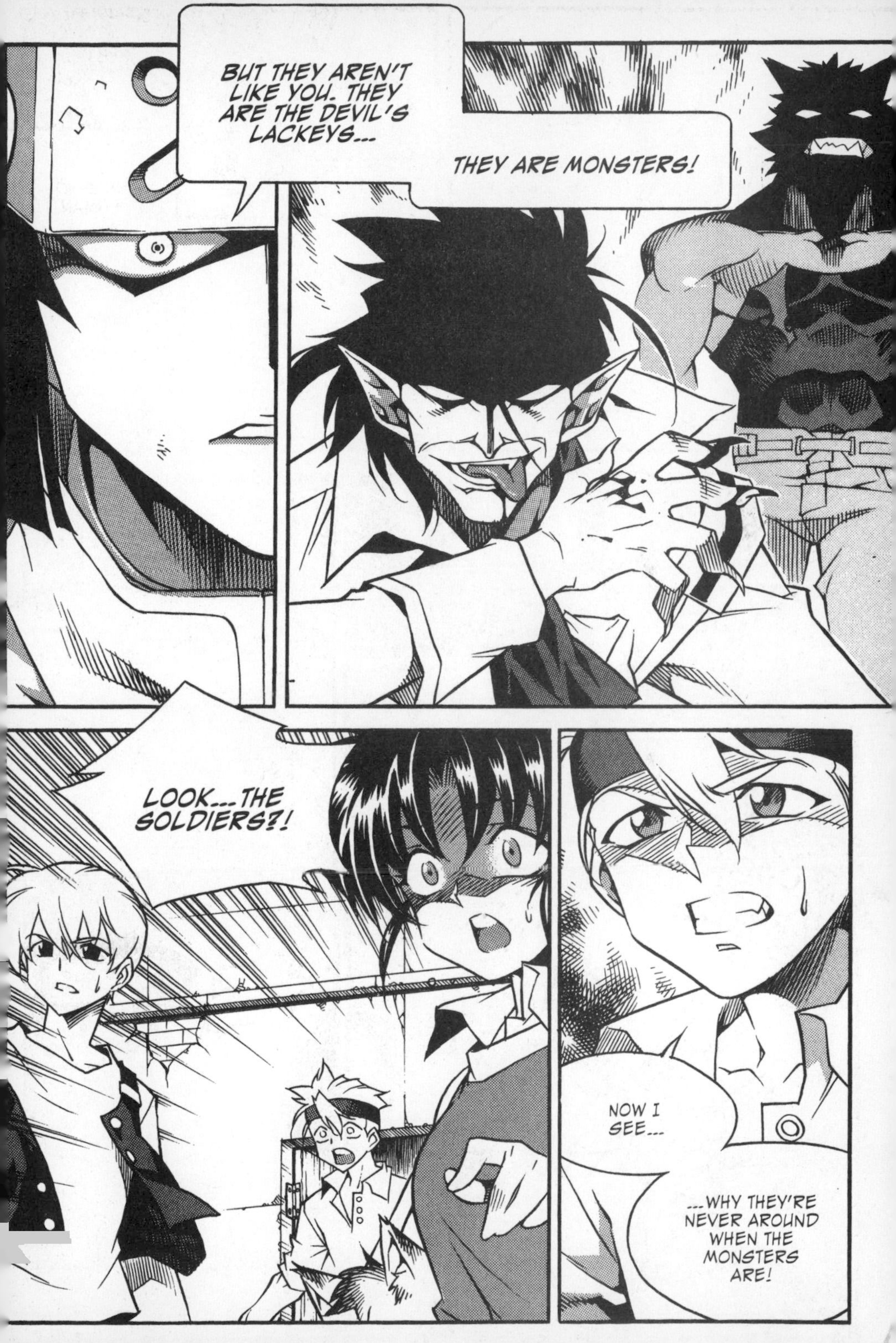
BUT THEY AREN'T LIKE YOU. THEY ARE THE DEVIL'S LACKEYS...
THEY ARE MONSTERS!
LOOK...THE SOLDIERS?!
NOW I SEE...
...WHY THEY'RE NEVER AROUND WHEN THE MONSTERS ARE!

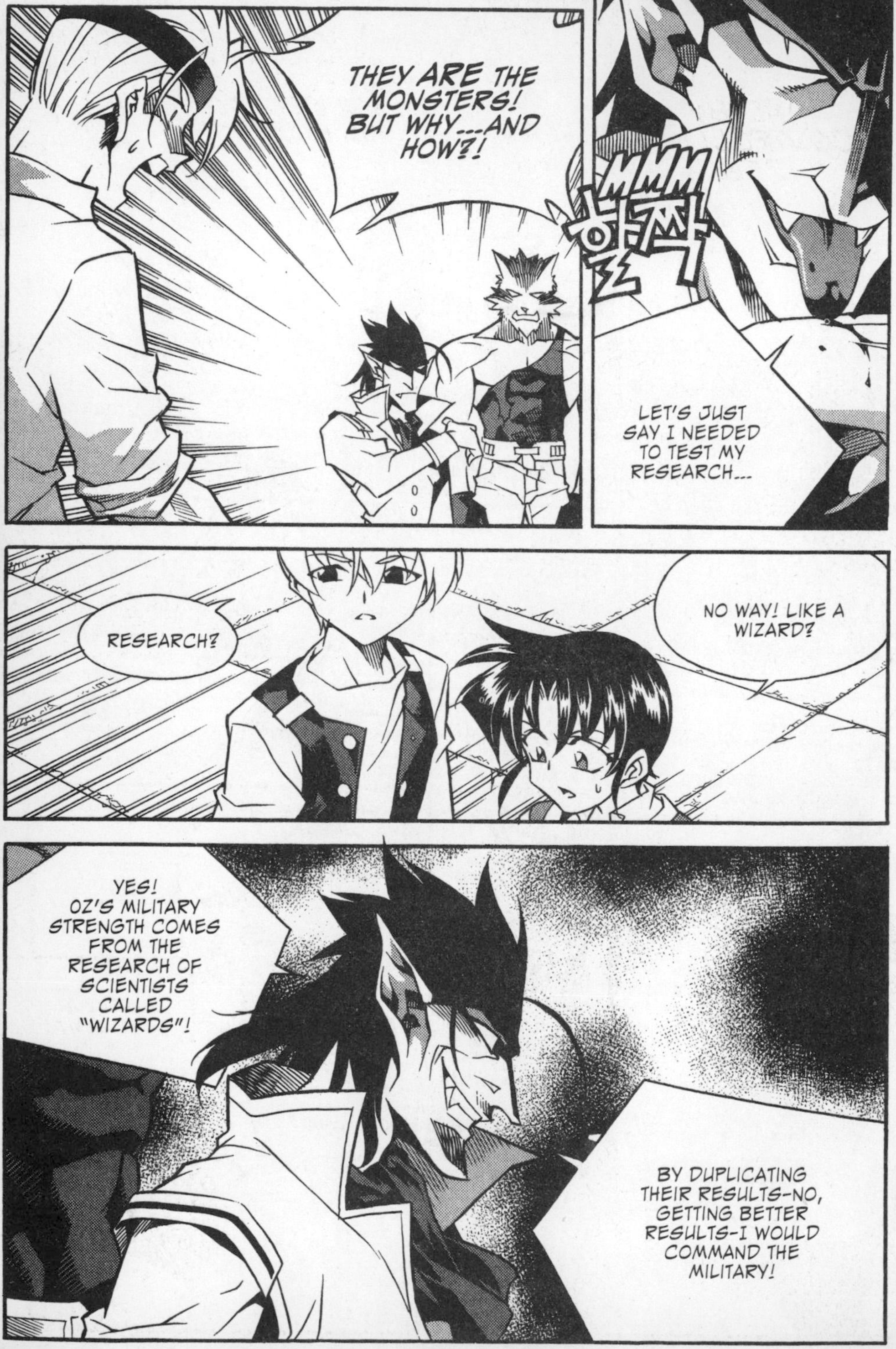
THEY ARE THE MONSTERS! BUT WHY...AND HOW?!
MMM
LET'S JUST SAY I NEEDED TO TEST MY RESEARCH...
RESEARCH?
NO WAY! LIKE A WIZARD?
YES! OZ'S MILITARY STRENGTH COMES FROM THE RESEARCH OF SCIENTISTS CALLED "WIZARDS"!
BY DUPLICATING THEIR RESULTS-NO, GETTING BETTER RESULTS-I WOULD COMMAND THE MILITARY!

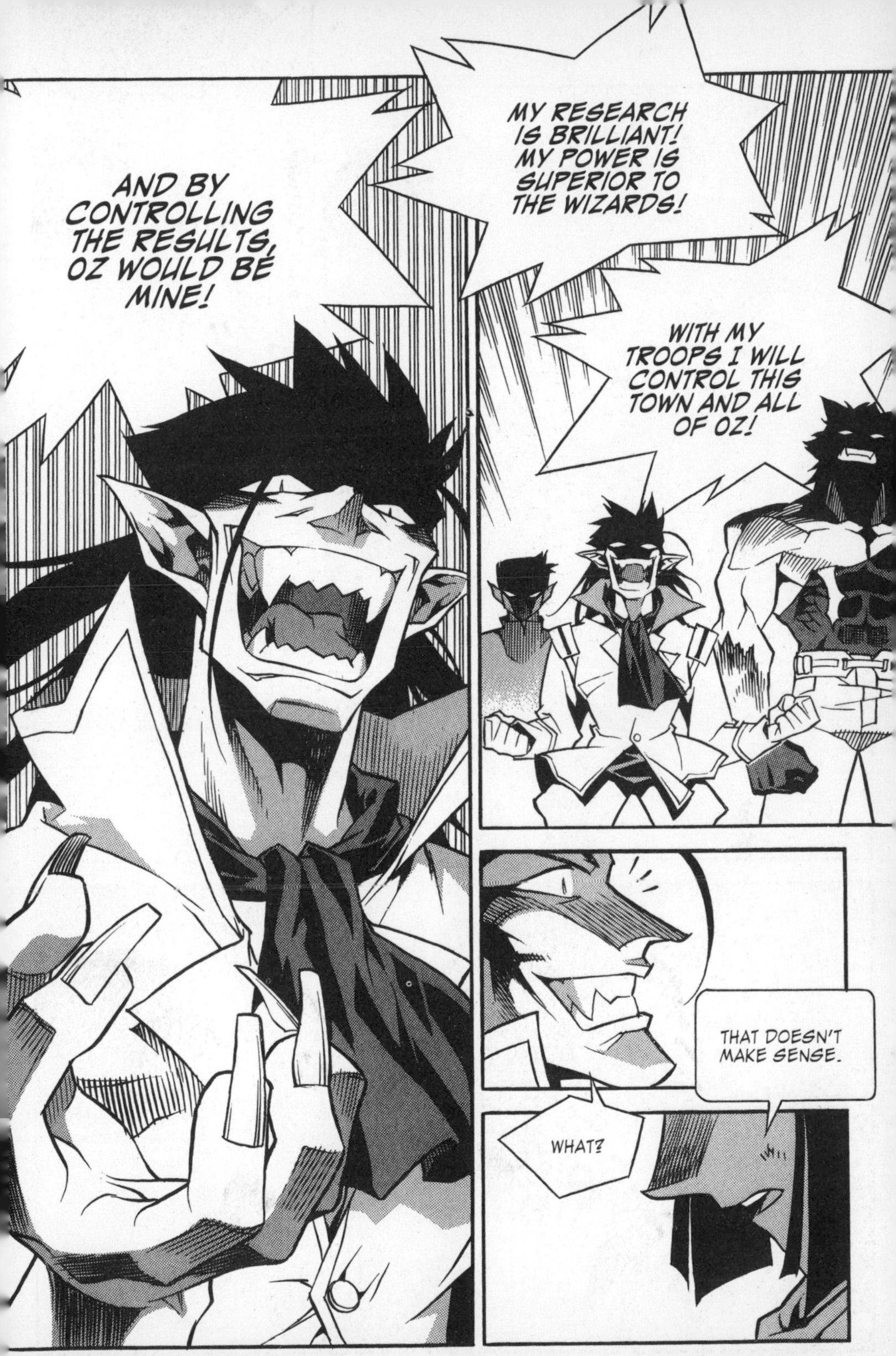
AND BY CONTROLLING THE RESULTS, OZ WOULD BE MINE!
MY RESEARCH IS BRILLIANT! MY POWER IS SUPERIOR TO THE WIZARDS!
WITH MY TROOPS I WILL CONTROL THIS TOWN AND ALL OF OZ!
THAT DOESN'T MAKE SENSE.
WHAT?

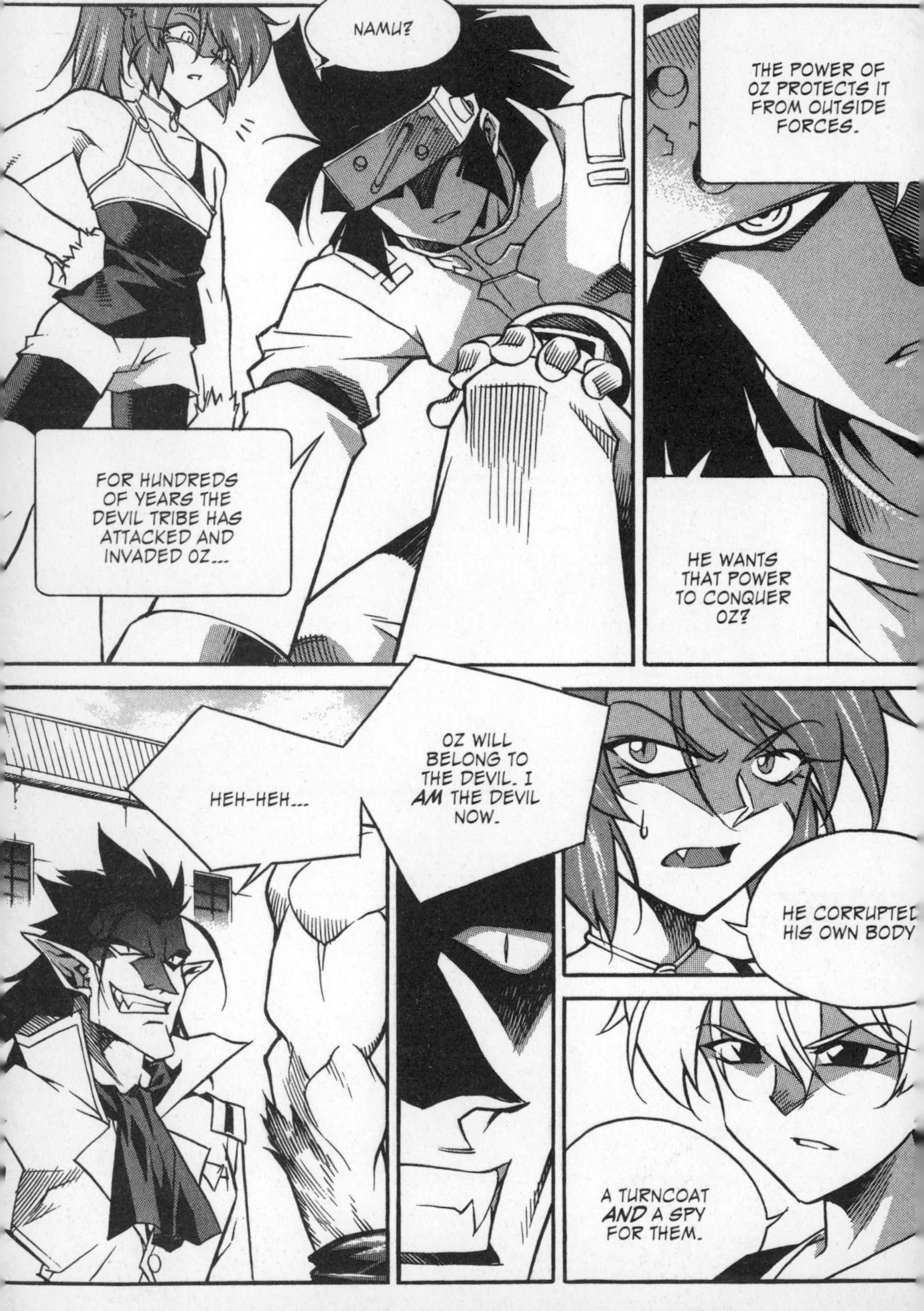
NAMU?
FOR HUNDREDS OF YEARS THE DEVIL TRIBE HAS ATTACKED AND INVADED OZ...
THE POWER OF OZ PROTECTS IT FROM OUTSIDE FORCES.
HE WANTS THAT POWER TO CONQUER OZ?
HEH-HEH...
OZ WILL BELONG TO THE DEVIL. I ***AM*** THE DEVIL NOW.
HE CORRUPTED HIS OWN BODY
A TURNCOAT ***AND*** A SPY FOR THEM.

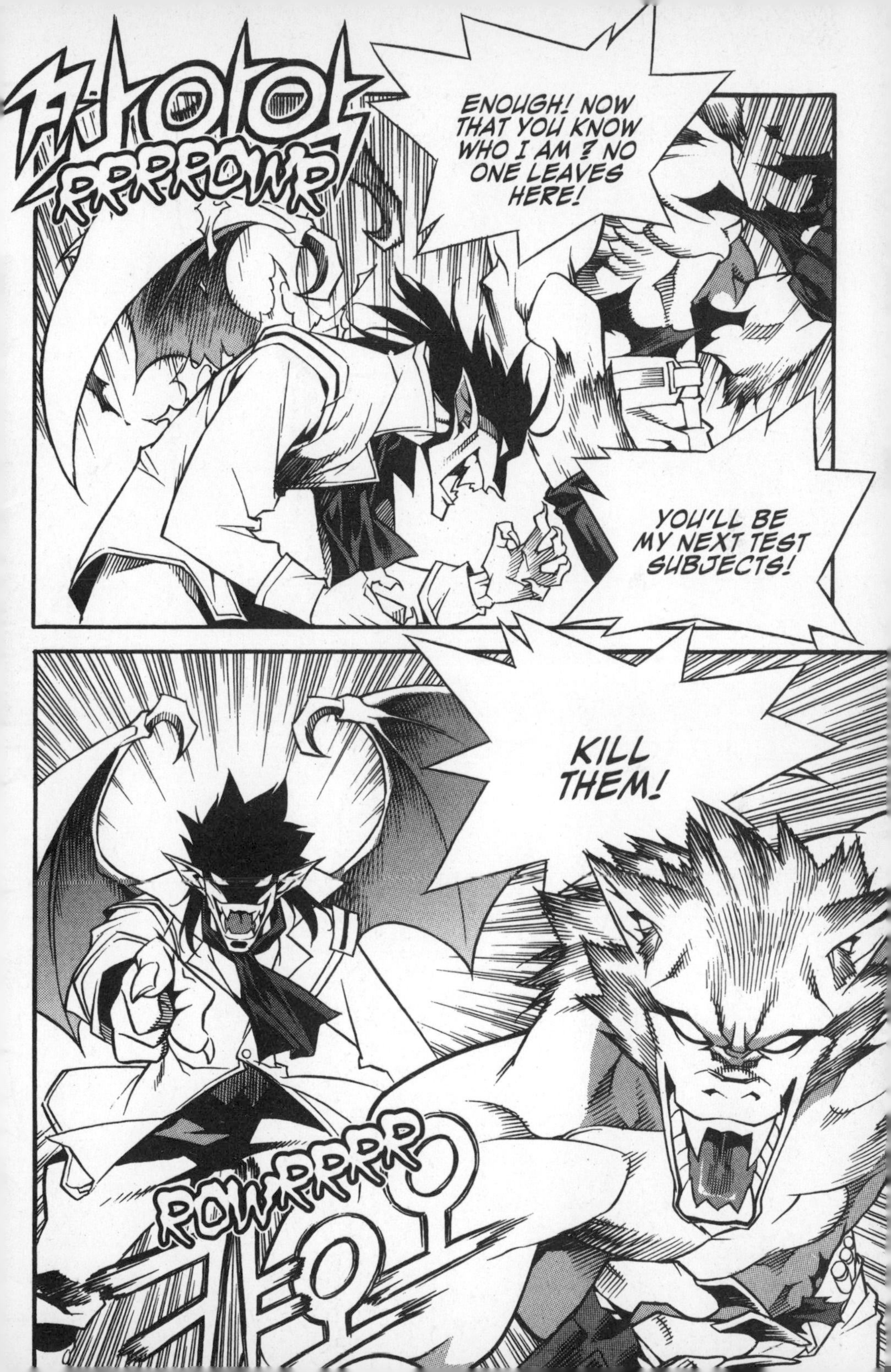
RRRROWR
ENOUGH! NOW THAT YOU KNOW WHO I AM ? NO ONE LEAVES HERE!
YOU'LL BE MY NEXT TEST SUBJECTS!
KILL THEM!
ROWRRRR

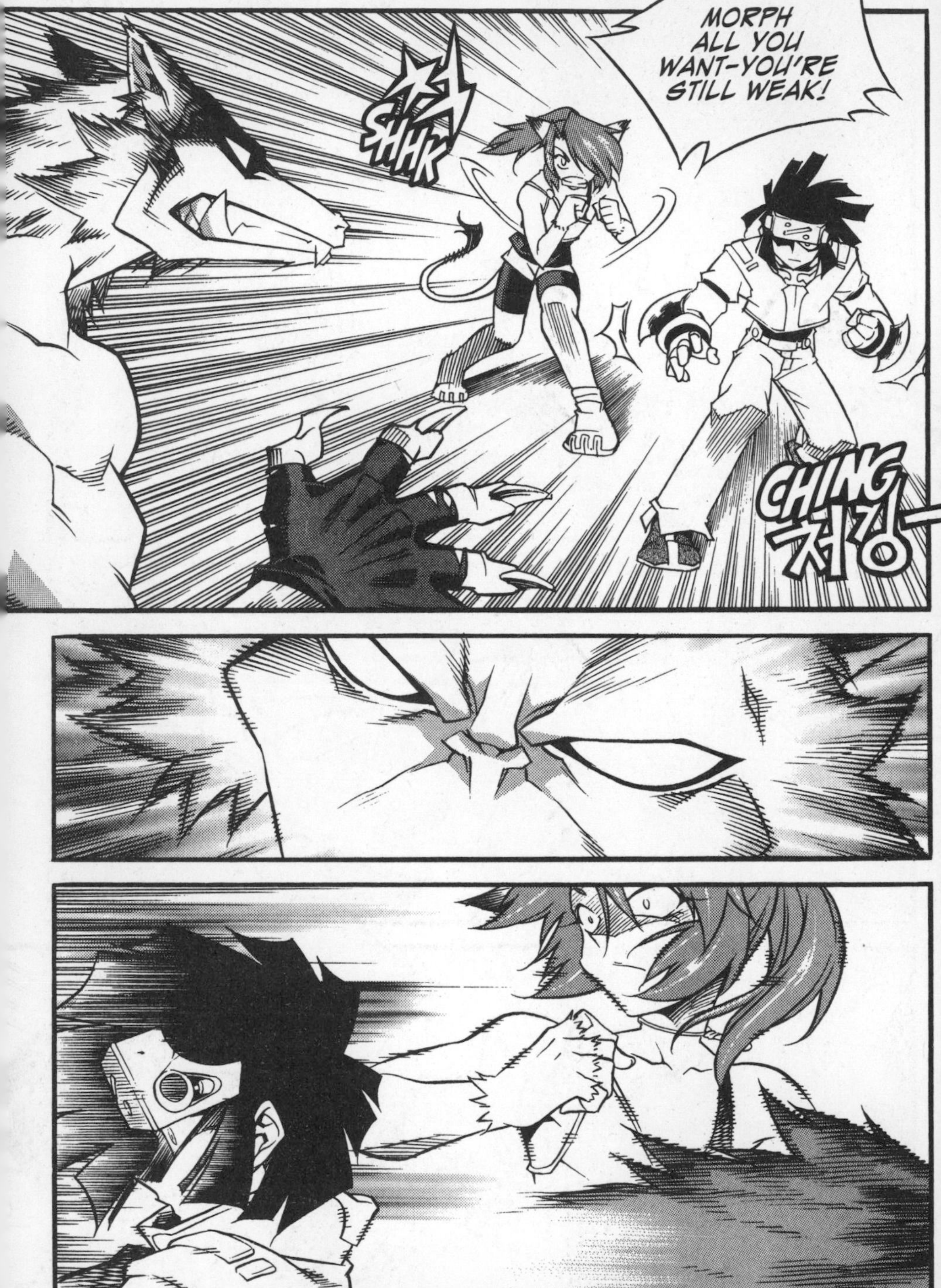
SHHK
MORPH ALL YOU WANT-YOU'RE STILL WEAK!
CHING

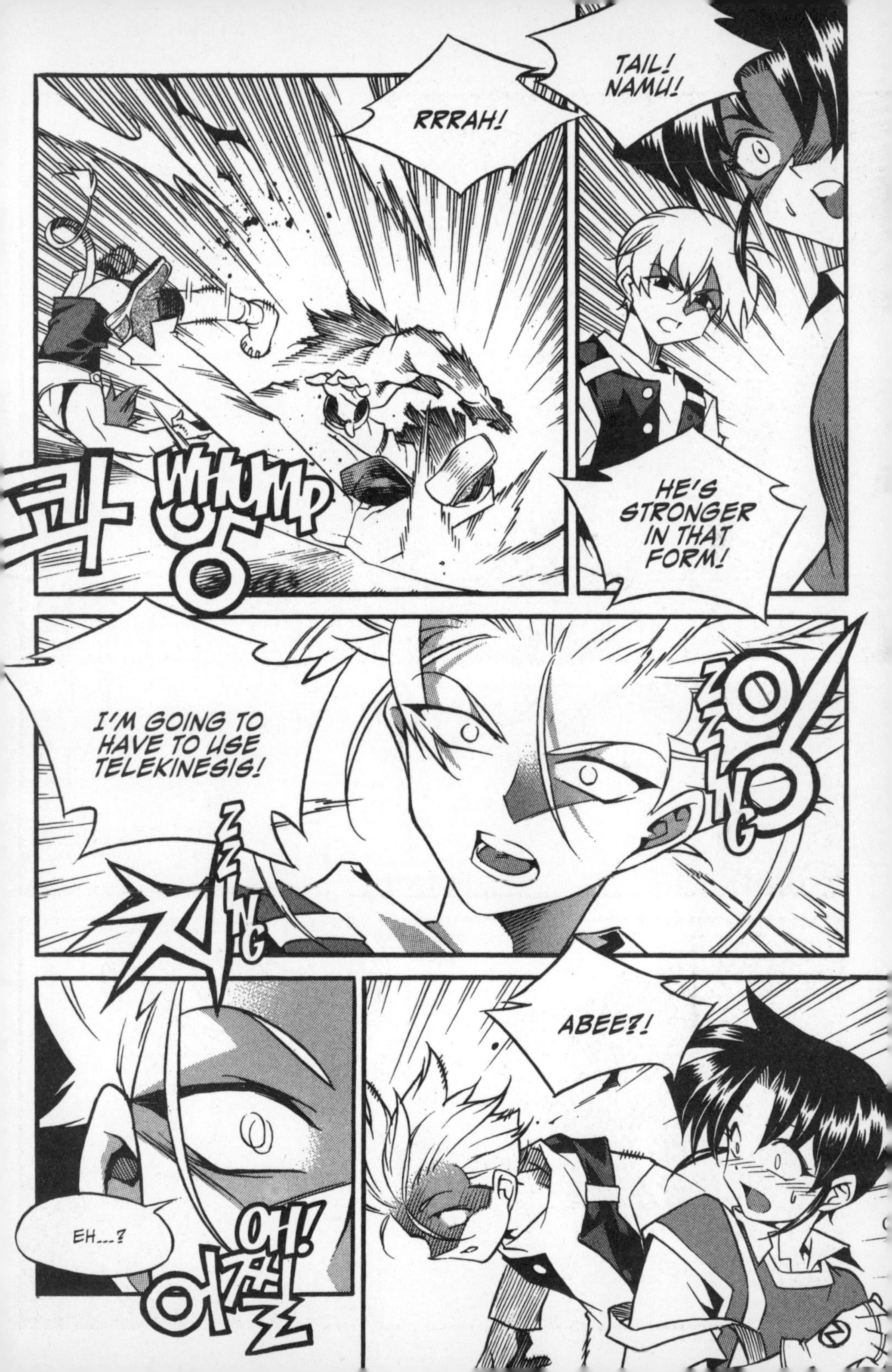

RRRAH!
WHUMP
TAIL! NAMU!
HE'S STRONGER IN THAT FORM!
I'M GOING TO HAVE TO USE TELEKINESIS!
ZZING
ZZING
EH...?
OH!
ABEE?!

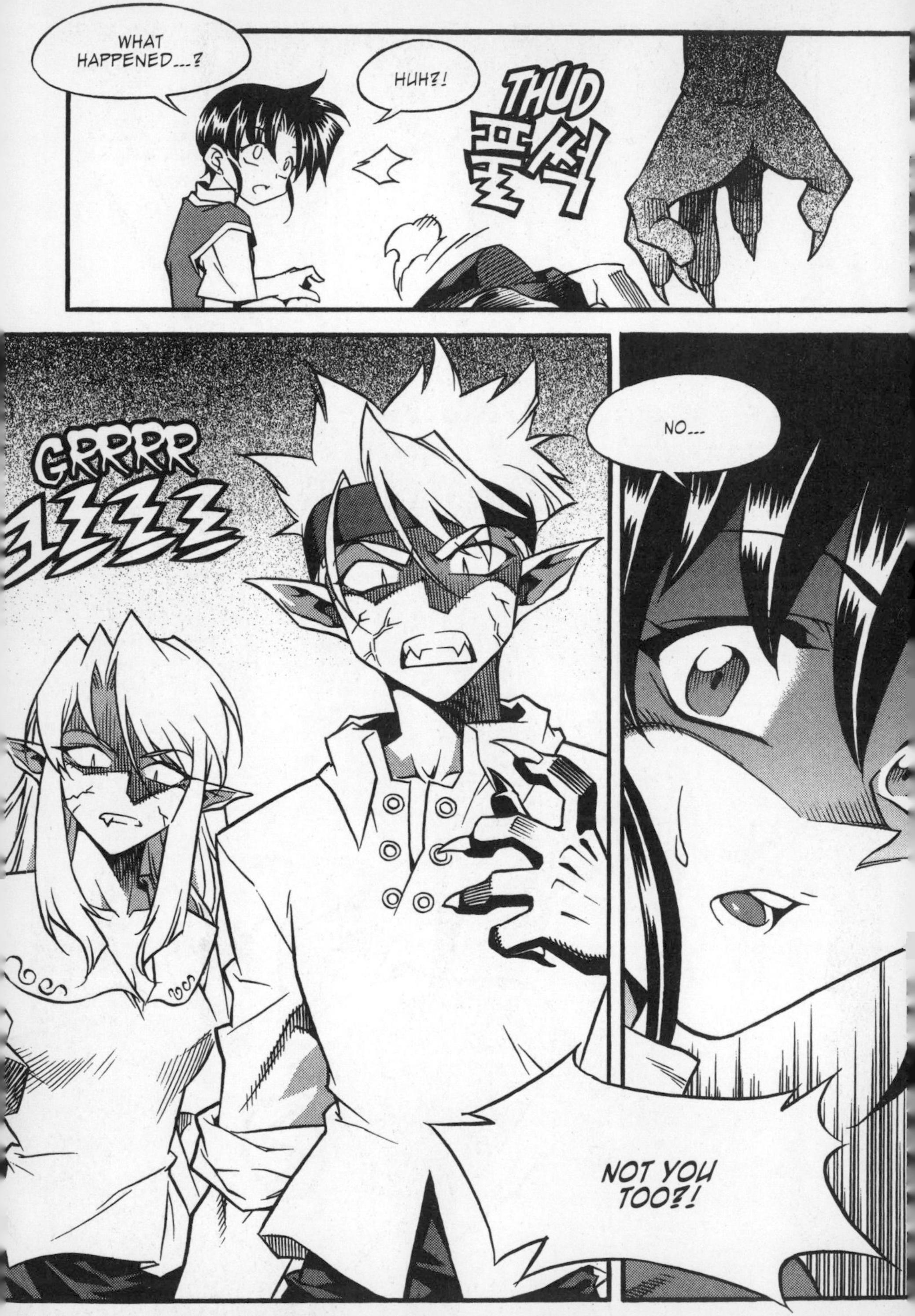
WHAT HAPPENED...?
HUH?!
THUD
풀썩
GRRRR
NO...
NOT YOU TOO?!

DOROTHY OF OZ
도로시

Step 2 TRANSFORMATION

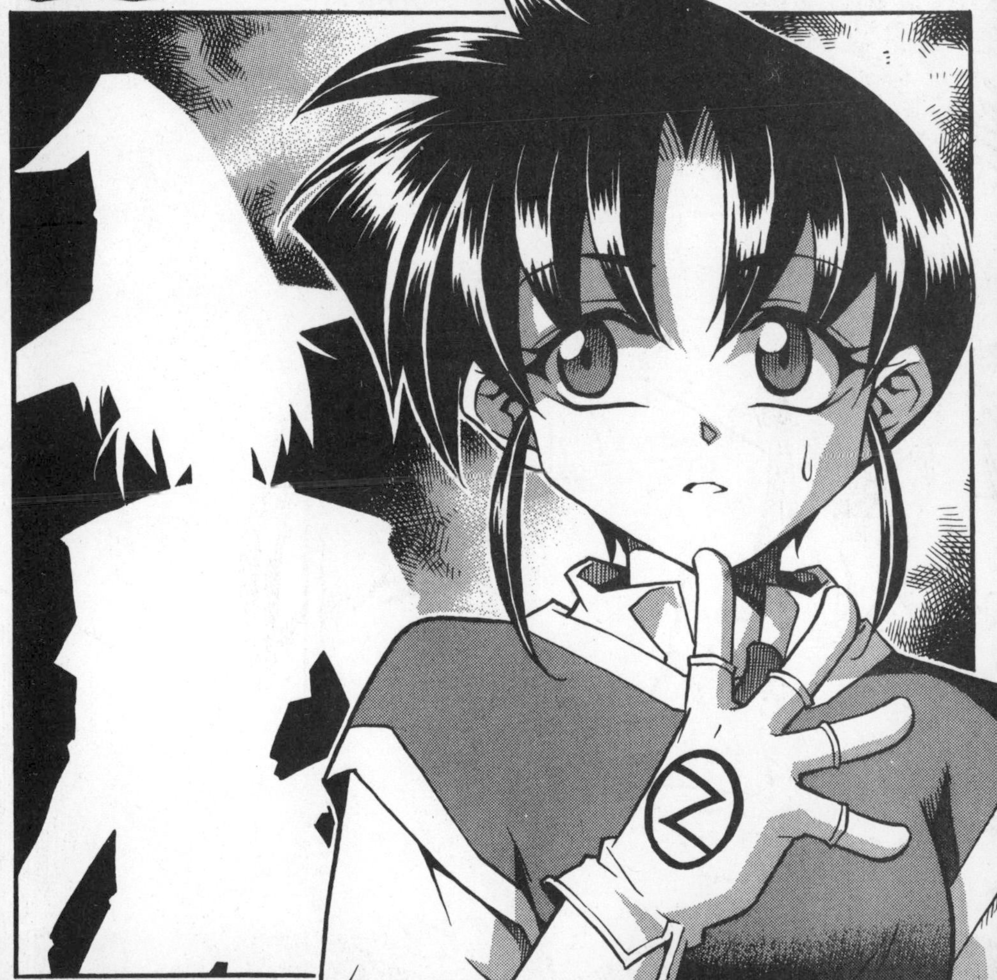

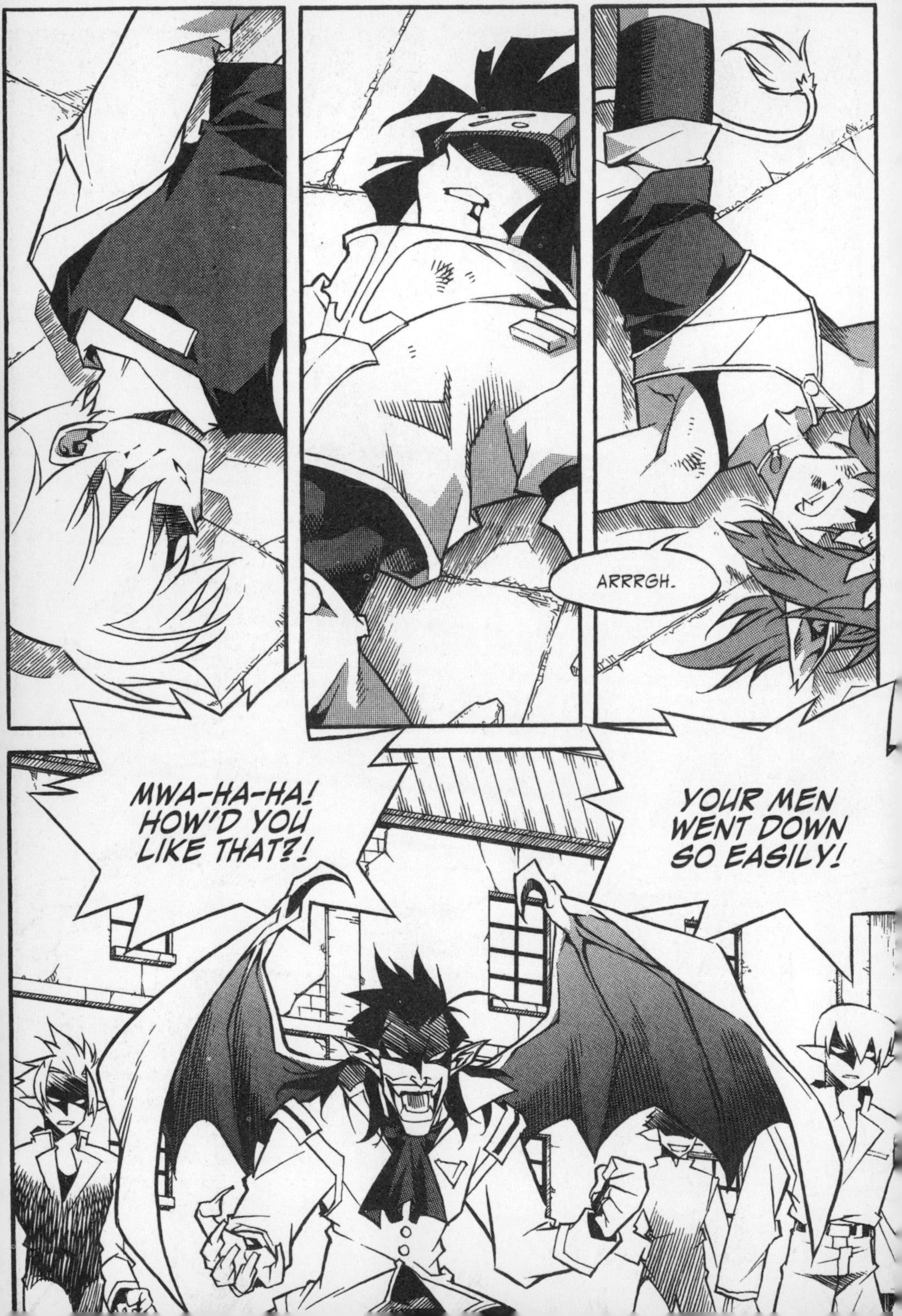
ARRRGH.
MWA-HA-HA! HOW'D YOU LIKE THAT?!
YOUR MEN WENT DOWN SO EASILY!

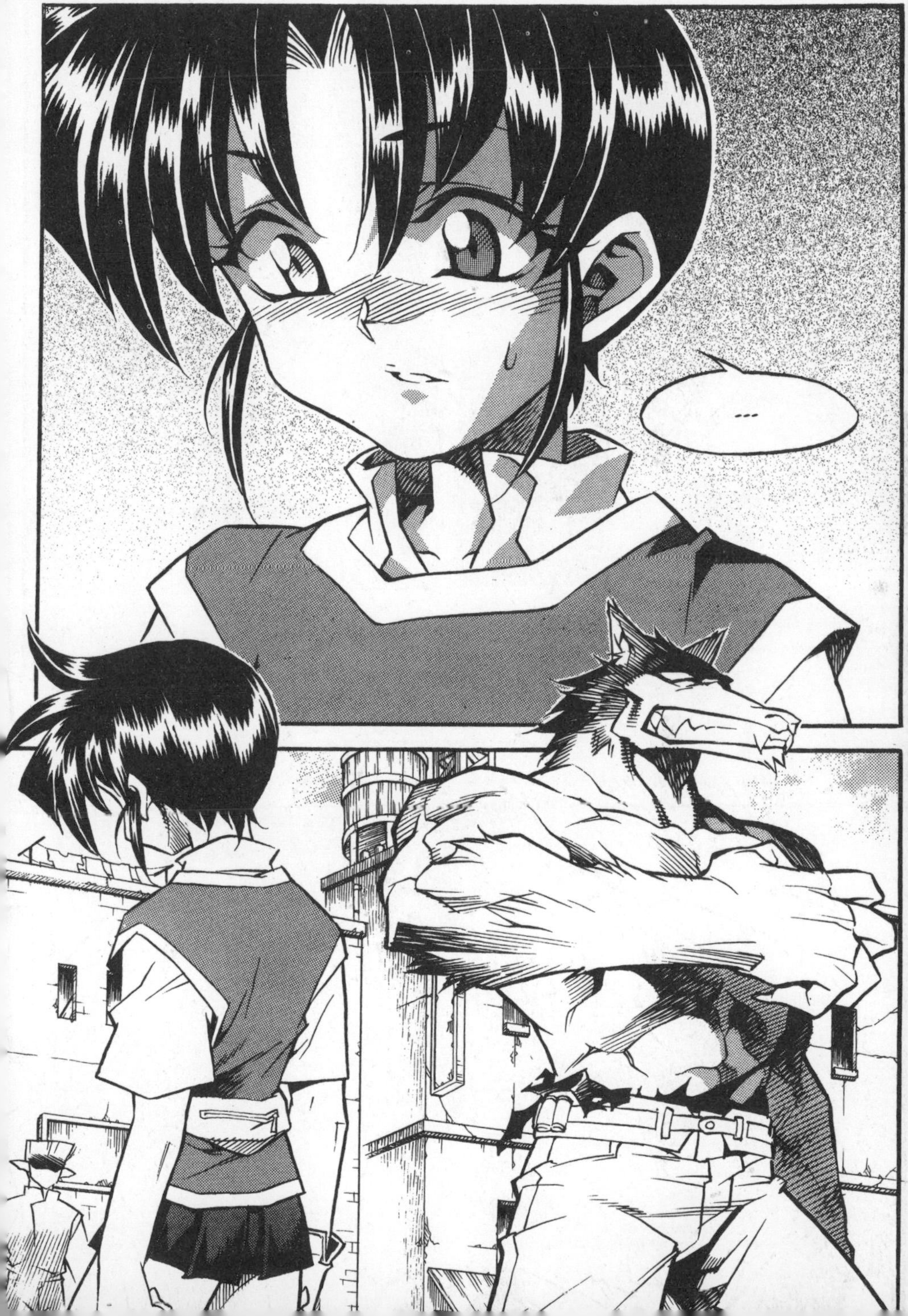
...

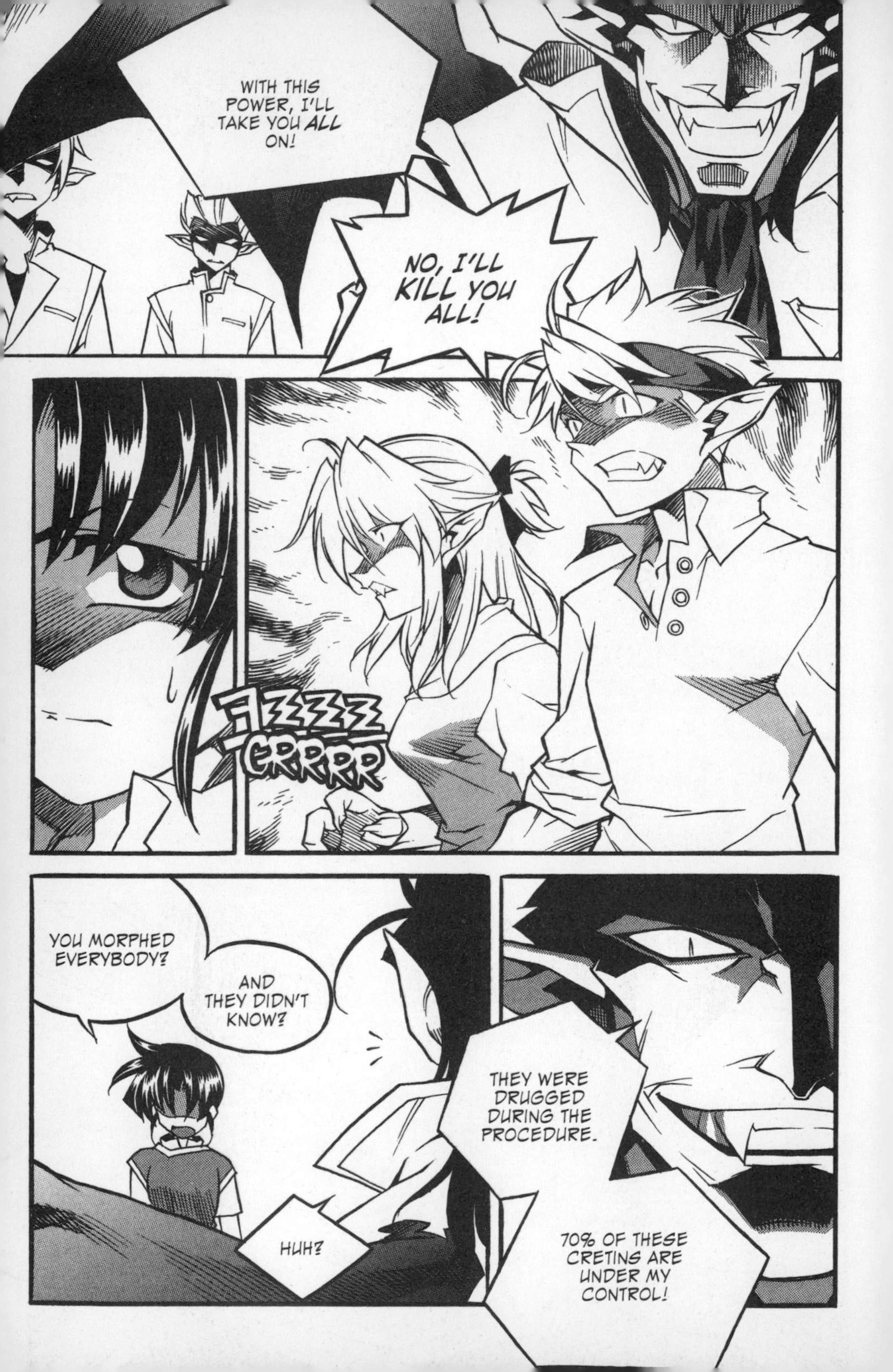
WITH THIS POWER, I'LL TAKE YOU *ALL* ON!
NO, I'LL *KILL* YOU ALL!
GRRRR
YOU MORPHED EVERYBODY?
AND THEY DIDN'T KNOW?
THEY WERE DRUGGED DURING THE PROCEDURE.
HUH?
70% OF THESE CRETINS ARE UNDER MY CONTROL!

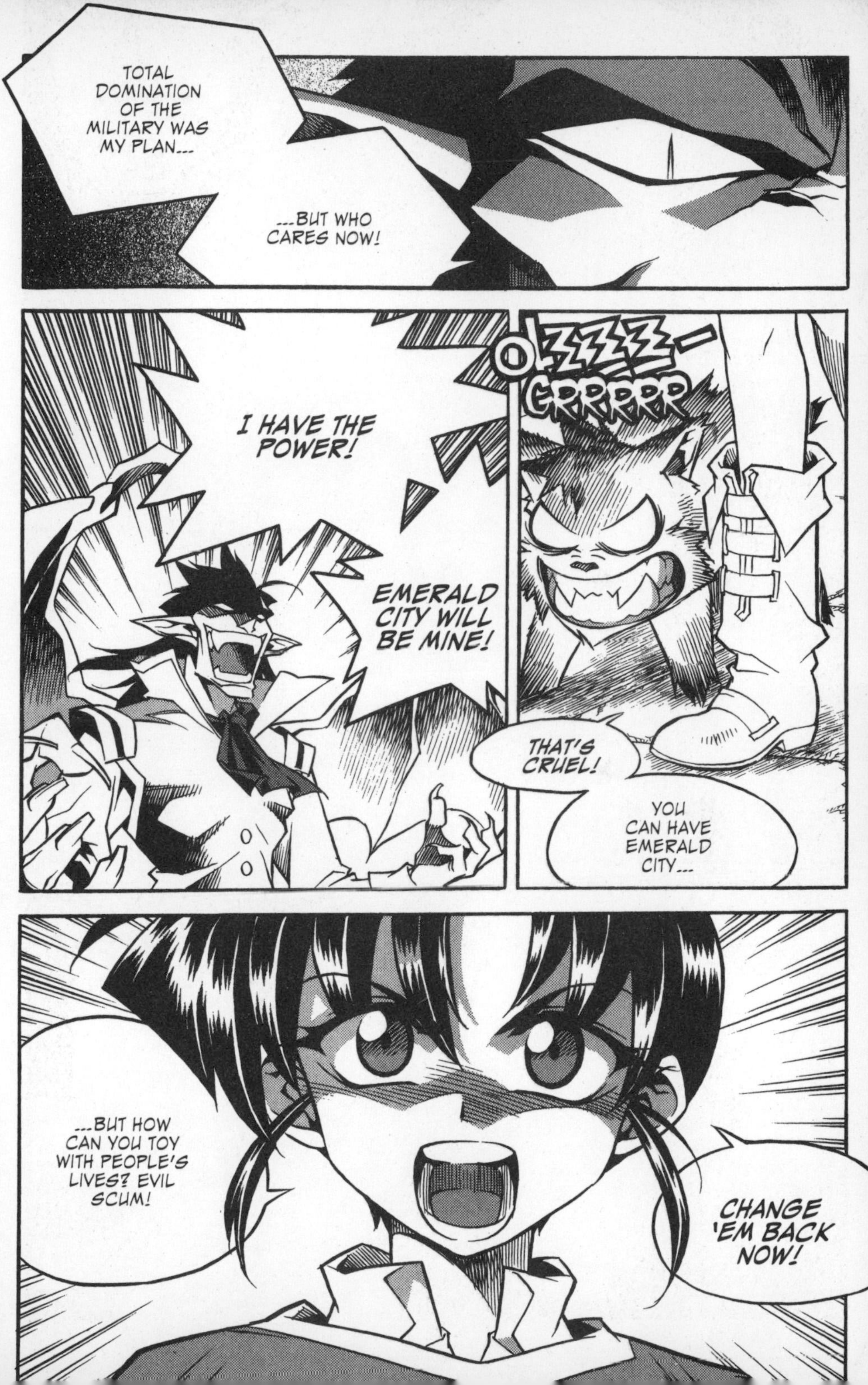
TOTAL DOMINATION OF THE MILITARY WAS MY PLAN...
...BUT WHO CARES NOW!
I HAVE THE POWER!
EMERALD CITY WILL BE MINE!
OIZZZZZ-GRRRRRR
THAT'S CRUEL!
YOU CAN HAVE EMERALD CITY...
...BUT HOW CAN YOU TOY WITH PEOPLE'S LIVES? EVIL SCUM!
CHANGE 'EM BACK NOW!

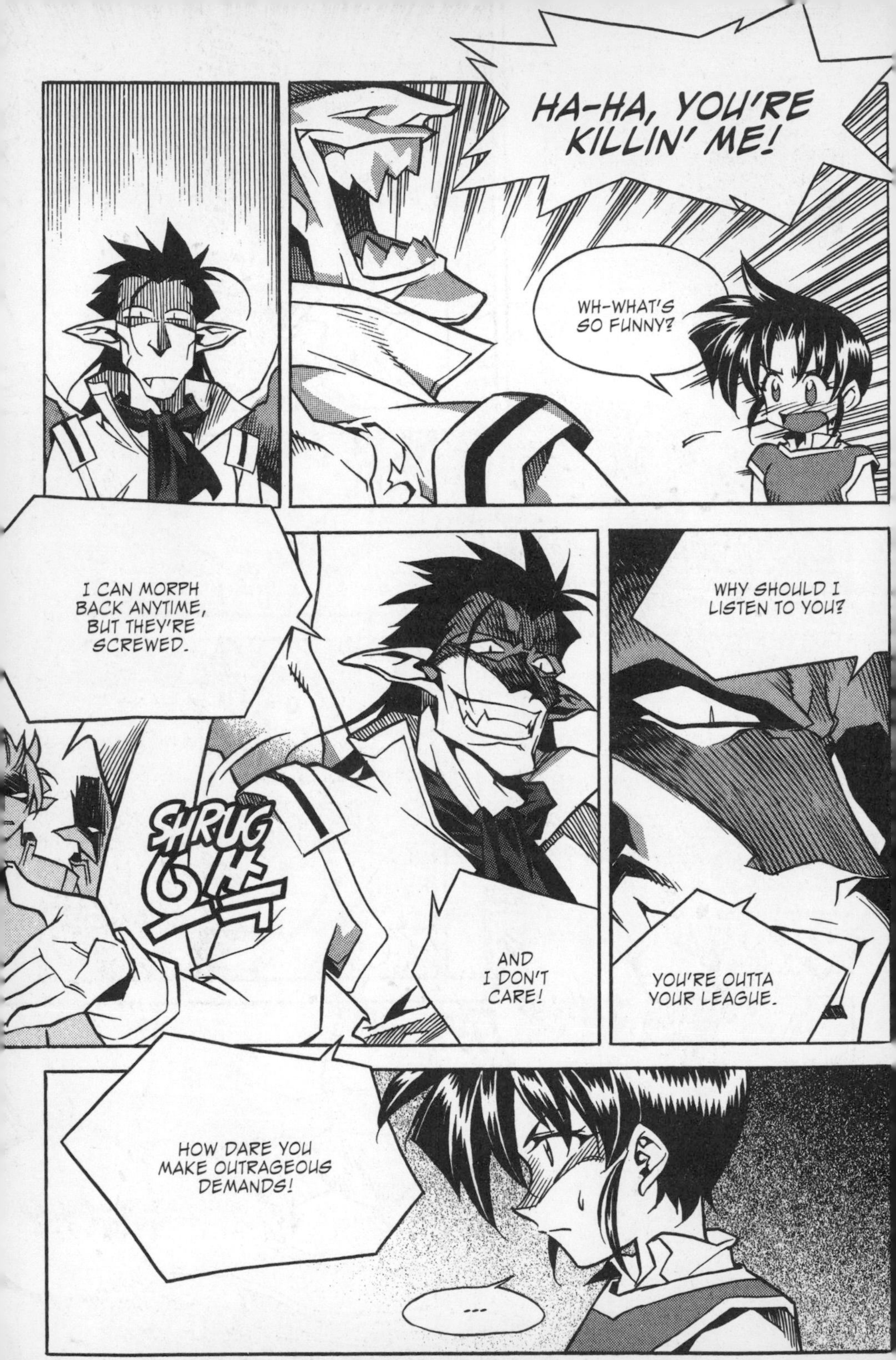
HA-HA, YOU'RE KILLIN' ME!
WH-WHAT'S SO FUNNY?
I CAN MORPH BACK ANYTIME, BUT THEY'RE SCREWED.
SHRUG
AND I DON'T CARE!
WHY SHOULD I LISTEN TO YOU?
YOU'RE OUTTA YOUR LEAGUE.
HOW DARE YOU MAKE OUTRAGEOUS DEMANDS!
...

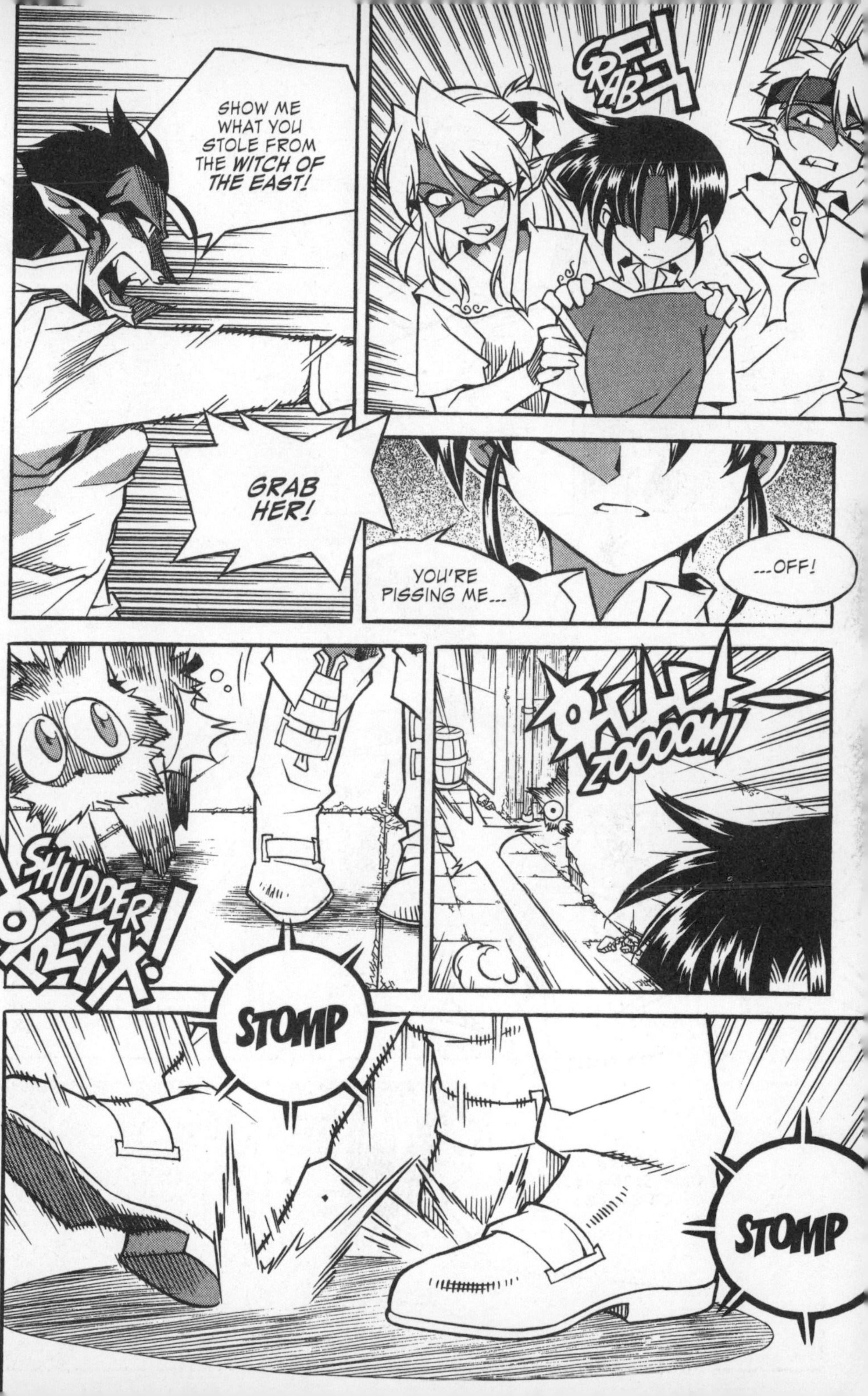
SHOW ME WHAT YOU STOLE FROM THE WITCH OF THE EAST!
GRAB
GRAB HER!
YOU'RE PISSING ME...
...OFF!
SHUDDER
ZOOOOOM!
STOMP
STOMP

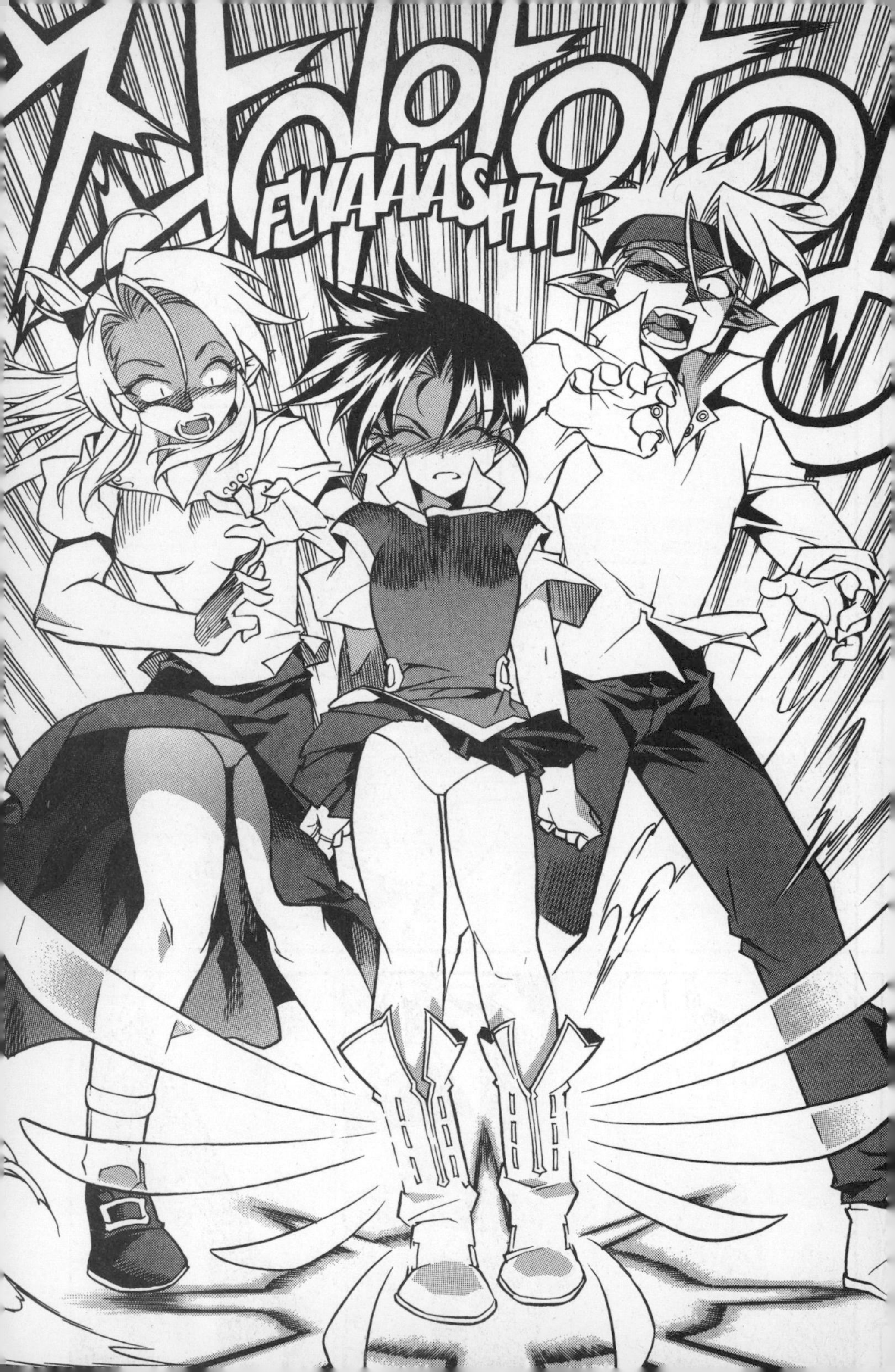
FWAAASHH

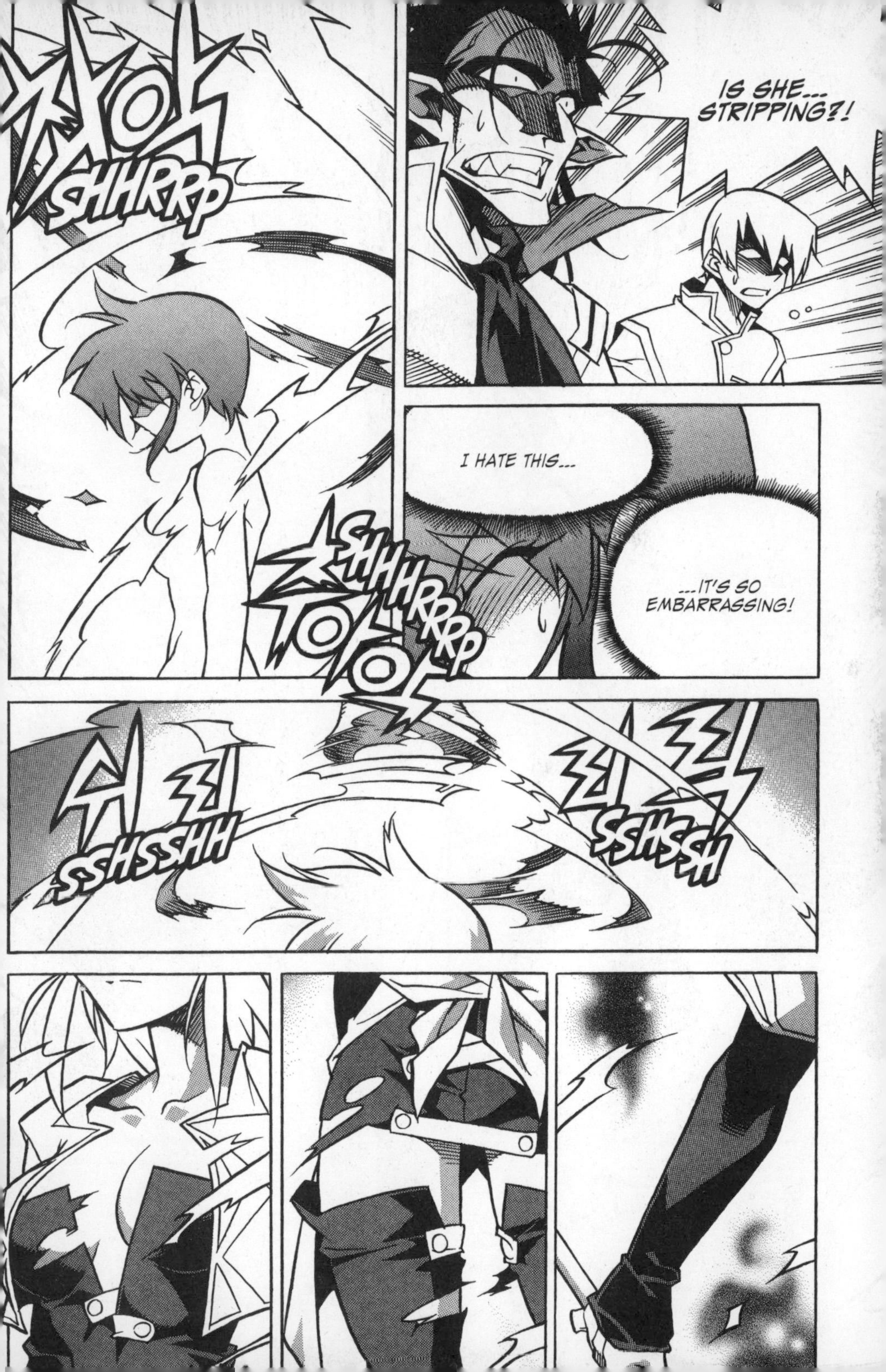
TOK
SHHRRP
IS SHE... STRIPPING?!
I HATE THIS...
...IT'S SO EMBARRASSING!
SHHHRRRP
TOK
SSHSSHH
SSHSSH

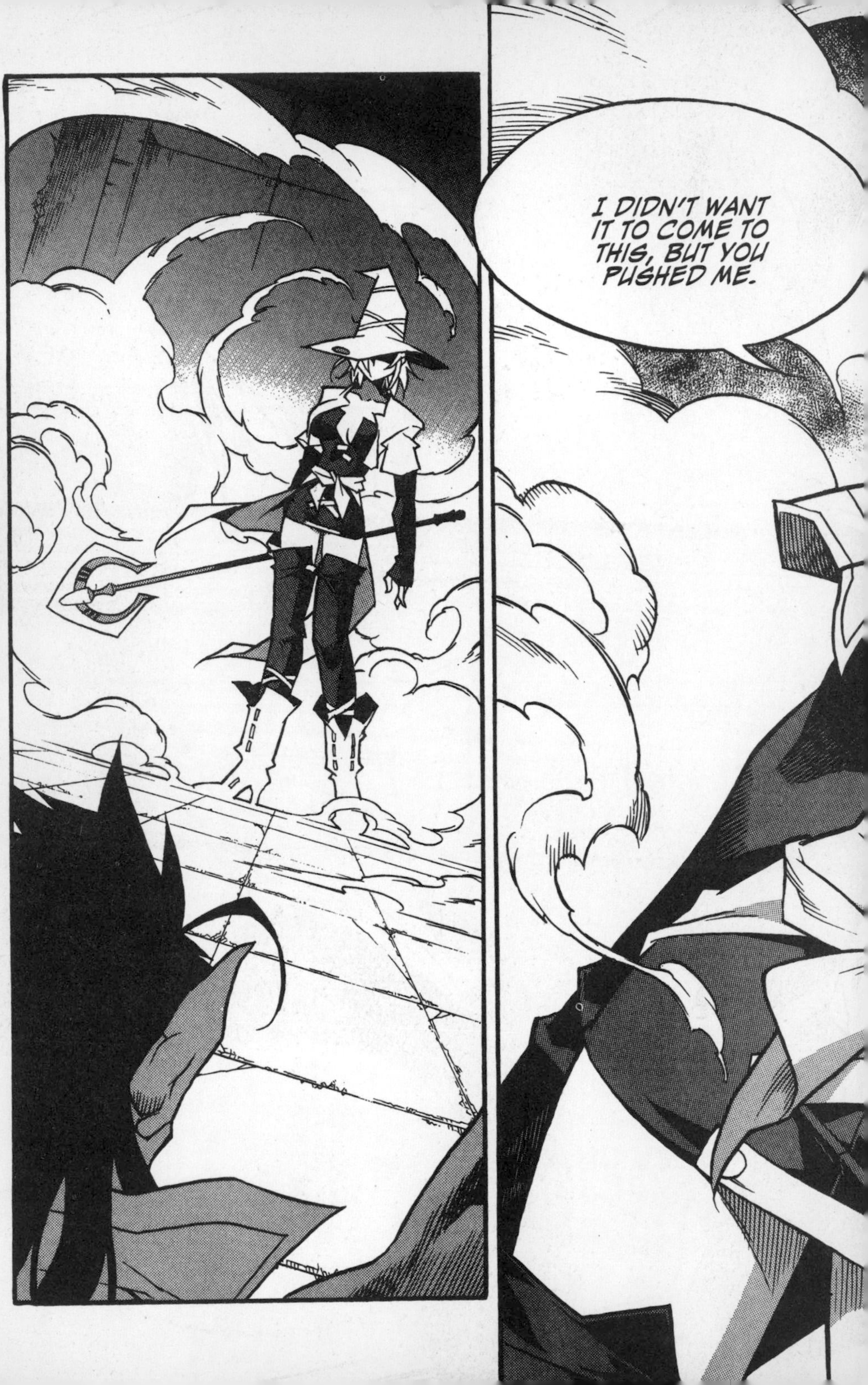
I DIDN'T WANT IT TO COME TO THIS, BUT YOU PUSHED ME.

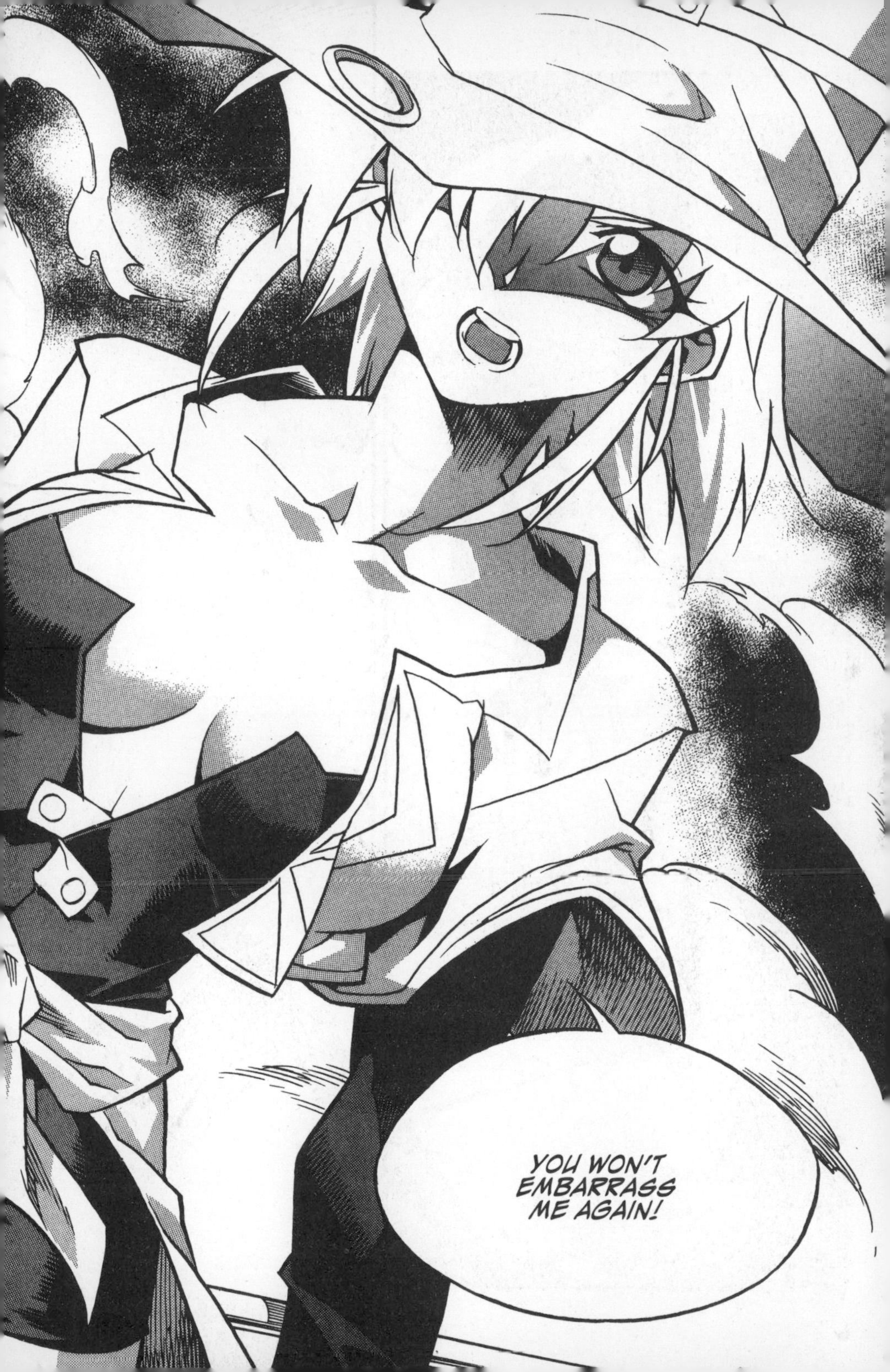
YOU WON'T EMBARRASS ME AGAIN!

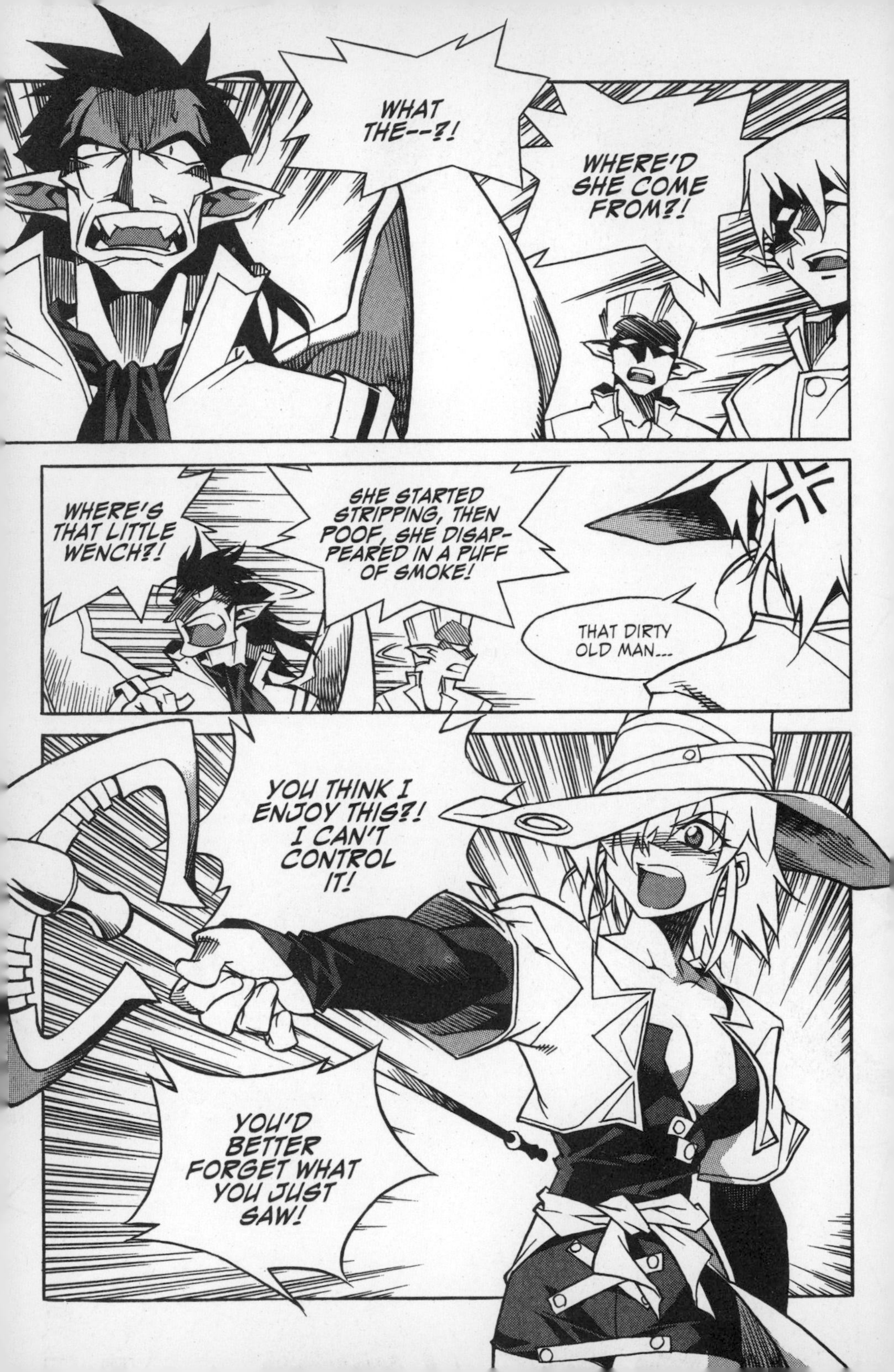
WHAT THE--?!
WHERE'D SHE COME FROM?!
WHERE'S THAT LITTLE WENCH?!
SHE STARTED STRIPPING, THEN POOF, SHE DISAPPEARED IN A PUFF OF SMOKE!
THAT DIRTY OLD MAN...
YOU THINK I ENJOY THIS?! I CAN'T CONTROL IT!
YOU'D BETTER FORGET WHAT YOU JUST SAW!

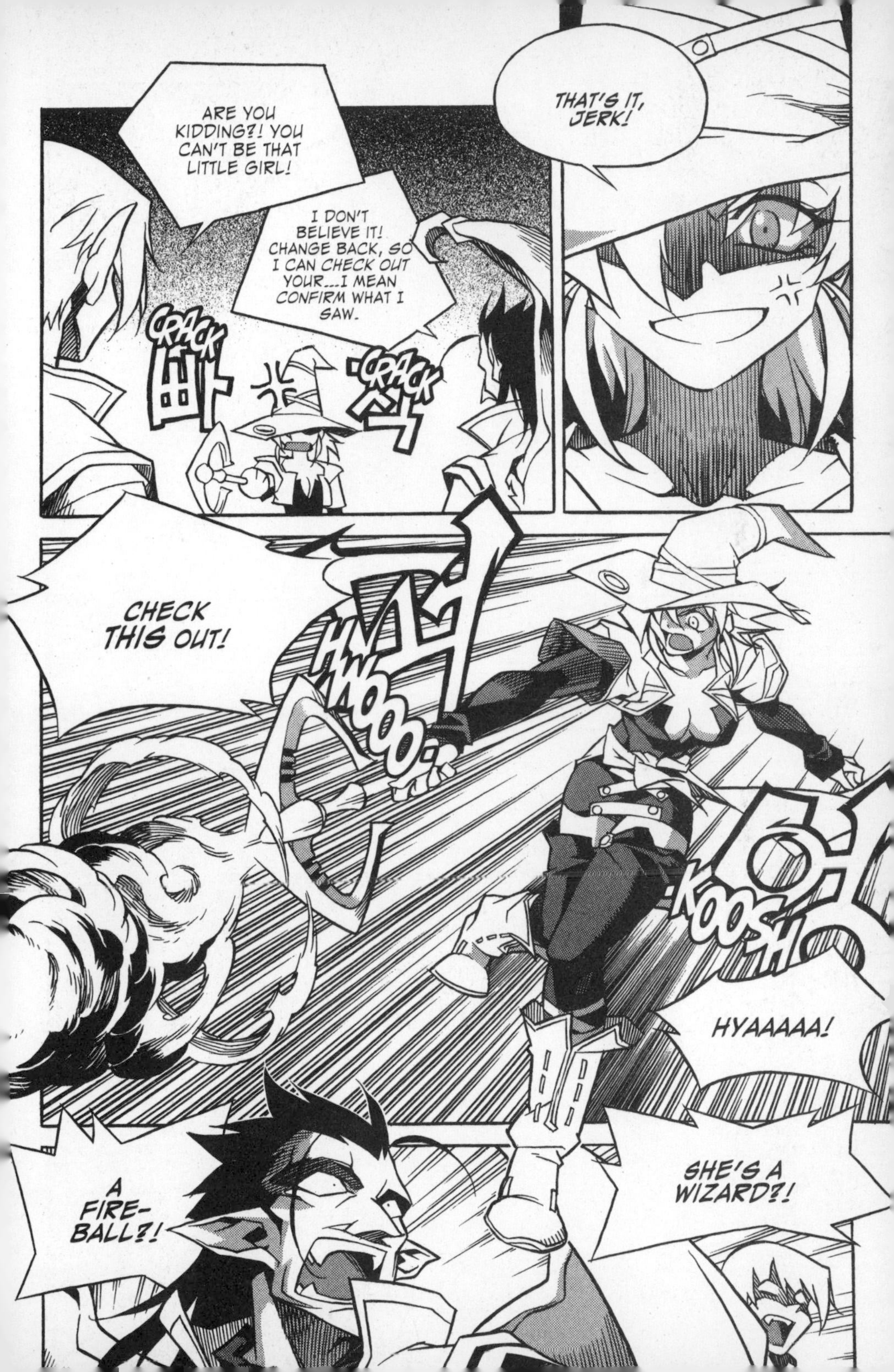
ARE YOU KIDDING?! YOU CAN'T BE THAT LITTLE GIRL!
I DON'T BELIEVE IT! CHANGE BACK, SO I CAN CHECK OUT YOUR...I MEAN CONFIRM WHAT I SAW.
CRACK
CRACK
THAT'S IT, JERK!
CHECK THIS OUT!
HWOOOO
KOOSH
HYAAAAA!
A FIRE-BALL?!
SHE'S A WIZARD?!

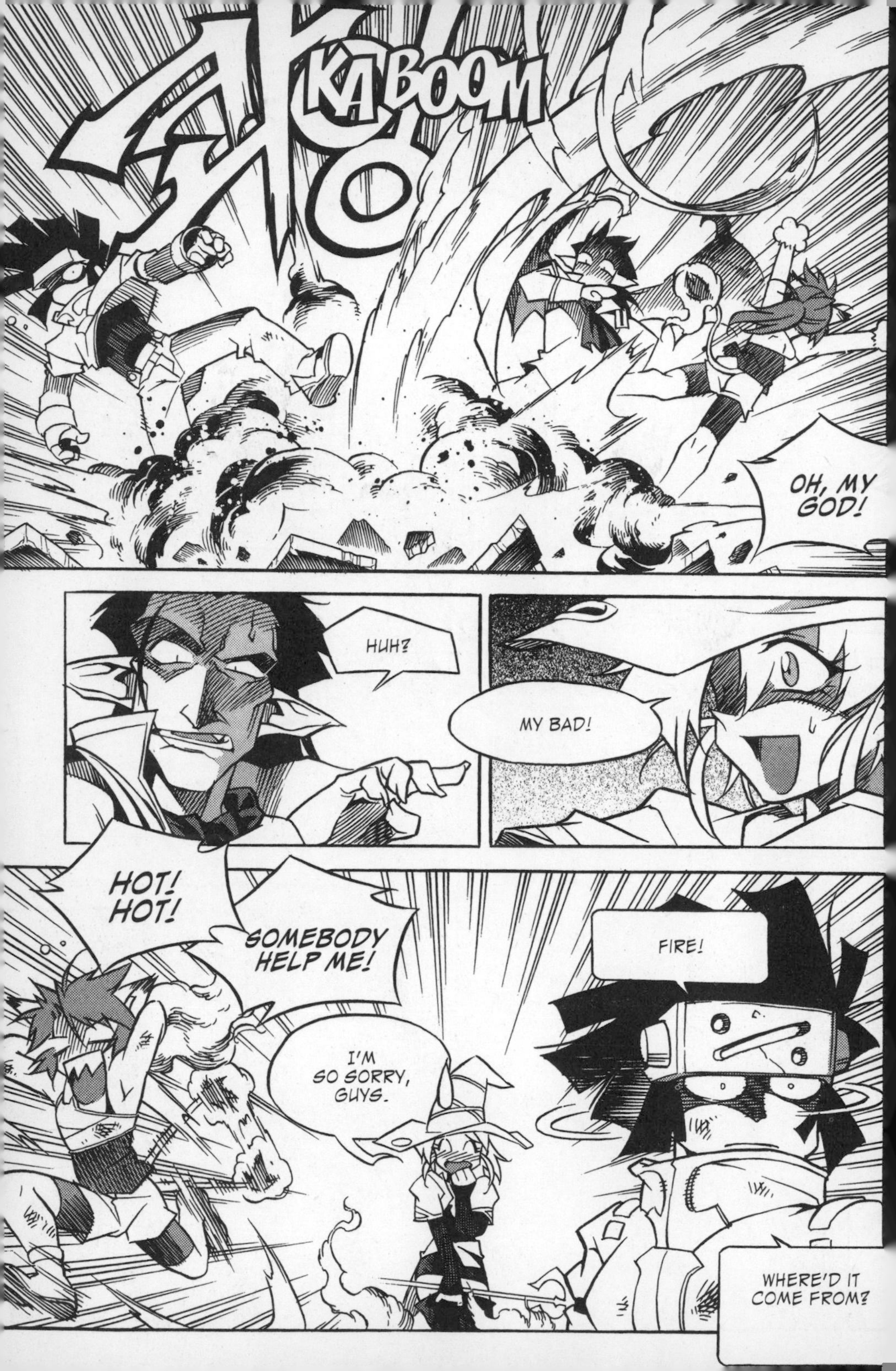
KA BOOM
OH, MY GOD!
HUH?
MY BAD!
HOT! HOT!
SOMEBODY HELP ME!
I'M SO SORRY, GUYS.
FIRE!
WHERE'D IT COME FROM?

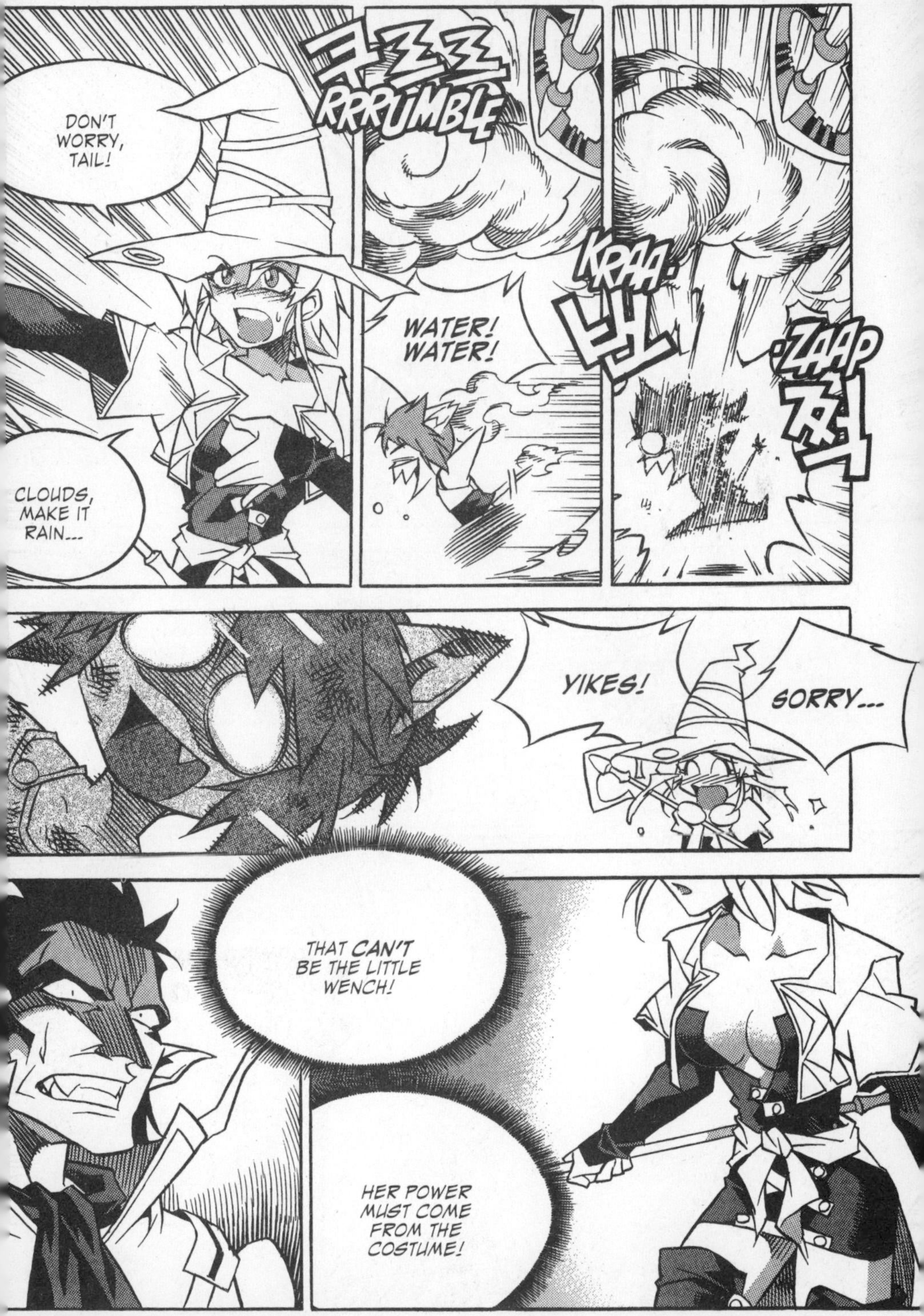
DON'T WORRY, TAIL!
CLOUDS, MAKE IT RAIN...
RRRUMBLE
WATER! WATER!
KRAA-
-ZAAP
YIKES!
SORRY...
THAT CAN'T BE THE LITTLE WENCH!
HER POWER MUST COME FROM THE COSTUME!

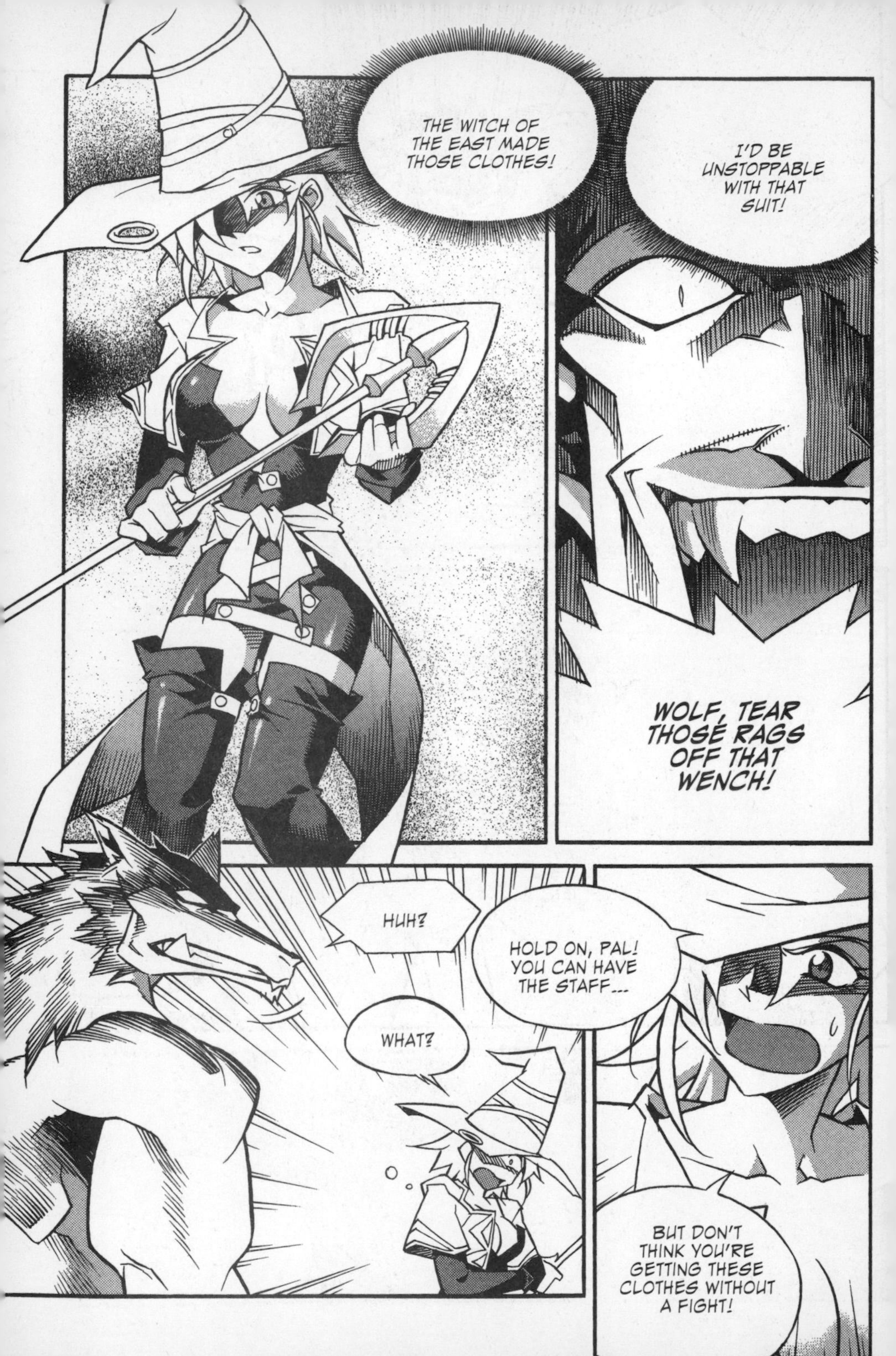
THE WITCH OF THE EAST MADE THOSE CLOTHES!
I'D BE UNSTOPPABLE WITH THAT SUIT!
WOLF, TEAR THOSE RAGS OFF THAT WENCH!
HUH?
HOLD ON, PAL! YOU CAN HAVE THE STAFF...
WHAT?
BUT DON'T THINK YOU'RE GETTING THESE CLOTHES WITHOUT A FIGHT!

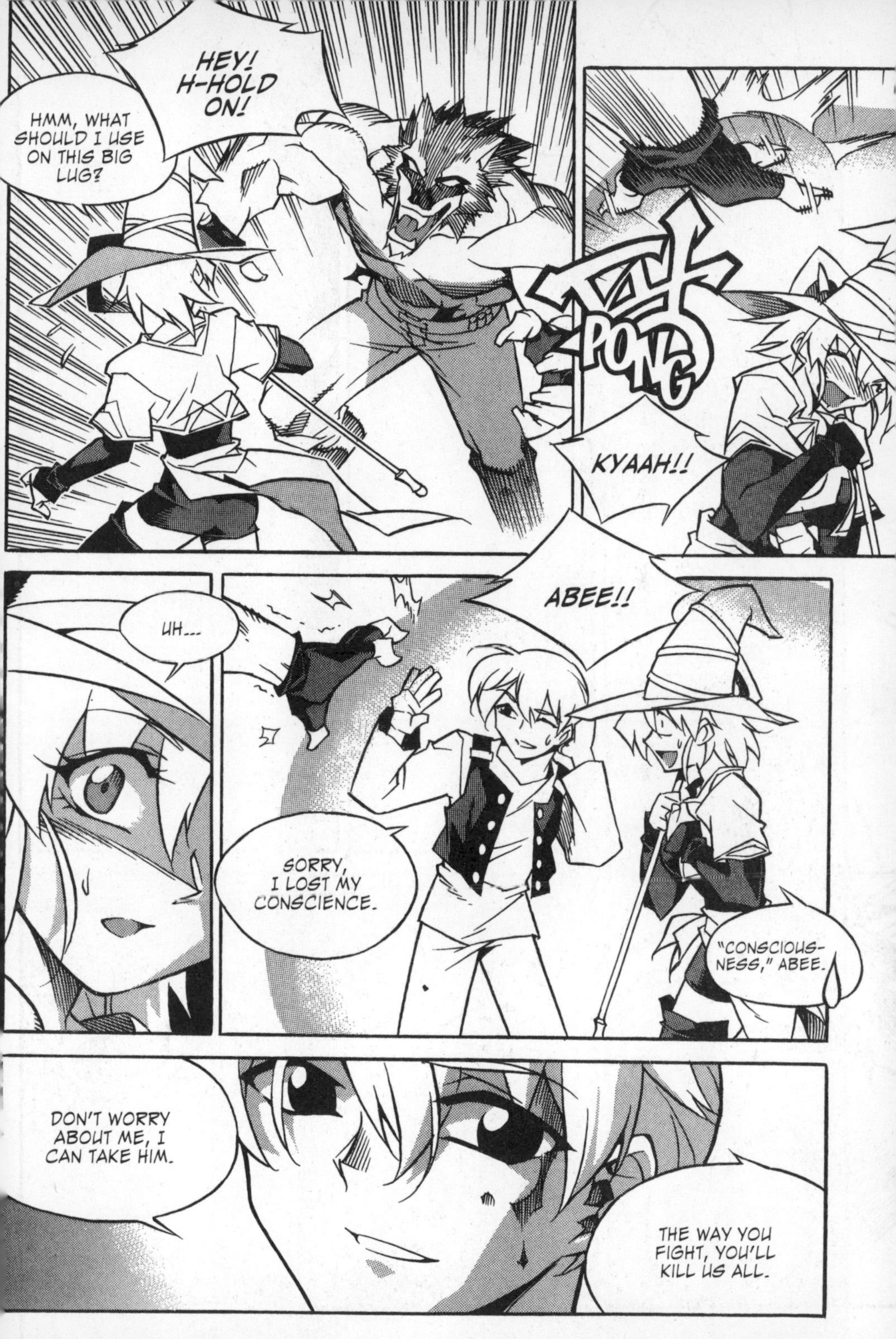
HMM, WHAT SHOULD I USE ON THIS BIG LUG?
HEY! H-HOLD ON!
TAK
PONG
KYAAH!!
UH...
ABEE!!
SORRY, I LOST MY CONSCIENCE.
"CONSCIOUSNESS," ABEE.
DON'T WORRY ABOUT ME, I CAN TAKE HIM.
THE WAY YOU FIGHT, YOU'LL KILL US ALL.

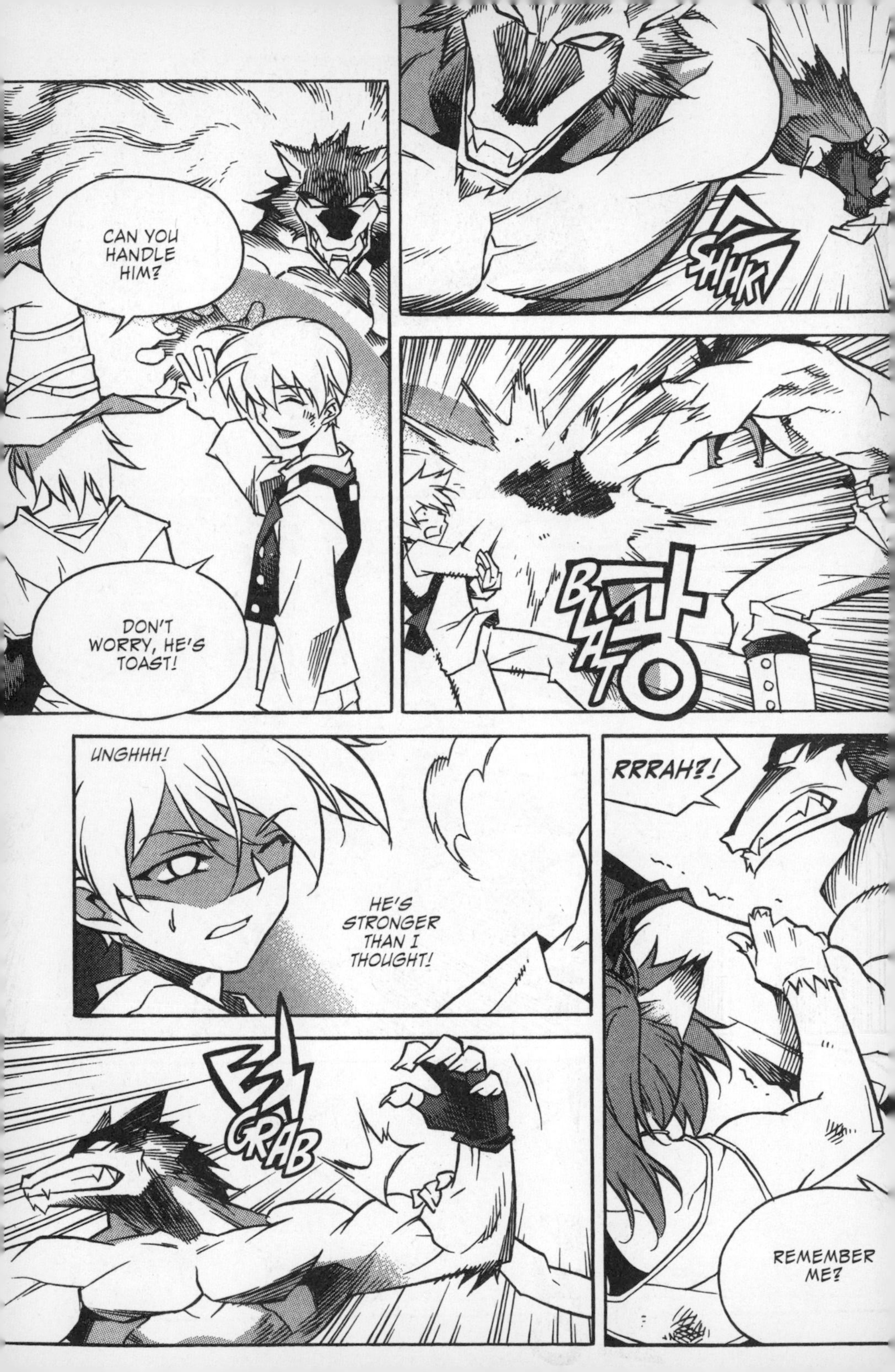
CAN YOU HANDLE HIM?
DON'T WORRY, HE'S TOAST!
SHHK
BLAT
UNGHHH!
HE'S STRONGER THAN I THOUGHT!
GRAB
RRRAH?!
REMEMBER ME?

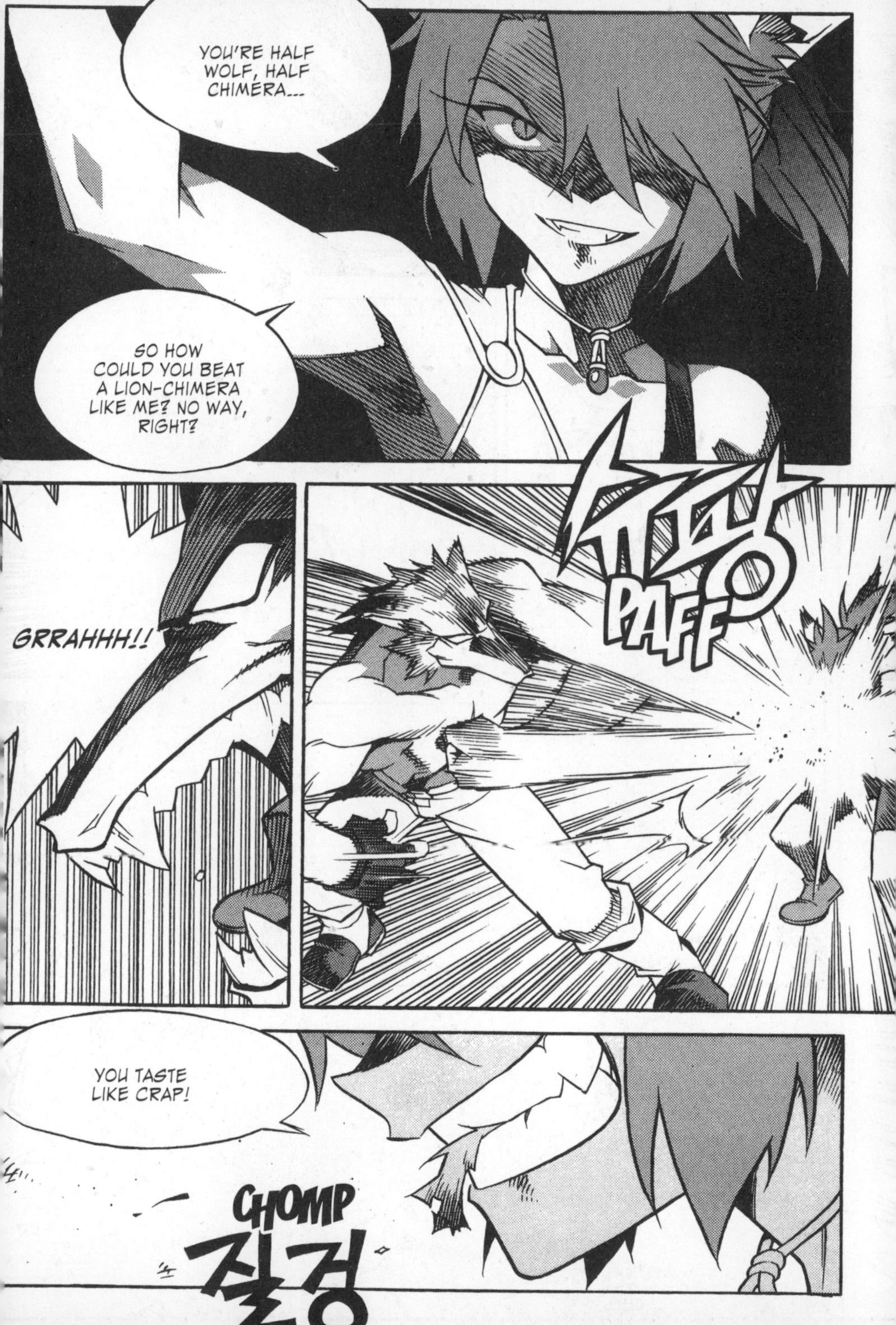
YOU'RE HALF WOLF, HALF CHIMERA...
SO HOW COULD YOU BEAT A LION-CHIMERA LIKE ME? NO WAY, RIGHT?
GRRAHHH!!
PAFF
YOU TASTE LIKE CRAP!
CHOMP
질겅

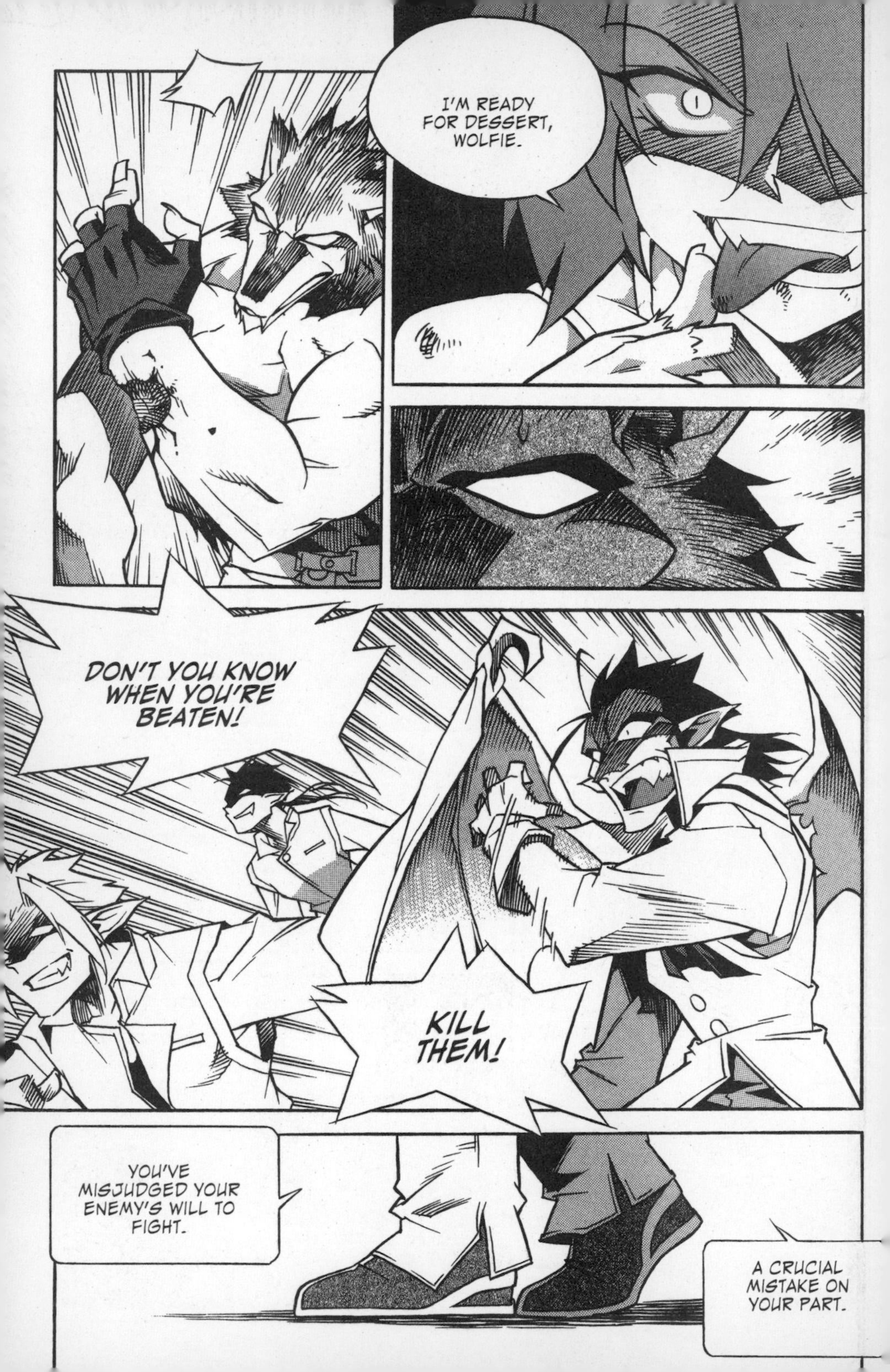

I'M READY FOR DESSERT, WOLFIE.
DON'T YOU KNOW WHEN YOU'RE BEATEN!
KILL THEM!
YOU'VE MISJUDGED YOUR ENEMY'S WILL TO FIGHT.
A CRUCIAL MISTAKE ON YOUR PART.

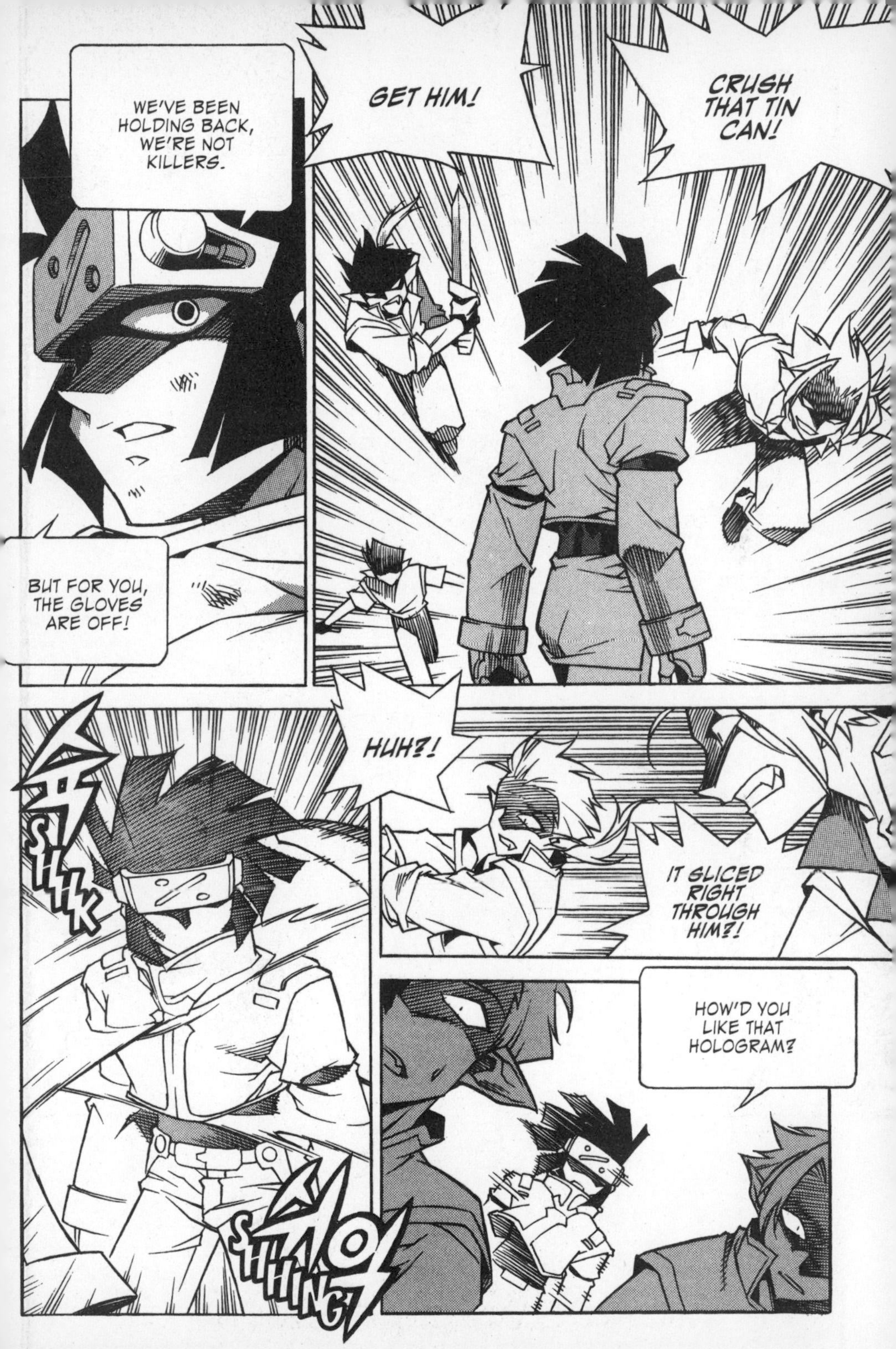
WE'VE BEEN HOLDING BACK, WE'RE NOT KILLERS.
BUT FOR YOU, THE GLOVES ARE OFF!
GET HIM!
CRUSH THAT TIN CAN!
SHIIK
SHHING
HUH?!
IT SLICED RIGHT THROUGH HIM?!
HOW'D YOU LIKE THAT HOLOGRAM?

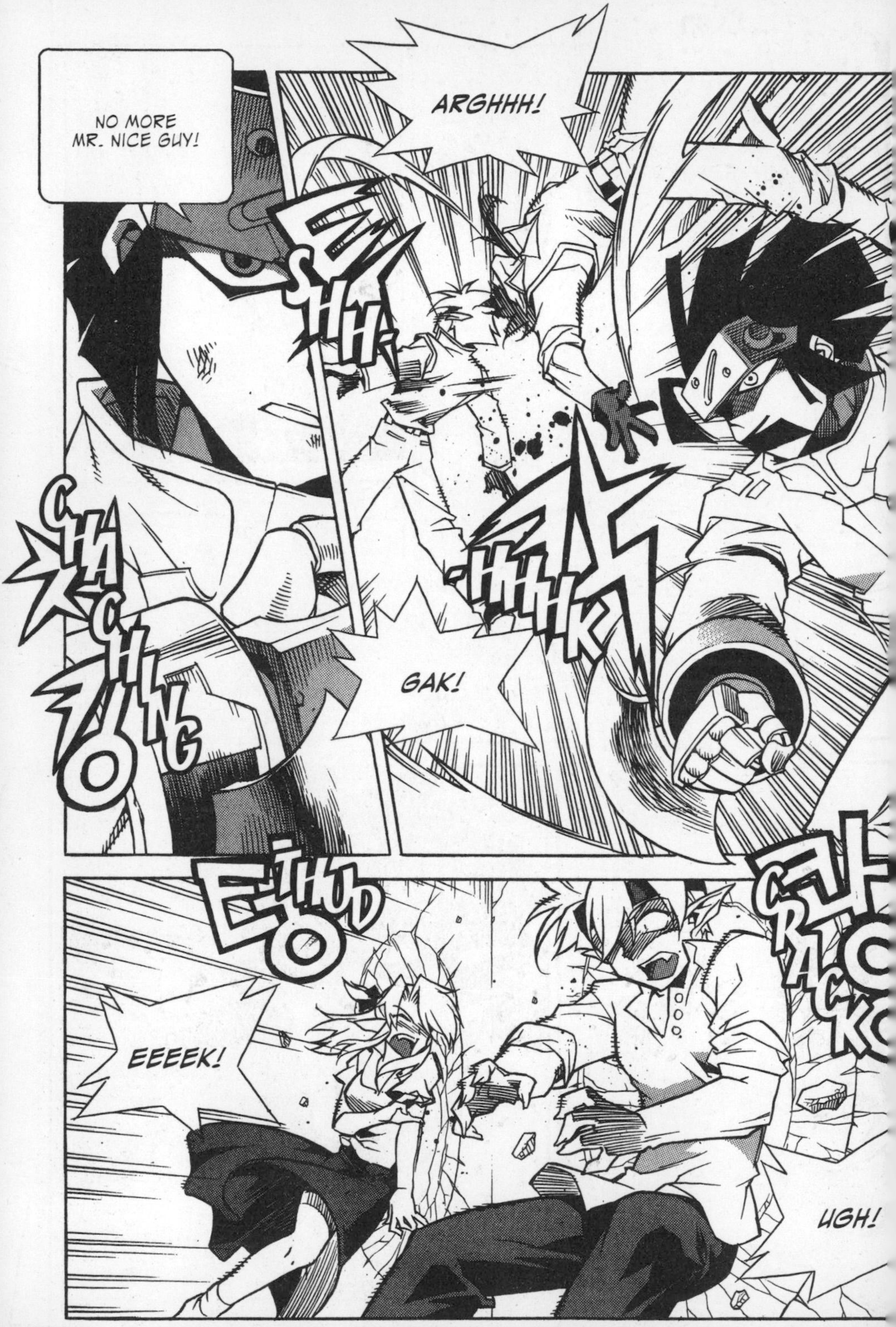
NO MORE MR. NICE GUY!
ARGHHH!
SHHH-
CHACHING
-HHHHK
GAK!
E-THUD
CRACK
EEEEK!
UGH!

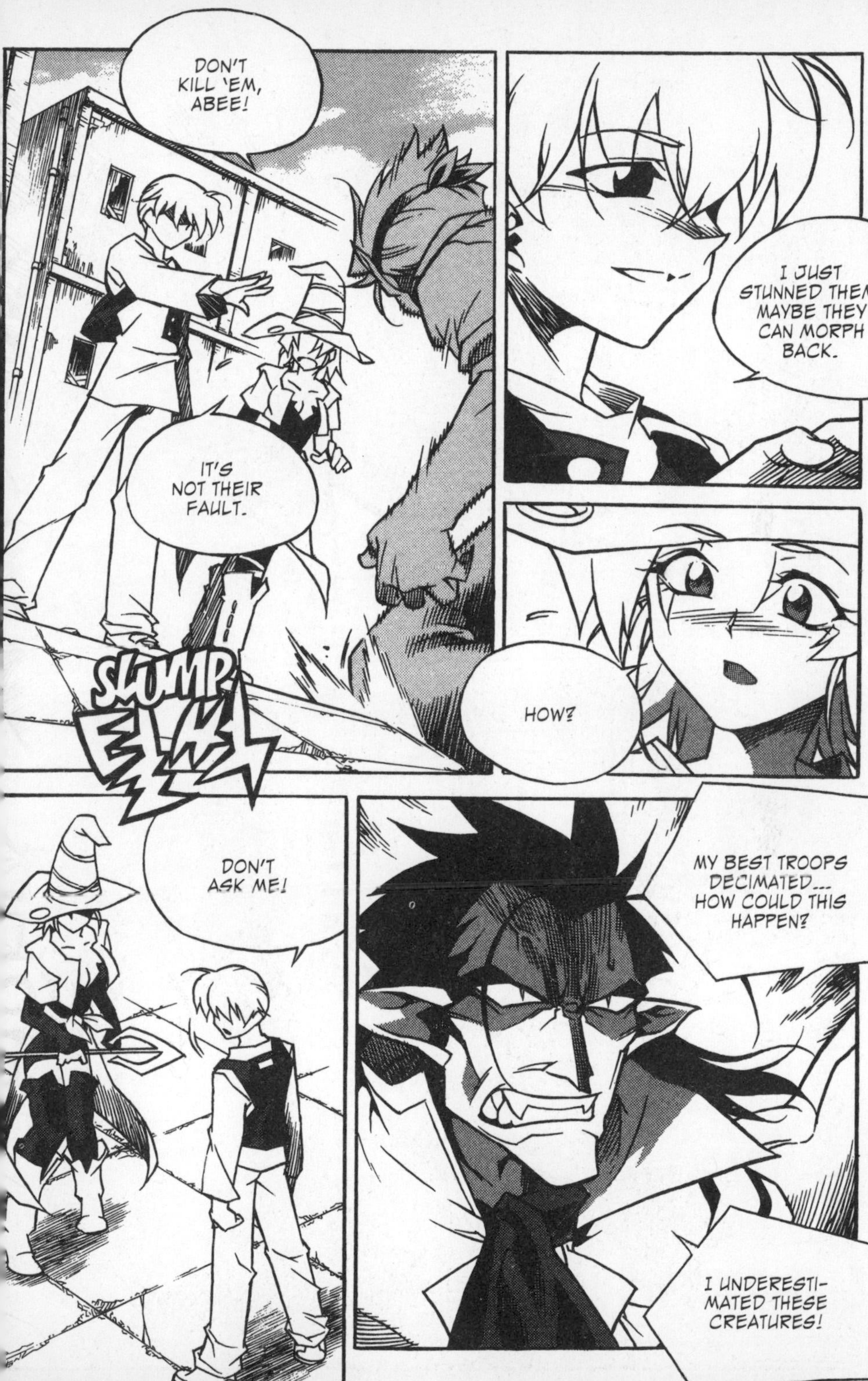
DON'T KILL 'EM, ABEE!
IT'S NOT THEIR FAULT.
SLUMP
I JUST STUNNED THEM. MAYBE THEY CAN MORPH BACK.
HOW?
DON'T ASK ME!
MY BEST TROOPS DECIMATED... HOW COULD THIS HAPPEN?
I UNDERESTI-MATED THESE CREATURES!

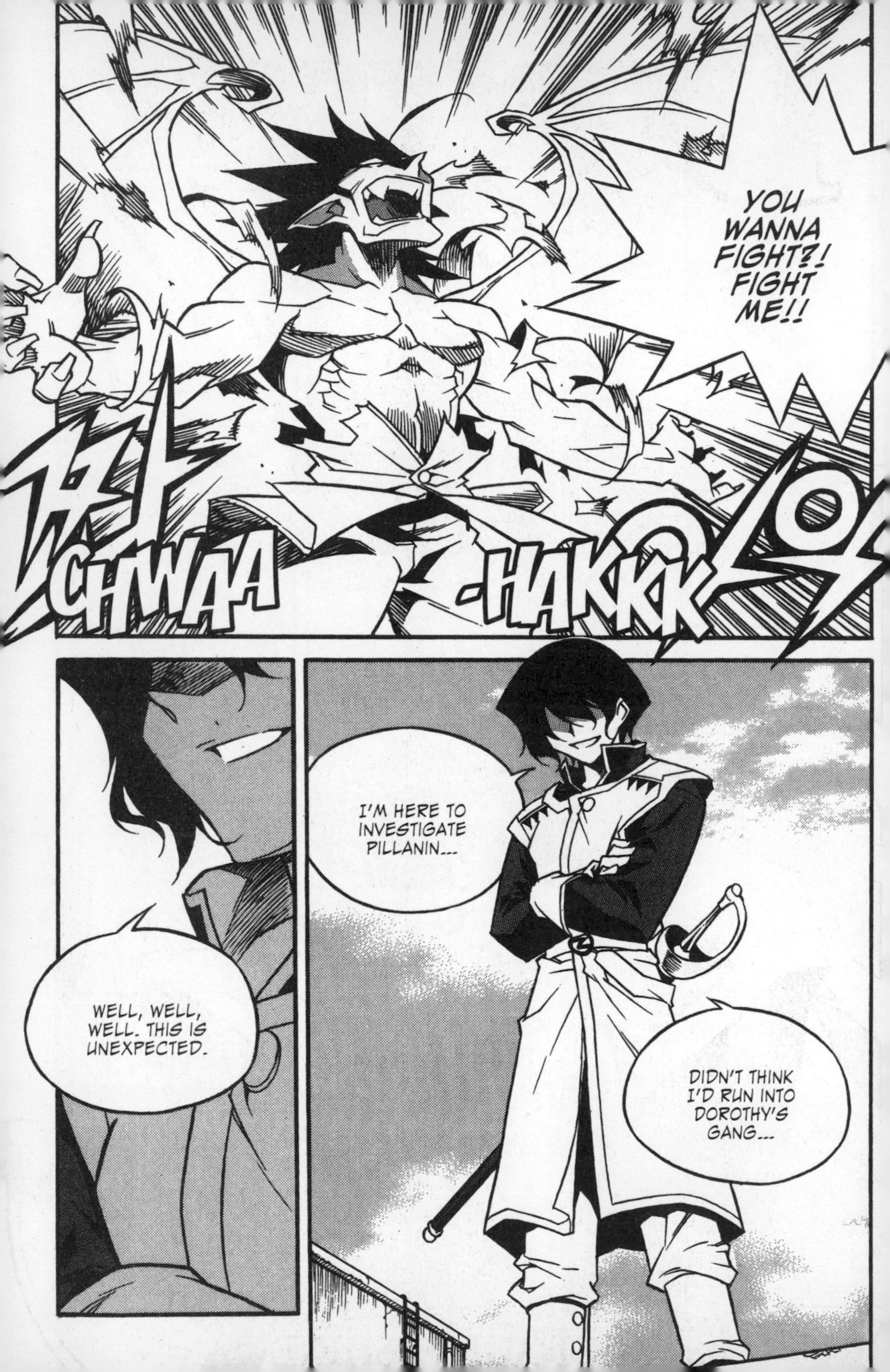
YOU WANNA FIGHT?! FIGHT ME!!
CHWAAA-HAKKK
WELL, WELL, WELL. THIS IS UNEXPECTED.
I'M HERE TO INVESTIGATE PILLANIN...
DIDN'T THINK I'D RUN INTO DOROTHY'S GANG...

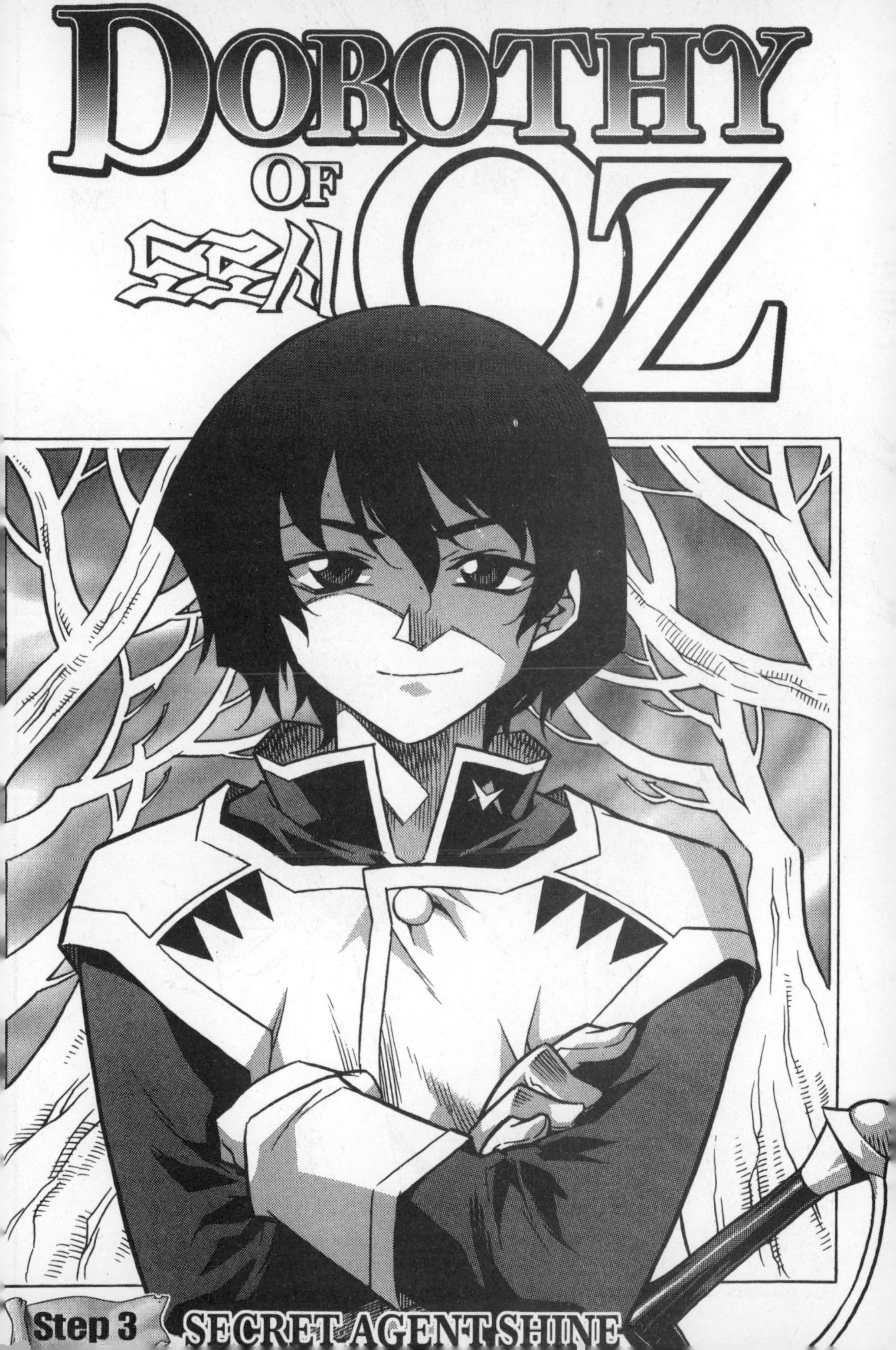
DOROTHY OF 오즈 OZ
Step 3
SECRET AGENT SHINE

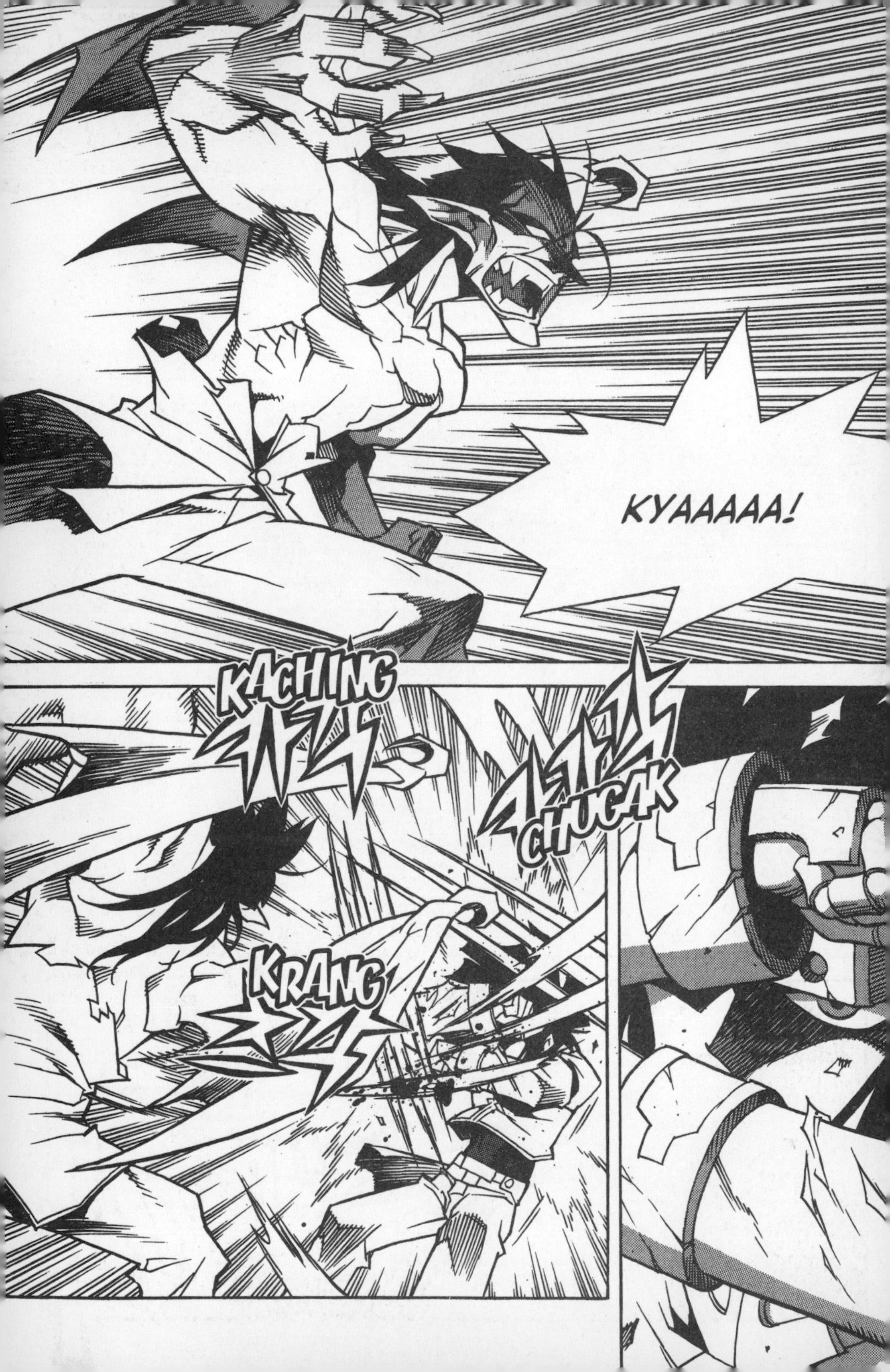
KYAAAAA!
KACHING
CHUCAK
KRANG

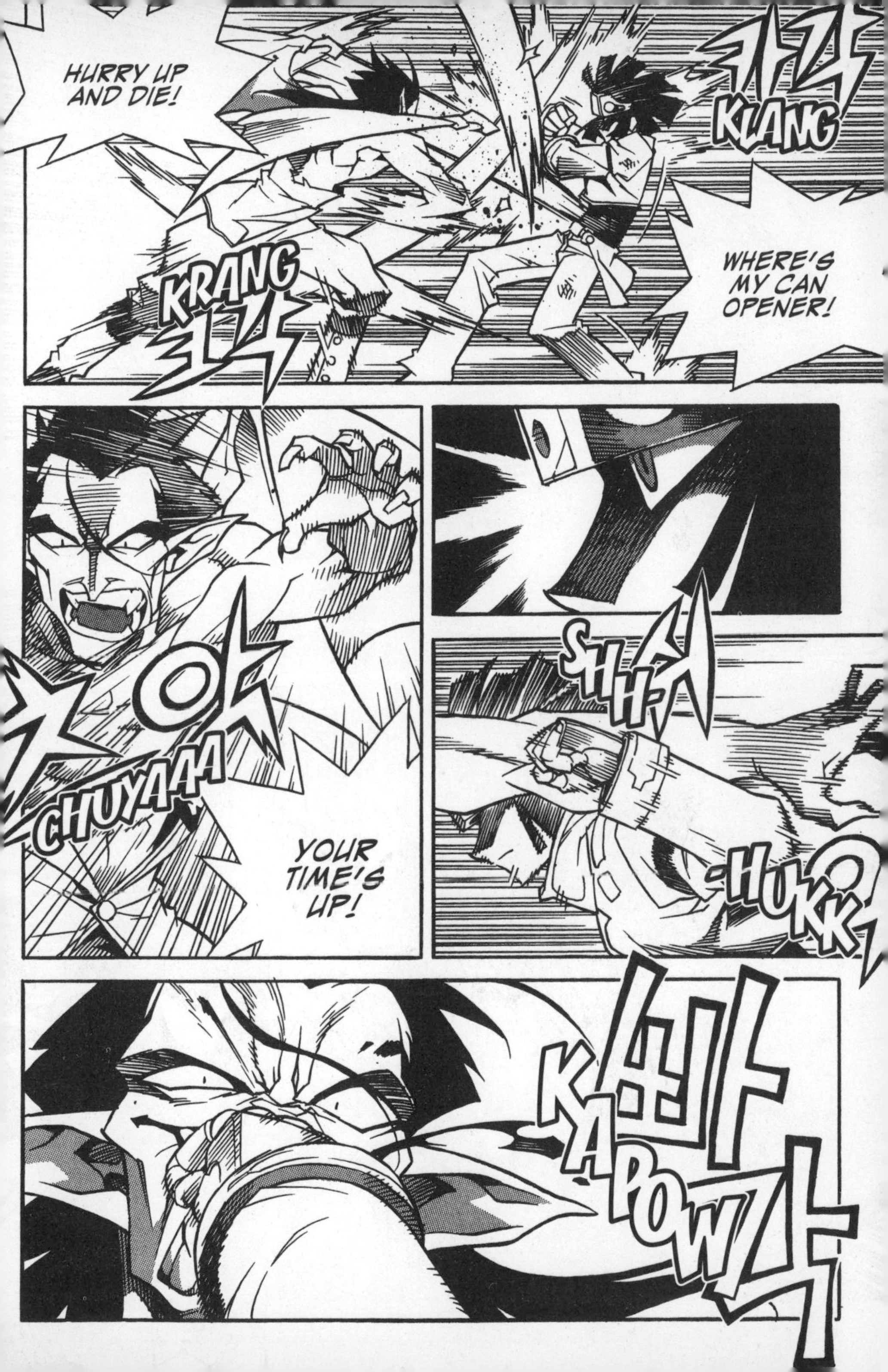
HURRY UP AND DIE!
KLANG
KRANG
WHERE'S MY CAN OPENER!
CHUYAAA
YOUR TIME'S UP!
SHH
HUKK
KAPOW

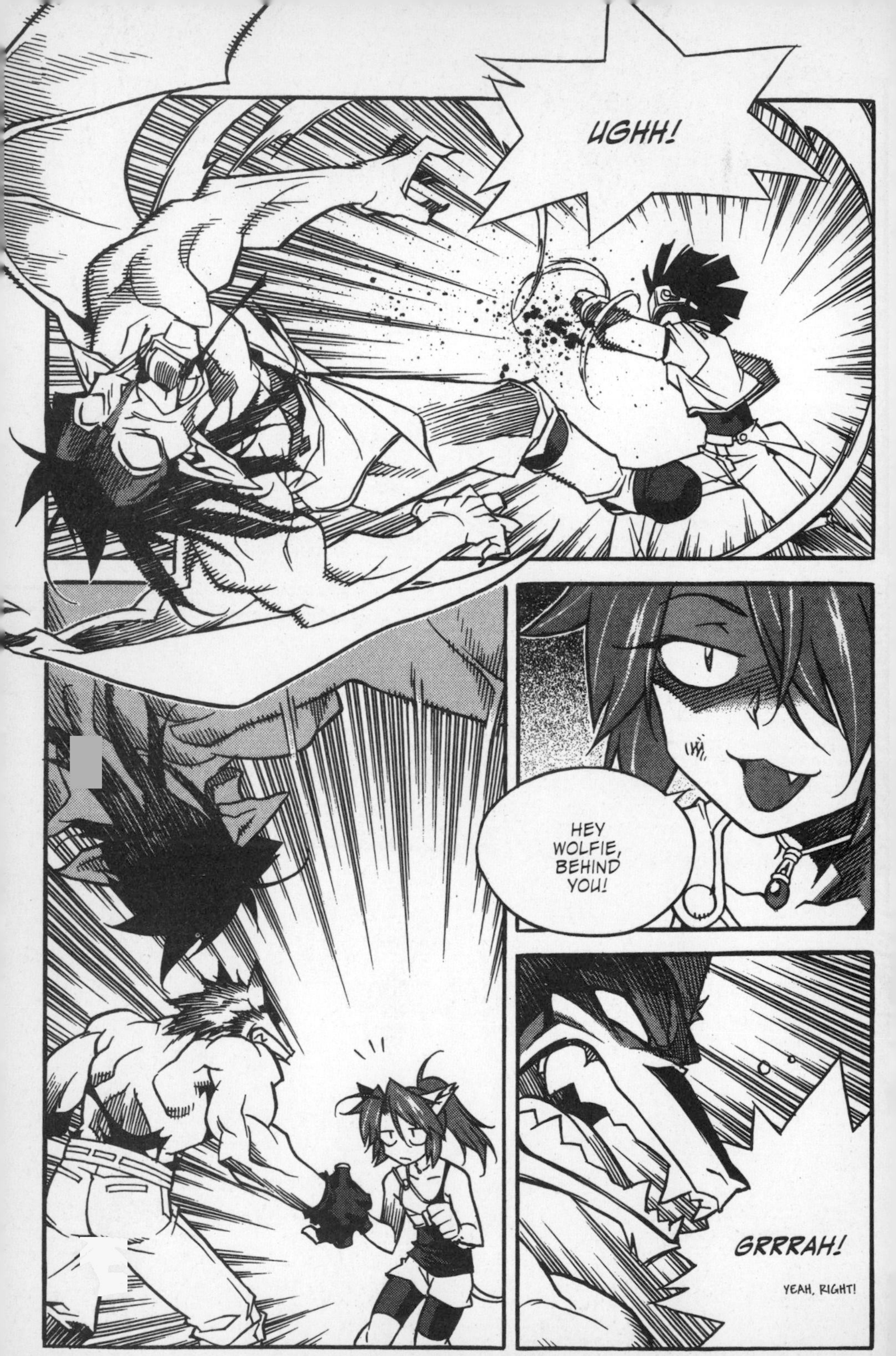
UGHH!
HEY WOLFIE, BEHIND YOU!
GRRRAH!
YEAH, RIGHT!

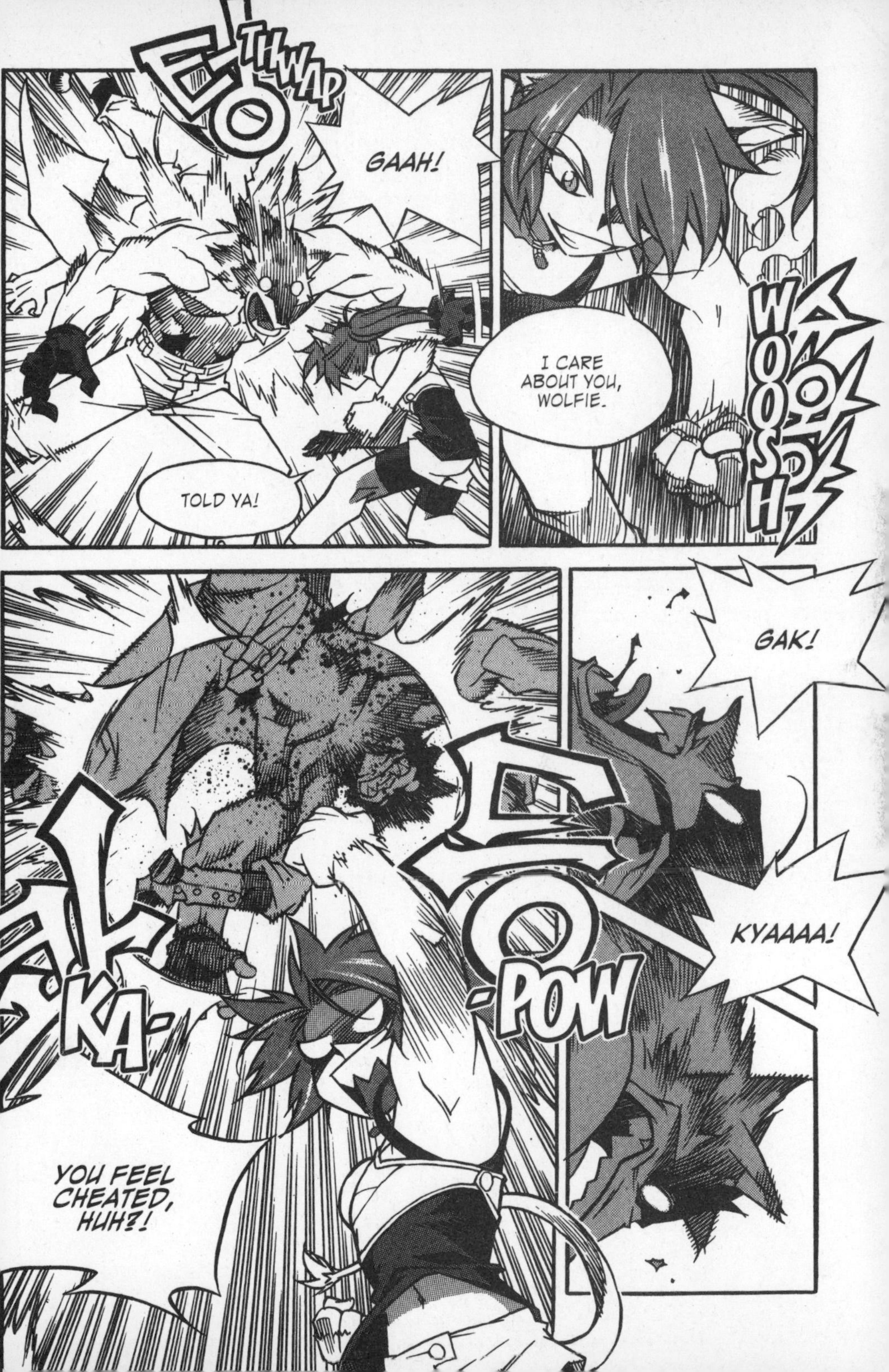
THWAP
GAAH!
TOLD YA!
I CARE ABOUT YOU, WOLFIE.
WOOSH
KA-
-POW
YOU FEEL CHEATED, HUH?!
GAK!
KYAAAA!

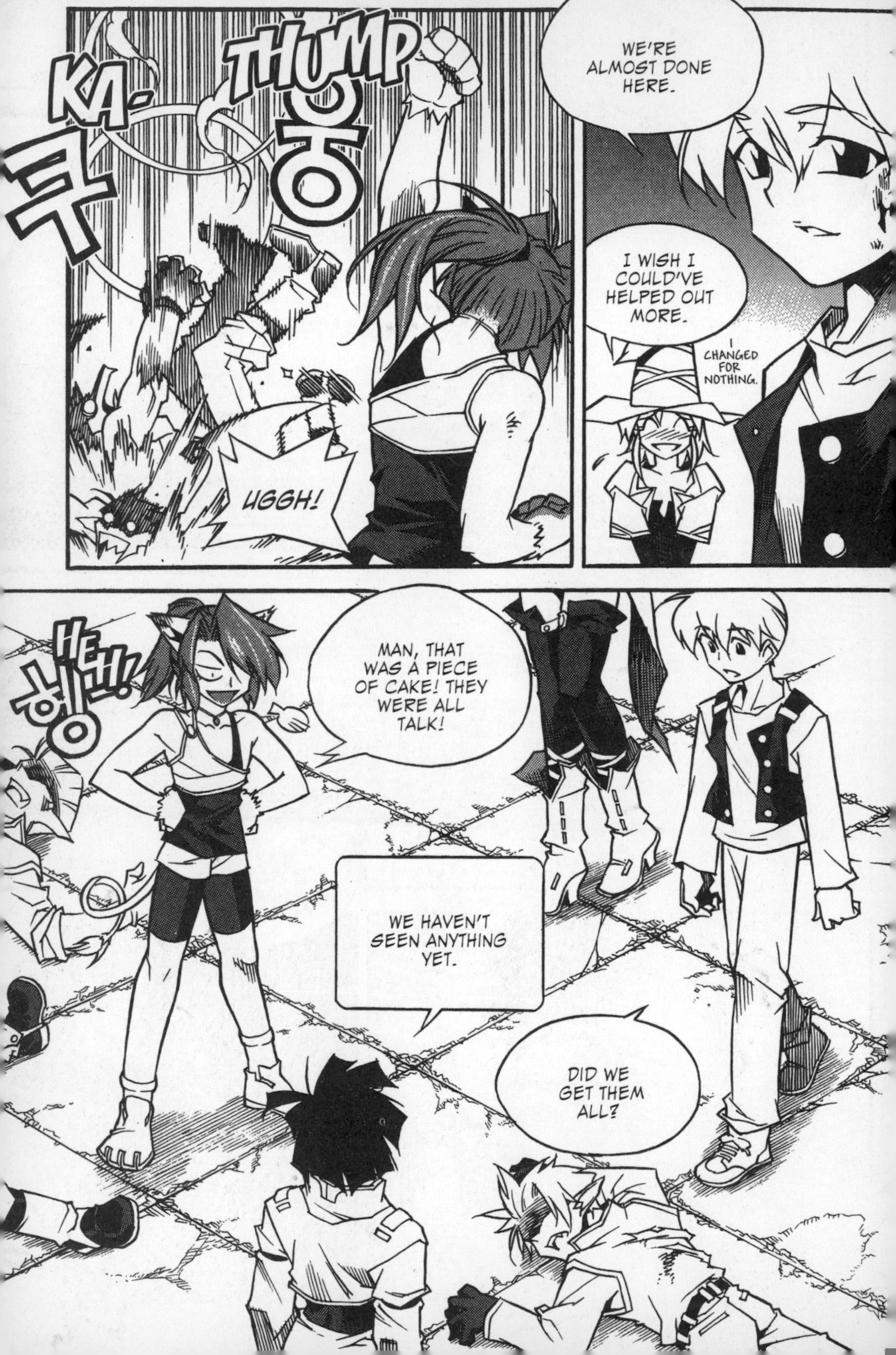
KA-
THUMP
쿠
웅
UGGH!
WE'RE ALMOST DONE HERE.
I WISH I COULD'VE HELPED OUT MORE.
I CHANGED FOR NOTHING.
HEHH!
헤
MAN, THAT WAS A PIECE OF CAKE! THEY WERE ALL TALK!
WE HAVEN'T SEEN ANYTHING YET.
DID WE GET THEM ALL?

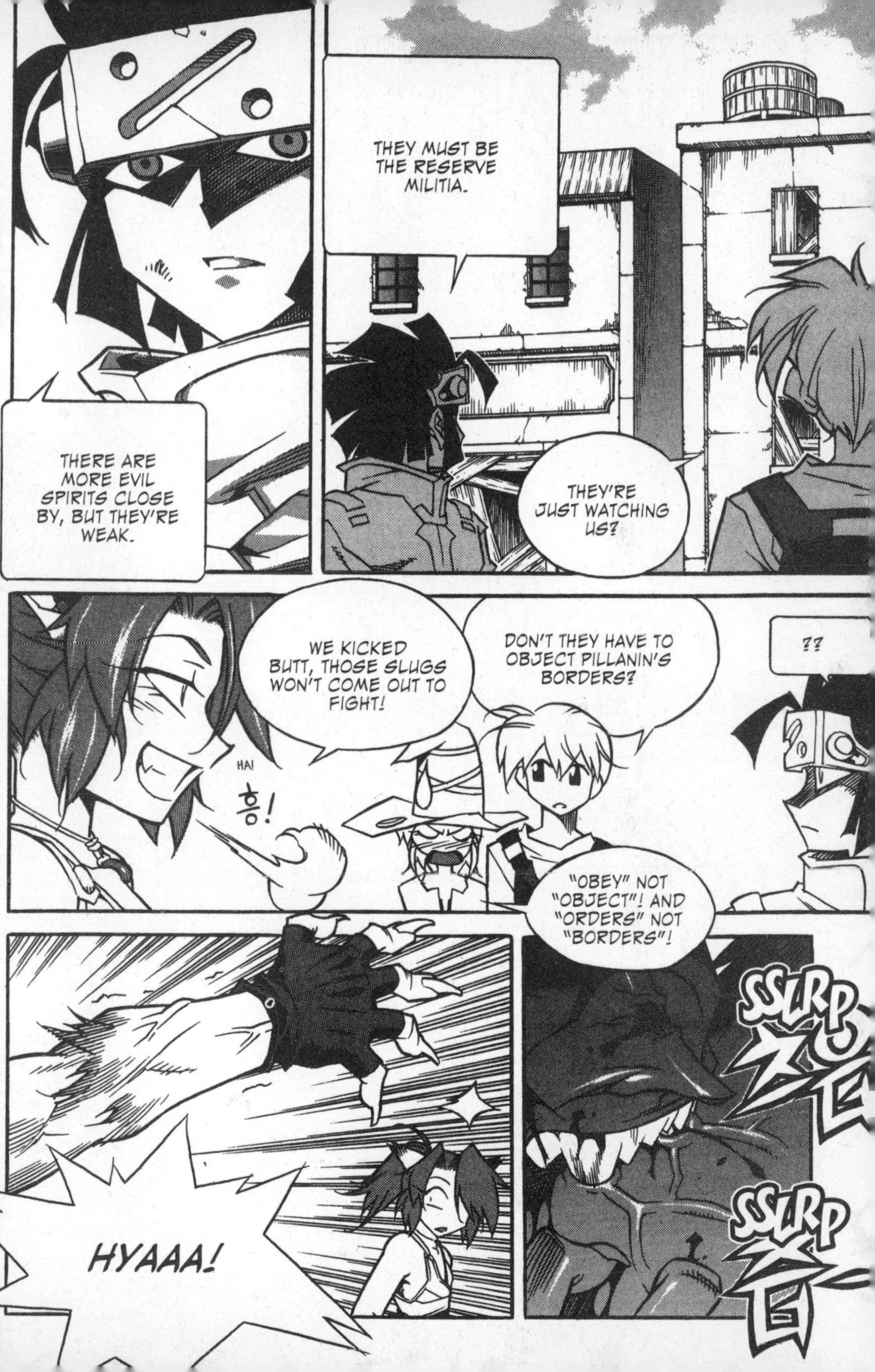
THERE ARE MORE EVIL SPIRITS CLOSE BY, BUT THEY'RE WEAK.
THEY MUST BE THE RESERVE MILITIA.
THEY'RE JUST WATCHING US?
WE KICKED BUTT, THOSE SLUGS WON'T COME OUT TO FIGHT!
HA!
흥!
DON'T THEY HAVE TO OBJECT PILLANIN'S BORDERS?
??
"OBEY" NOT "OBJECT"! AND "ORDERS" NOT "BORDERS"!
HYAAA!
SSLRP
SSLRP

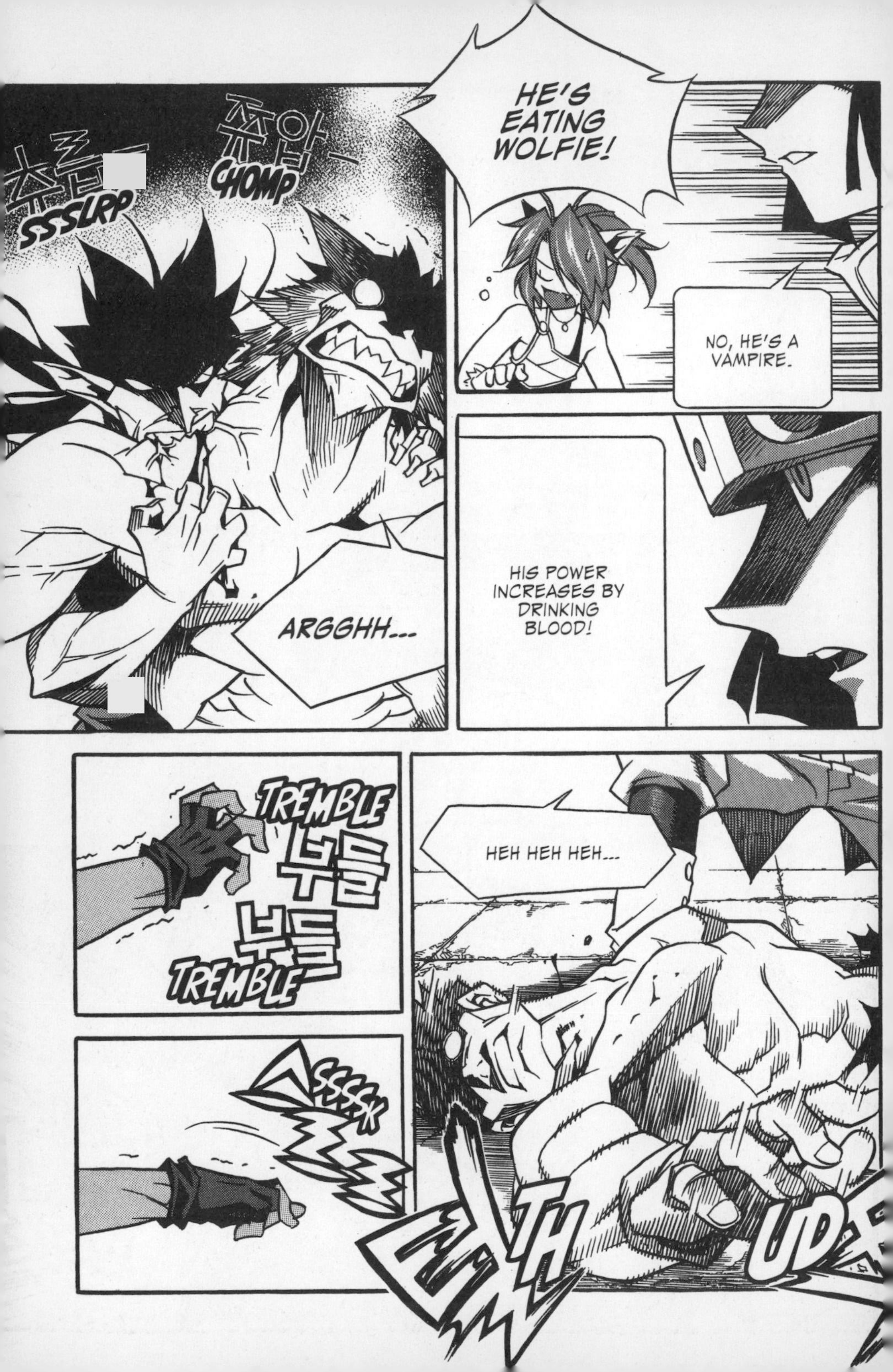
SSSLRP
CHOMP
ARGGHH...
HE'S EATING WOLFIE!
NO, HE'S A VAMPIRE.
HIS POWER INCREASES BY DRINKING BLOOD!
TREMBLE
부들
부들
TREMBLE
SSSSK
HEH HEH HEH...
THUD

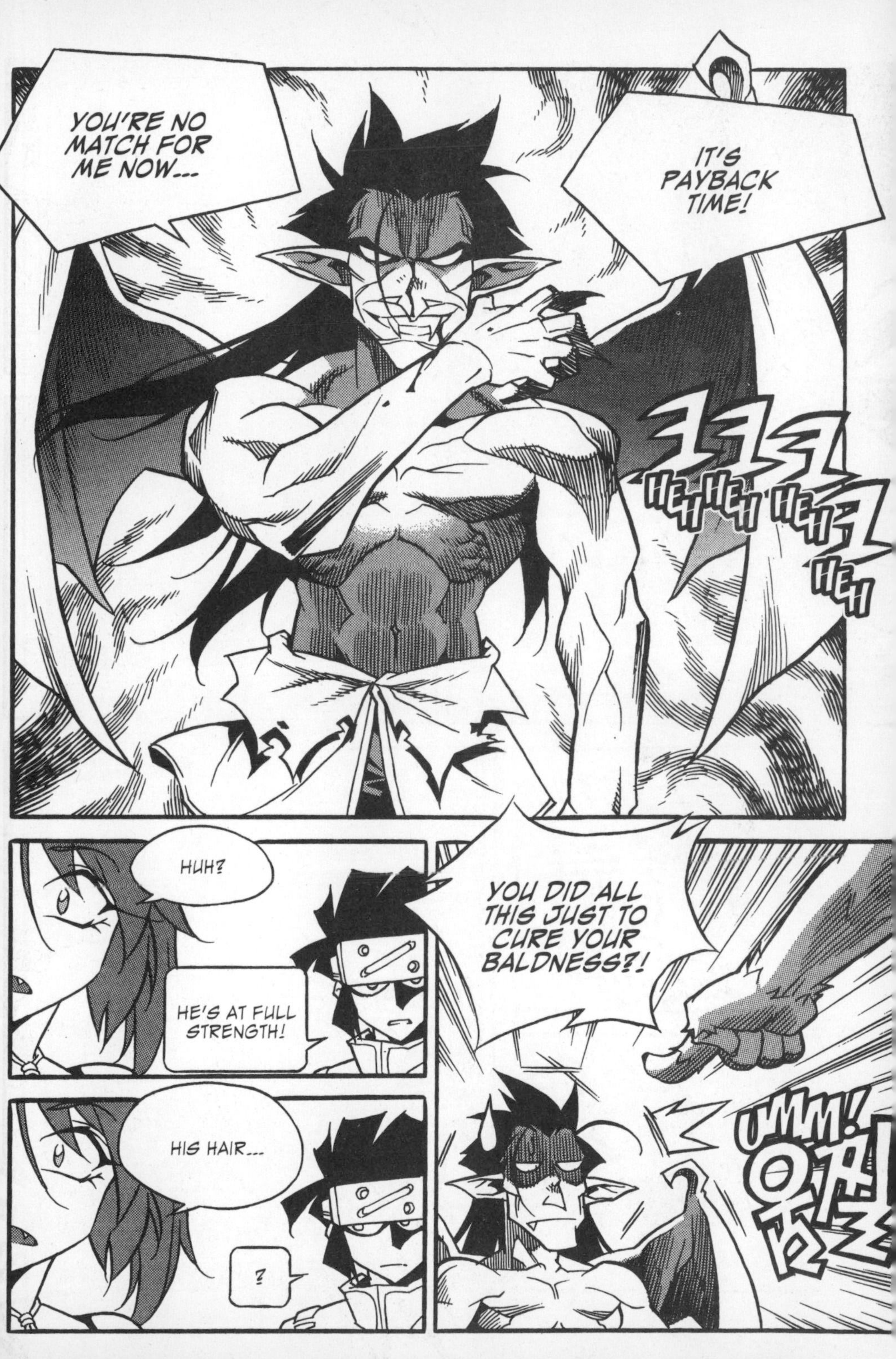
YOU'RE NO MATCH FOR ME NOW...
IT'S PAYBACK TIME!
HEH HEH HEH HEH HEH
HUH?
HE'S AT FULL STRENGTH!
HIS HAIR...
?
YOU DID ALL THIS JUST TO CURE YOUR BALDNESS?!
UMM!

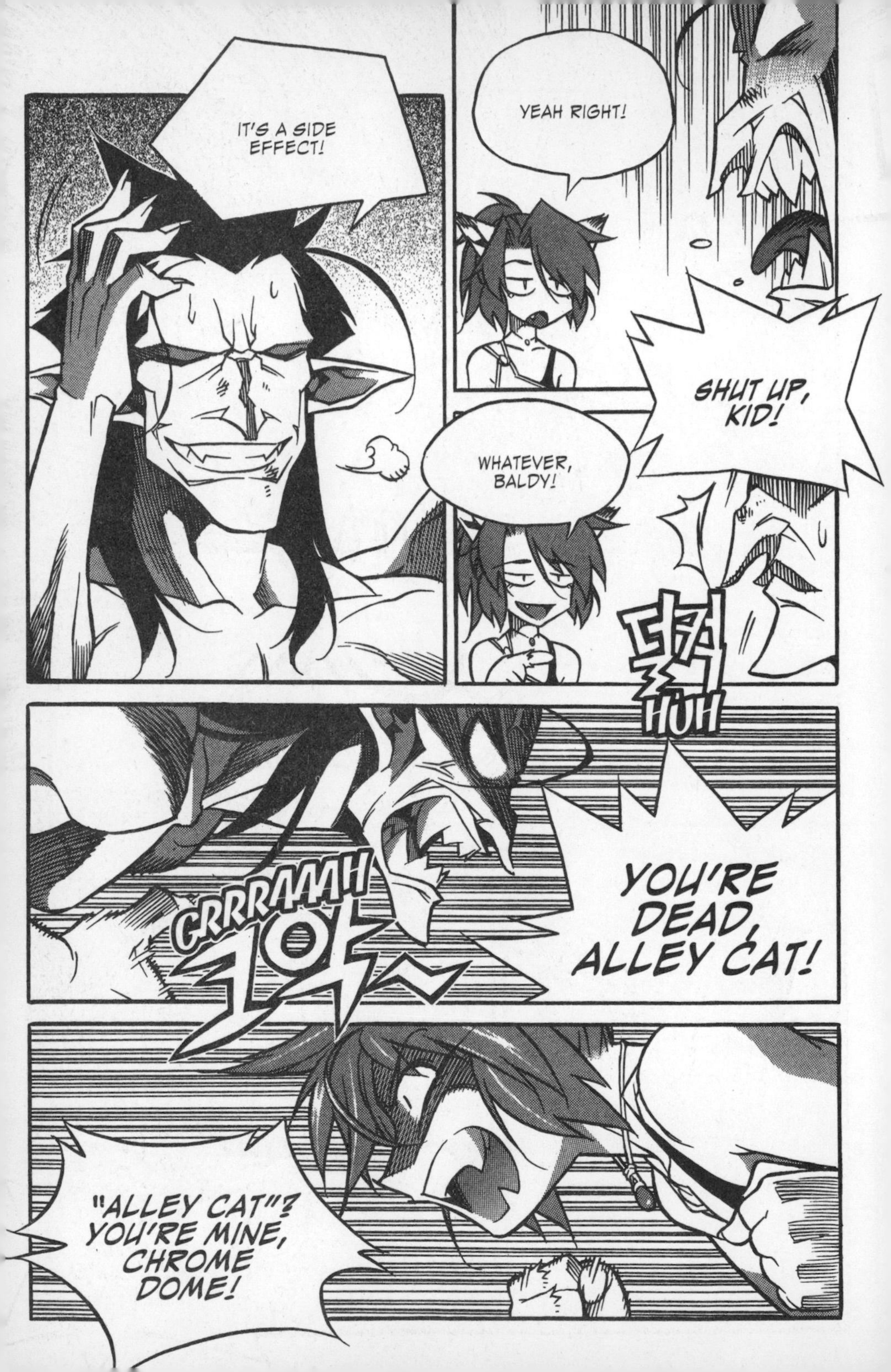
IT'S A SIDE EFFECT!
YEAH RIGHT!
SHUT UP, KID!
WHATEVER, BALDY!
HUH
GRRRAAAH
YOU'RE DEAD, ALLEY CAT!
"ALLEY CAT"? YOU'RE MINE, CHROME DOME!

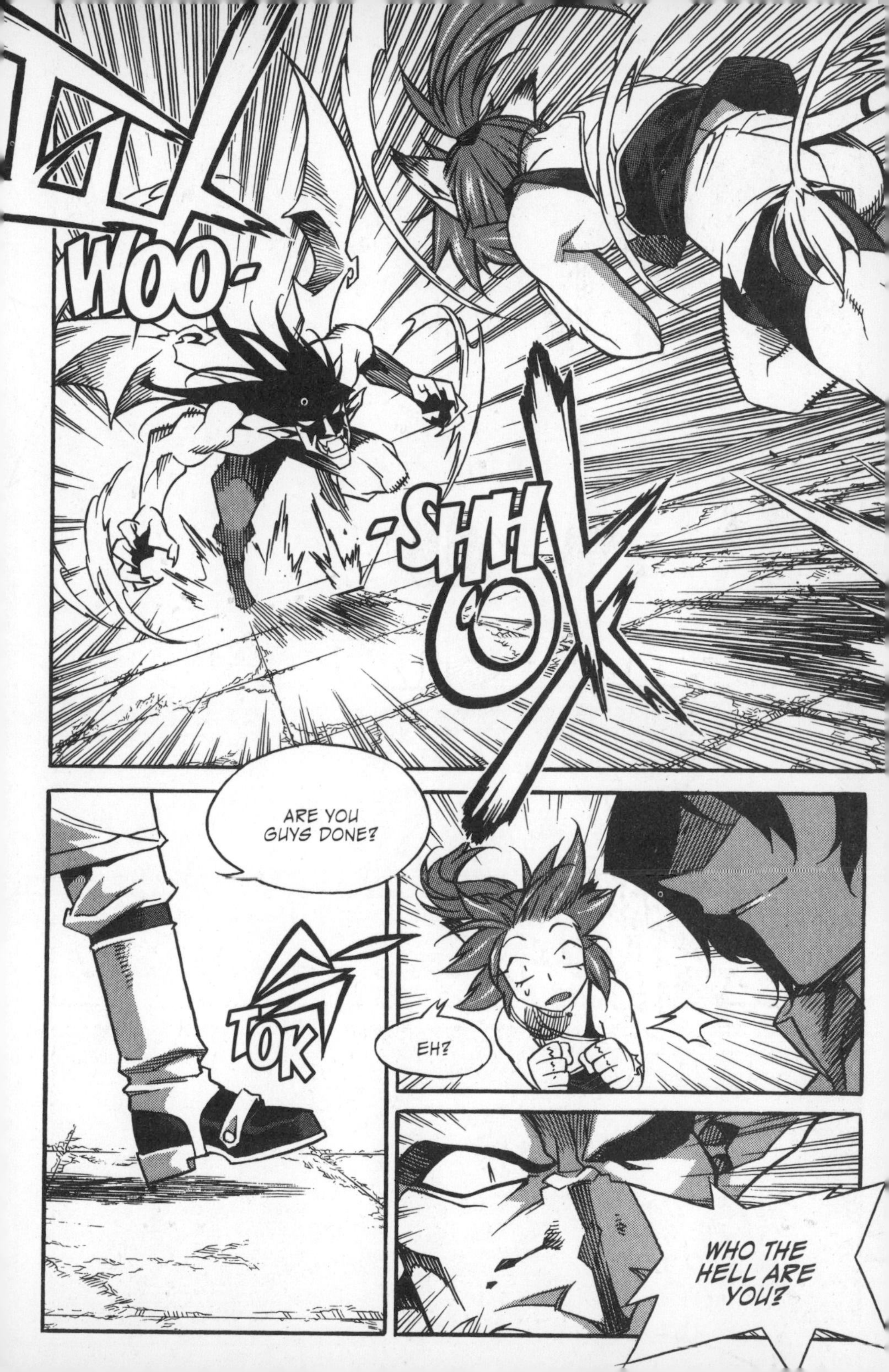
WOO-
-SHH
ARE YOU GUYS DONE?
TOK
EH?
WHO THE HELL ARE YOU?

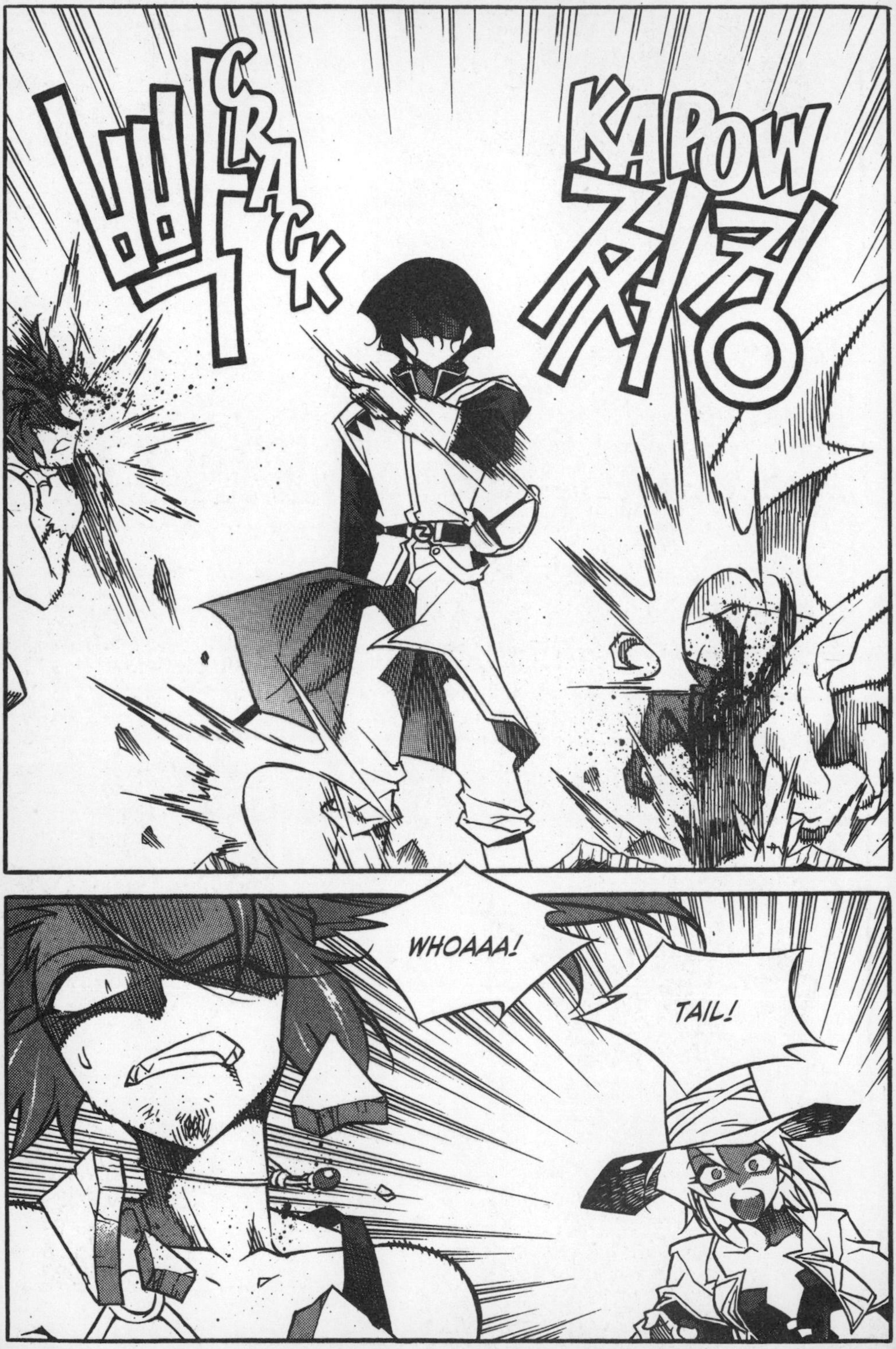
!!
CRACK
KAPOW
WHOAAA!
TAIL!

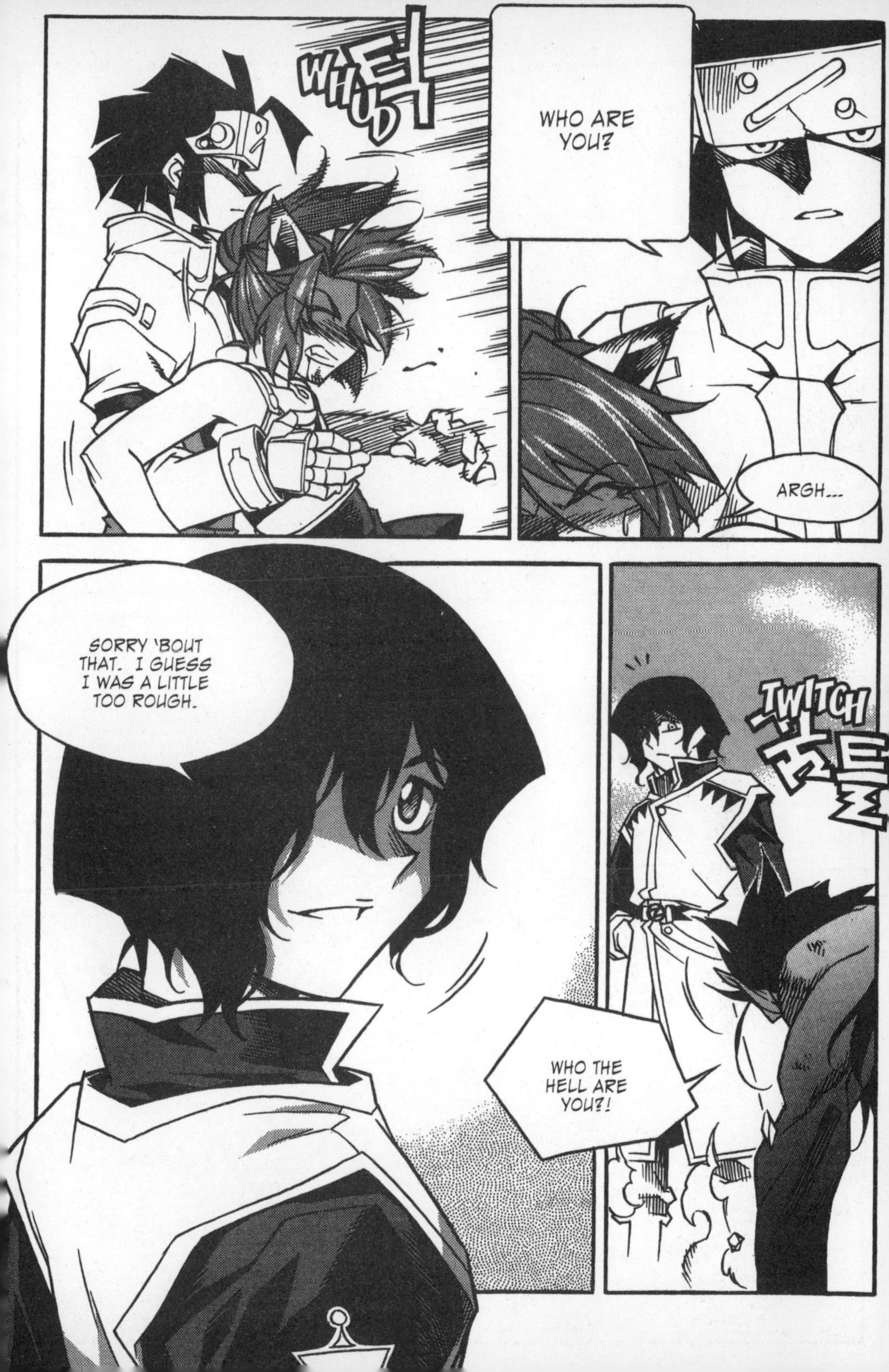
WHUD
WHO ARE YOU?
ARGH...
SORRY 'BOUT THAT. I GUESS I WAS A LITTLE TOO ROUGH.
TWITCH
WHO THE HELL ARE YOU?!

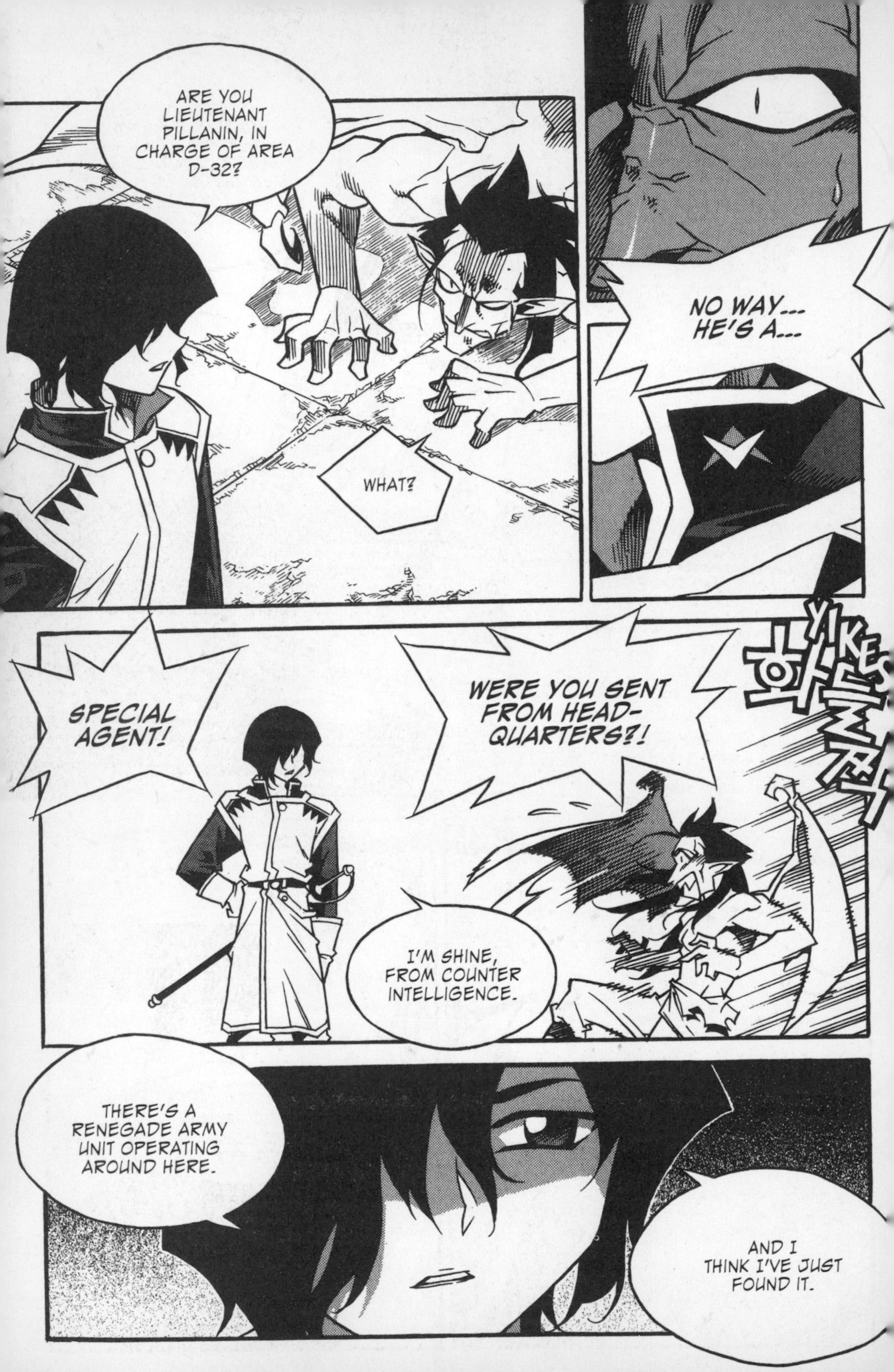
ARE YOU LIEUTENANT PILLANIN, IN CHARGE OF AREA D-32?
WHAT?
NO WAY... HE'S A...
SPECIAL AGENT!
WERE YOU SENT FROM HEAD-QUARTERS?!
YAKES!
I'M SHINE, FROM COUNTER INTELLIGENCE.
THERE'S A RENEGADE ARMY UNIT OPERATING AROUND HERE.
AND I THINK I'VE JUST FOUND IT.

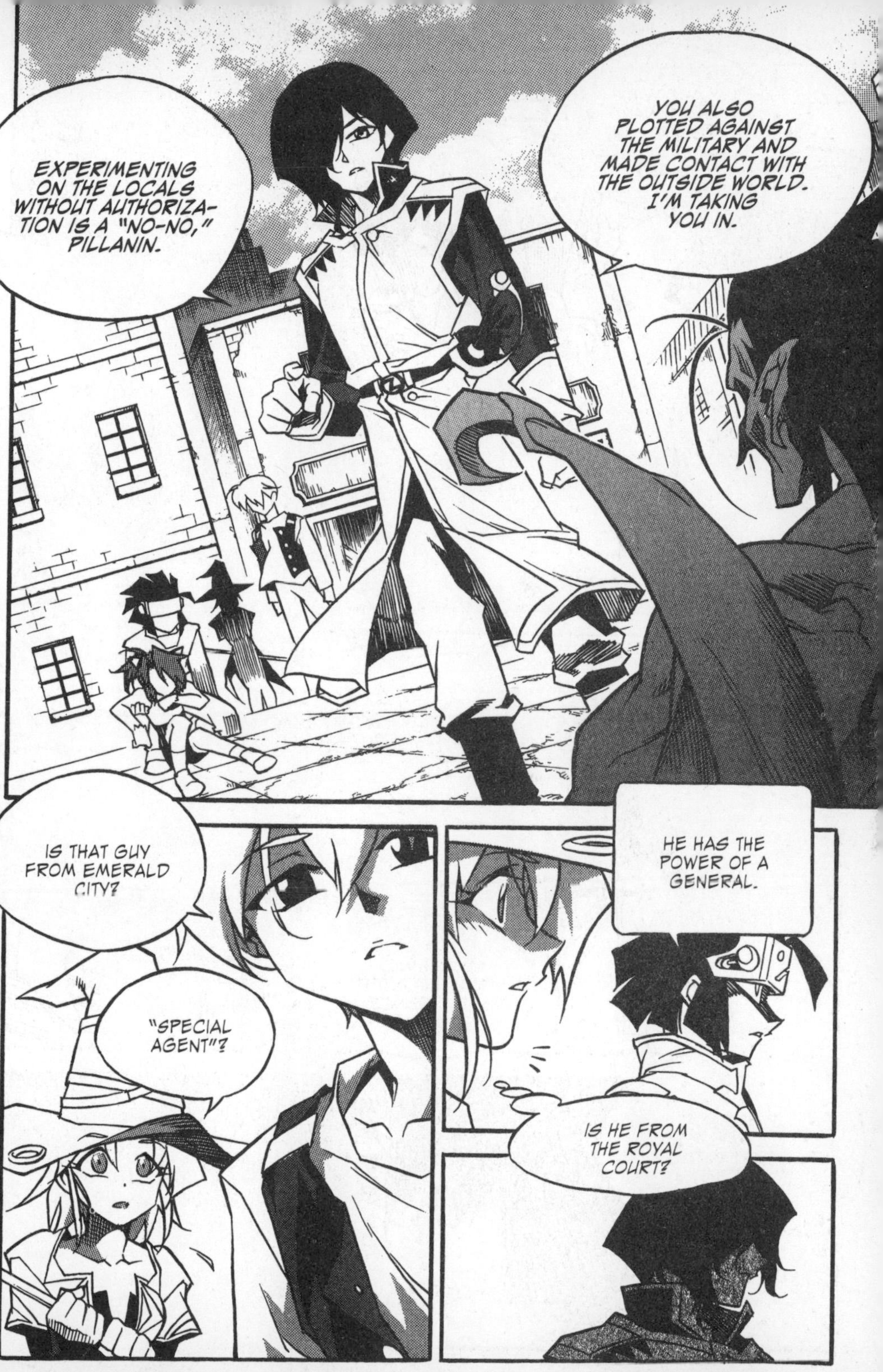
EXPERIMENTING ON THE LOCALS WITHOUT AUTHORIZATION IS A "NO-NO," PILLANIN.
YOU ALSO PLOTTED AGAINST THE MILITARY AND MADE CONTACT WITH THE OUTSIDE WORLD. I'M TAKING YOU IN.
IS THAT GUY FROM EMERALD CITY?
"SPECIAL AGENT"?
HE HAS THE POWER OF A GENERAL.
IS HE FROM THE ROYAL COURT?

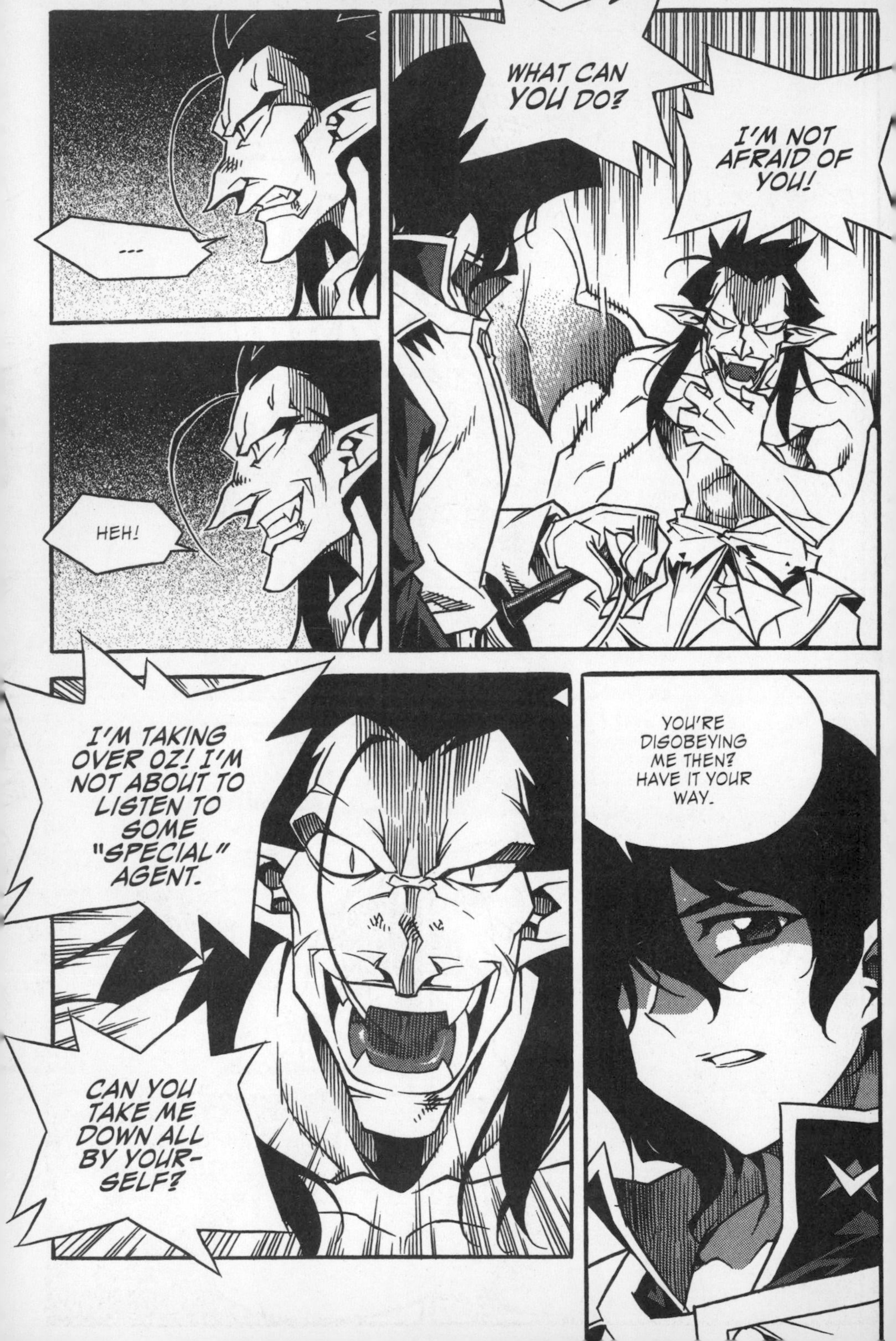
...
HEH!
WHAT CAN YOU DO?
I'M NOT AFRAID OF YOU!
I'M TAKING OVER OZ! I'M NOT ABOUT TO LISTEN TO SOME "SPECIAL" AGENT.
CAN YOU TAKE ME DOWN ALL BY YOUR-SELF?
YOU'RE DISOBEYING ME THEN? HAVE IT YOUR WAY.

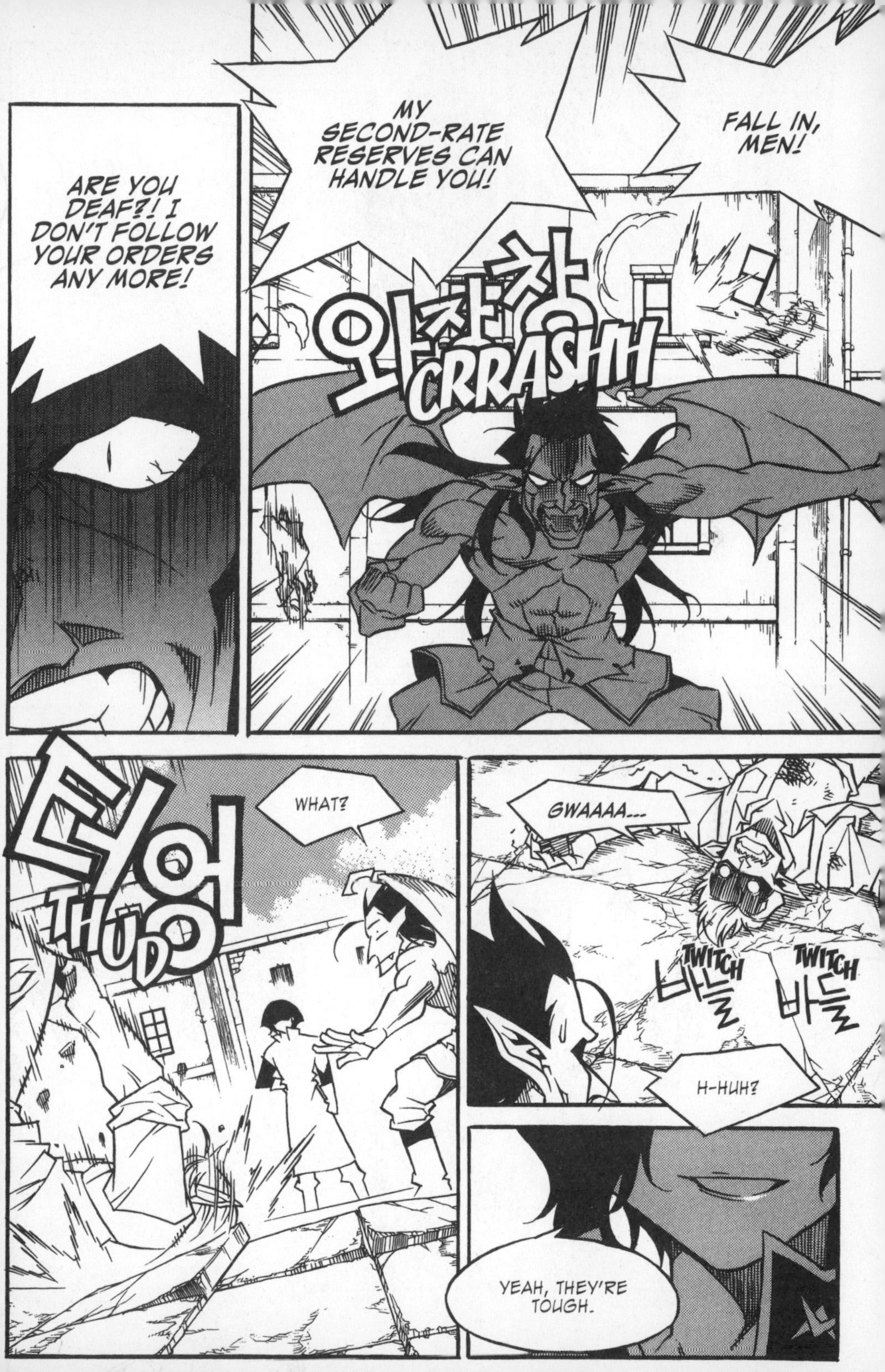
ARE YOU DEAF?! I DON'T FOLLOW YOUR ORDERS ANY MORE!
MY SECOND-RATE RESERVES CAN HANDLE YOU!
FALL IN, MEN!
CRRASHH
텅
THUD
WHAT?
GWAAAA...
TWITCH
바들
TWITCH
바들
H-HUH?
YEAH, THEY'RE TOUGH.

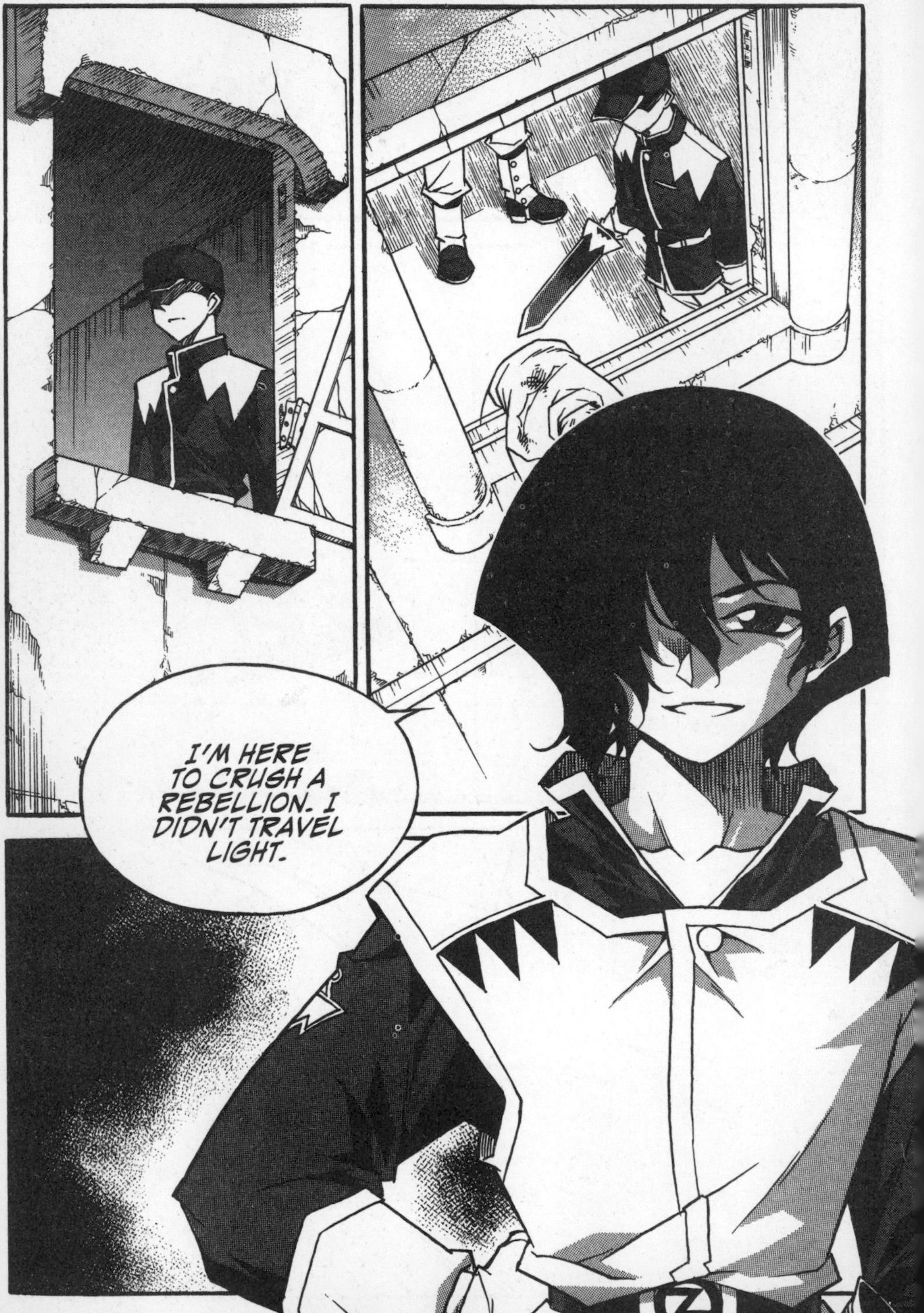
I'M HERE TO CRUSH A REBELLION. I DIDN'T TRAVEL LIGHT.

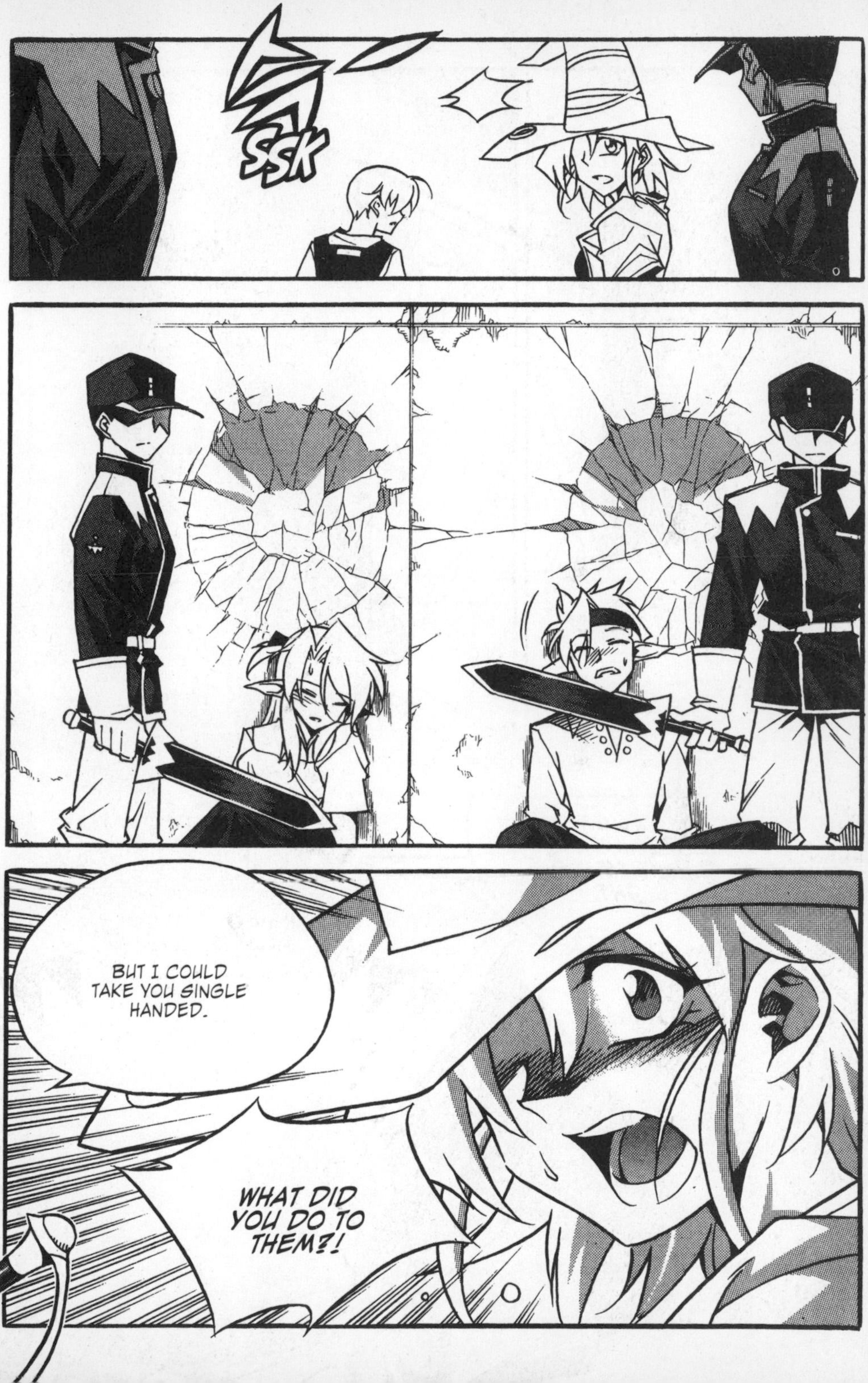
SSK
BUT I COULD TAKE YOU SINGLE HANDED.
WHAT DID YOU DO TO THEM?!

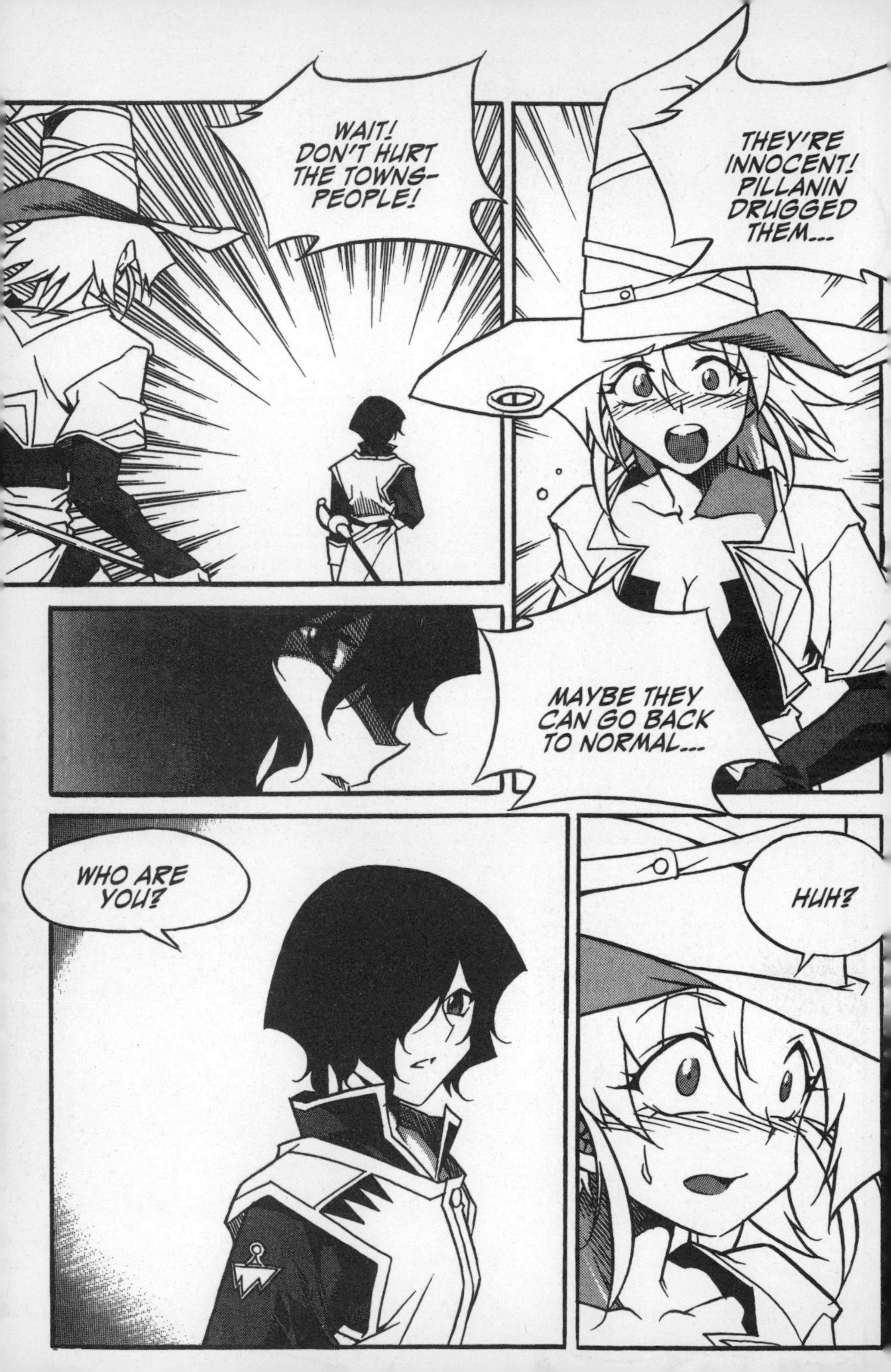
WAIT! DON'T HURT THE TOWNS-PEOPLE!
THEY'RE INNOCENT! PILLANIN DRUGGED THEM...
MAYBE THEY CAN GO BACK TO NORMAL...
WHO ARE YOU?
HUH?

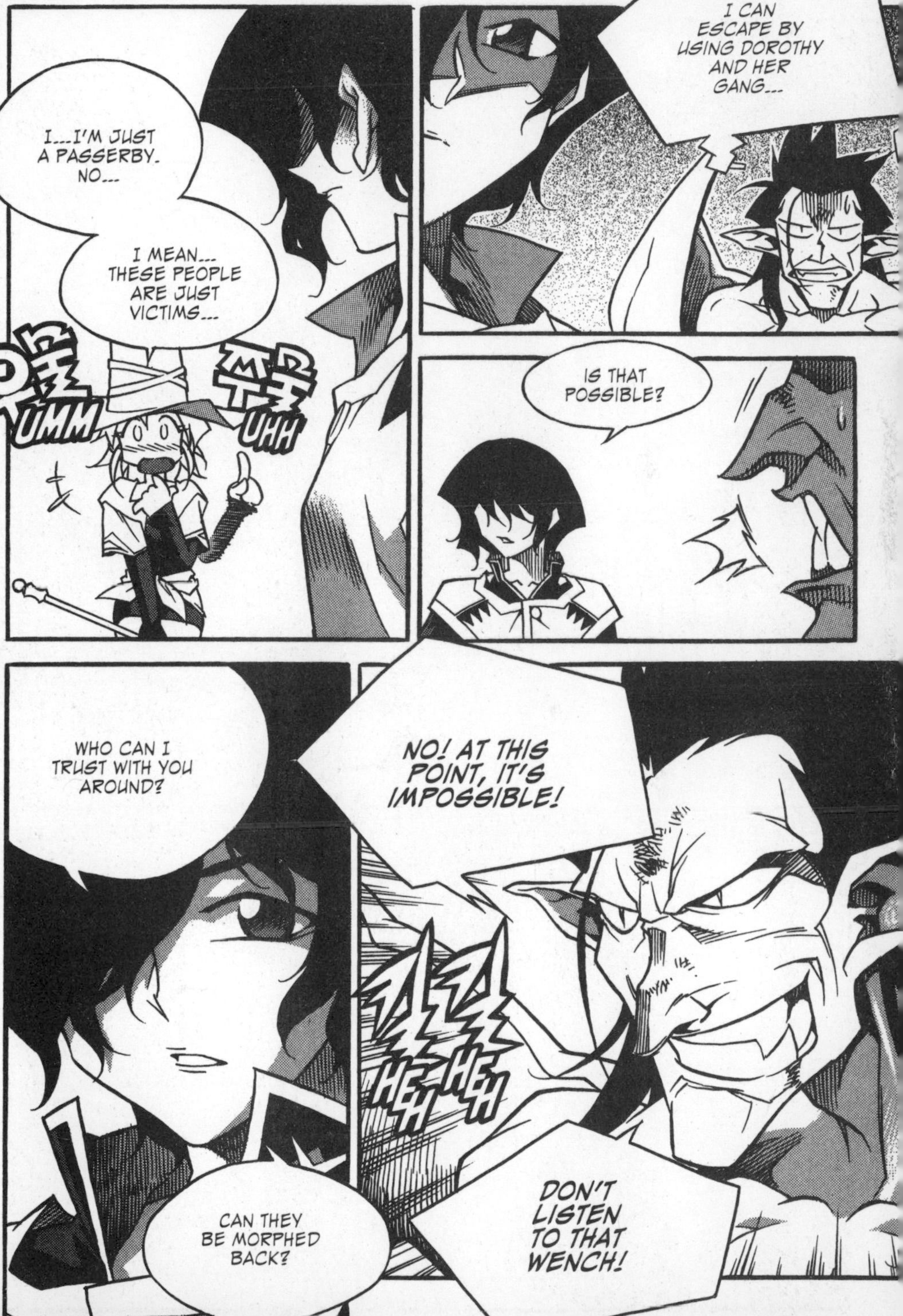
I...I'M JUST A PASSERBY. NO...
I MEAN... THESE PEOPLE ARE JUST VICTIMS...
UMM
UHH
I CAN ESCAPE BY USING DOROTHY AND HER GANG...
IS THAT POSSIBLE?
WHO CAN I TRUST WITH YOU AROUND?
CAN THEY BE MORPHED BACK?
NO! AT THIS POINT, IT'S IMPOSSIBLE!
HEH HEH
HEH HEH
DON'T LISTEN TO THAT WENCH!

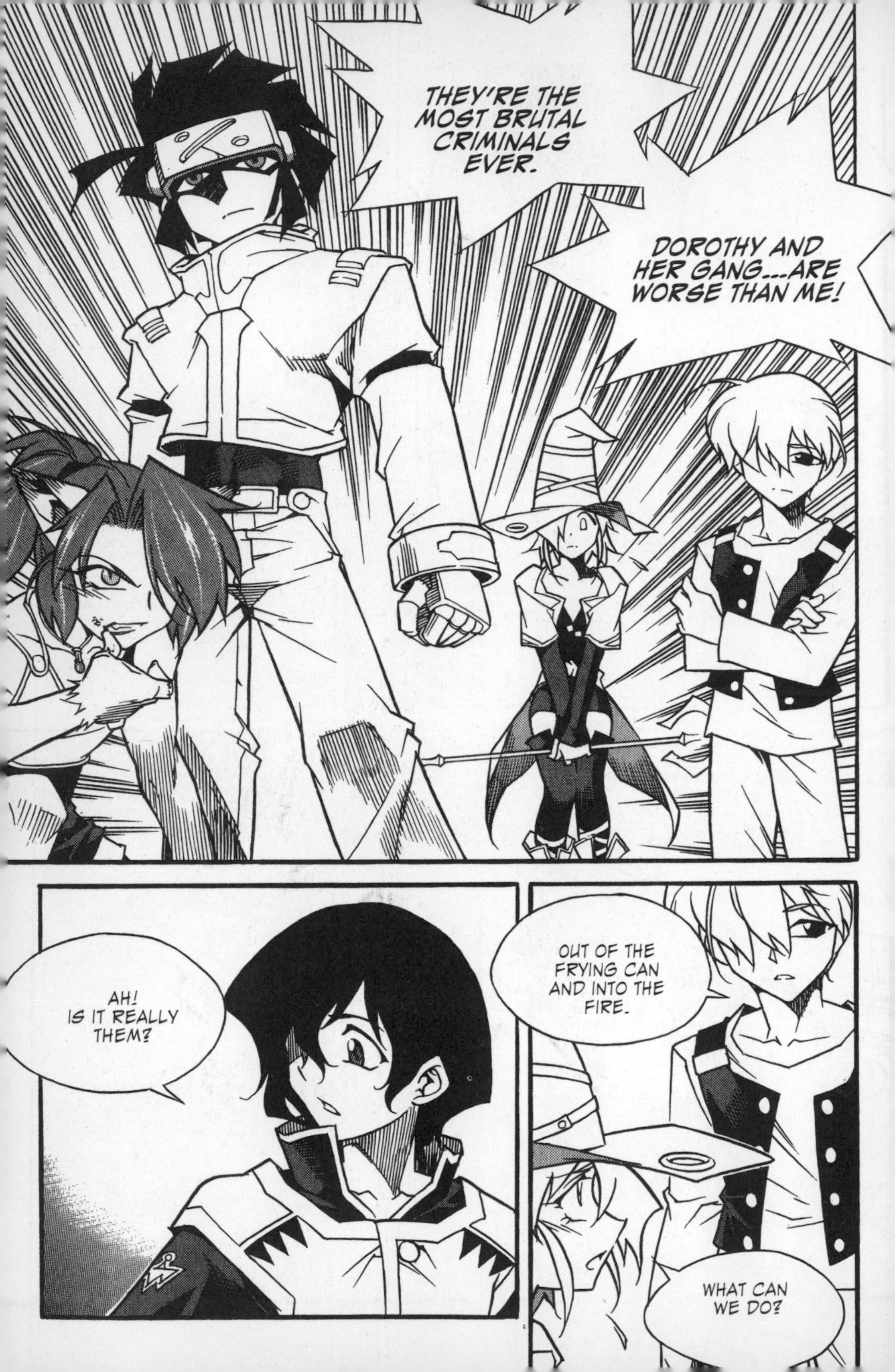

THEY'RE THE MOST BRUTAL CRIMINALS EVER.
DOROTHY AND HER GANG...ARE WORSE THAN ME!
AH! IS IT REALLY THEM?
OUT OF THE FRYING CAN AND INTO THE FIRE.
WHAT CAN WE DO?

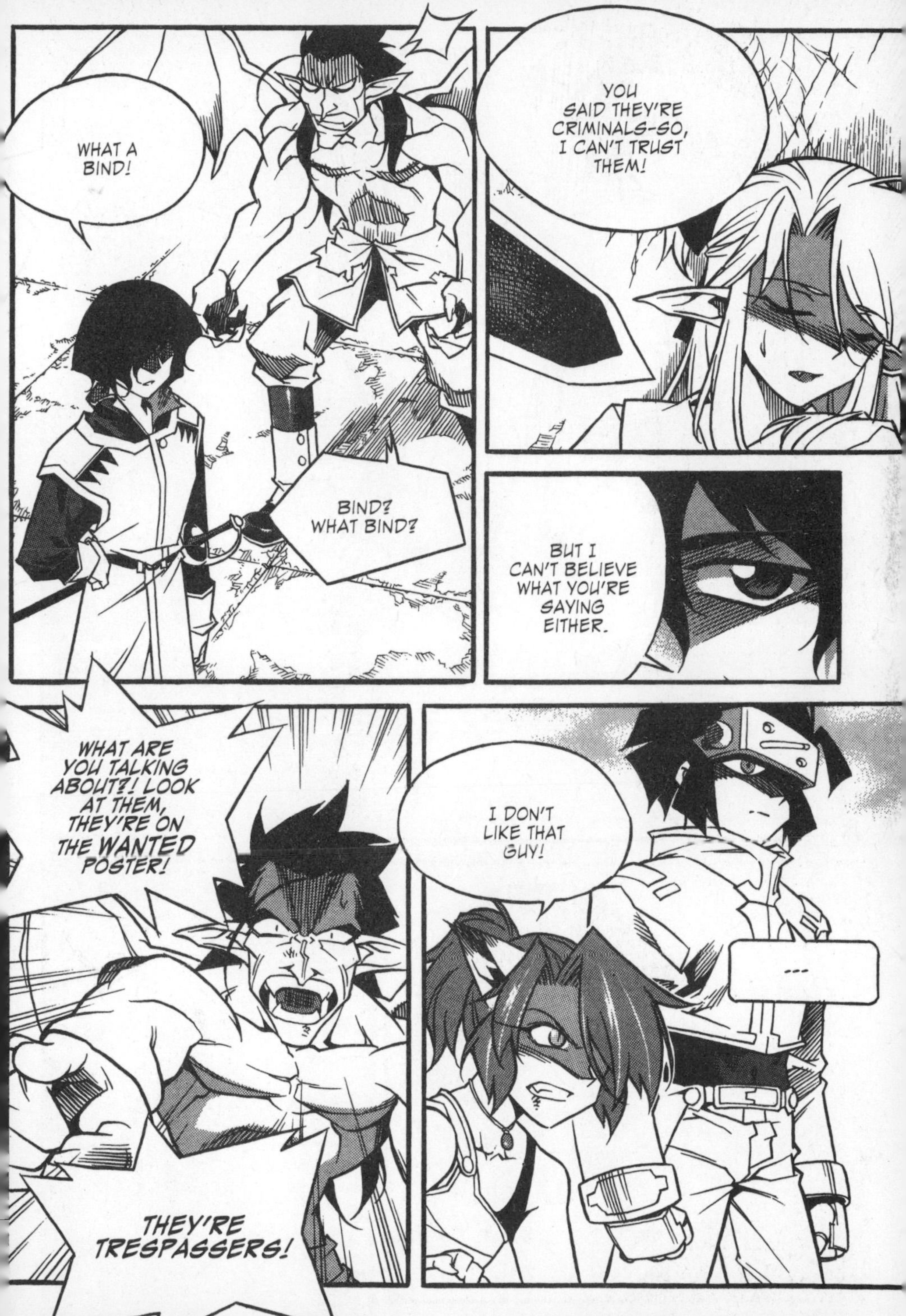
WHAT A BIND!
YOU SAID THEY'RE CRIMINALS-SO, I CAN'T TRUST THEM!
BIND? WHAT BIND?
BUT I CAN'T BELIEVE WHAT YOU'RE SAYING EITHER.
WHAT ARE YOU TALKING ABOUT?! LOOK AT THEM, THEY'RE ON THE WANTED POSTER!
THEY'RE TRESPASSERS!
I DON'T LIKE THAT GUY!
...

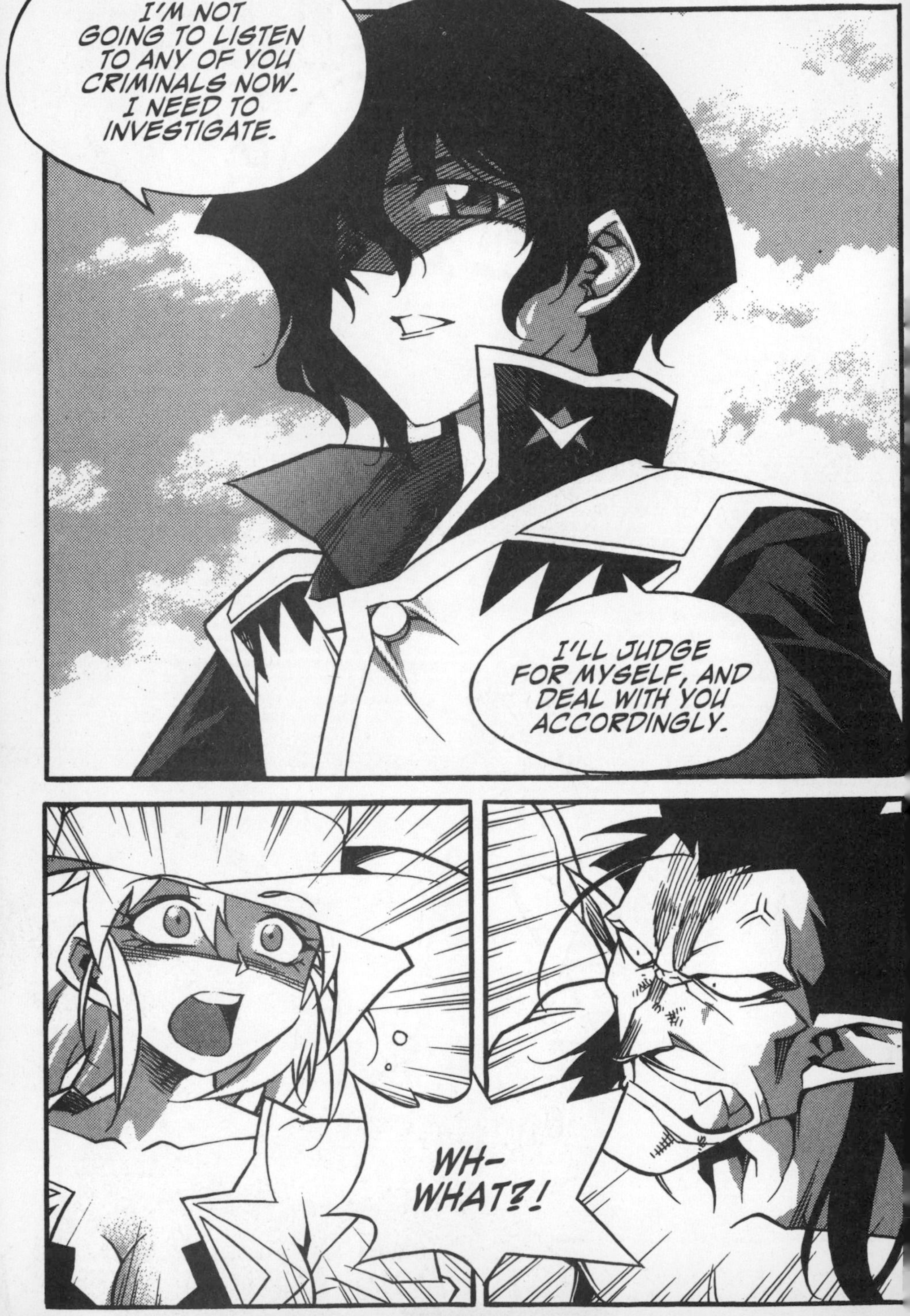
I'M NOT GOING TO LISTEN TO ANY OF YOU CRIMINALS NOW. I NEED TO INVESTIGATE.
I'LL JUDGE FOR MYSELF, AND DEAL WITH YOU ACCORDINGLY.
WH- WHAT?!

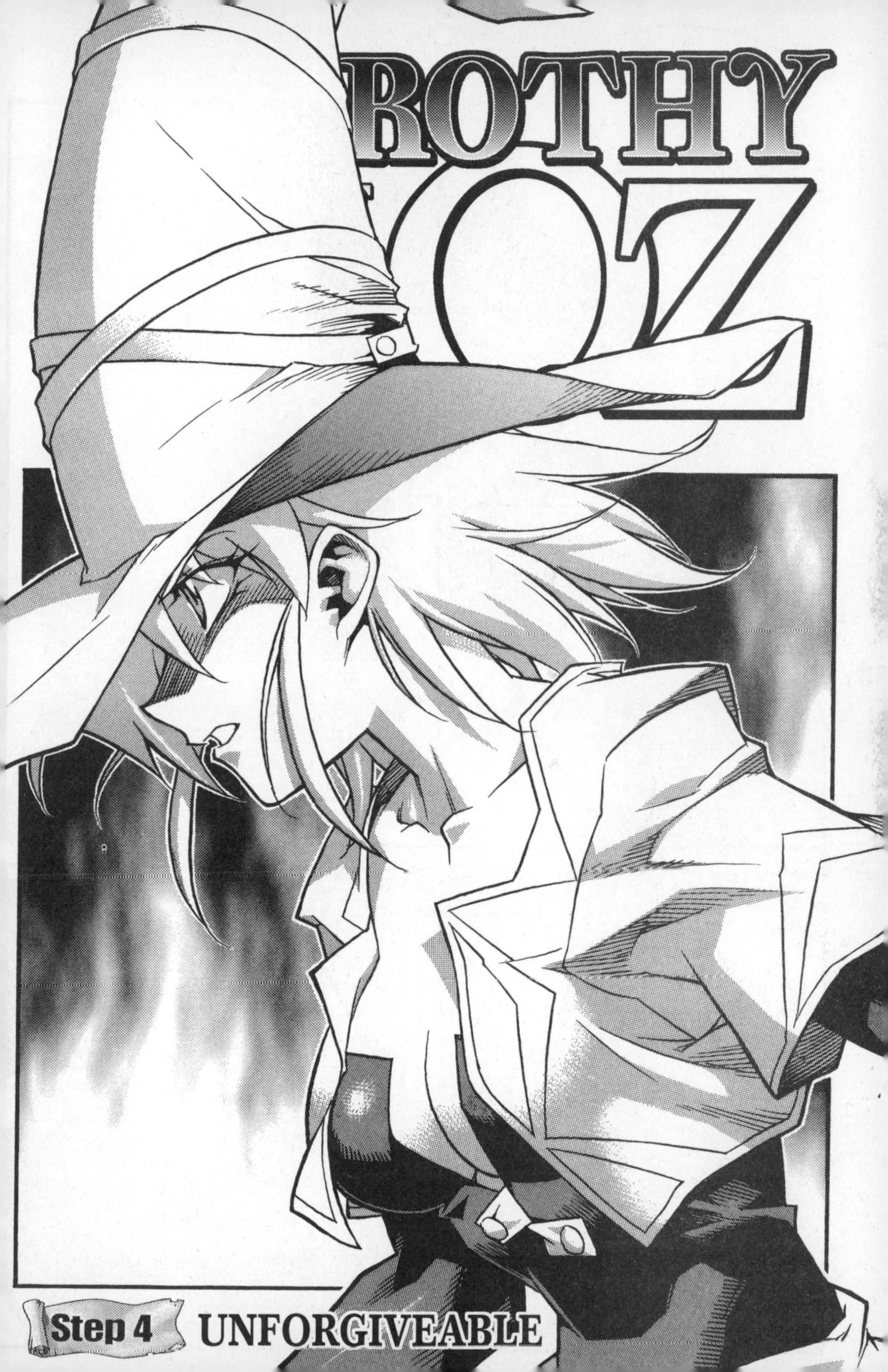
ROTHY
OZ
Step 4
UNFORGIVEABLE

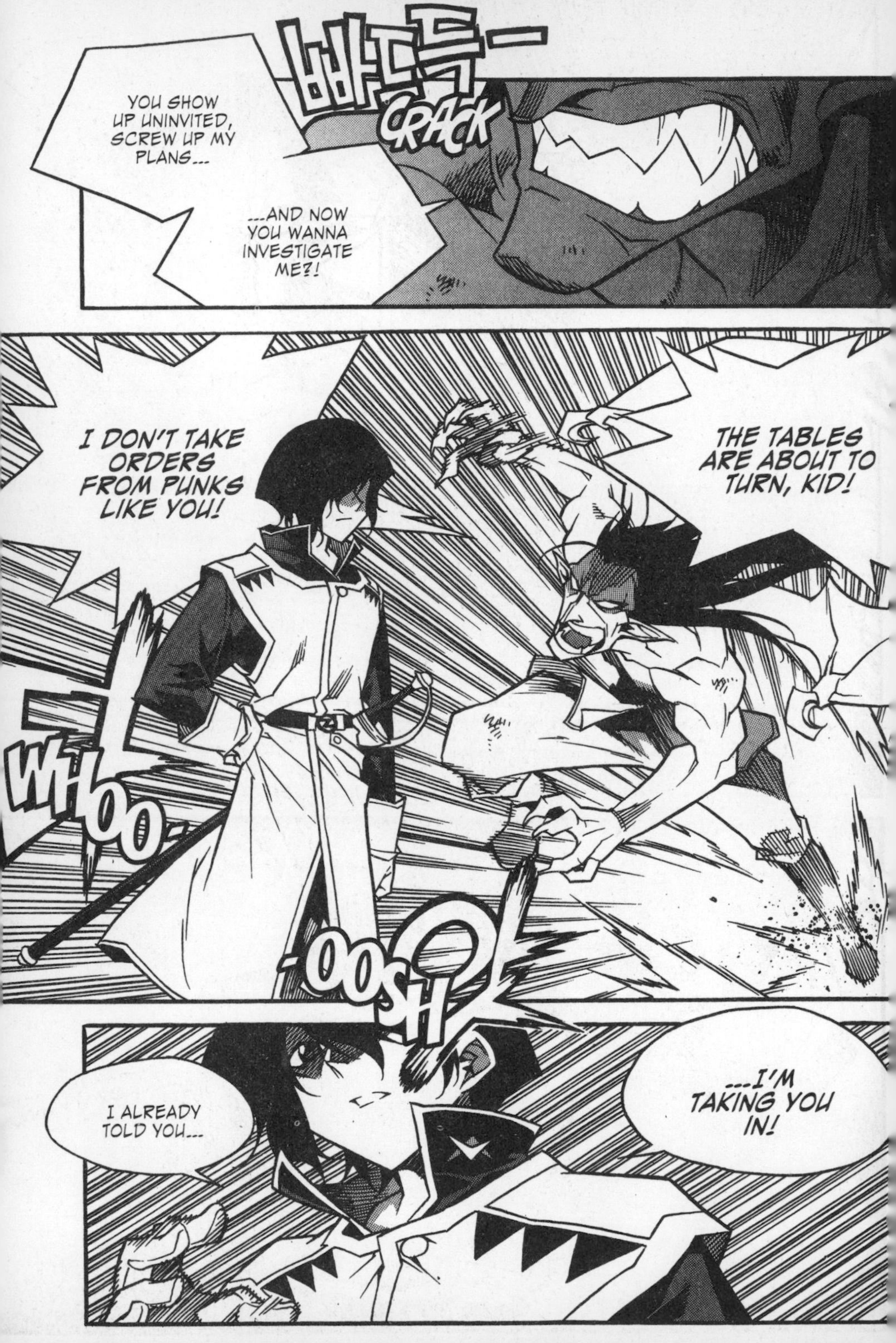
YOU SHOW UP UNINVITED, SCREW UP MY PLANS...
...AND NOW YOU WANNA INVESTIGATE ME?!
빠드득 -
CRACK
I DON'T TAKE ORDERS FROM PUNKS LIKE YOU!
THE TABLES ARE ABOUT TO TURN, KID!
WHOO-
-OOSH
I ALREADY TOLD YOU...
...I'M TAKING YOU IN!

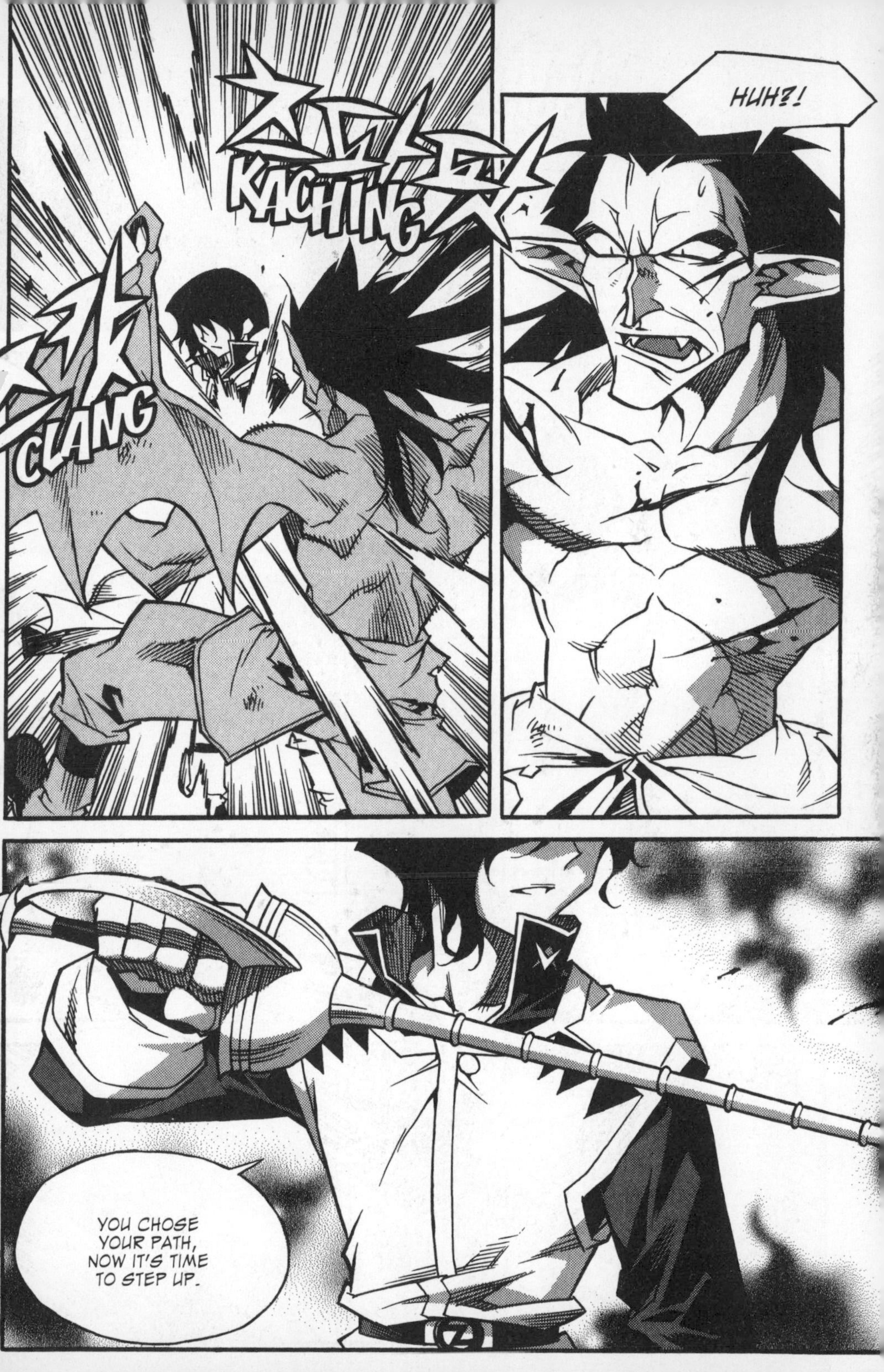
KACHING
CLANG
HUH?!
YOU CHOSE YOUR PATH, NOW IT'S TIME TO STEP UP.

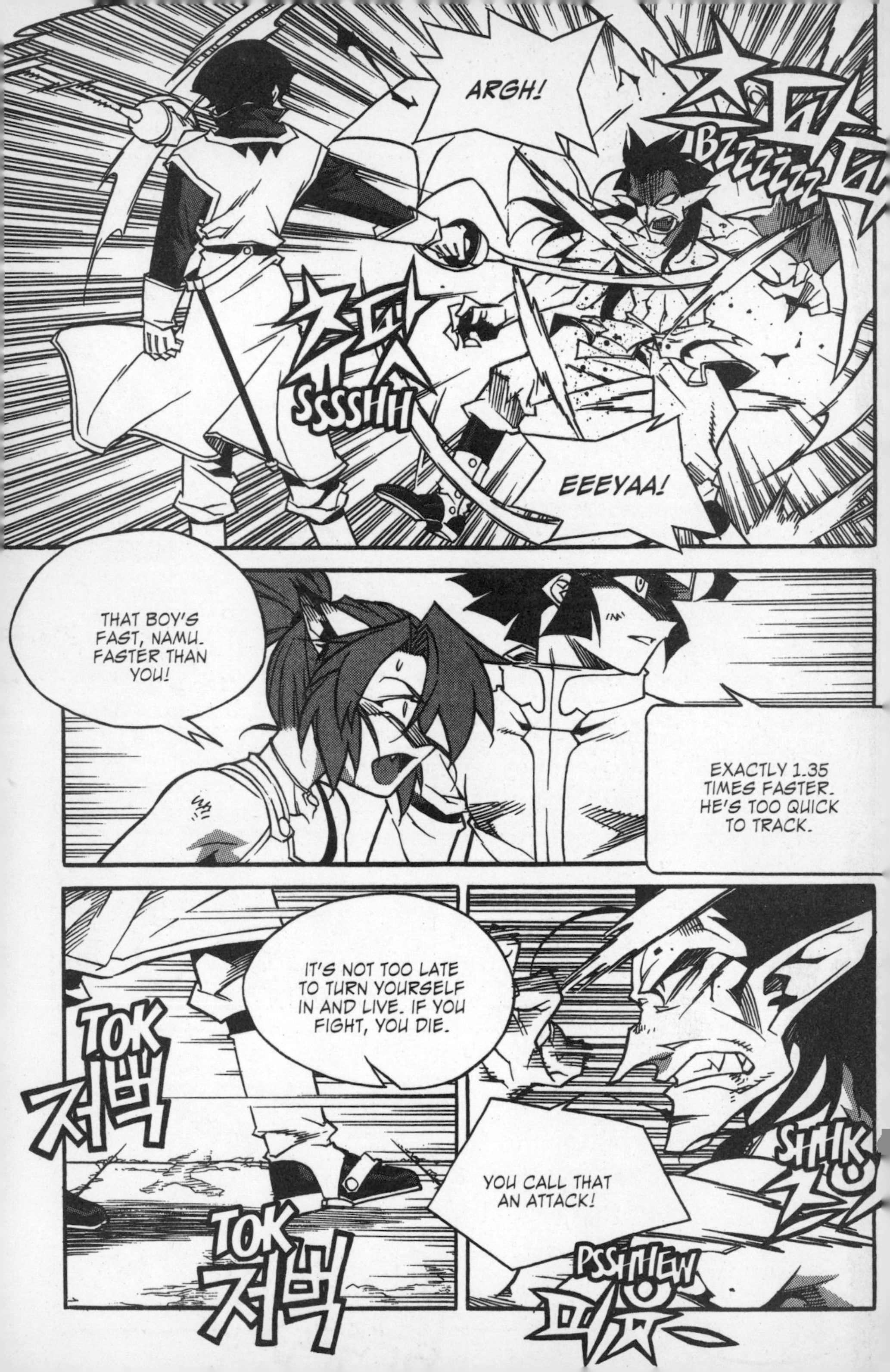
ARGH!
BZZZZZZ
SSSSHH
EEEYAA!
THAT BOY'S FAST, NAMU. FASTER THAN YOU!
EXACTLY 1.35 TIMES FASTER. HE'S TOO QUICK TO TRACK.
TOK
저벅
IT'S NOT TOO LATE TO TURN YOURSELF IN AND LIVE. IF YOU FIGHT, YOU DIE.
TOK
저벅
YOU CALL THAT AN ATTACK!
SHHK
PSSHHEW

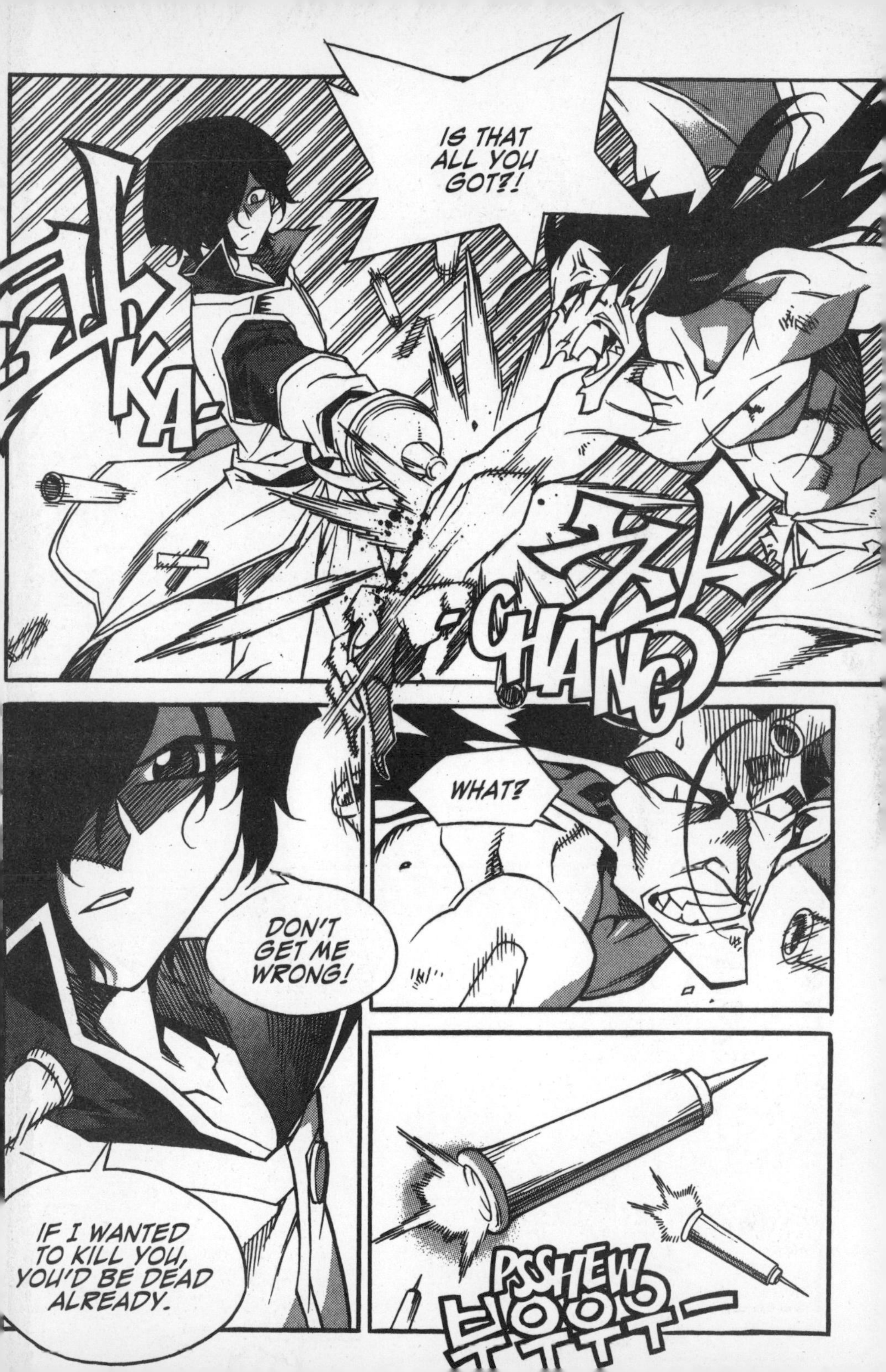
IS THAT ALL YOU GOT?!
KA-
-CHANG
DON'T GET ME WRONG!
IF I WANTED TO KILL YOU, YOU'D BE DEAD ALREADY.
WHAT?
PSSHEW

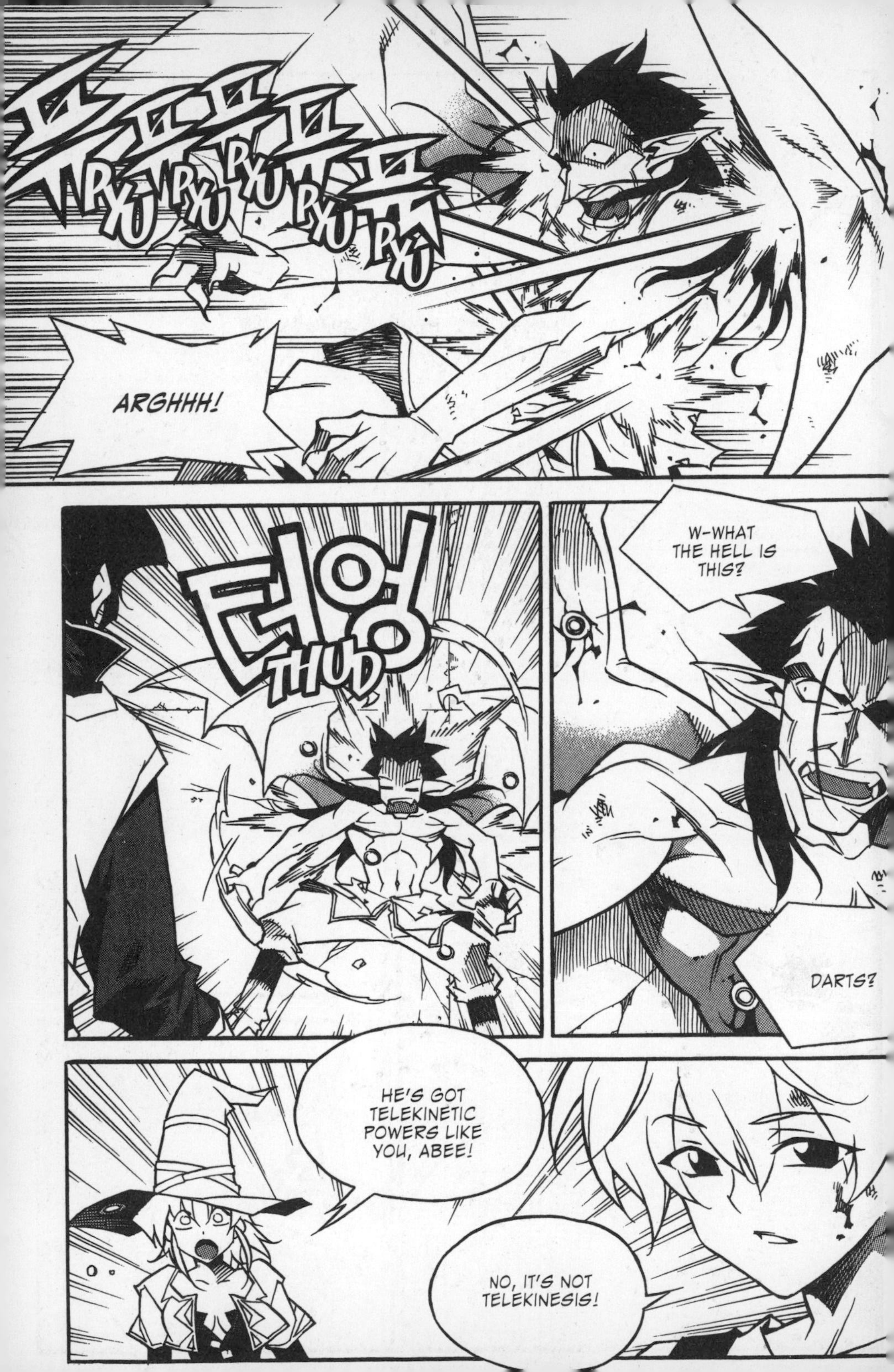
PYU PYU PYU PYU PYU
ARGHHH!
THUD
W-WHAT THE HELL IS THIS?
DARTS?
HE'S GOT TELEKINETIC POWERS LIKE YOU, ABEE!
NO, IT'S NOT TELEKINESIS!

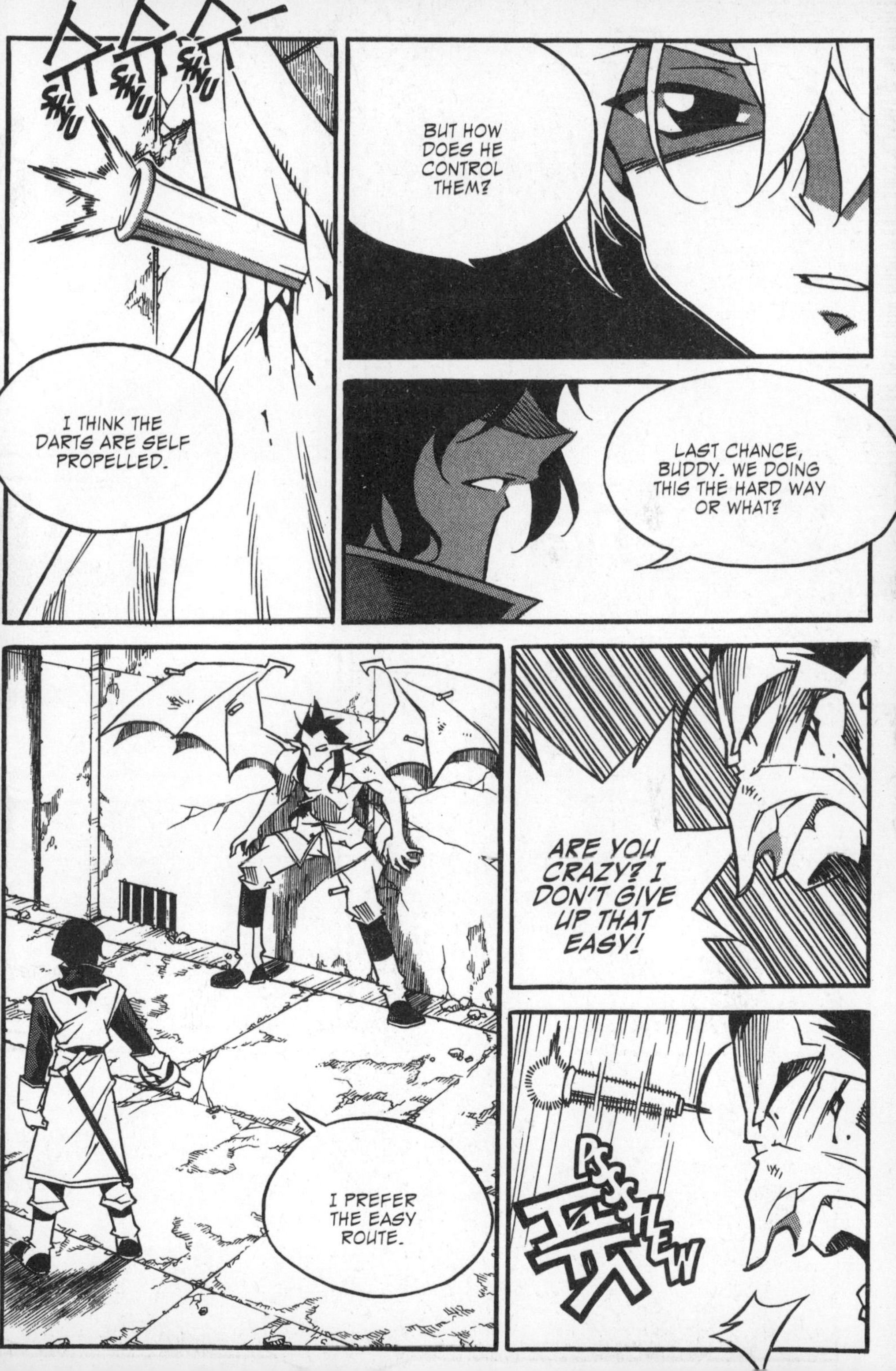

D-D-D-
SHU SHU SHU
I THINK THE DARTS ARE SELF PROPELLED.
BUT HOW DOES HE CONTROL THEM?
LAST CHANCE, BUDDY. WE DOING THIS THE HARD WAY OR WHAT?
I PREFER THE EASY ROUTE.
ARE YOU CRAZY? I DON'T GIVE UP THAT EASY!
PSSSHEW

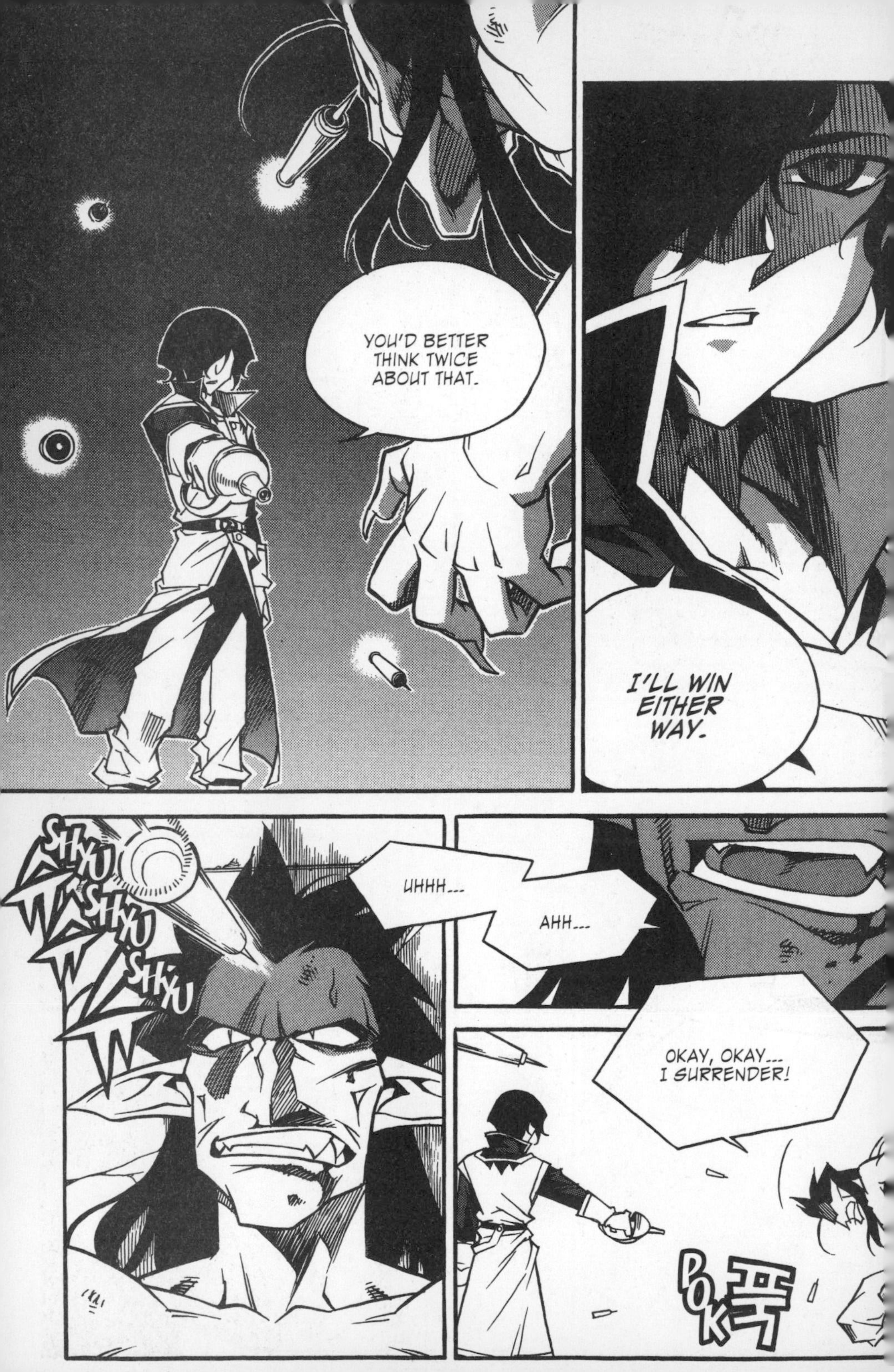
YOU'D BETTER THINK TWICE ABOUT THAT.
I'LL WIN EITHER WAY.
SHYU SHYU SHYU
UHHH...
AHH...
OKAY, OKAY... I SURRENDER!
POK

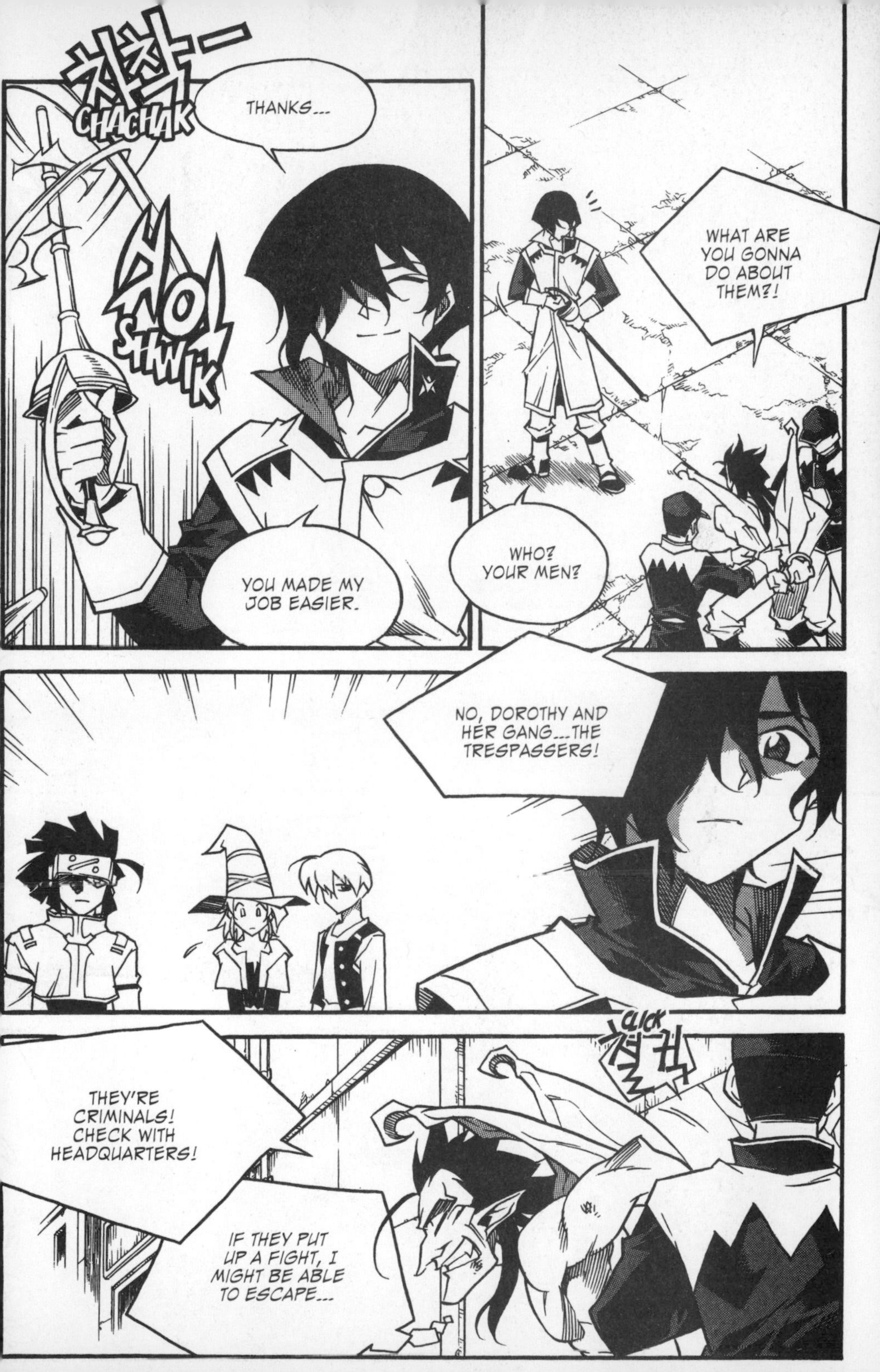

CHACHAK
THANKS...
SHWIK
YOU MADE MY JOB EASIER.
WHAT ARE YOU GONNA DO ABOUT THEM?!
WHO? YOUR MEN?
NO, DOROTHY AND HER GANG...THE TRESPASSERS!
THEY'RE CRIMINALS! CHECK WITH HEADQUARTERS!
CLICK
IF THEY PUT UP A FIGHT, I MIGHT BE ABLE TO ESCAPE...

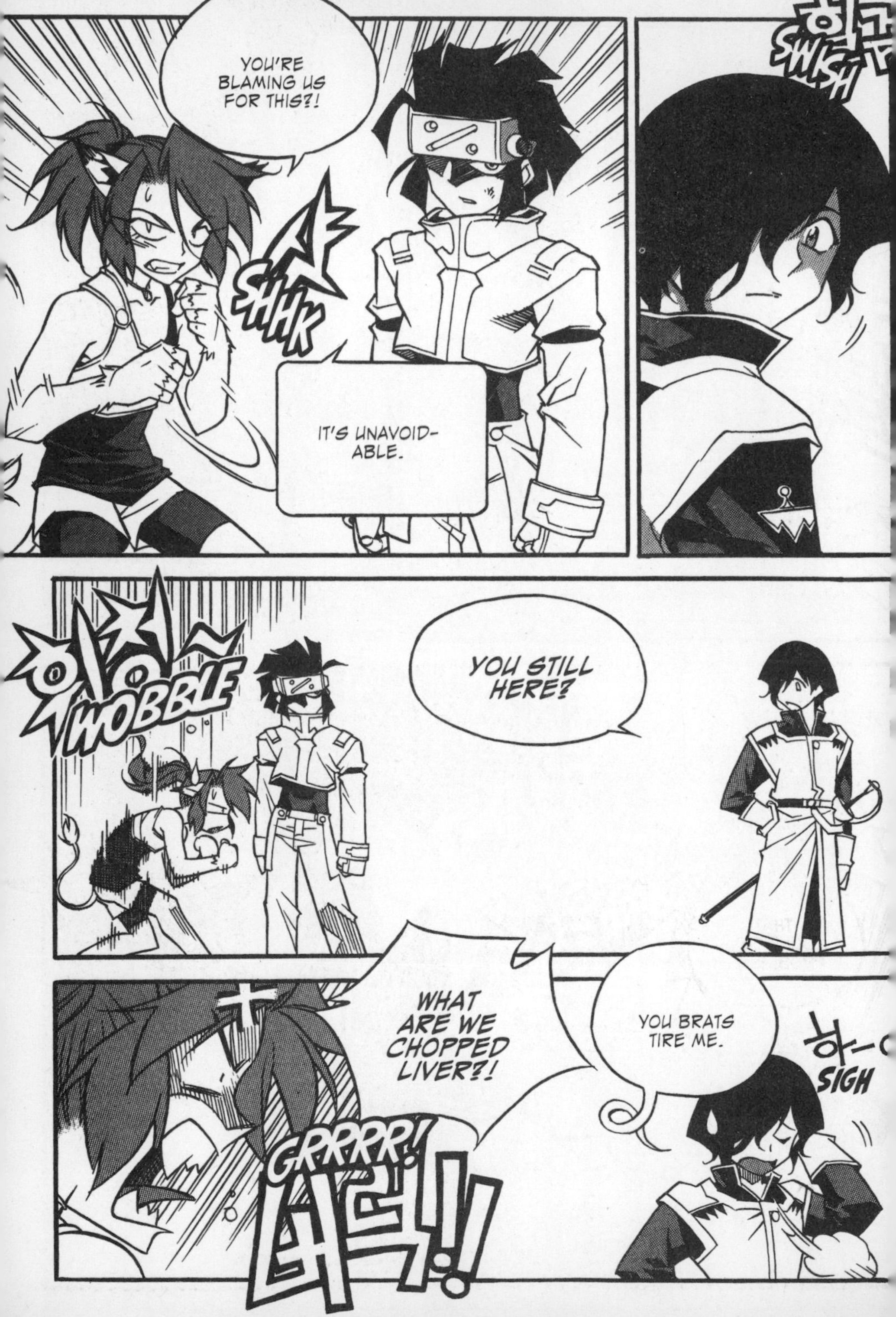
YOU'RE BLAMING US FOR THIS?!
SHHK
IT'S UNAVOID-ABLE.
SWISH
WOBBLE
YOU STILL HERE?
WHAT ARE WE CHOPPED LIVER?!
GRRRR!
YOU BRATS TIRE ME.
SIGH

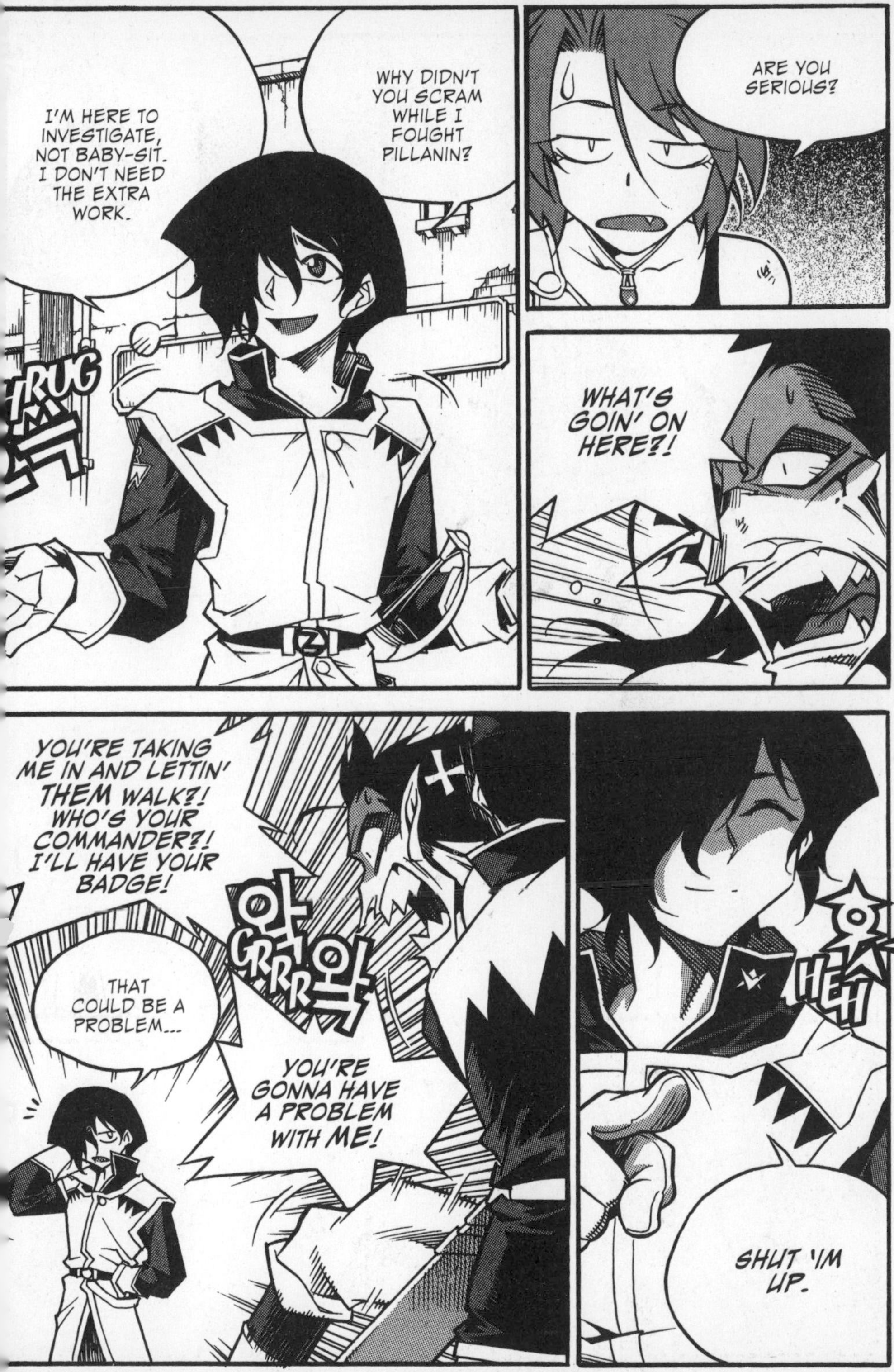
I'M HERE TO INVESTIGATE, NOT BABY-SIT. I DON'T NEED THE EXTRA WORK.
WHY DIDN'T YOU SCRAM WHILE I FOUGHT PILLANIN?
HRUG
ARE YOU SERIOUS?
WHAT'S GOIN' ON HERE?!
YOU'RE TAKING ME IN AND LETTIN' THEM WALK?! WHO'S YOUR COMMANDER?! I'LL HAVE YOUR BADGE!
GRRR
THAT COULD BE A PROBLEM...
YOU'RE GONNA HAVE A PROBLEM WITH ME!
HEH
SHUT 'IM UP.

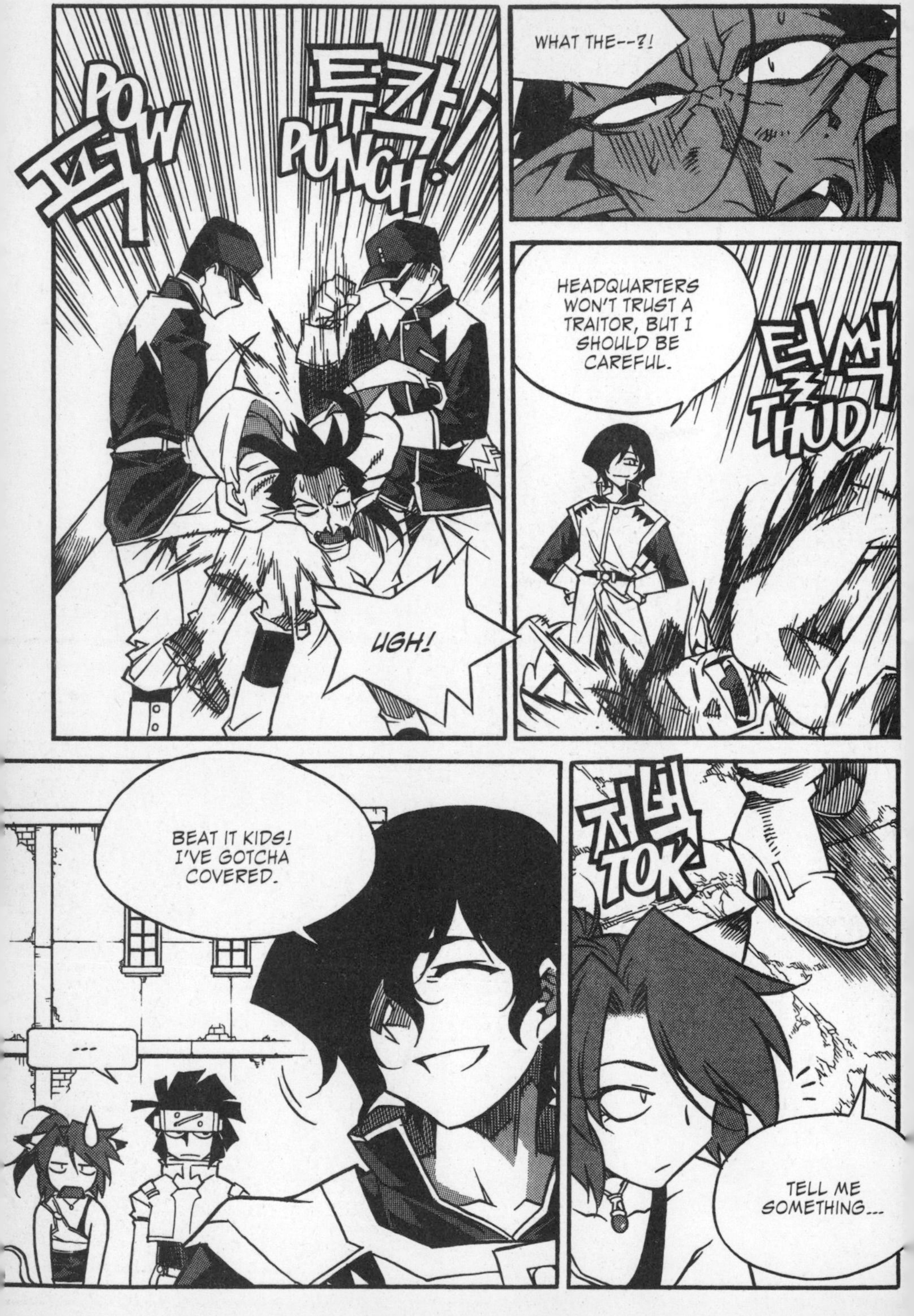
POW
PUNCH!
UGH!
WHAT THE--?!
HEADQUARTERS WON'T TRUST A TRAITOR, BUT I SHOULD BE CAREFUL.
THUD
BEAT IT KIDS! I'VE GOTCHA COVERED.
...
TOK
TELL ME SOMETHING...

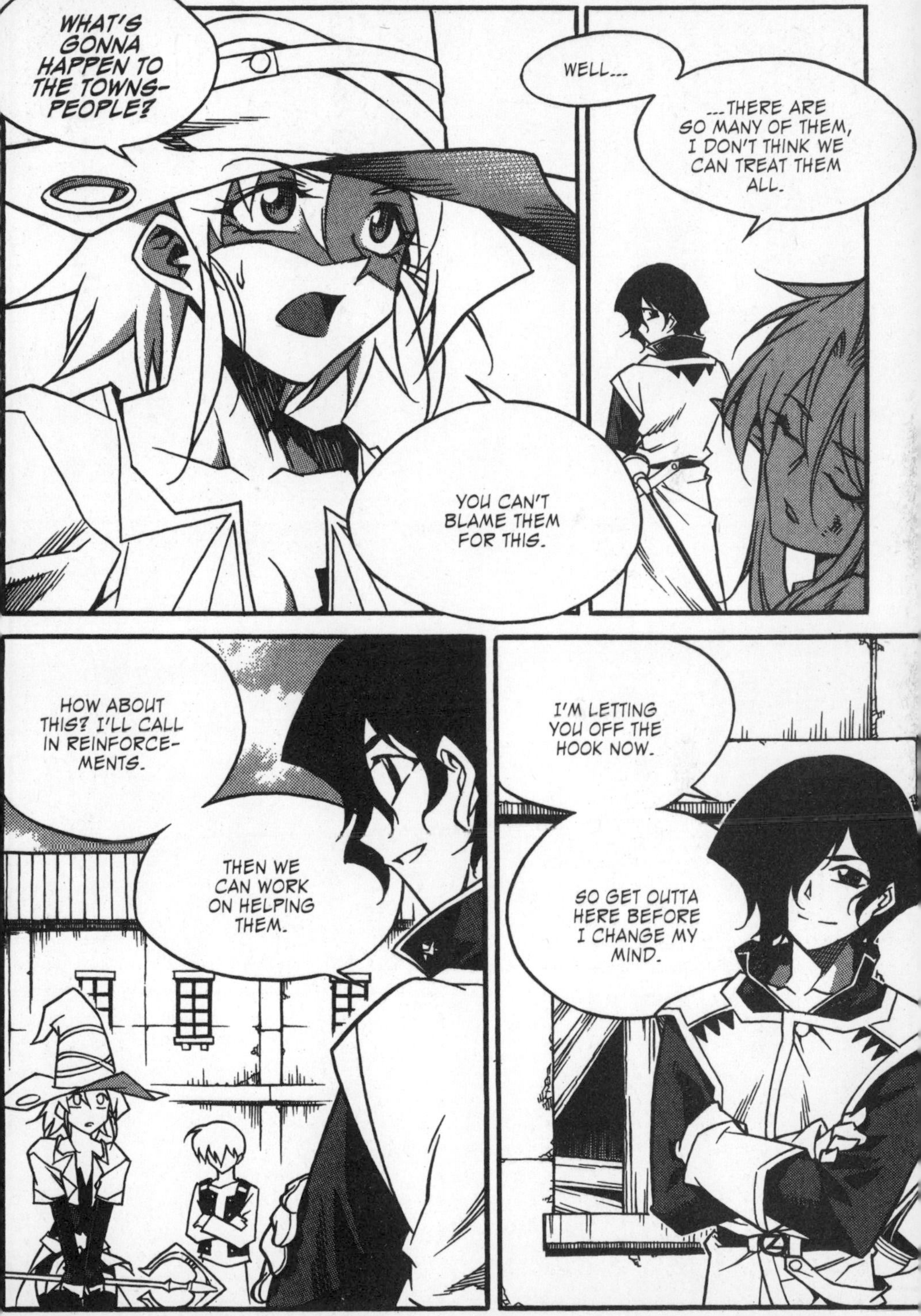
WHAT'S GONNA HAPPEN TO THE TOWNS-PEOPLE?
WELL...
...THERE ARE SO MANY OF THEM, I DON'T THINK WE CAN TREAT THEM ALL.
YOU CAN'T BLAME THEM FOR THIS.
HOW ABOUT THIS? I'LL CALL IN REINFORCE-MENTS.
THEN WE CAN WORK ON HELPING THEM.
I'M LETTING YOU OFF THE HOOK NOW.
SO GET OUTTA HERE BEFORE I CHANGE MY MIND.

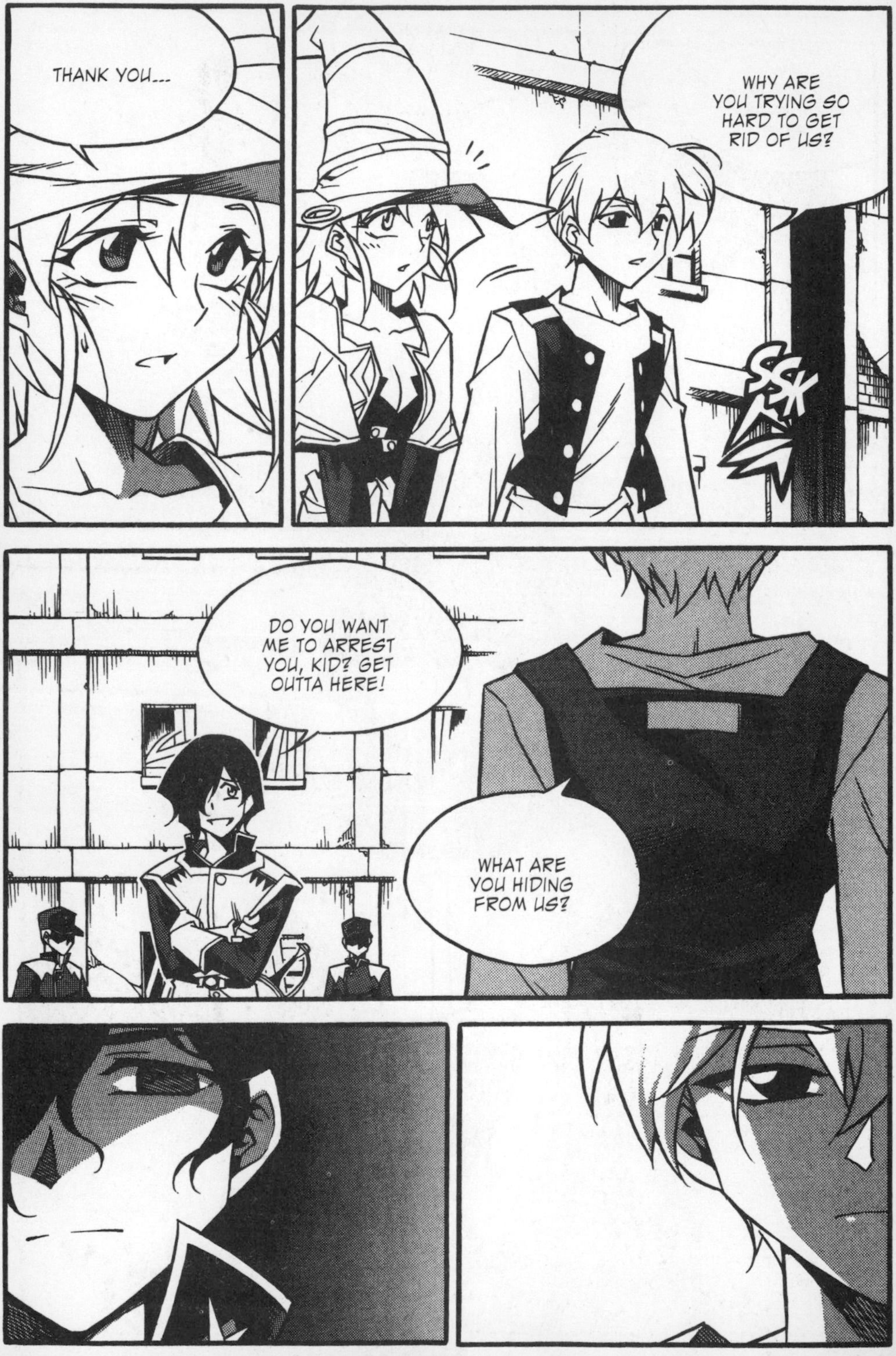
THANK YOU...
WHY ARE YOU TRYING SO HARD TO GET RID OF US?
SSK
DO YOU WANT ME TO ARREST YOU, KID? GET OUTTA HERE!
WHAT ARE YOU HIDING FROM US?

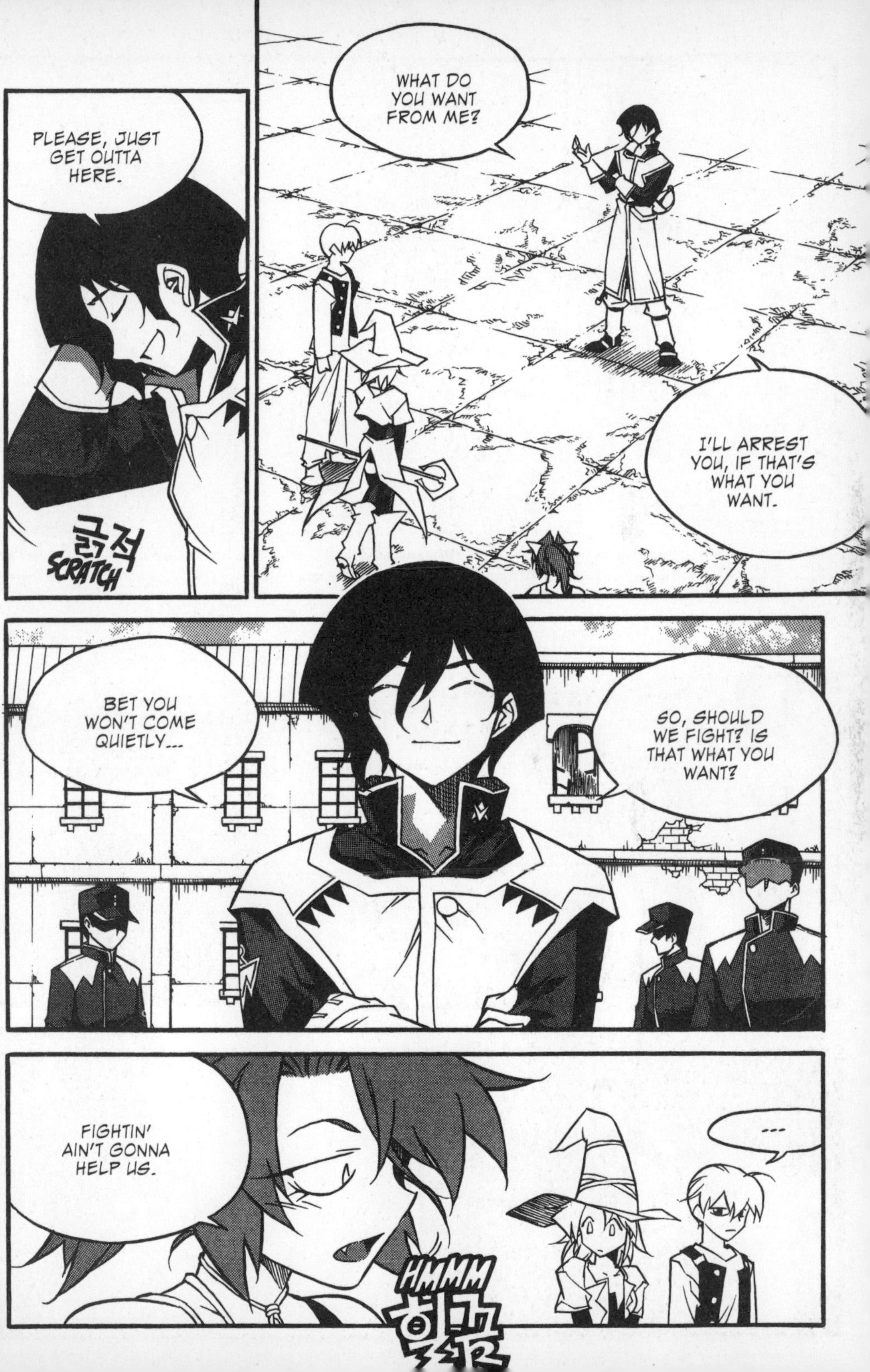
PLEASE, JUST GET OUTTA HERE.
긁적
SCRATCH
WHAT DO YOU WANT FROM ME?
I'LL ARREST YOU, IF THAT'S WHAT YOU WANT.
BET YOU WON'T COME QUIETLY...
SO, SHOULD WE FIGHT? IS THAT WHAT YOU WANT?
FIGHTIN' AIN'T GONNA HELP US.
HMMM
...

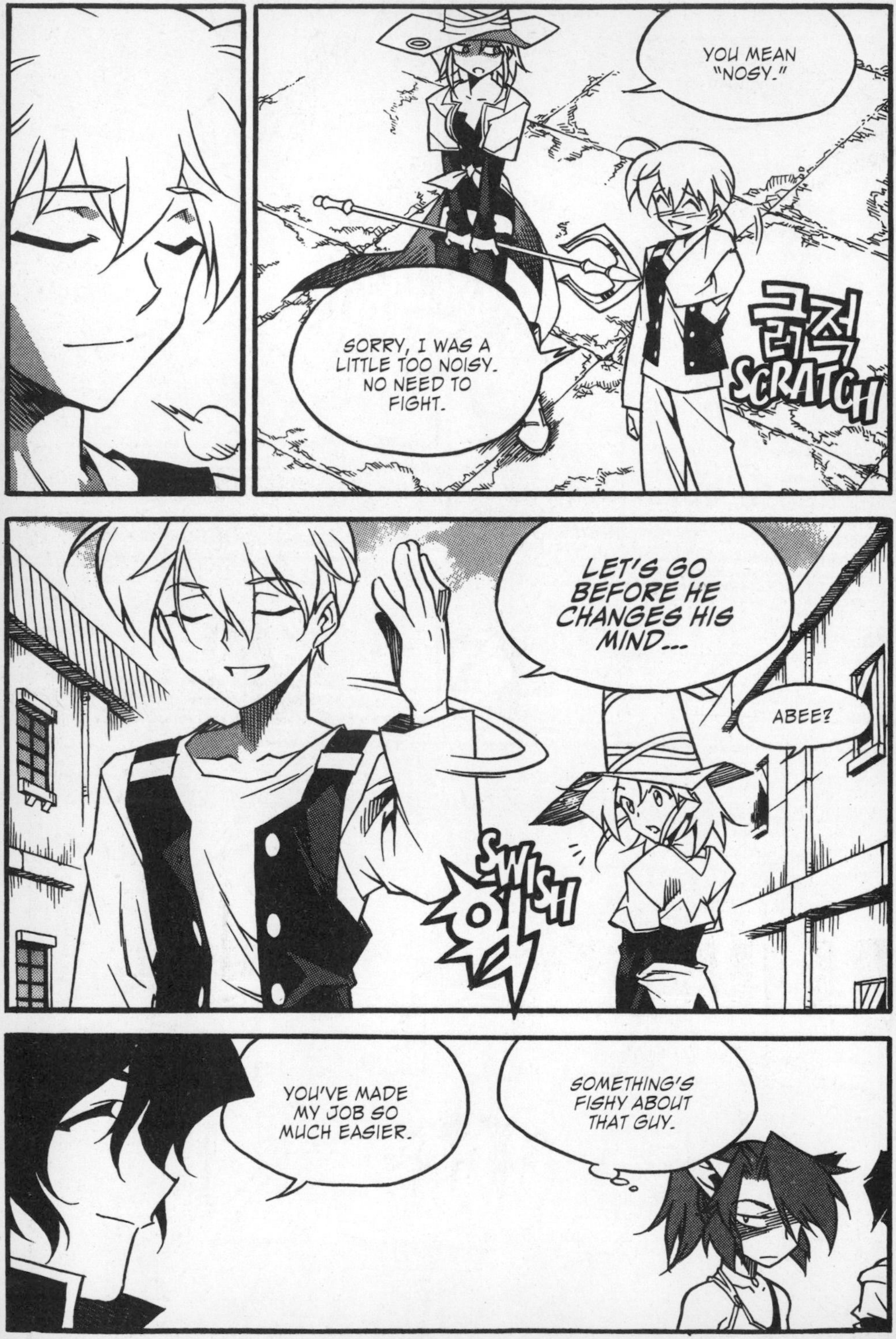
YOU MEAN "NOSY."
SORRY, I WAS A LITTLE TOO NOISY. NO NEED TO FIGHT.
긁적
SCRATCH
LET'S GO BEFORE HE CHANGES HIS MIND...
휙
SWISH
ABEE?
YOU'VE MADE MY JOB SO MUCH EASIER.
SOMETHING'S FISHY ABOUT THAT GUY.

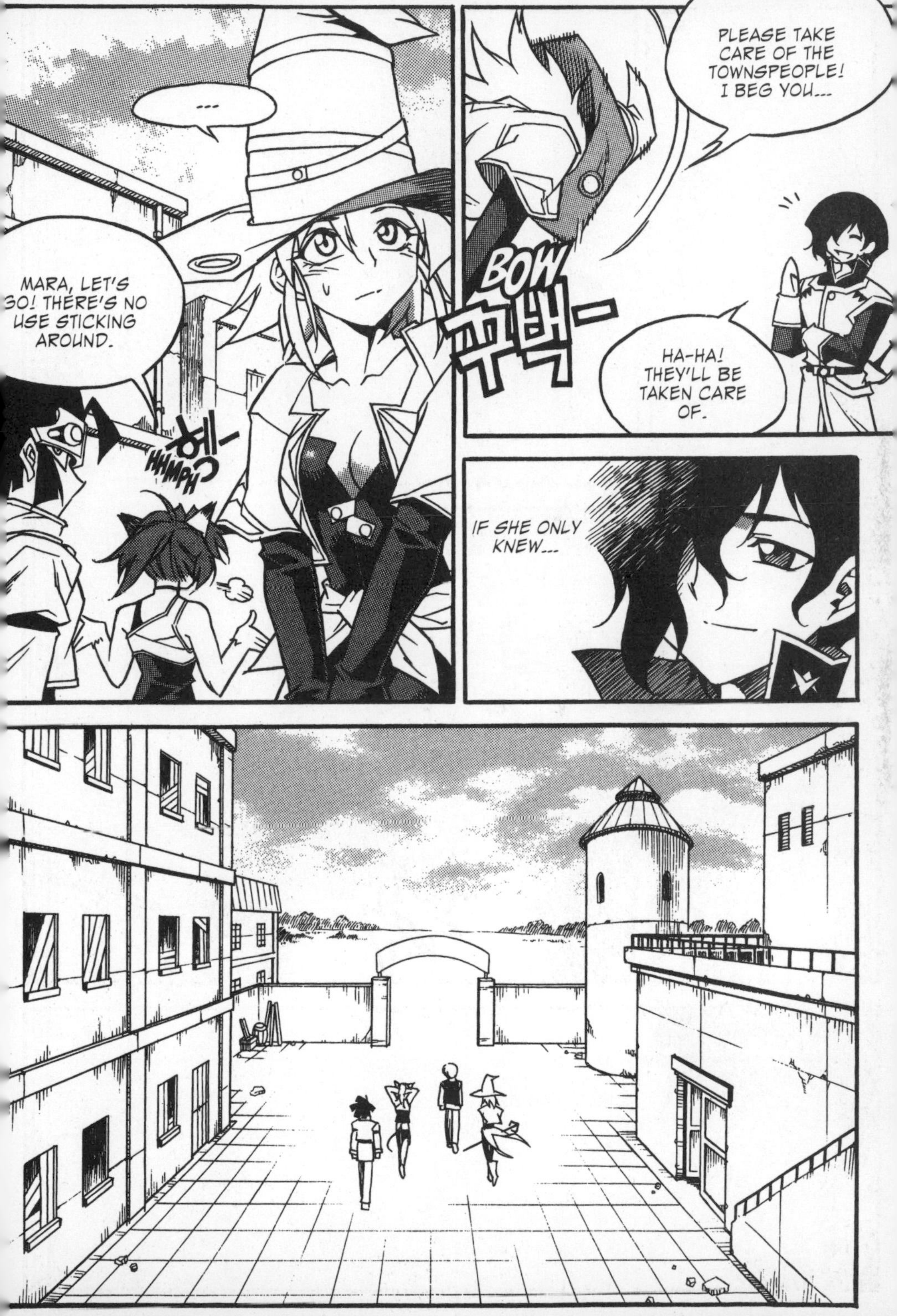
...
MARA, LET'S GO! THERE'S NO USE STICKING AROUND.
HMMPH
PLEASE TAKE CARE OF THE TOWNSPEOPLE! I BEG YOU...
BOW
꾸벅-
HA-HA! THEY'LL BE TAKEN CARE OF.
IF SHE ONLY KNEW...

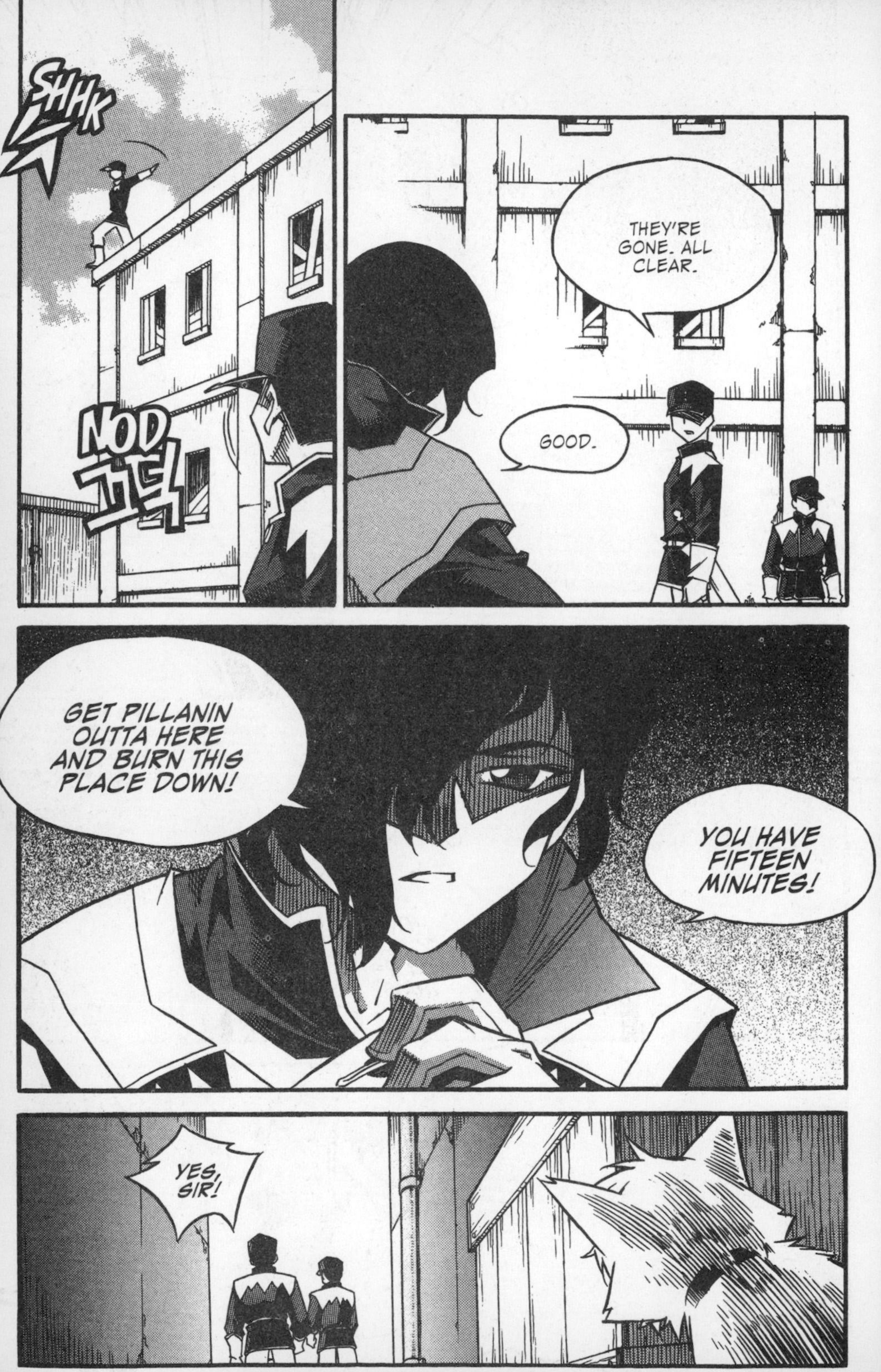
SHHK
NOD
끄덕
THEY'RE GONE. ALL CLEAR.
GOOD.
GET PILLANIN OUTTA HERE AND BURN THIS PLACE DOWN!
YOU HAVE FIFTEEN MINUTES!
YES, SIR!

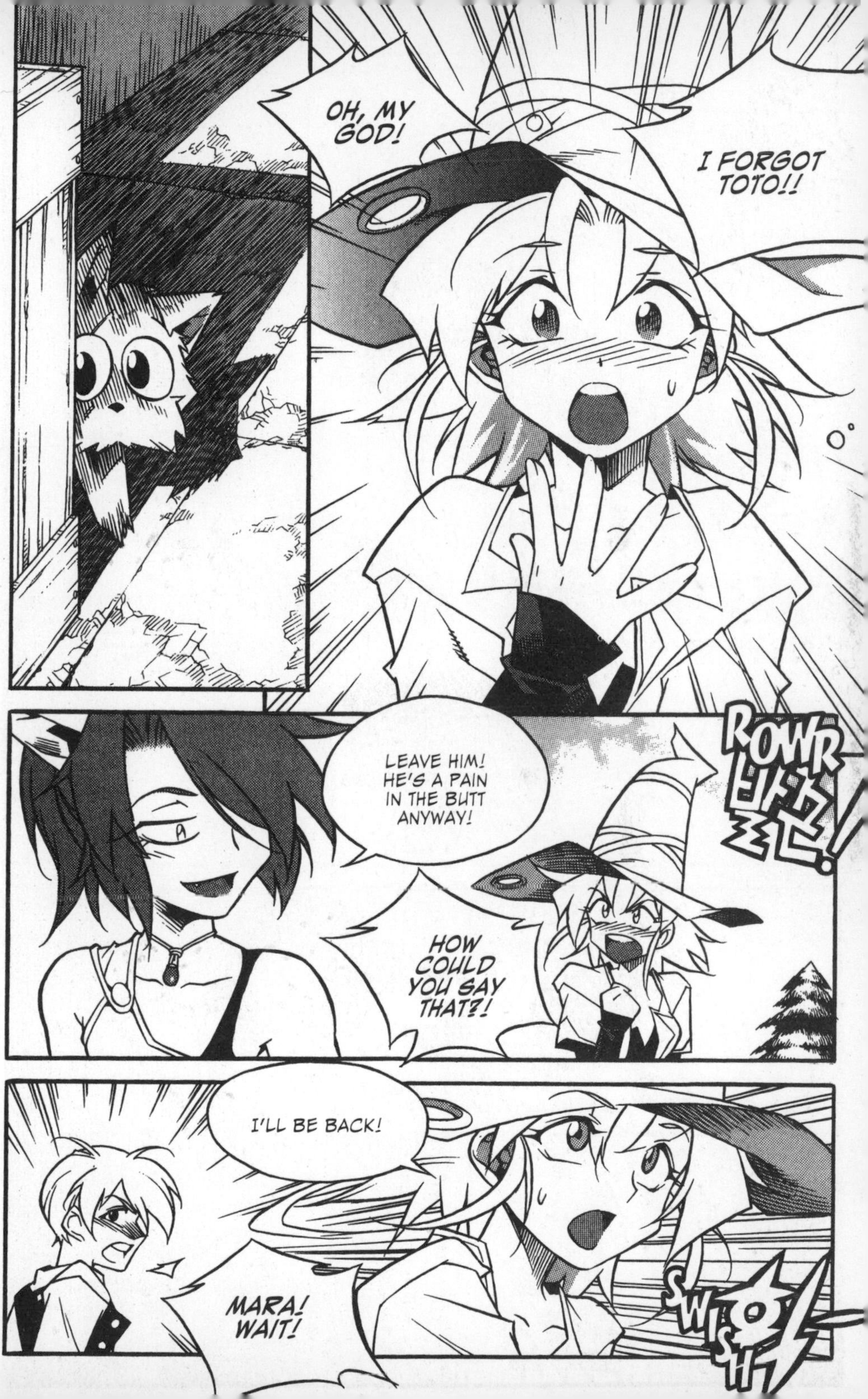
OH, MY GOD!
I FORGOT TOTO!!
LEAVE HIM! HE'S A PAIN IN THE BUTT ANYWAY!
HOW COULD YOU SAY THAT?!
ROWR
I'LL BE BACK!
MARA! WAIT!
SWISH

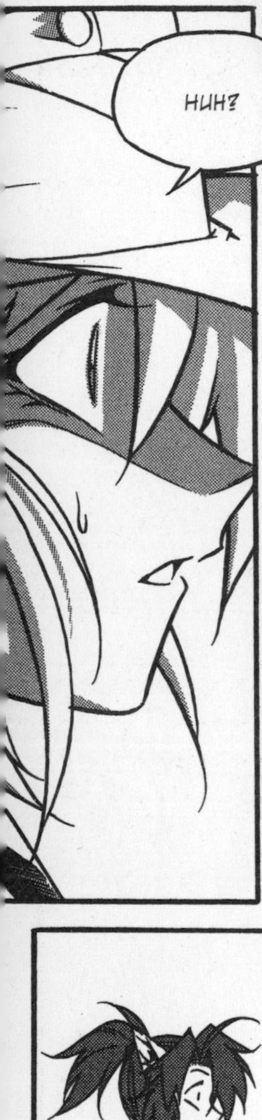
HUH?
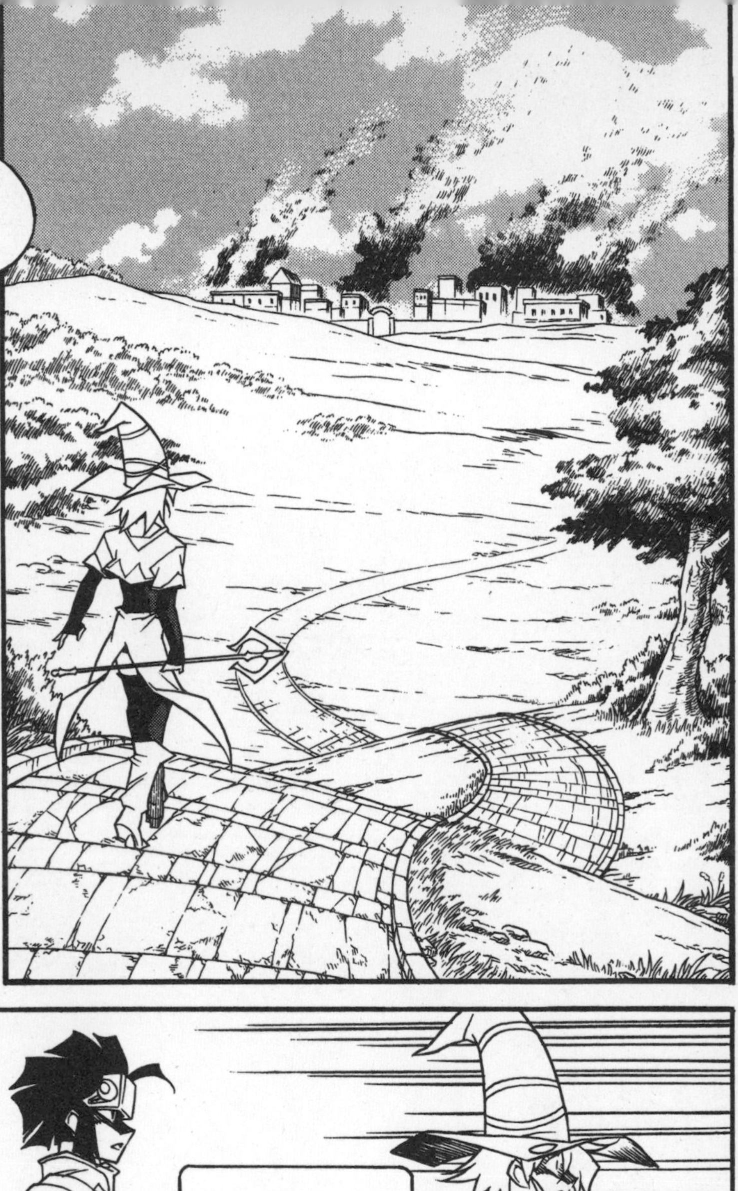
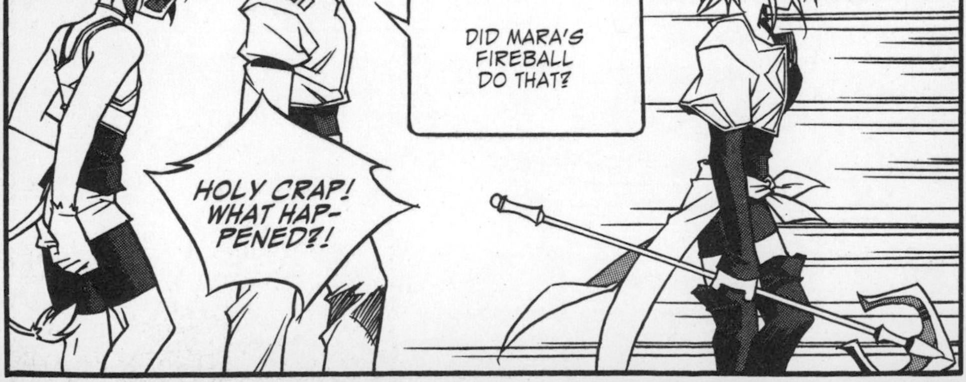
HOLY CRAP! WHAT HAP-PENED?!
DID MARA'S FIREBALL DO THAT?

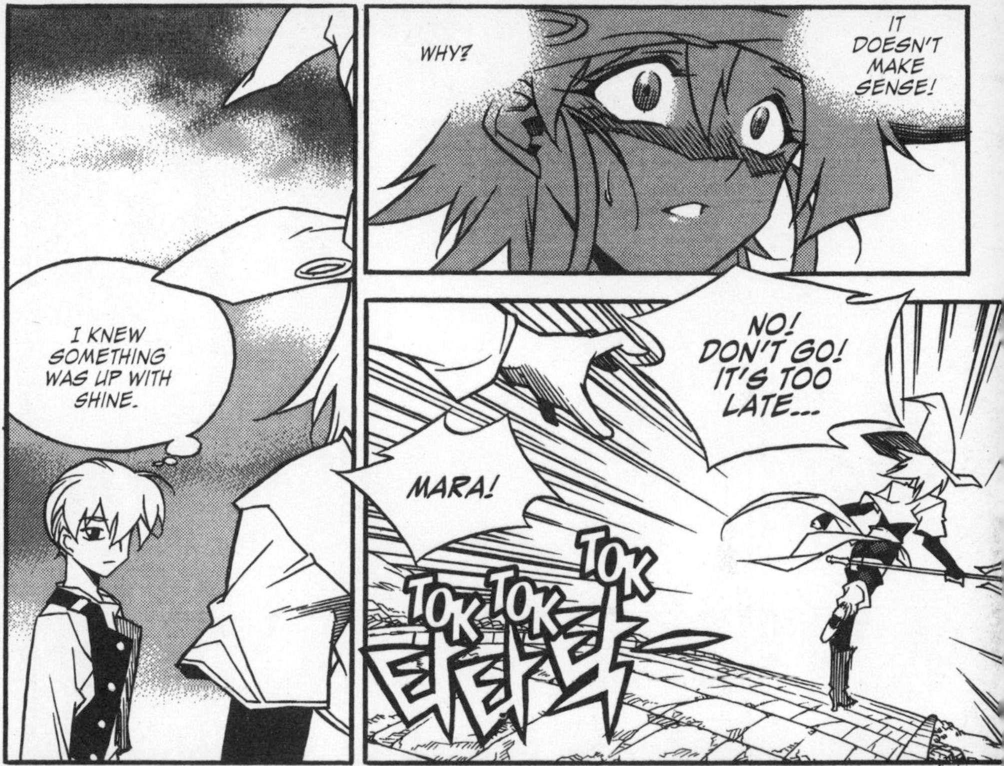
I KNEW SOMETHING WAS UP WITH SHINE.
WHY?
IT DOESN'T MAKE SENSE!
NO! DON'T GO! IT'S TOO LATE...
MARA!
TOK TOK TOK
타타닥

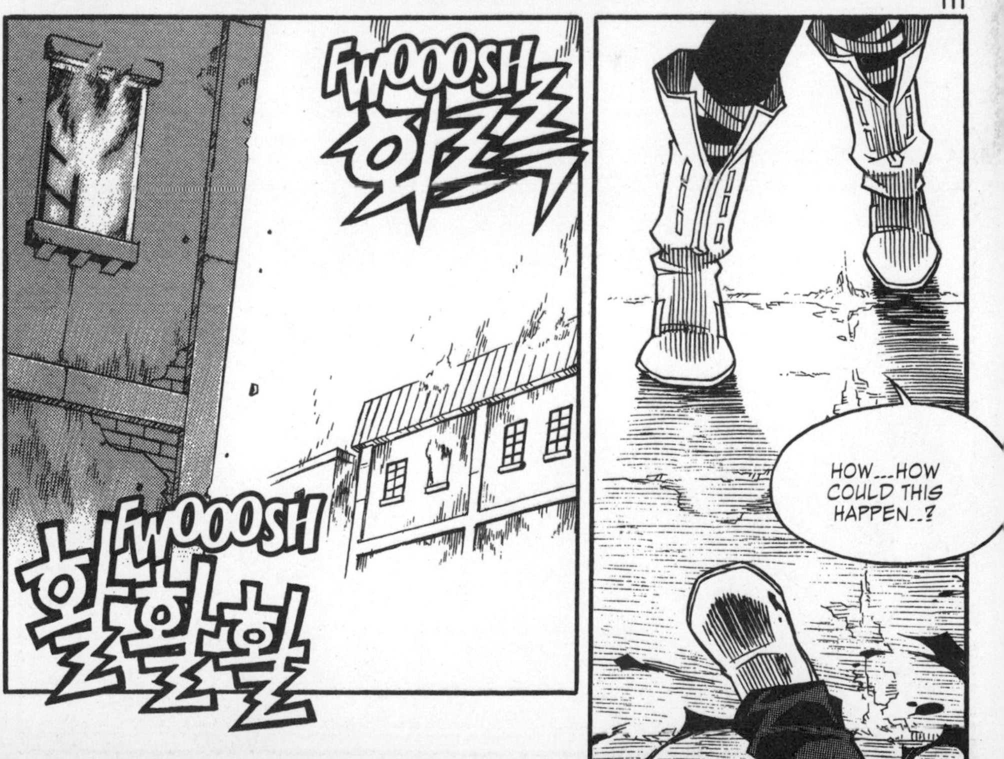
FWOOOSH
FWOOOSH
활활활
HOW...HOW COULD THIS HAPPEN..?

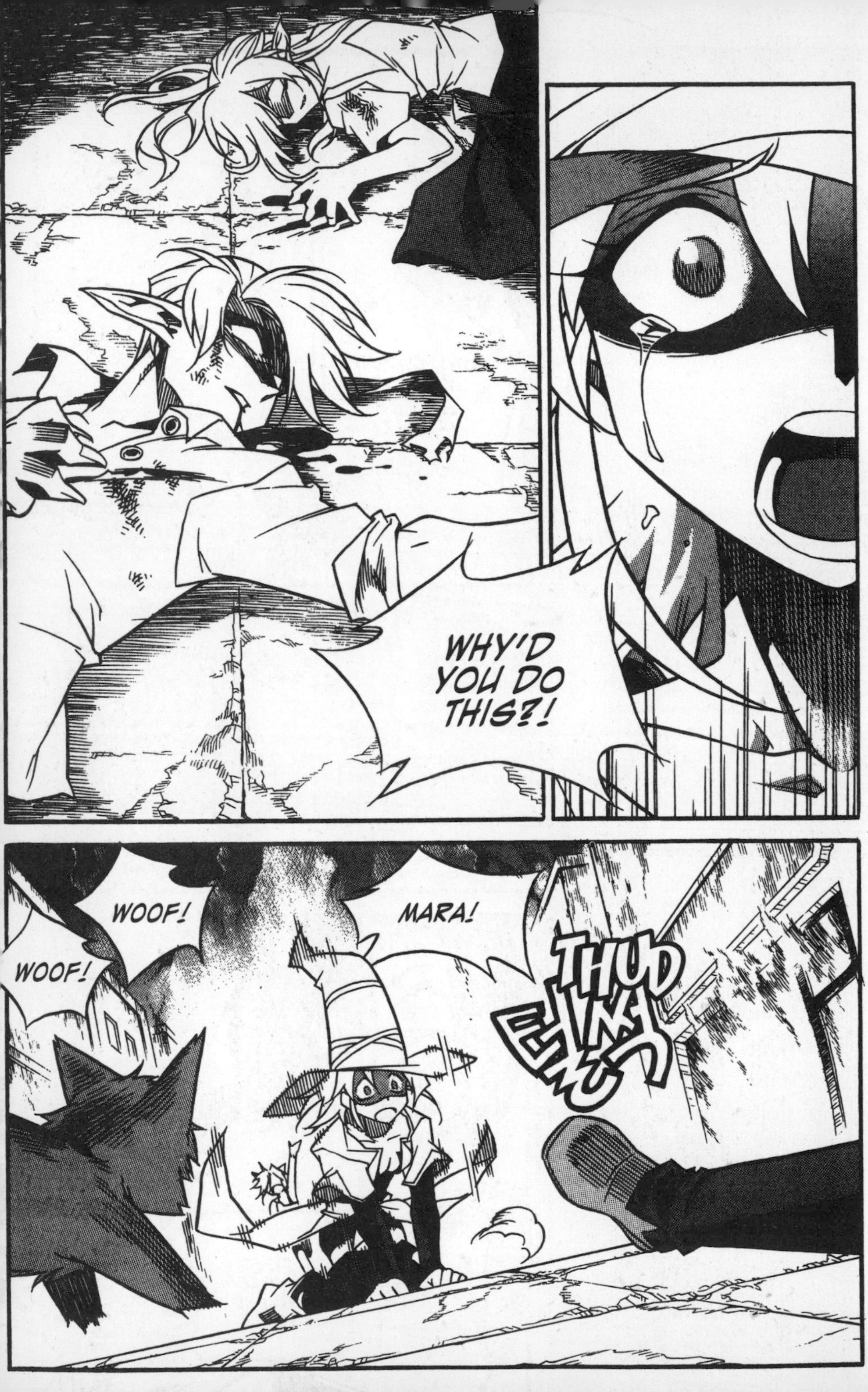
WHY'D YOU DO THIS?!
WOOF!
WOOF!
MARA!
THUD

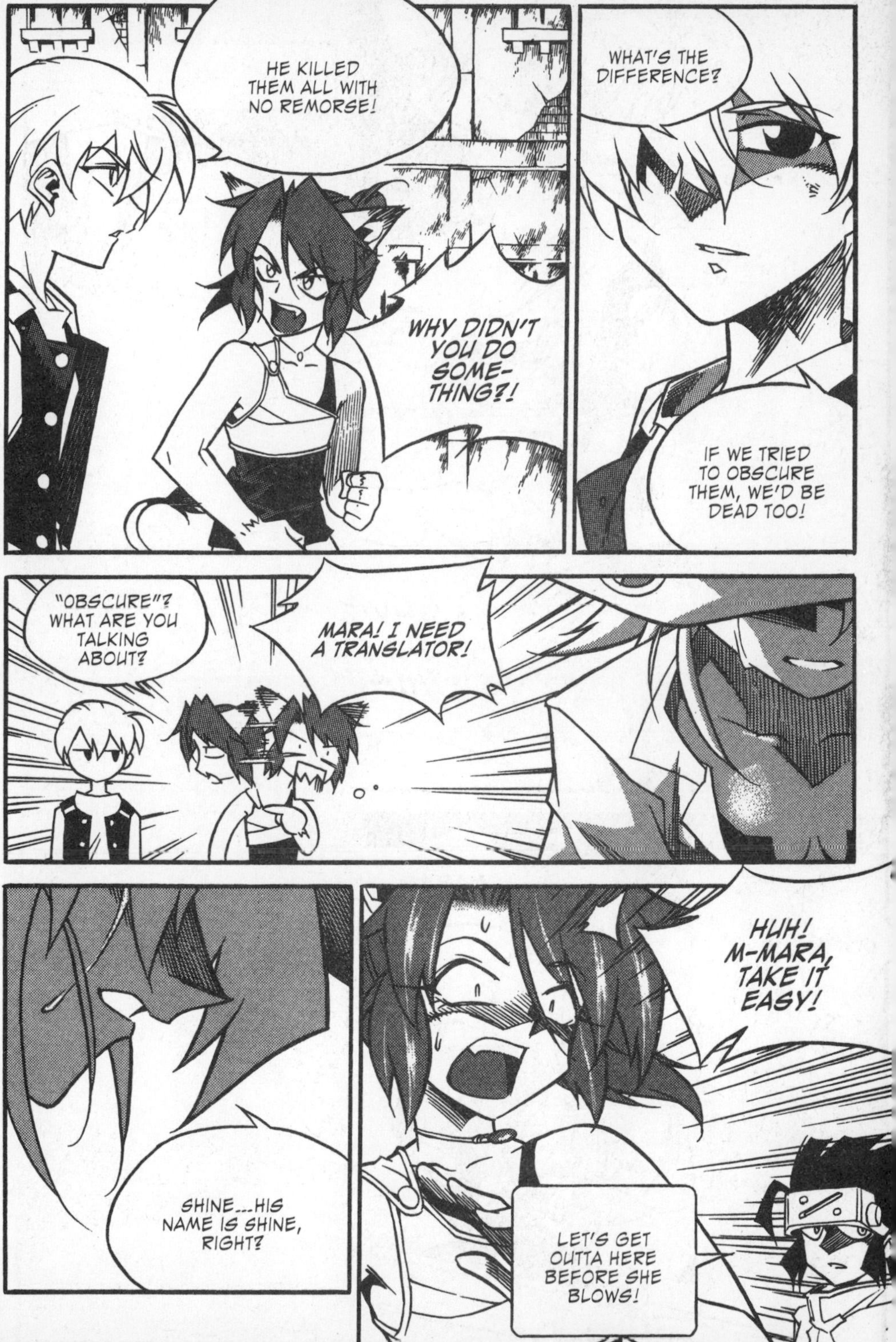
HE KILLED THEM ALL WITH NO REMORSE!
WHY DIDN'T YOU DO SOME-THING?!
WHAT'S THE DIFFERENCE?
IF WE TRIED TO OBSCURE THEM, WE'D BE DEAD TOO!
"OBSCURE"? WHAT ARE YOU TALKING ABOUT?
MARA! I NEED A TRANSLATOR!
SHINE...HIS NAME IS SHINE, RIGHT?
HUH! M-MARA, TAKE IT EASY!
LET'S GET OUTTA HERE BEFORE SHE BLOWS!

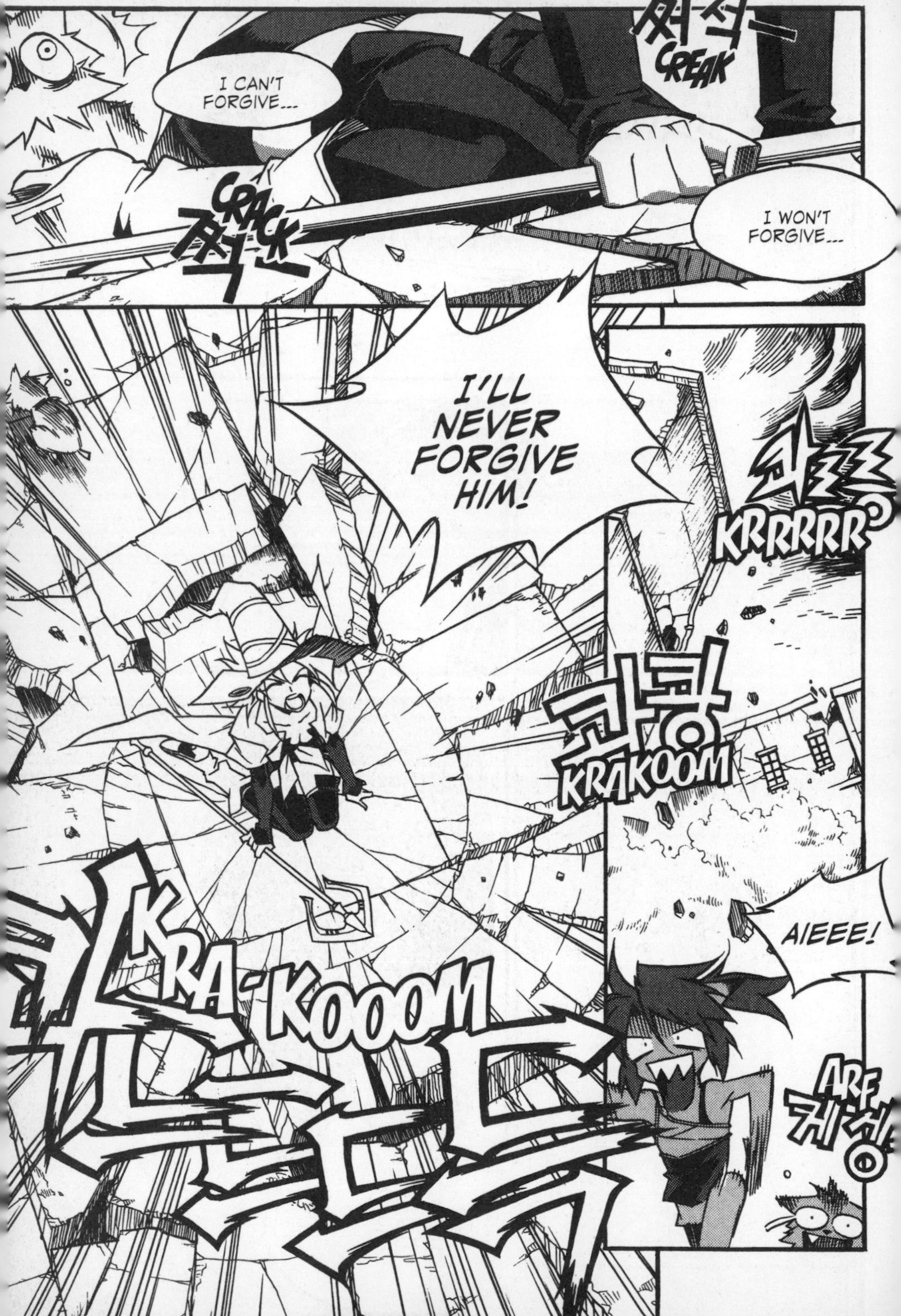
쩌적-
CREAK
I CAN'T FORGIVE...
CRACK
I WON'T FORGIVE...
I'LL NEVER FORGIVE HIM!
KRA-KOOOM
KRRRRR
KRAKOOM
AIEEE!
ARF

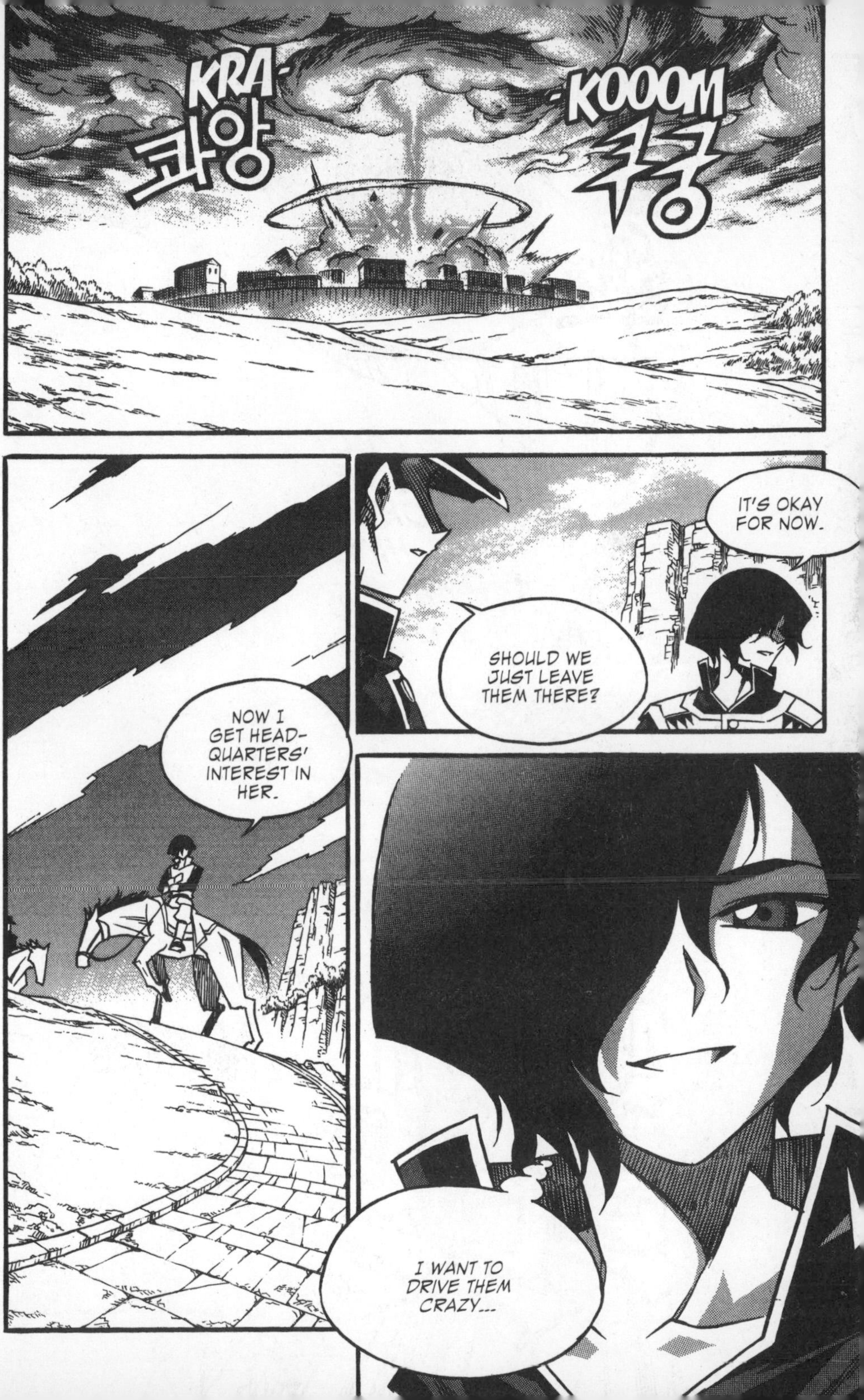
KRA-
콰앙
-KOOOM
쿠궁
NOW I GET HEAD-QUARTERS' INTEREST IN HER.
SHOULD WE JUST LEAVE THEM THERE?
IT'S OKAY FOR NOW.
I WANT TO DRIVE THEM CRAZY...

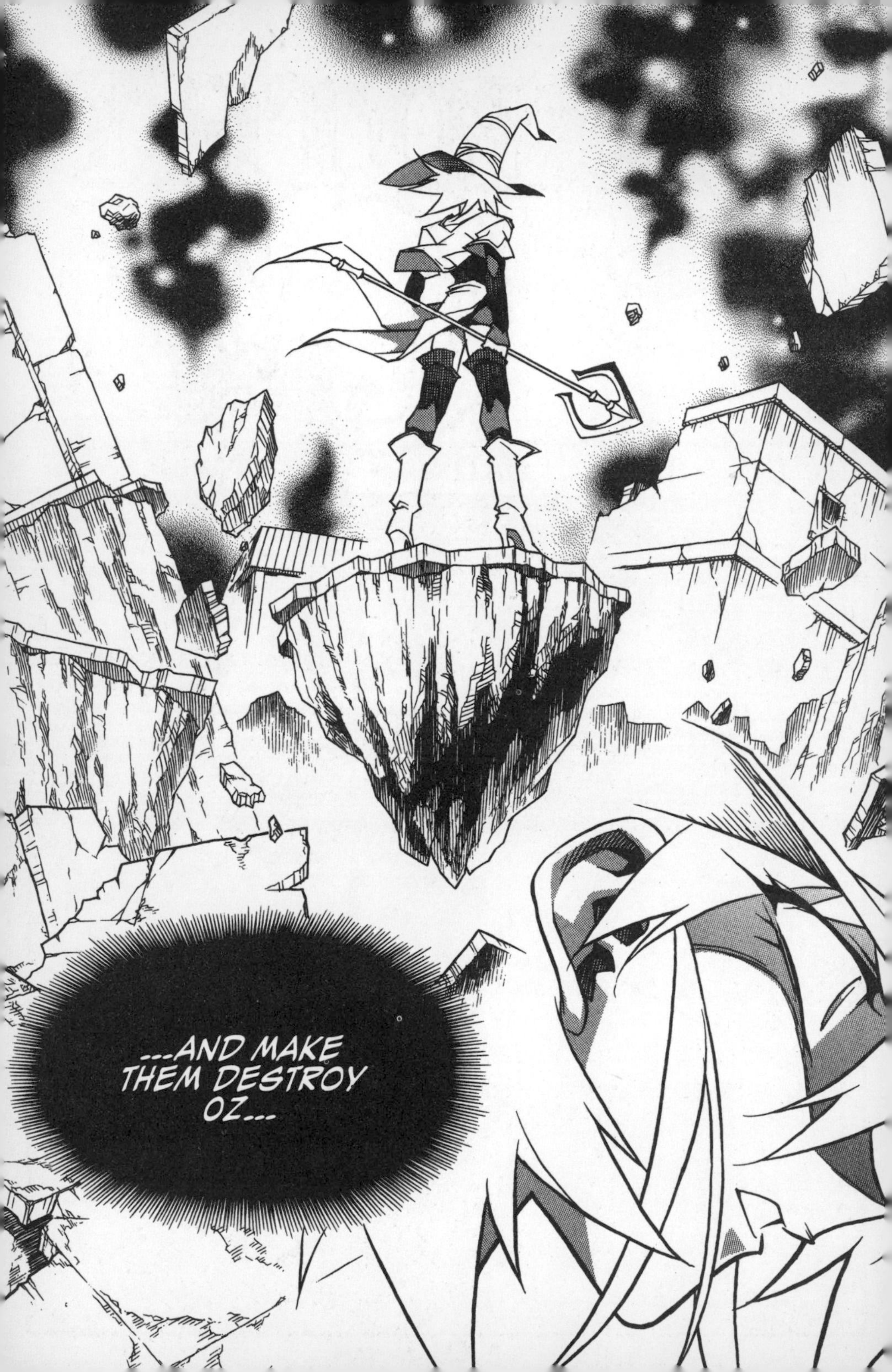
...AND MAKE THEM DESTROY OZ...

DOROTHY OF OZ

도로시

Step 5 YELLOW BRICK ROAD

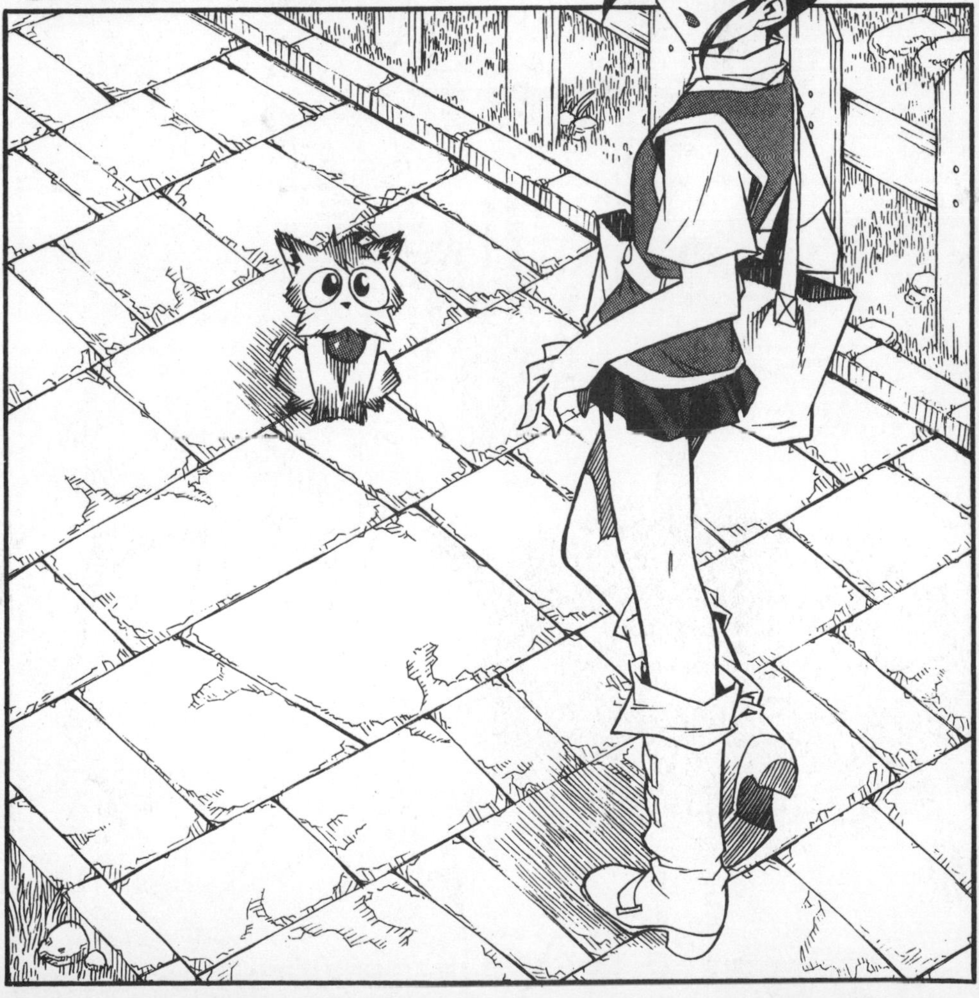

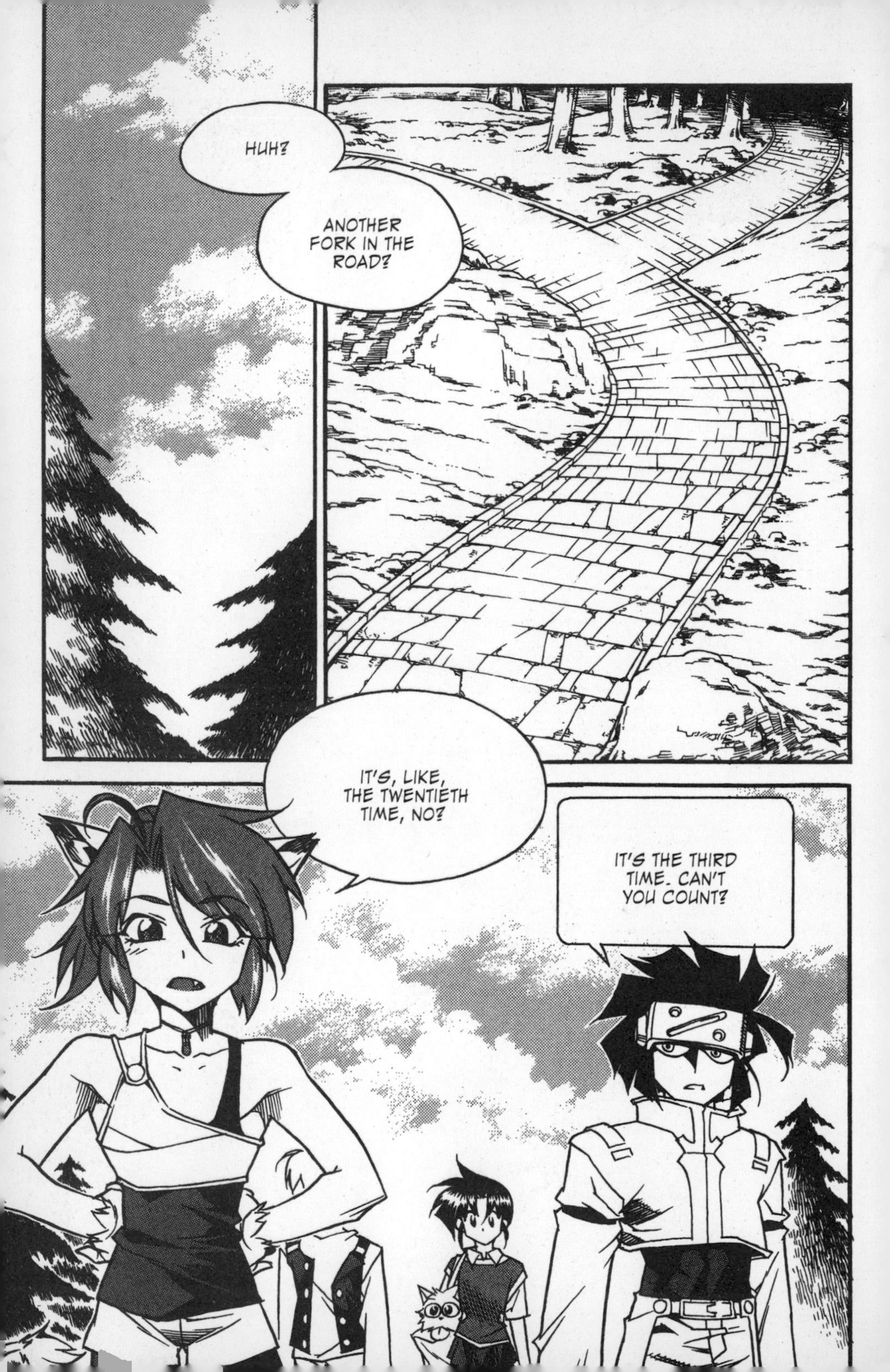
HUH?
ANOTHER FORK IN THE ROAD?
IT'S, LIKE, THE TWENTIETH TIME, NO?
IT'S THE THIRD TIME. CAN'T YOU COUNT?

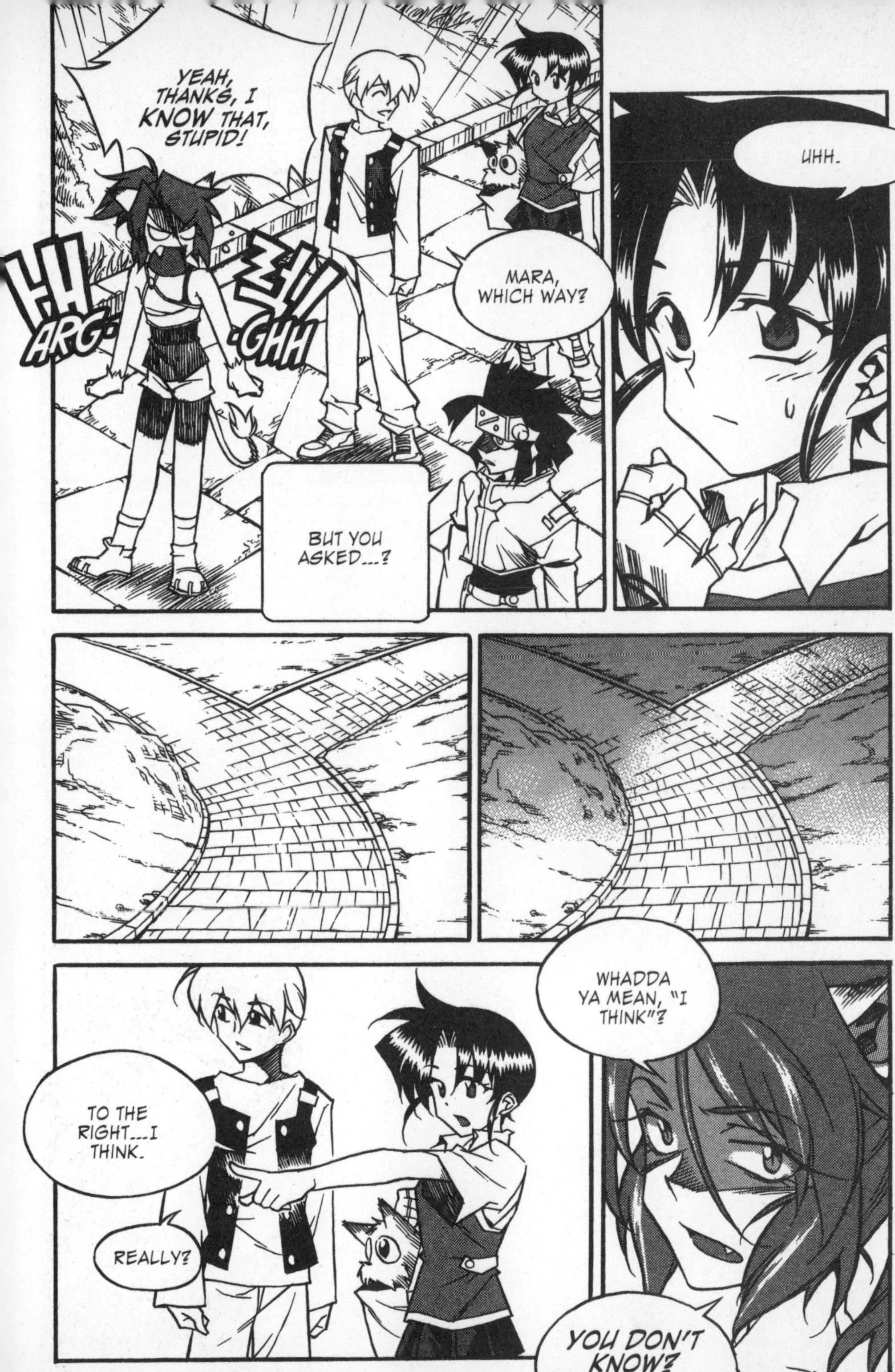
YEAH, THANKS, I KNOW THAT, STUPID!
ARG-
-GHH
MARA, WHICH WAY?
BUT YOU ASKED...?
UHH.
TO THE RIGHT...I THINK.
REALLY?
WHADDA YA MEAN, "I THINK"?
YOU DON'T KNOW?

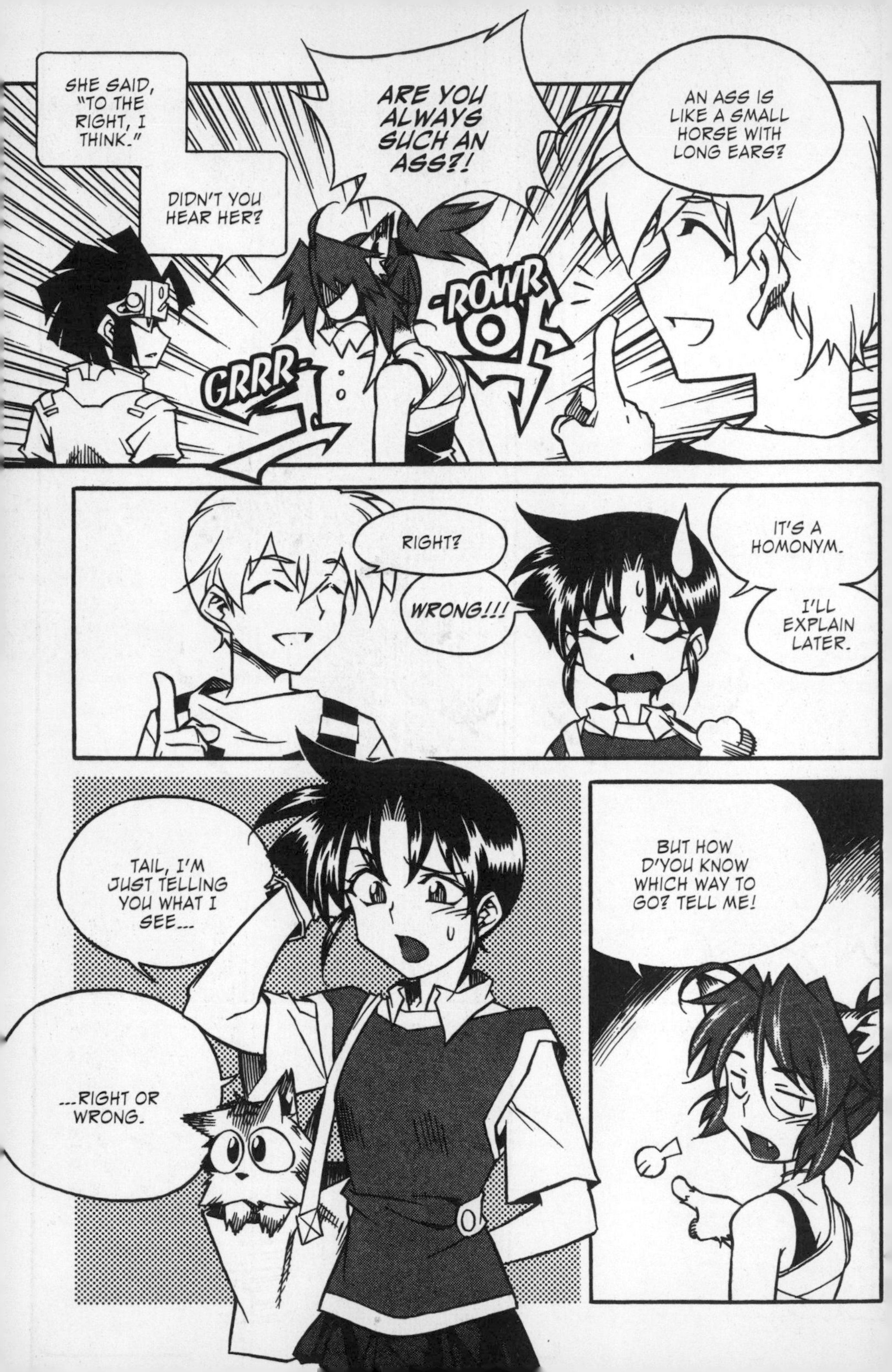

SHE SAID, "TO THE RIGHT, I THINK."
DIDN'T YOU HEAR HER?
ARE YOU ALWAYS SUCH AN ASS?!
AN ASS IS LIKE A SMALL HORSE WITH LONG EARS?
GRRR-
-ROWR
RIGHT?
WRONG!!!
IT'S A HOMONYM.
I'LL EXPLAIN LATER.
TAIL, I'M JUST TELLING YOU WHAT I SEE...
...RIGHT OR WRONG.
BUT HOW D'YOU KNOW WHICH WAY TO GO? TELL ME!

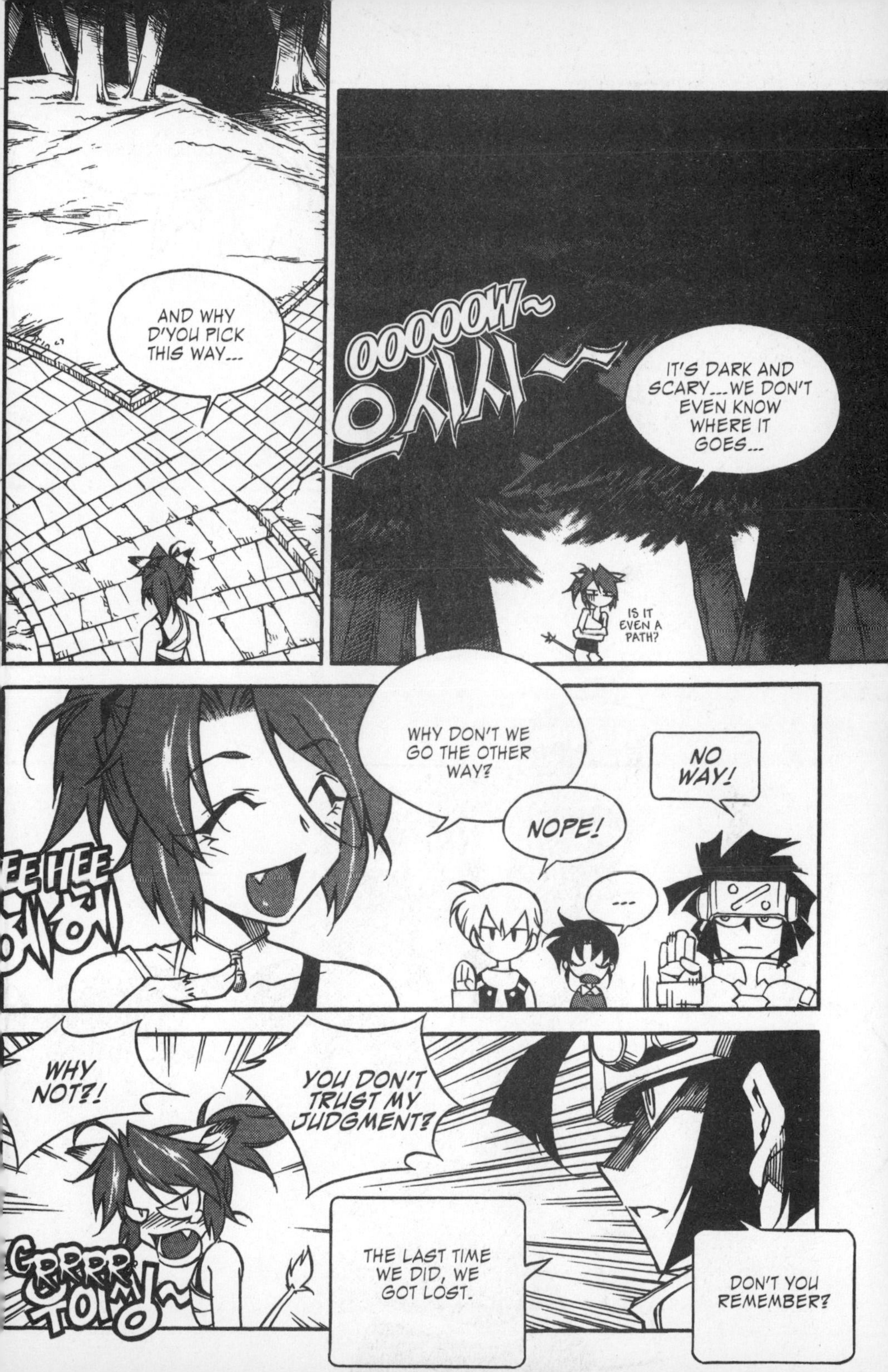
AND WHY D'YOU PICK THIS WAY...
OOOOOW~
으시시~
IT'S DARK AND SCARY... WE DON'T EVEN KNOW WHERE IT GOES...
IS IT EVEN A PATH?
HEE HEE
헤헤
WHY DON'T WE GO THE OTHER WAY?
NOPE!
...
NO WAY!
WHY NOT?!
YOU DON'T TRUST MY JUDGMENT?
GRRR.
THE LAST TIME WE DID, WE GOT LOST.
DON'T YOU REMEMBER?

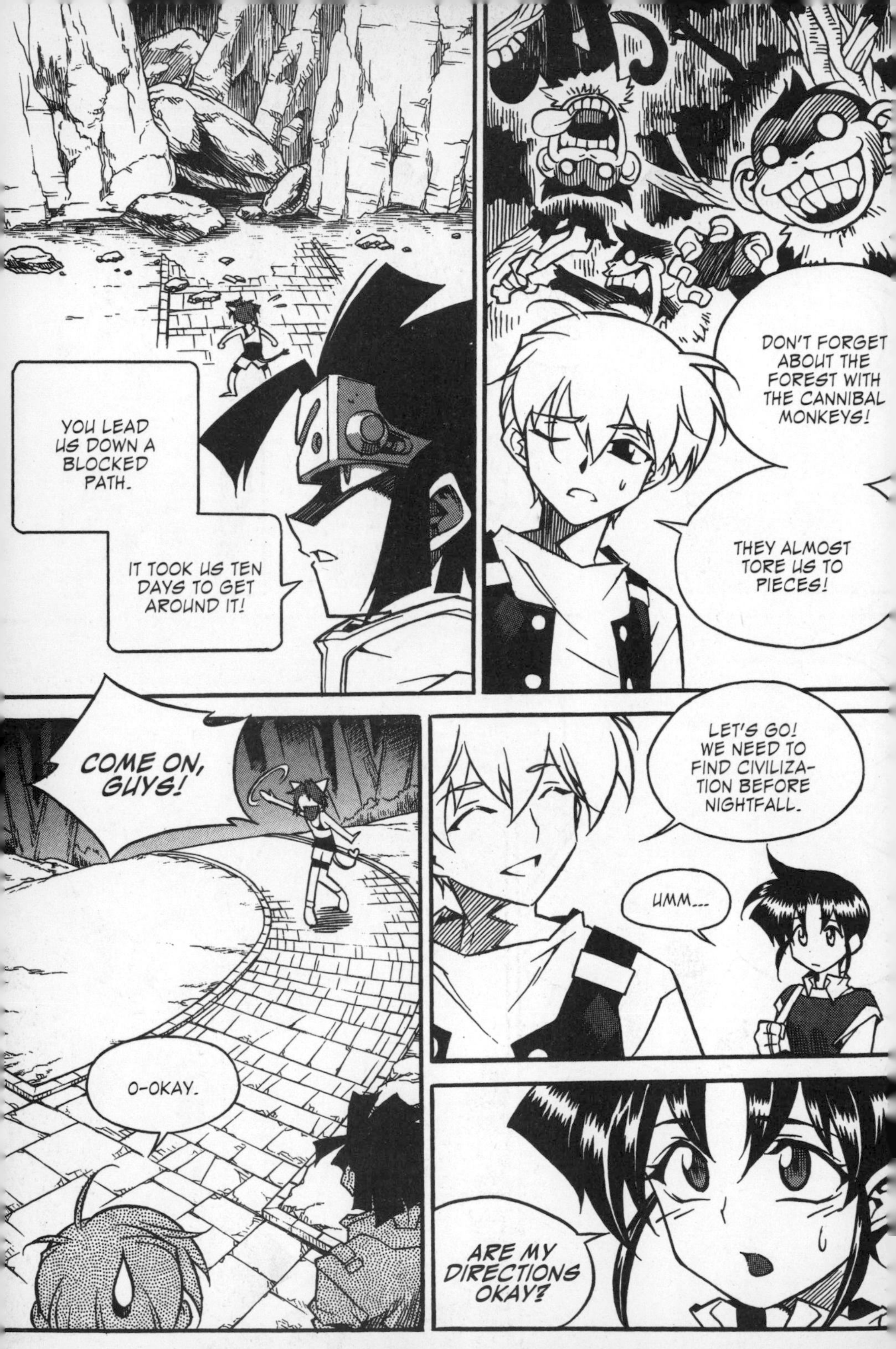
YOU LEAD US DOWN A BLOCKED PATH.
IT TOOK US TEN DAYS TO GET AROUND IT!
DON'T FORGET ABOUT THE FOREST WITH THE CANNIBAL MONKEYS!
THEY ALMOST TORE US TO PIECES!
COME ON, GUYS!
O-OKAY.
LET'S GO! WE NEED TO FIND CIVILIZA-TION BEFORE NIGHTFALL.
UMM...
ARE MY DIRECTIONS OKAY?

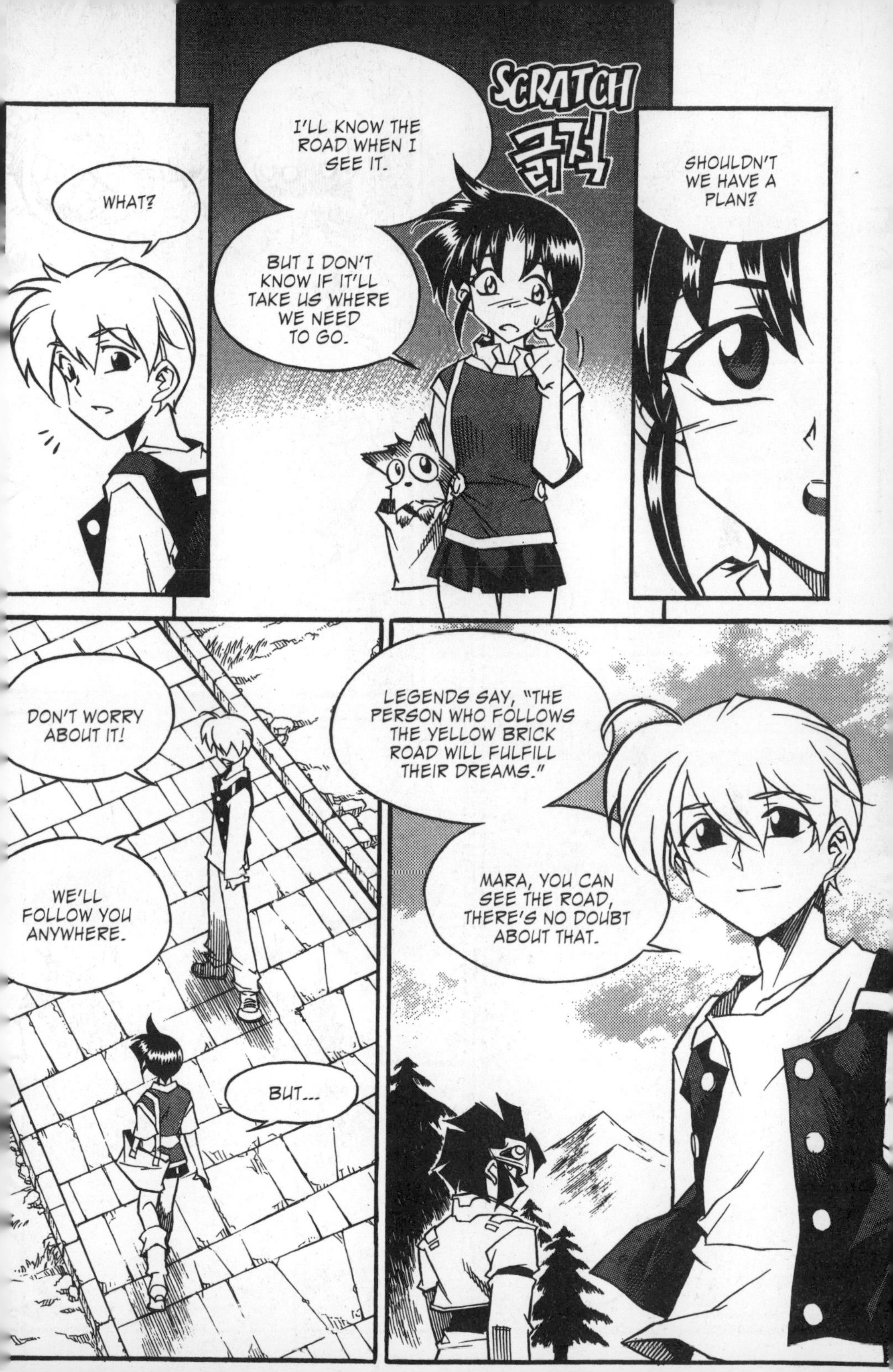
WHAT?
I'LL KNOW THE ROAD WHEN I SEE IT.
BUT I DON'T KNOW IF IT'LL TAKE US WHERE WE NEED TO GO.
SCRATCH
긁적
SHOULDN'T WE HAVE A PLAN?
DON'T WORRY ABOUT IT!
WE'LL FOLLOW YOU ANYWHERE.
BUT...
LEGENDS SAY, "THE PERSON WHO FOLLOWS THE YELLOW BRICK ROAD WILL FULFILL THEIR DREAMS."
MARA, YOU CAN SEE THE ROAD, THERE'S NO DOUBT ABOUT THAT.

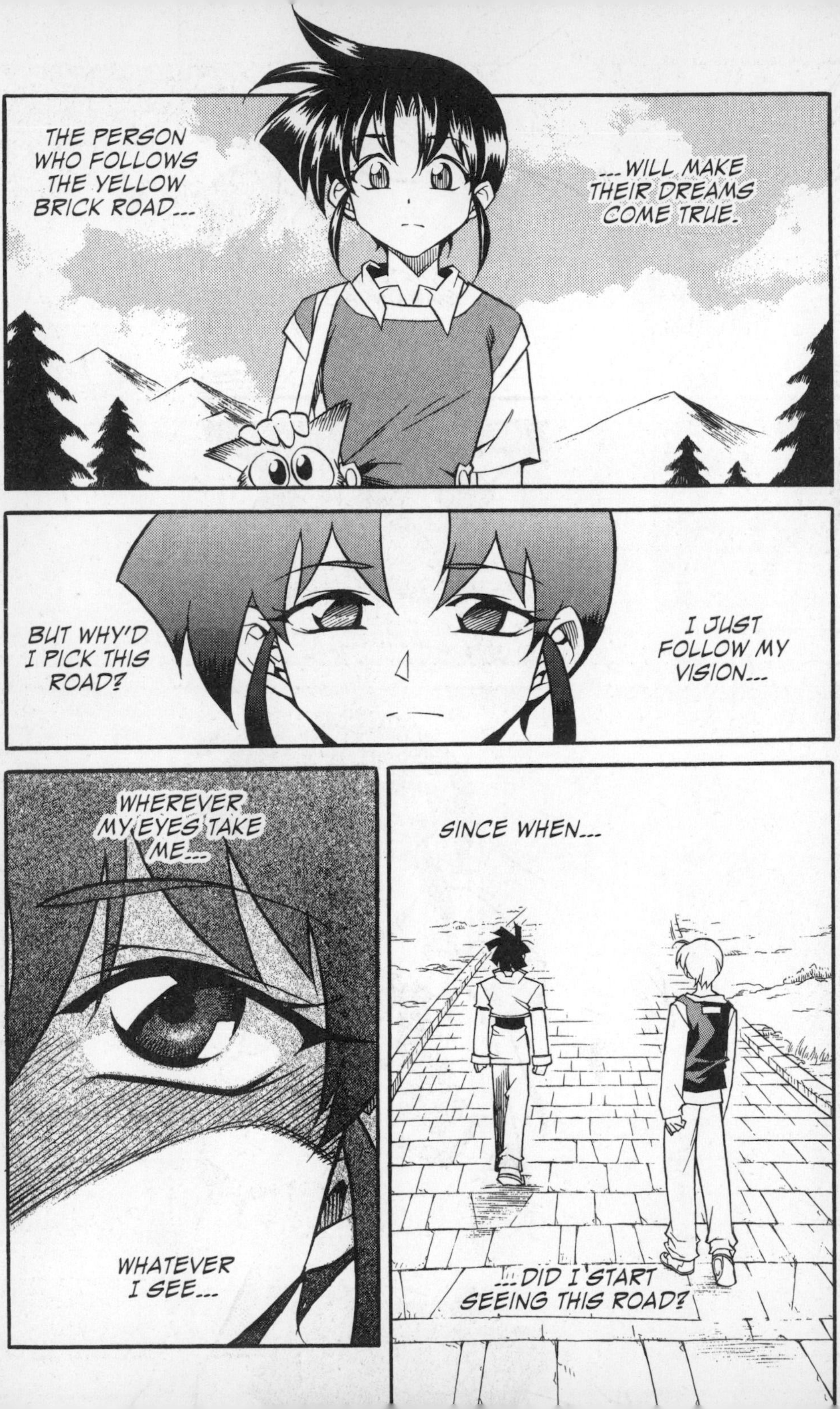
THE PERSON WHO FOLLOWS THE YELLOW BRICK ROAD...
...WILL MAKE THEIR DREAMS COME TRUE.
BUT WHY'D I PICK THIS ROAD?
I JUST FOLLOW MY VISION...
WHEREVER MY EYES TAKE ME...
WHATEVER I SEE...
SINCE WHEN...
...DID I START SEEING THIS ROAD?

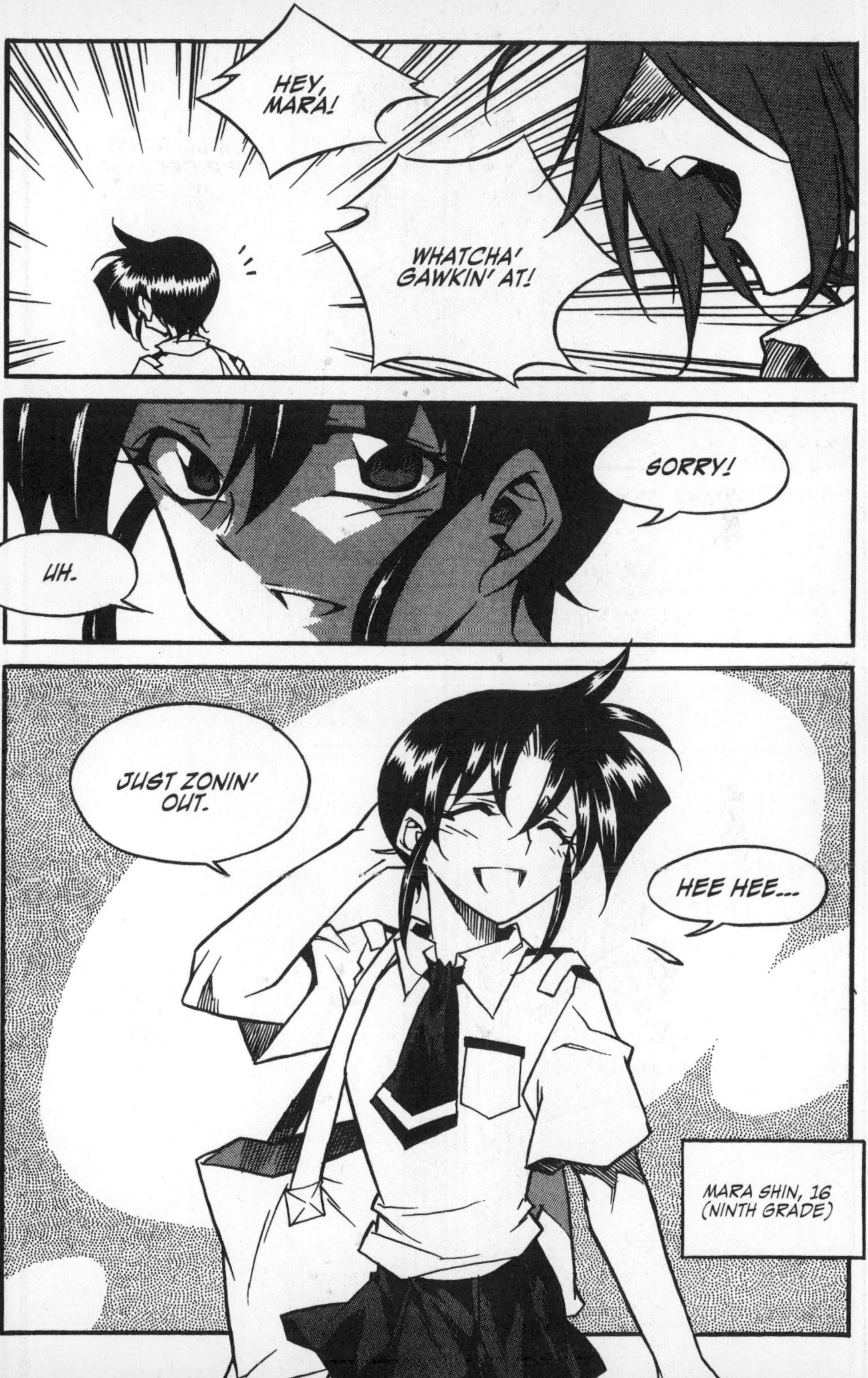
HEY, MARA!
WHATCHA' GAWKIN' AT!
UH.
SORRY!
JUST ZONIN' OUT.
HEE HEE...
MARA SHIN, 16 (NINTH GRADE)

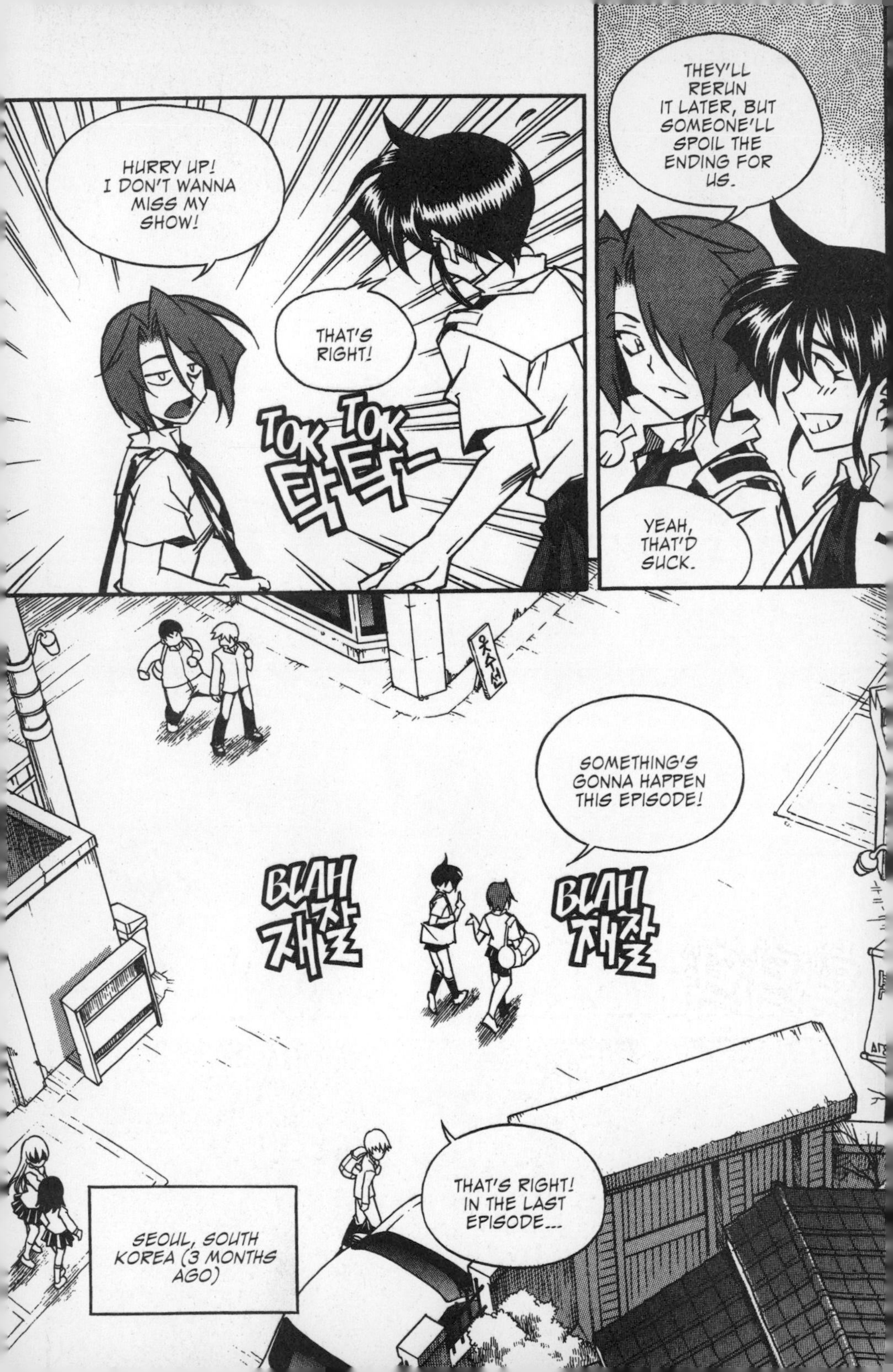
HURRY UP! I DON'T WANNA MISS MY SHOW!
THAT'S RIGHT!
TOK TOK
타닥 타닥
THEY'LL RERUN IT LATER, BUT SOMEONE'LL SPOIL THE ENDING FOR US.
YEAH, THAT'D SUCK.
옷수선
SOMETHING'S GONNA HAPPEN THIS EPISODE!
BLAH
재잘
BLAH
재잘
SEOUL, SOUTH KOREA (3 MONTHS AGO)
THAT'S RIGHT! IN THE LAST EPISODE...

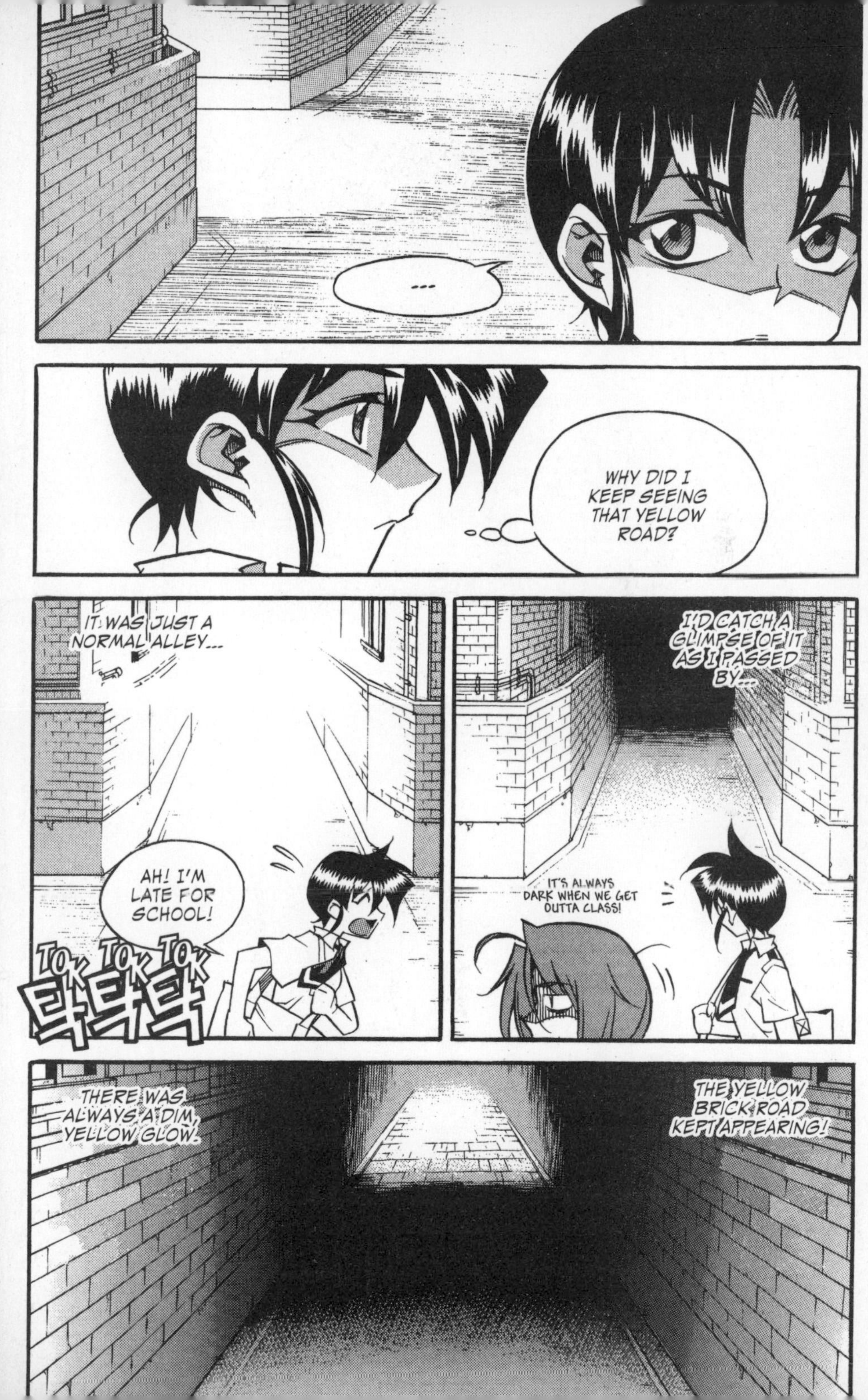
...
WHY DID I KEEP SEEING THAT YELLOW ROAD?
IT WAS JUST A NORMAL ALLEY...
AH! I'M LATE FOR SCHOOL!
TOK TOK TOK
탁탁탁
I'D CATCH A GLIMPSE OF IT AS I PASSED BY...
IT'S ALWAYS DARK WHEN WE GET OUTTA CLASS!
THERE WAS ALWAYS A DIM, YELLOW GLOW.
THE YELLOW BRICK ROAD KEPT APPEARING!

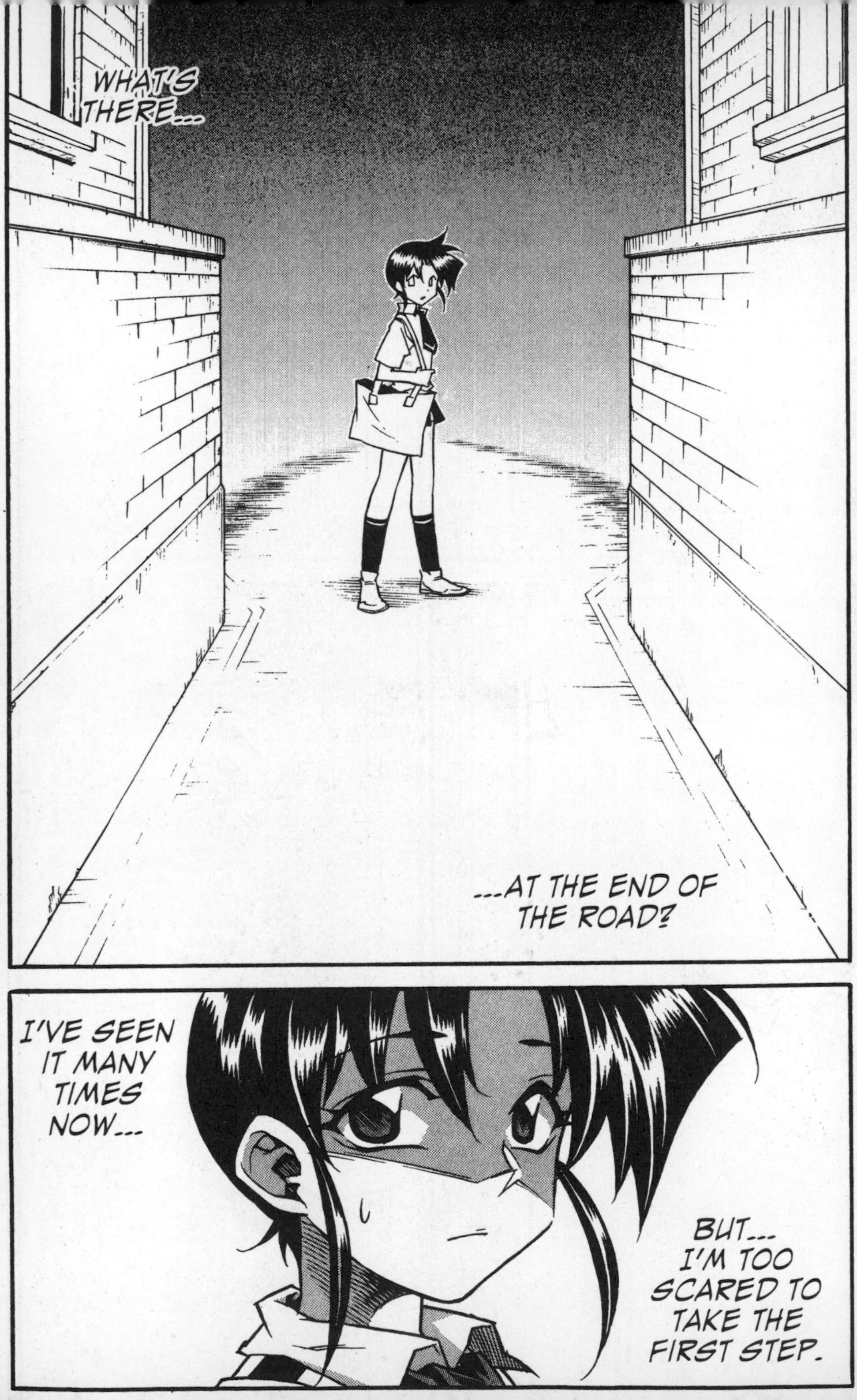
WHAT'S THERE...
...AT THE END OF THE ROAD?
I'VE SEEN IT MANY TIMES NOW...
BUT... I'M TOO SCARED TO TAKE THE FIRST STEP.

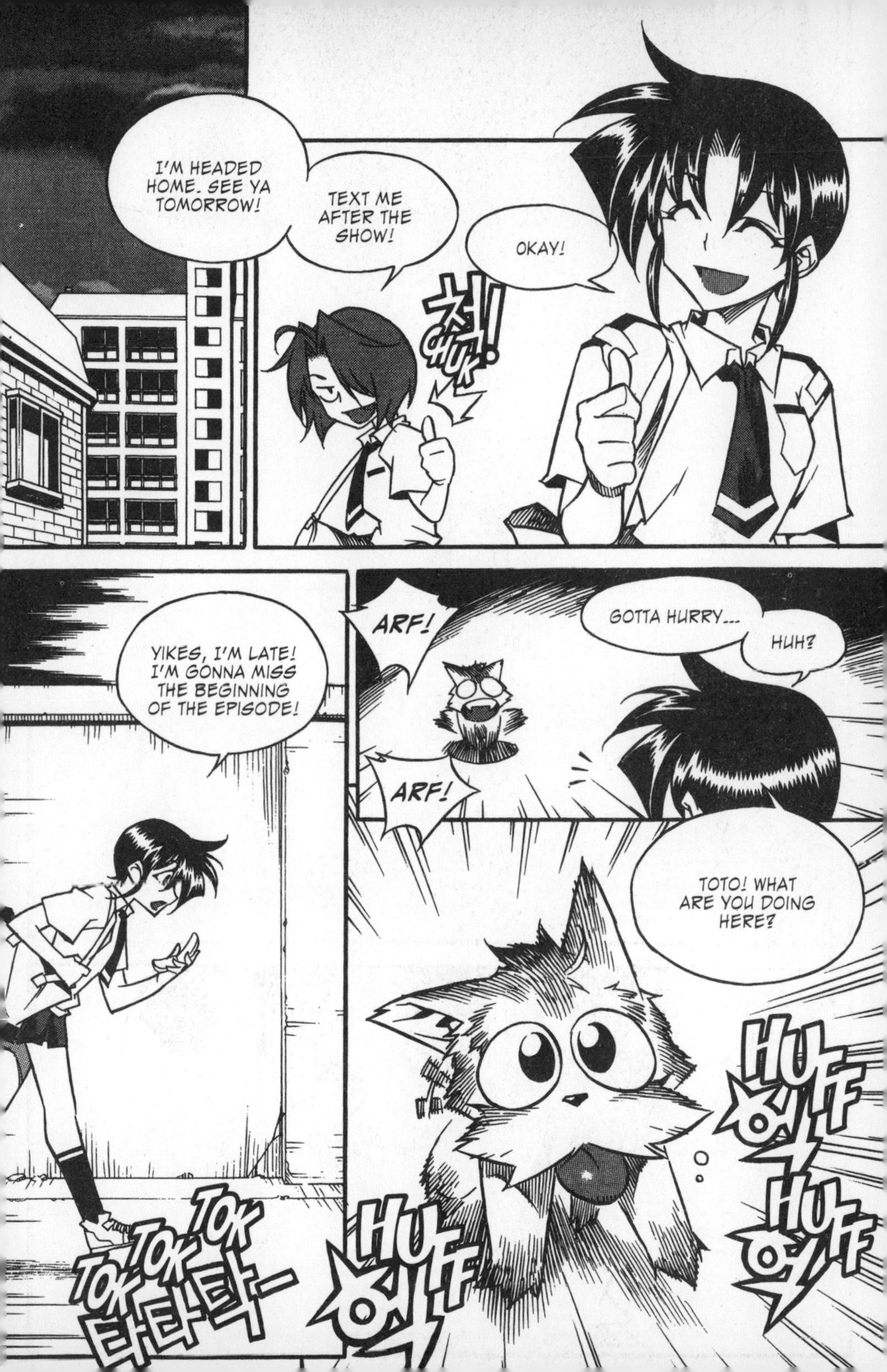

I'M HEADED HOME. SEE YA TOMORROW!
TEXT ME AFTER THE SHOW!
척 CHUK!
OKAY!
YIKES, I'M LATE! I'M GONNA MISS THE BEGINNING OF THE EPISODE!
TOK TOK TOK
타타타-
ARF!
ARF!
GOTTA HURRY...
HUH?
TOTO! WHAT ARE YOU DOING HERE?
HUFF 헉
HUFF 헉
HUFF 헉

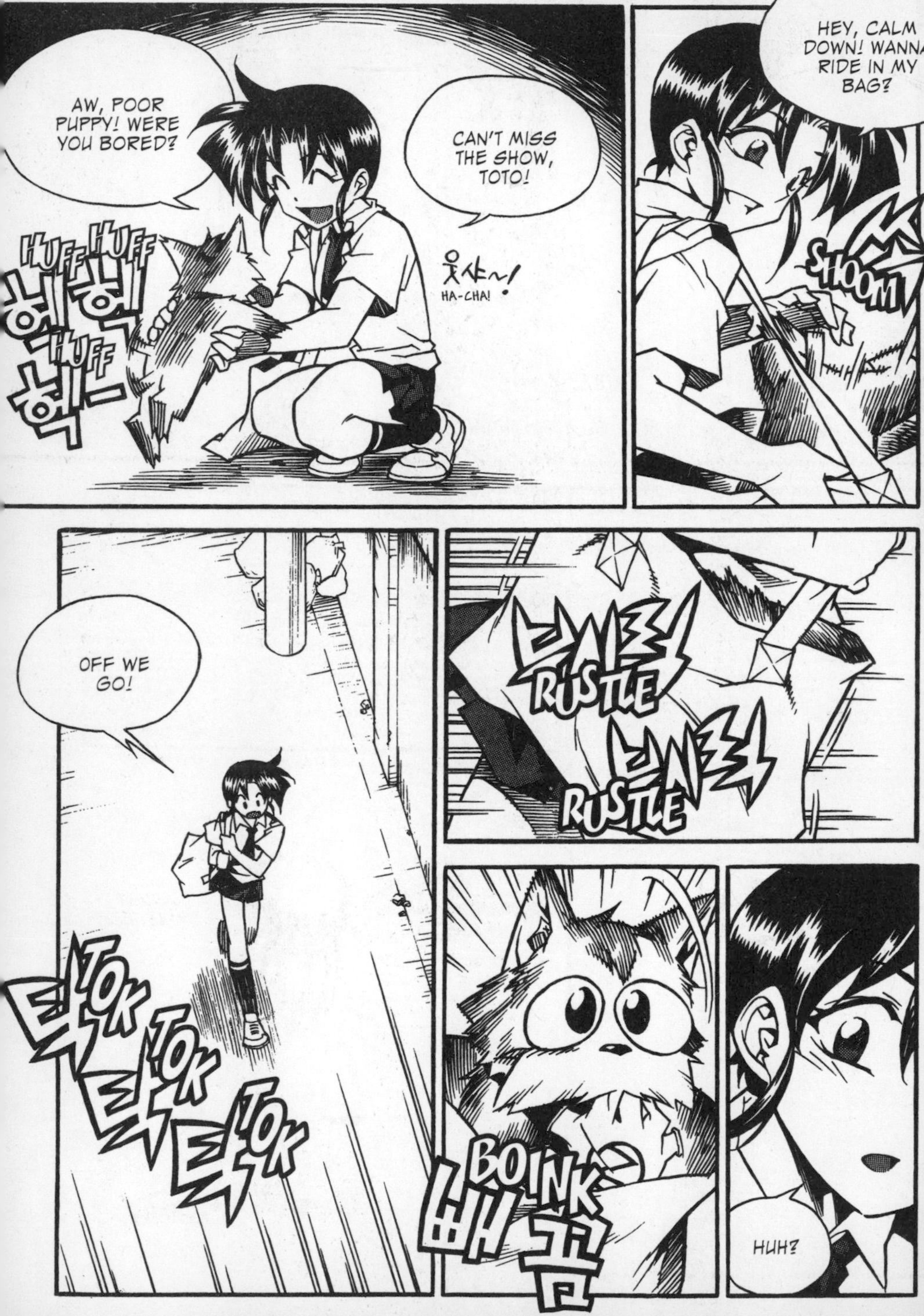
AW, POOR PUPPY! WERE YOU BORED?
HUFF HUFF
HUFF
CAN'T MISS THE SHOW, TOTO!
읏샤~!
HA-CHA!
HEY, CALM DOWN! WANNA RIDE IN MY BAG?
SHOOM
OFF WE GO!
TOK TOK TOK
RUSTLE
RUSTLE
BOINK
HUH?

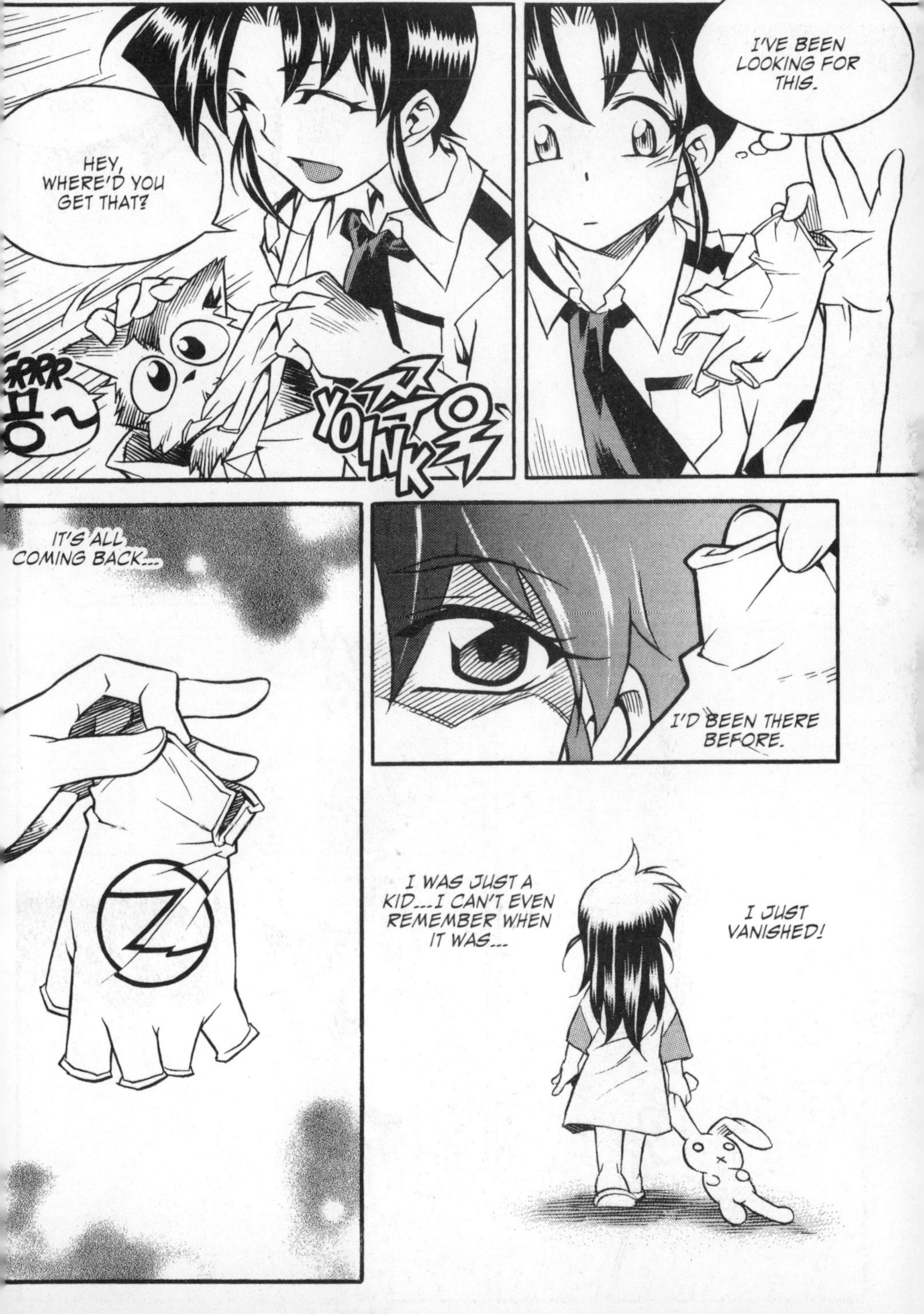
HEY, WHERE'D YOU GET THAT?
GRRR
YOINK
I'VE BEEN LOOKING FOR THIS.
IT'S ALL COMING BACK...
I'D BEEN THERE BEFORE.
I WAS JUST A KID...I CAN'T EVEN REMEMBER WHEN IT WAS...
I JUST VANISHED!

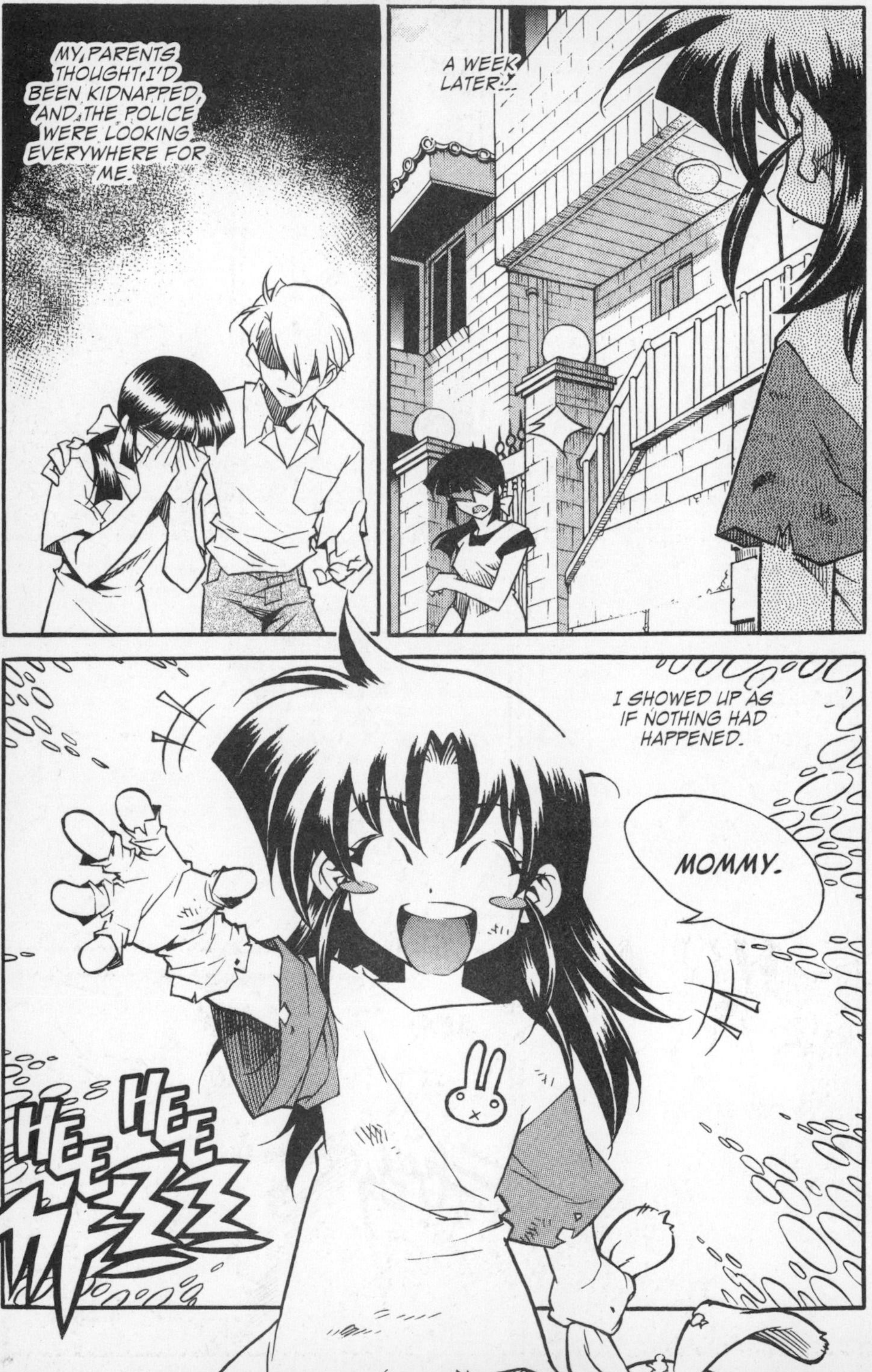
MY PARENTS THOUGHT I'D BEEN KIDNAPPED, AND THE POLICE WERE LOOKING EVERYWHERE FOR ME.
A WEEK LATER...
I SHOWED UP AS IF NOTHING HAD HAPPENED.
MOMMY.
HEE HEE
HEEZZZ

WEARING A TATTERED GLOVE ON MY RIGHT HAND....

THIS IS THE GAME GLOVE.

I FIXED IT BECAUSE IT WAS SO TATTERED....

IS IT A Z OR AN N?

NOW THAT I THINK ABOUT IT...

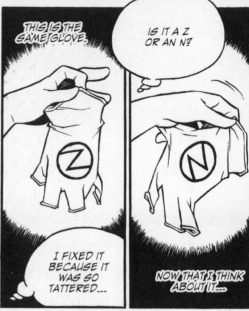

I'D BEEN DOWN THE YELLOW BRICK ROAD.

HMM

I'M JUST KEEPING IT FOR GOOD LUCK!

ARF!

AH!

TOK TOK

SHIK

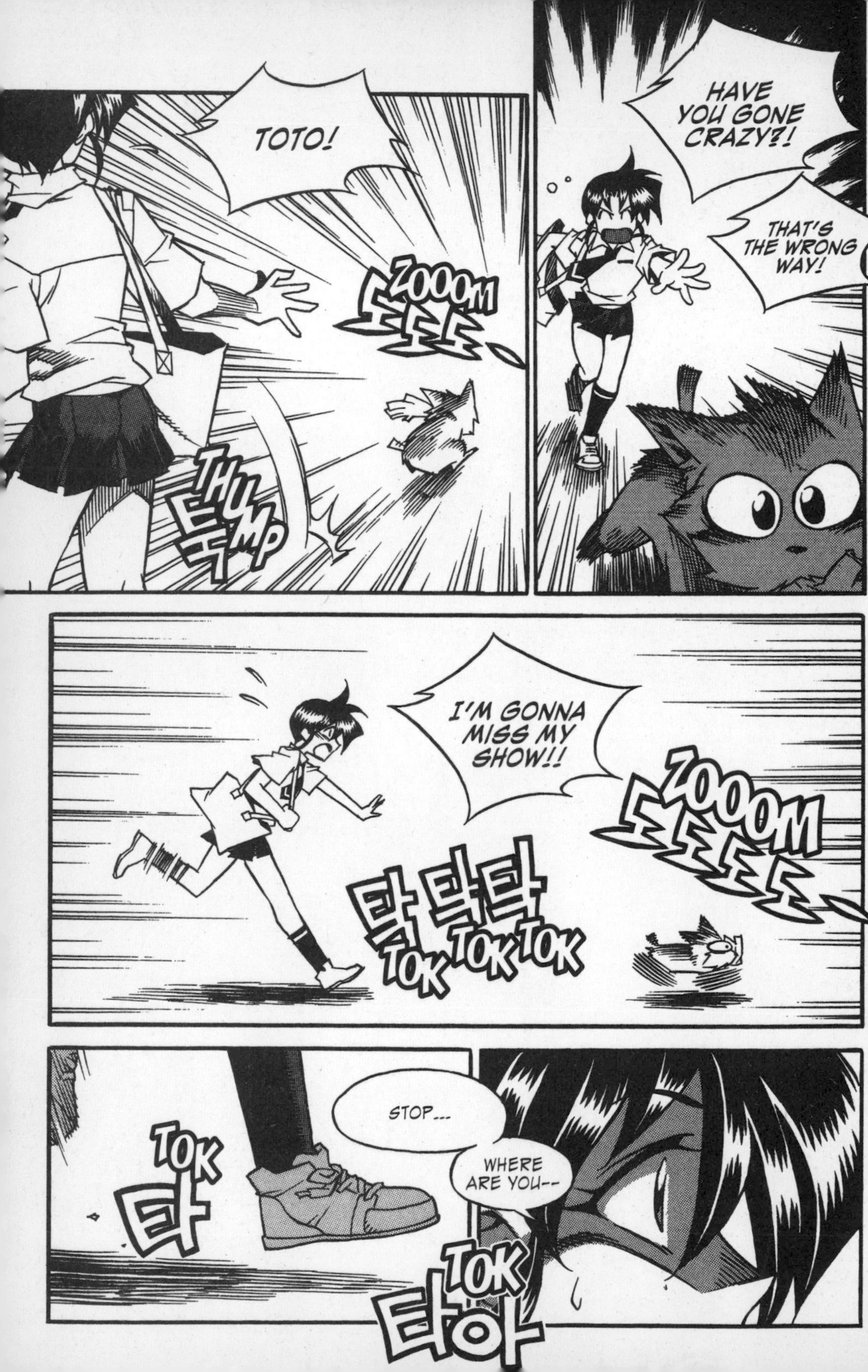
TOTO!
ZOOOM
THUMP
HAVE YOU GONE CRAZY?!
THAT'S THE WRONG WAY!
I'M GONNA MISS MY SHOW!!
ZOOOM
TOK TOK TOK
STOP...
TOK
WHERE ARE YOU--
TOK

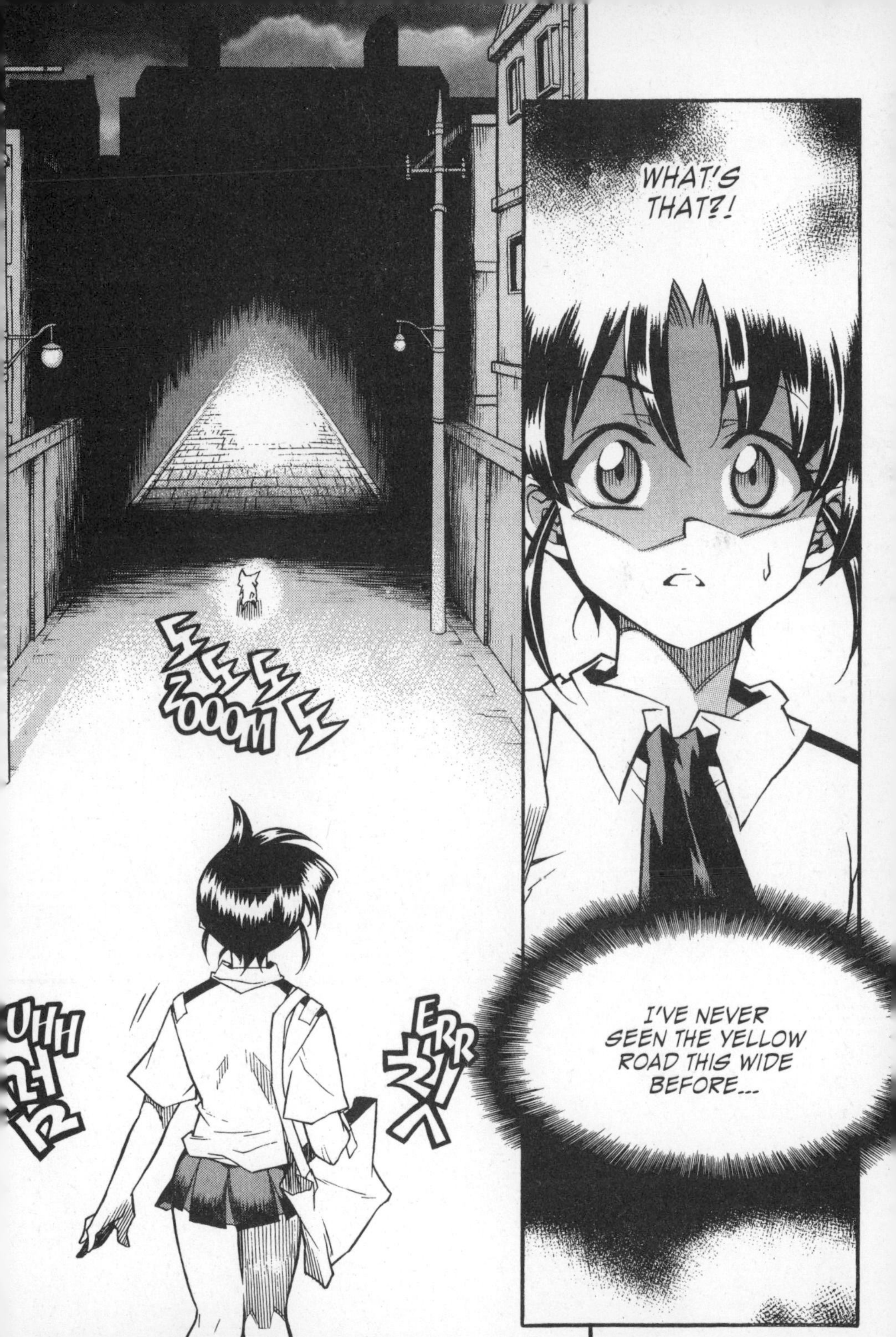
ZOOOM
UHH
ERR
WHAT'S THAT?!
I'VE NEVER SEEN THE YELLOW ROAD THIS WIDE BEFORE...

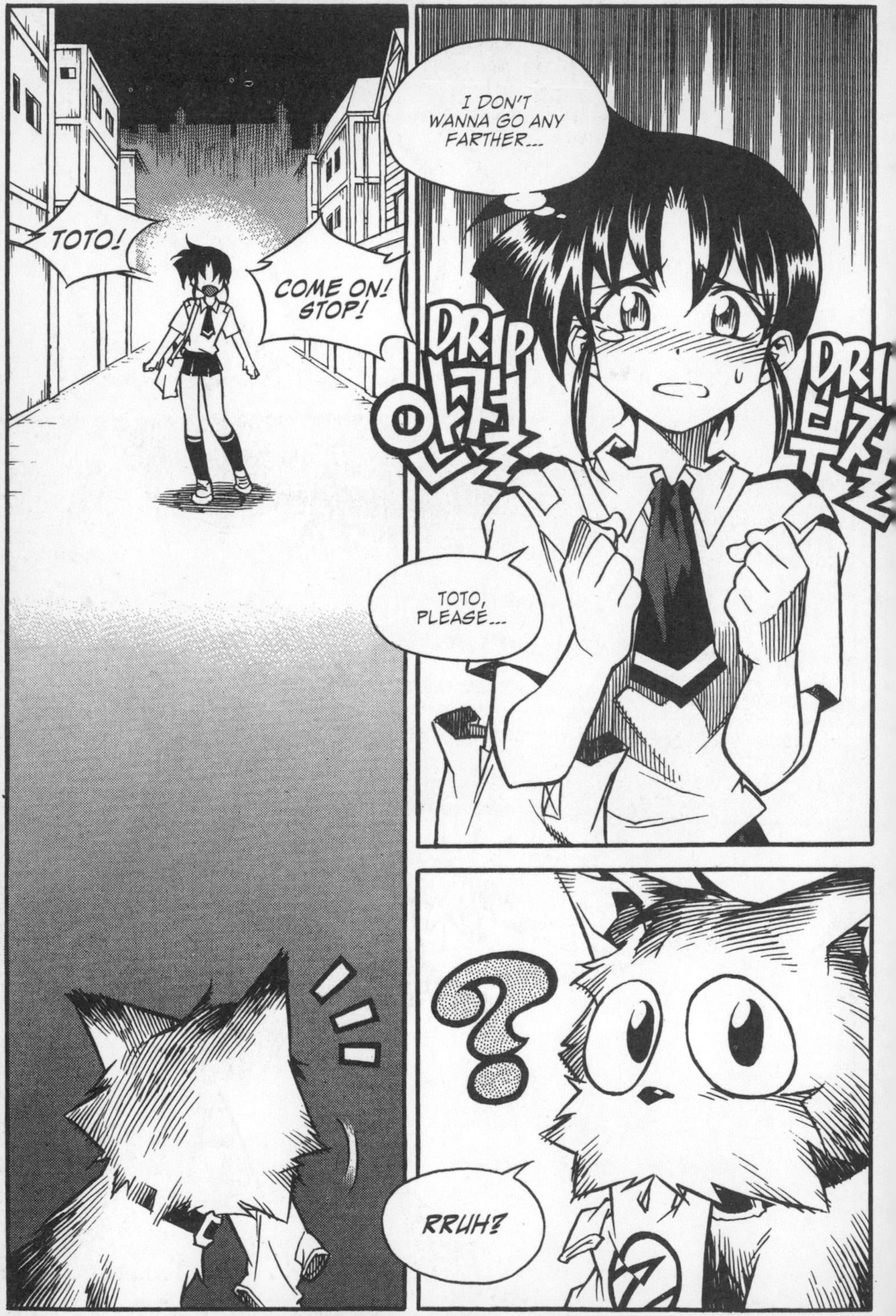
TOTO!
COME ON! STOP!
I DON'T WANNA GO ANY FARTHER...
DRIP
DRI
TOTO, PLEASE...
RRUH?

DOROTHY OF 도로시 OZ

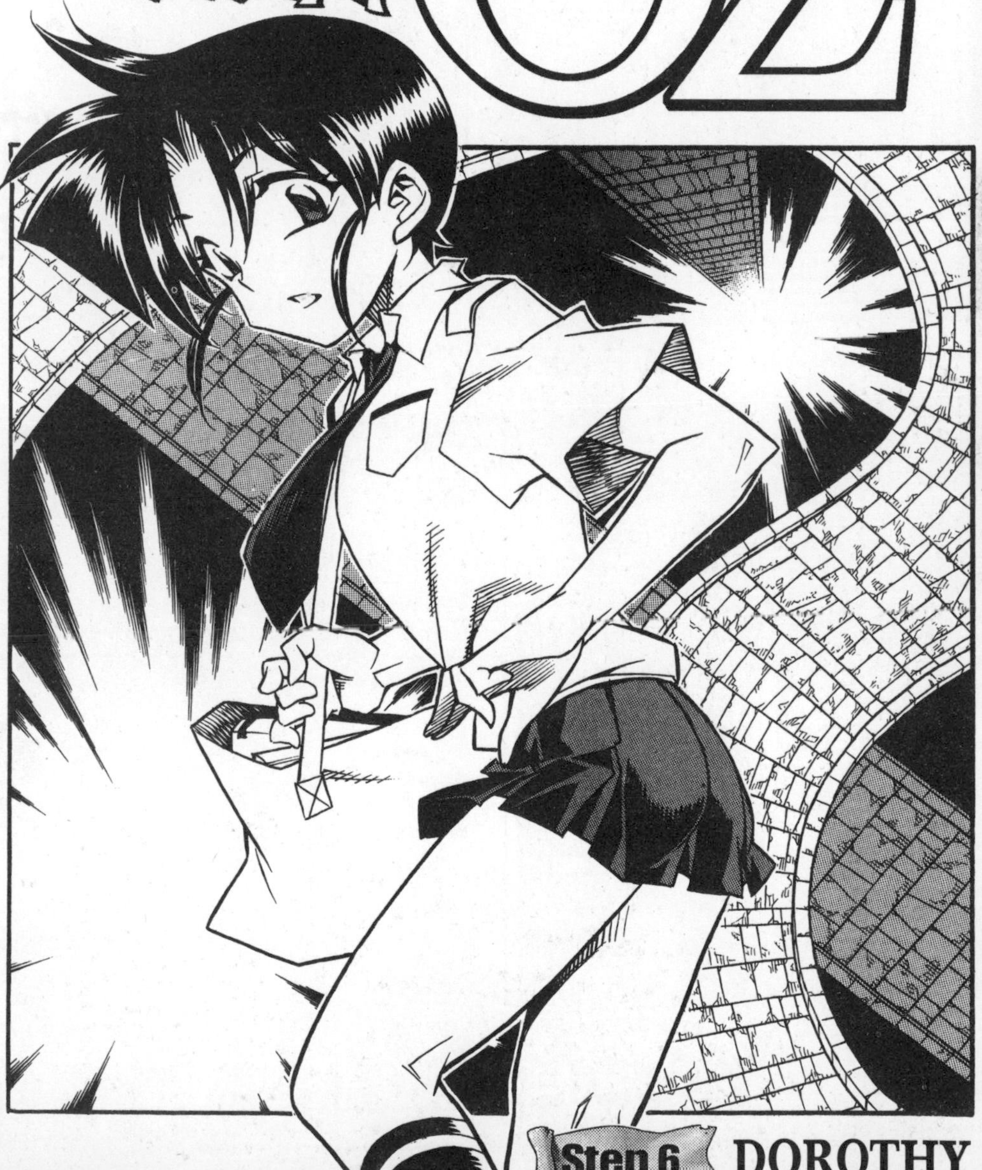

Step 6 DOROTHY

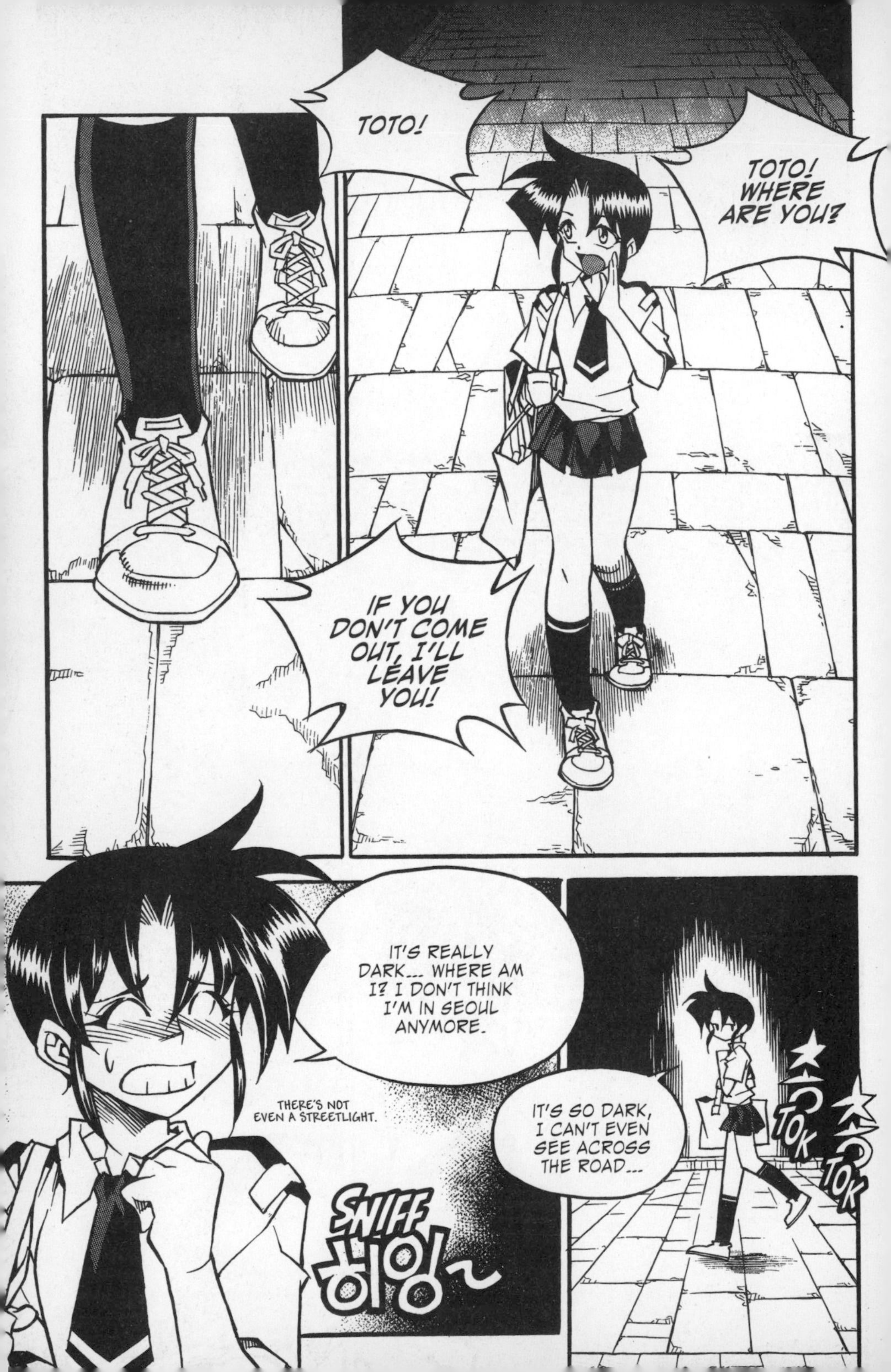
TOTO!
TOTO! WHERE ARE YOU?
IF YOU DON'T COME OUT, I'LL LEAVE YOU!
IT'S REALLY DARK... WHERE AM I? I DON'T THINK I'M IN SEOUL ANYMORE.
THERE'S NOT EVEN A STREETLIGHT.
SNIFF
히잉~
IT'S SO DARK, I CAN'T EVEN SEE ACROSS THE ROAD...
TOK
TOK

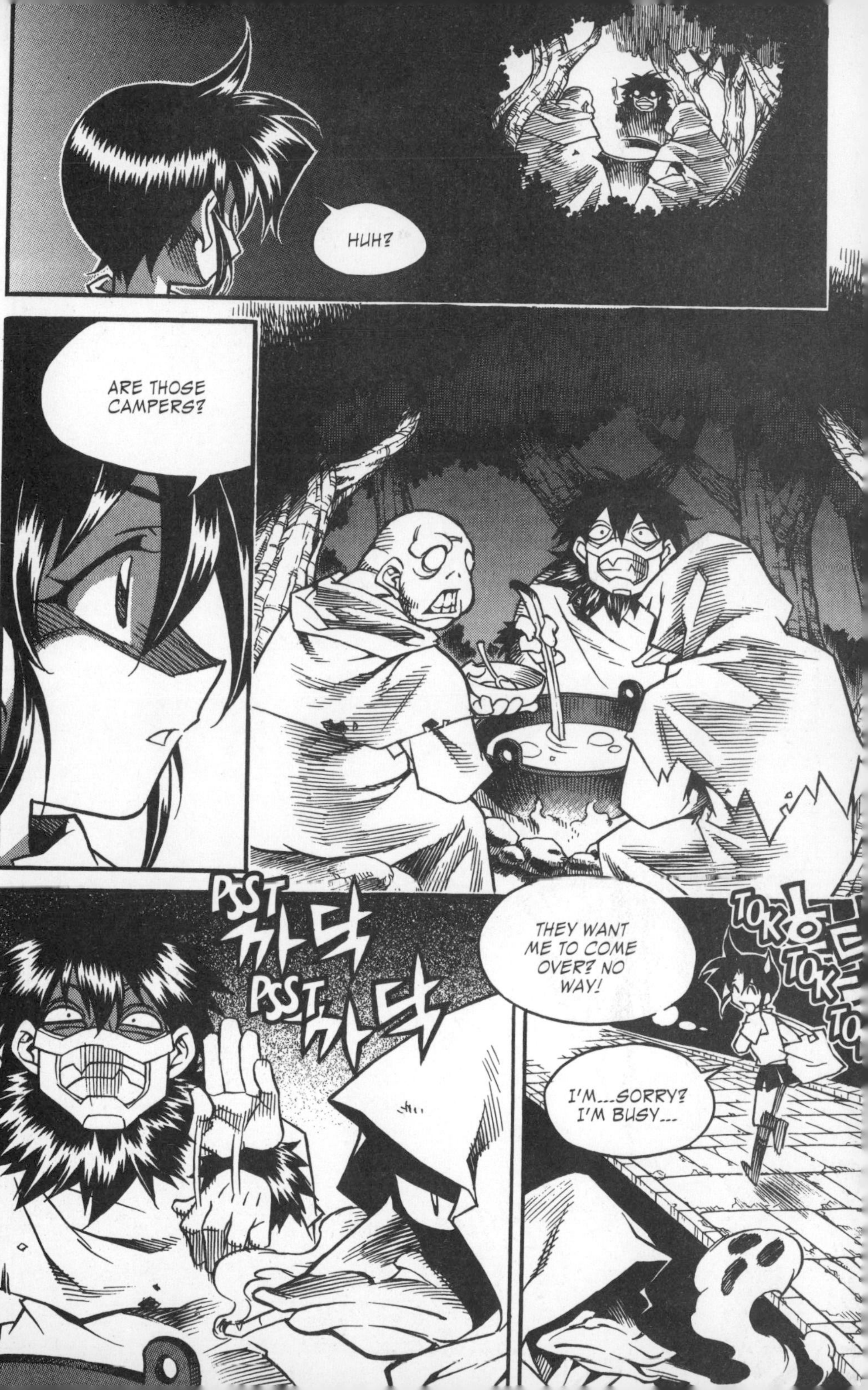
HUH?
ARE THOSE CAMPERS?
PSST 까닥
PSST 까닥
THEY WANT ME TO COME OVER? NO WAY!
I'M...SORRY? I'M BUSY...
TOK TOK

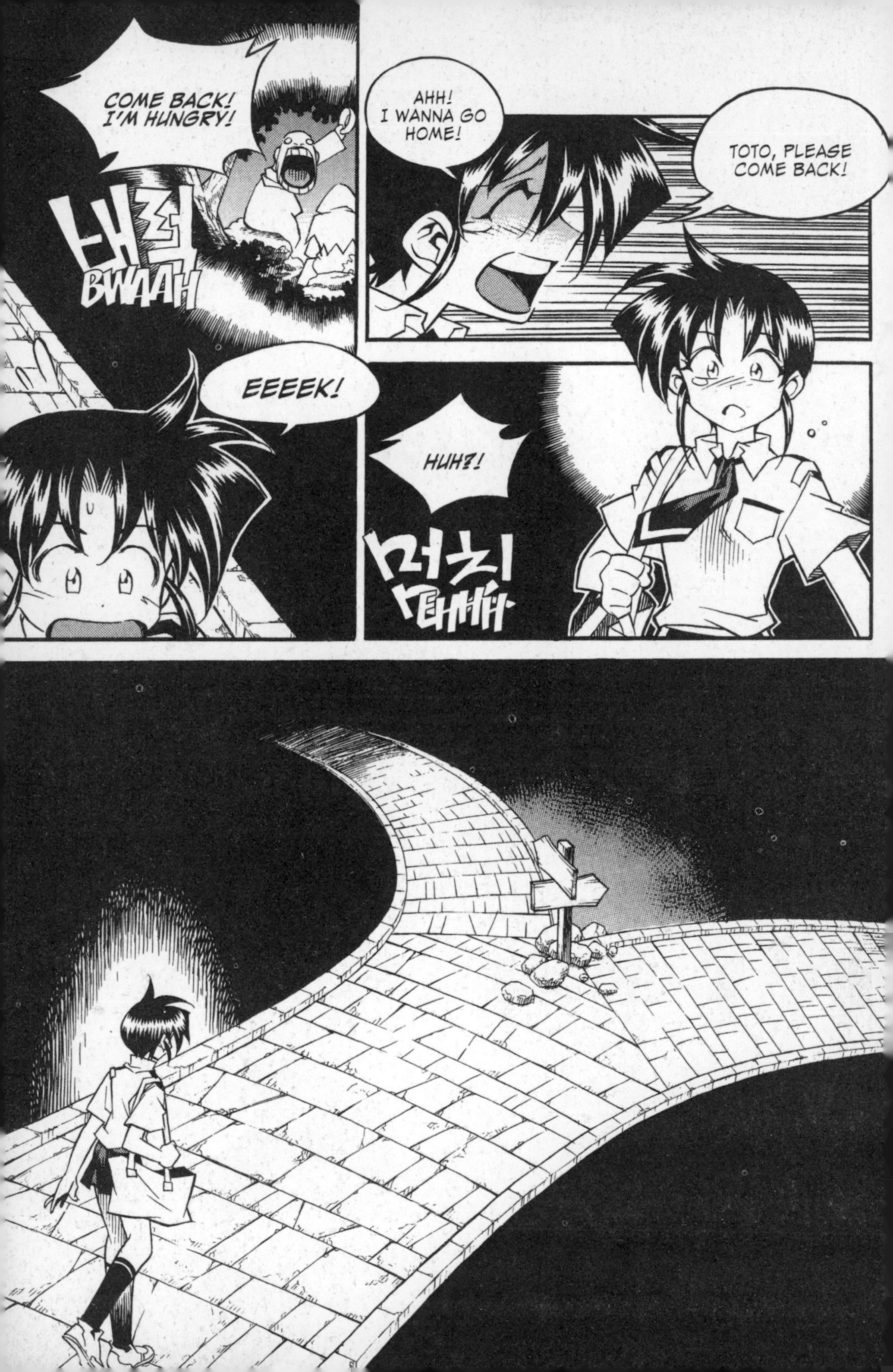
COME BACK! I'M HUNGRY!
BWAAH
AHH! I WANNA GO HOME!
TOTO, PLEASE COME BACK!
EEEEK!
HUH?!

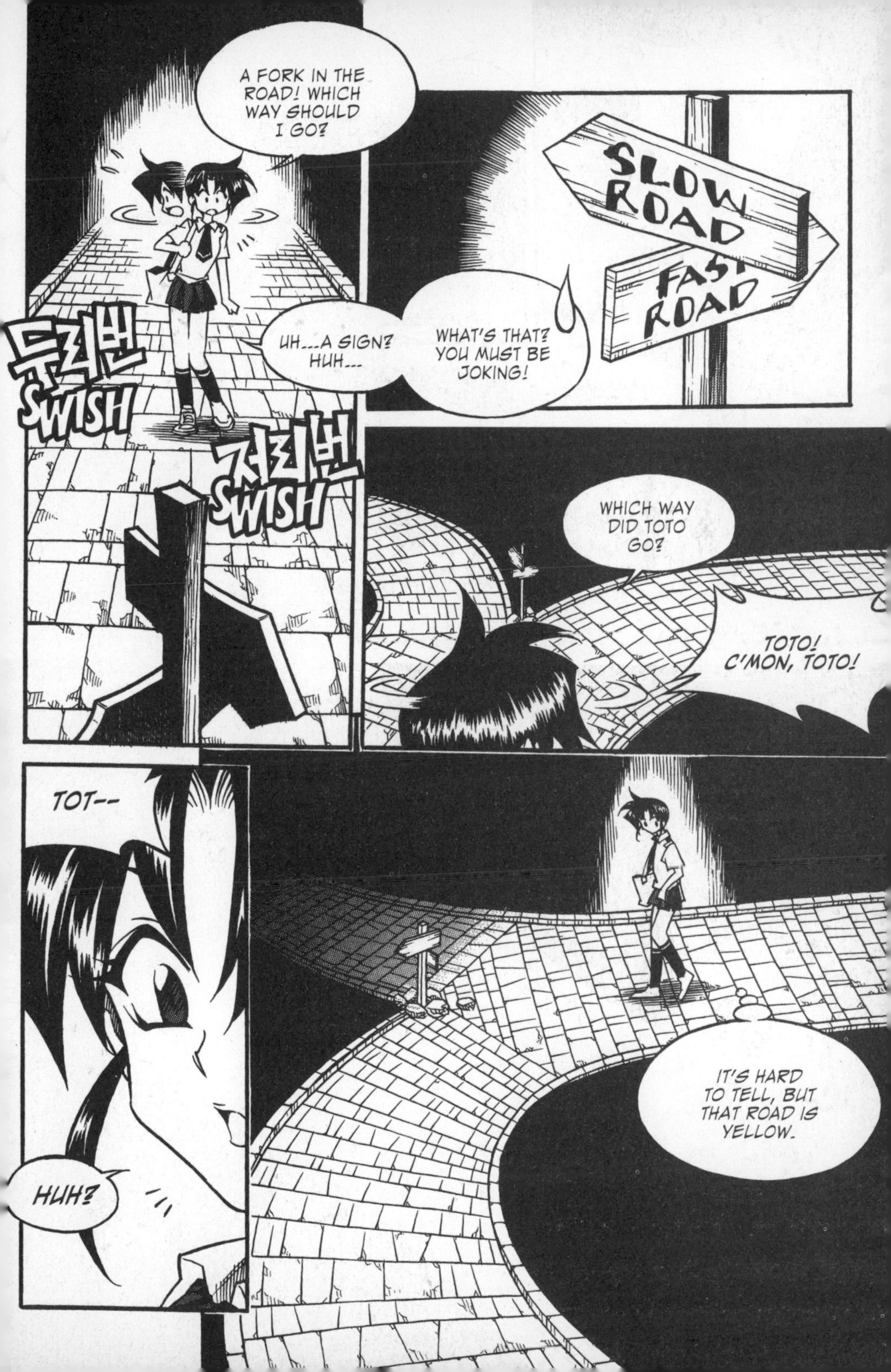

A FORK IN THE ROAD! WHICH WAY SHOULD I GO?
두리번
SWISH
UH...A SIGN? HUH...
SLOW ROAD
FAST ROAD
WHAT'S THAT? YOU MUST BE JOKING!
저리번
SWISH
WHICH WAY DID TOTO GO?
TOTO! C'MON, TOTO!
TOT--
HUH?
IT'S HARD TO TELL, BUT THAT ROAD IS YELLOW.

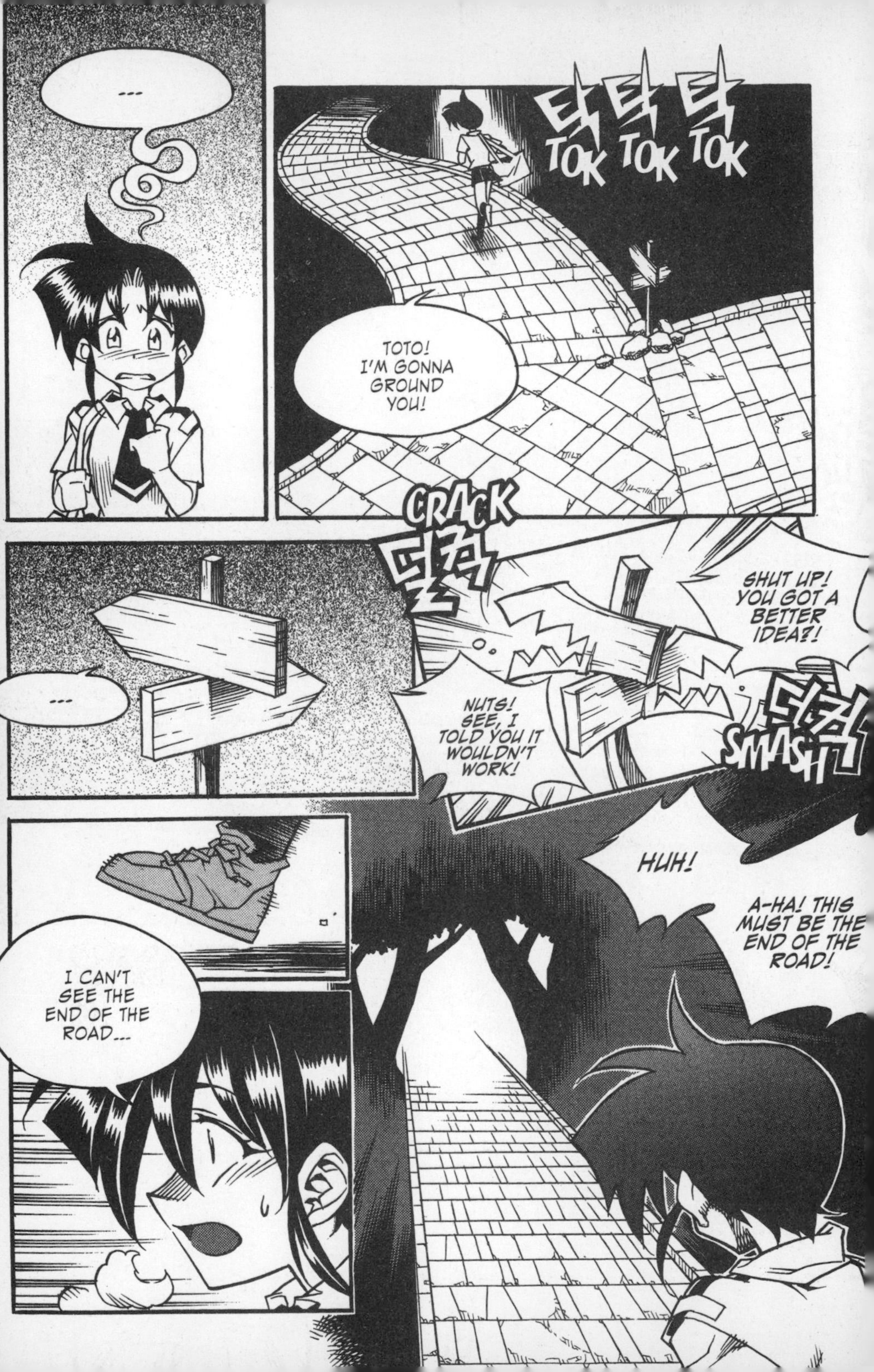
...
TOK TOK TOK
TOTO! I'M GONNA GROUND YOU!
...
CRACK
SHUT UP! YOU GOT A BETTER IDEA?!
NUTS! SEE, I TOLD YOU IT WOULDN'T WORK!
SMASH
I CAN'T SEE THE END OF THE ROAD...
HUH!
A-HA! THIS MUST BE THE END OF THE ROAD!

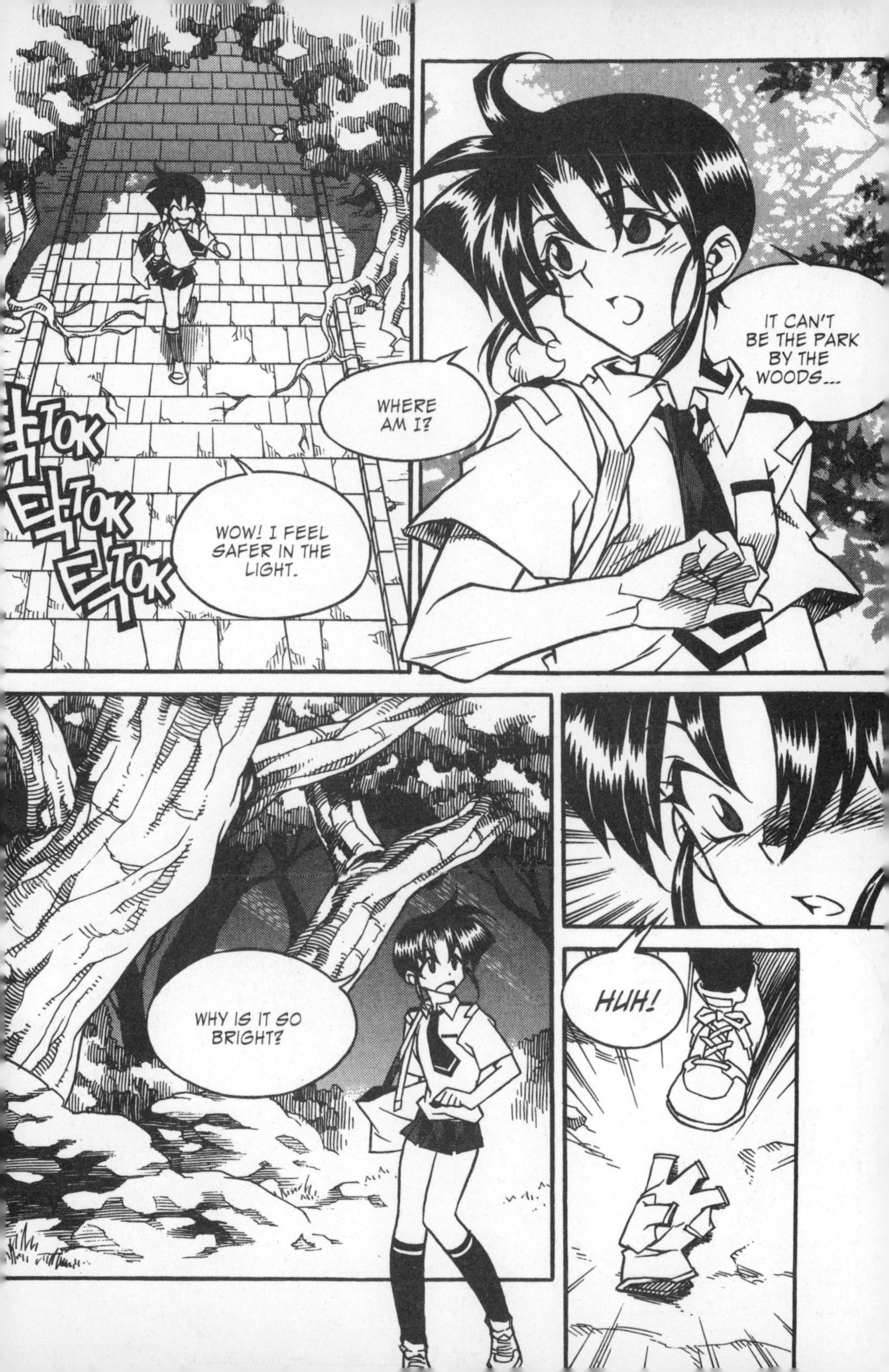
TOK
TOK
TOK
WOW! I FEEL SAFER IN THE LIGHT.
WHERE AM I?
IT CAN'T BE THE PARK BY THE WOODS...
WHY IS IT SO BRIGHT?
HUH!

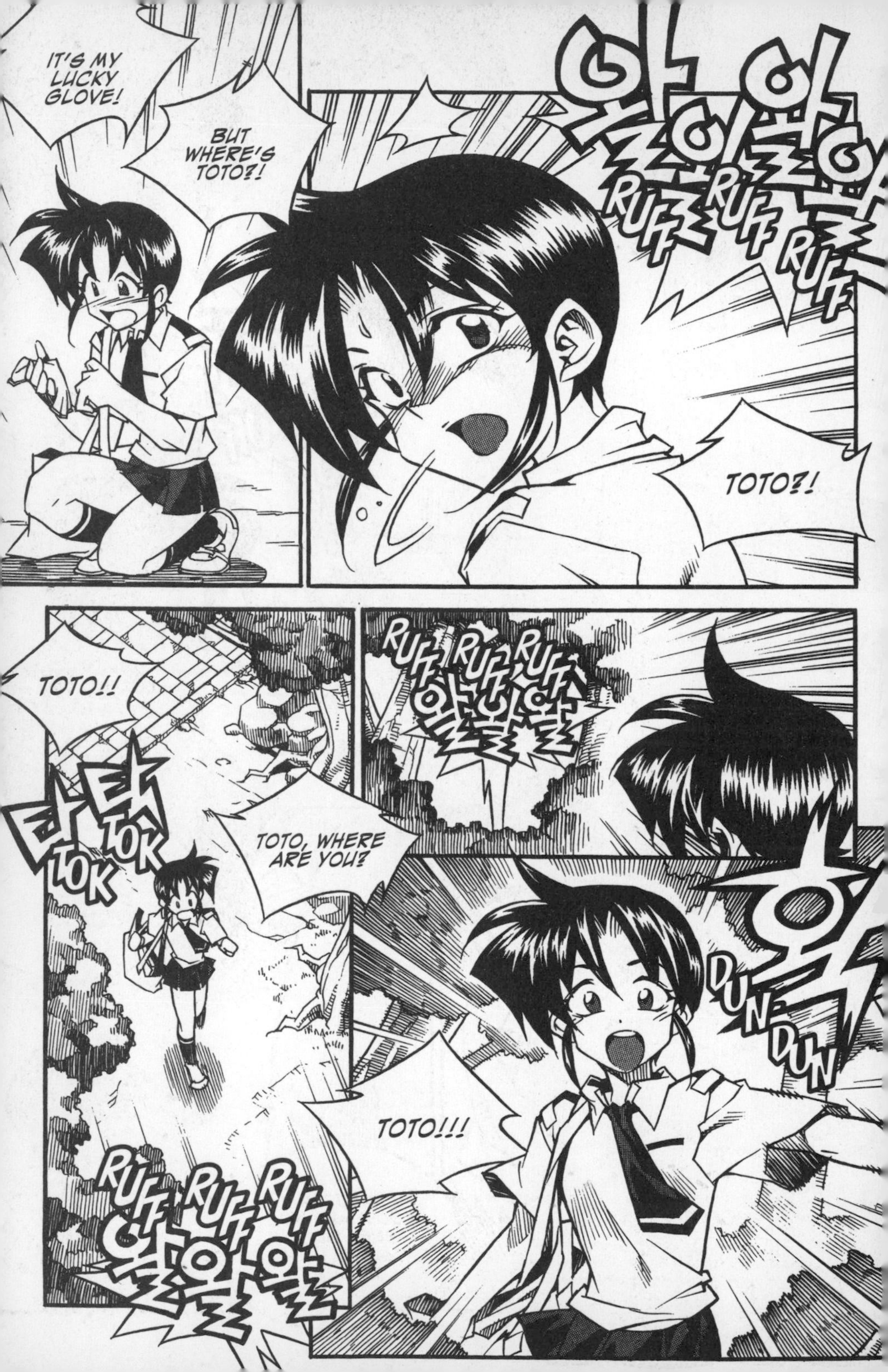
IT'S MY LUCKY GLOVE!
BUT WHERE'S TOTO?!
RUFF RUFF RUFF
TOTO?!
TOTO!!
TOK TOK
TOTO, WHERE ARE YOU?
RUFF RUFF RUFF
RUFF RUFF RUFF
DUN DUN
TOTO!!!

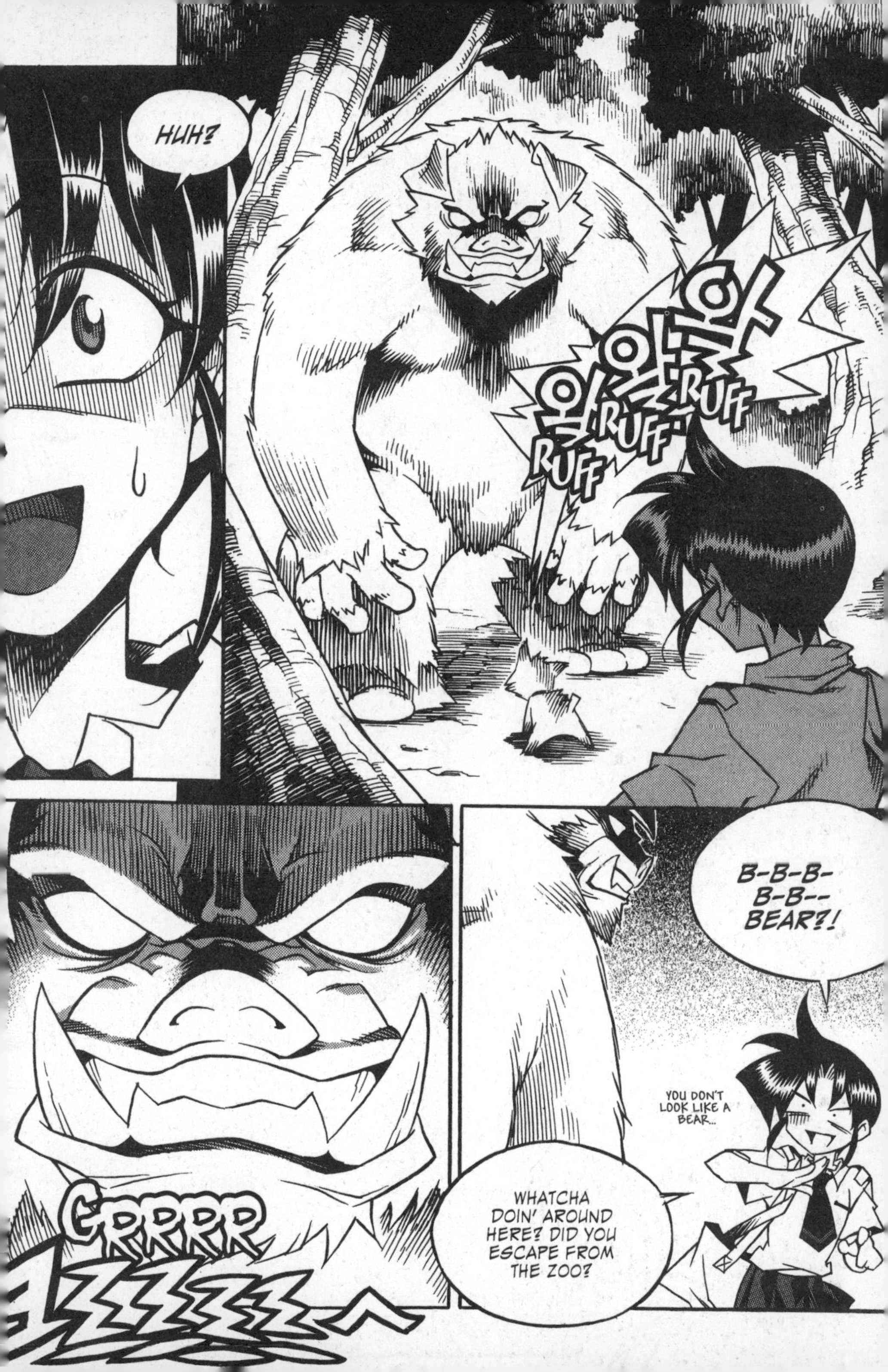
HUH?
RUFF RUFF RUFF RUFF
GRRRR
B-B-B-
B-B--
BEAR?!
YOU DON'T LOOK LIKE A BEAR...
WHATCHA DOIN' AROUND HERE? DID YOU ESCAPE FROM THE ZOO?

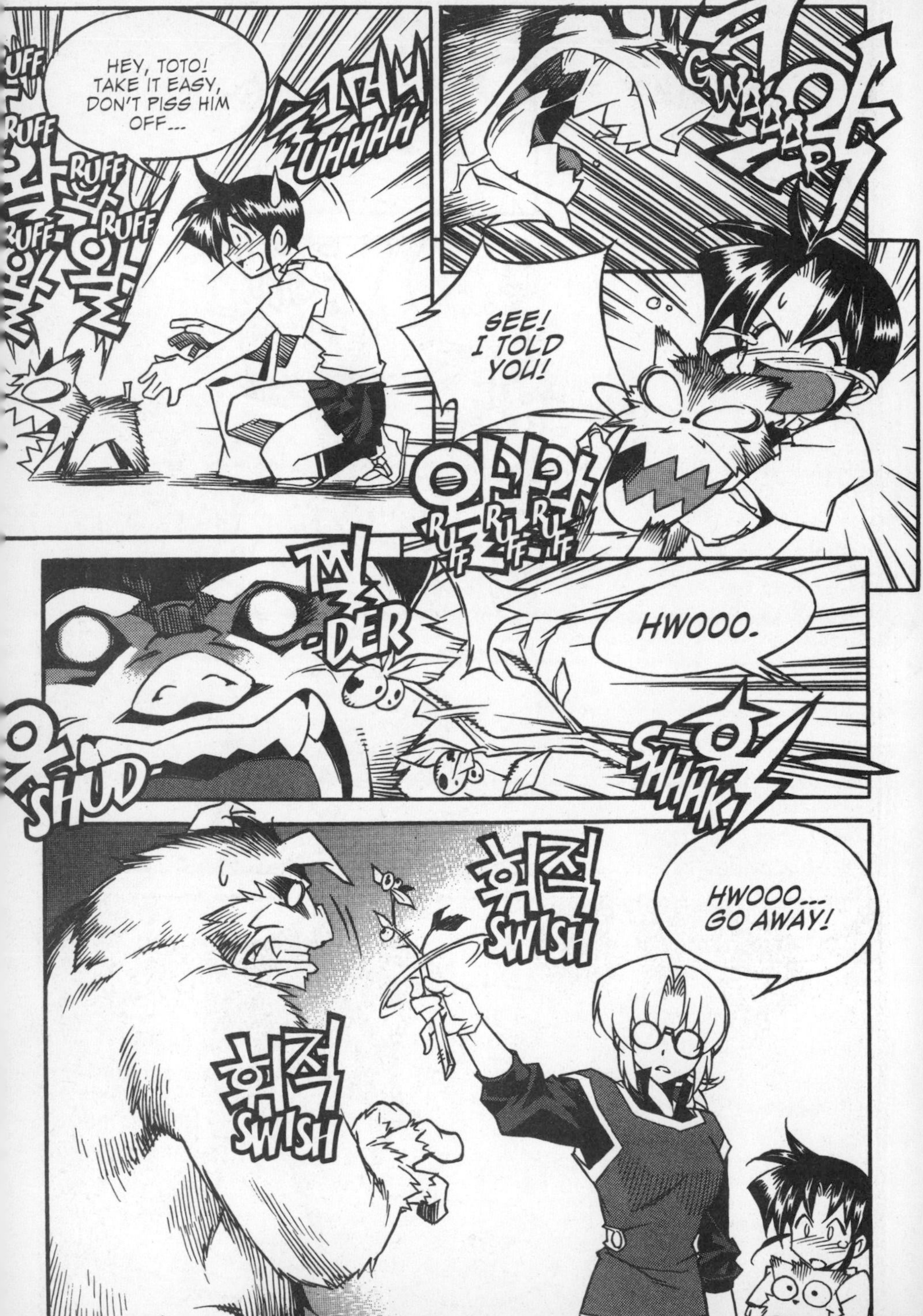
RUFF
RUFF
RUFF
RUFF
HEY, TOTO! TAKE IT EASY, DON'T PISS HIM OFF...
UHHHH
CWAAARR
SEE! I TOLD YOU!
RUFF RUFF RUFF
-DER
SHUD
HWOOO.
SHHHK
휘적
SWISH
HWOOO... GO AWAY!
휘적
SWISH

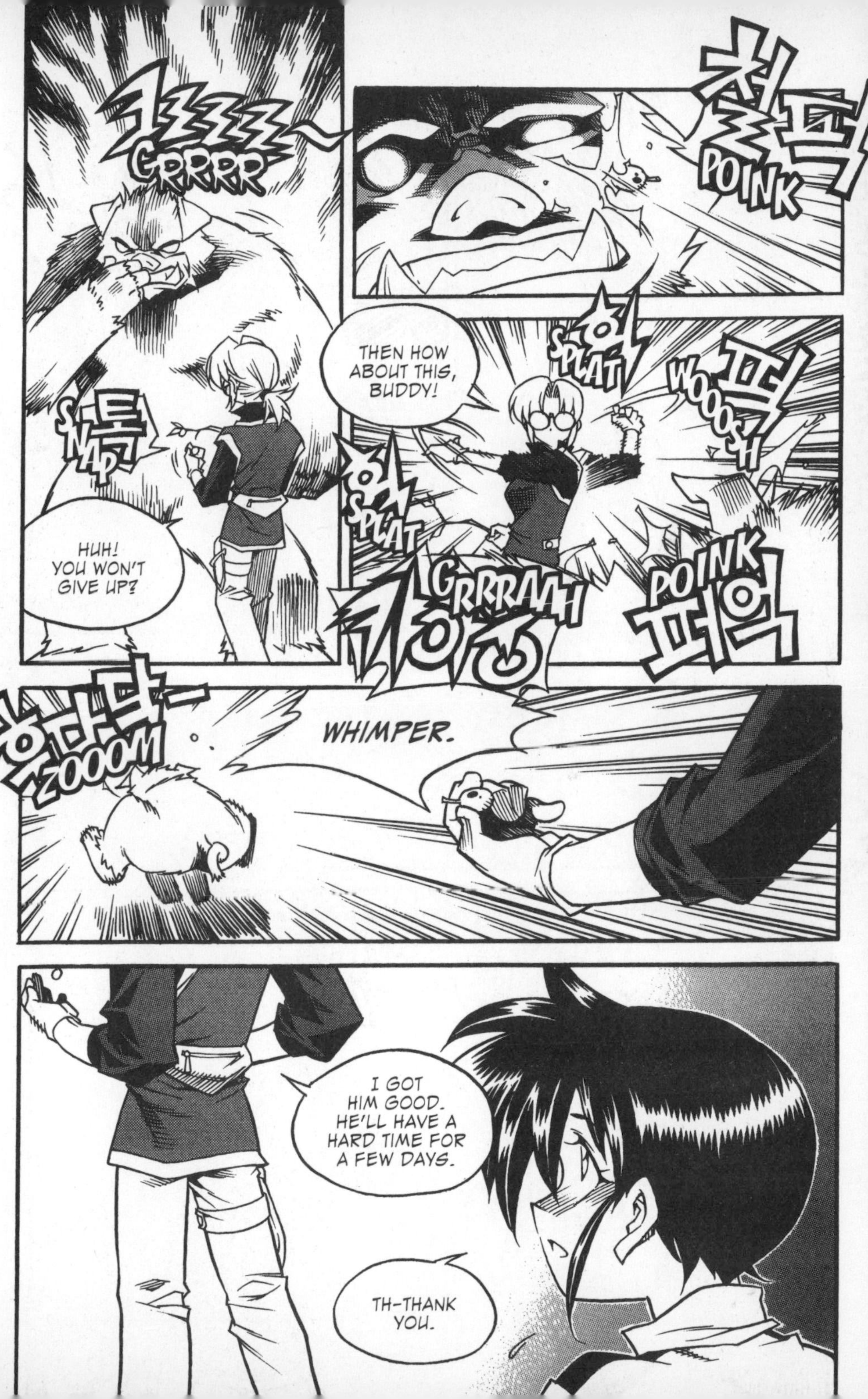
크르르르~
GRRRRR
철퍽
POINK
THEN HOW ABOUT THIS, BUDDY!
툭
SNAP
HUH! YOU WON'T GIVE UP?
SPLAT
퍽
WOOOOSH
SPLAT
GRRRAAAH
POINK
퍼억
WHIMPER.
ZOOOOM
I GOT HIM GOOD. HE'LL HAVE A HARD TIME FOR A FEW DAYS.
TH-THANK YOU.

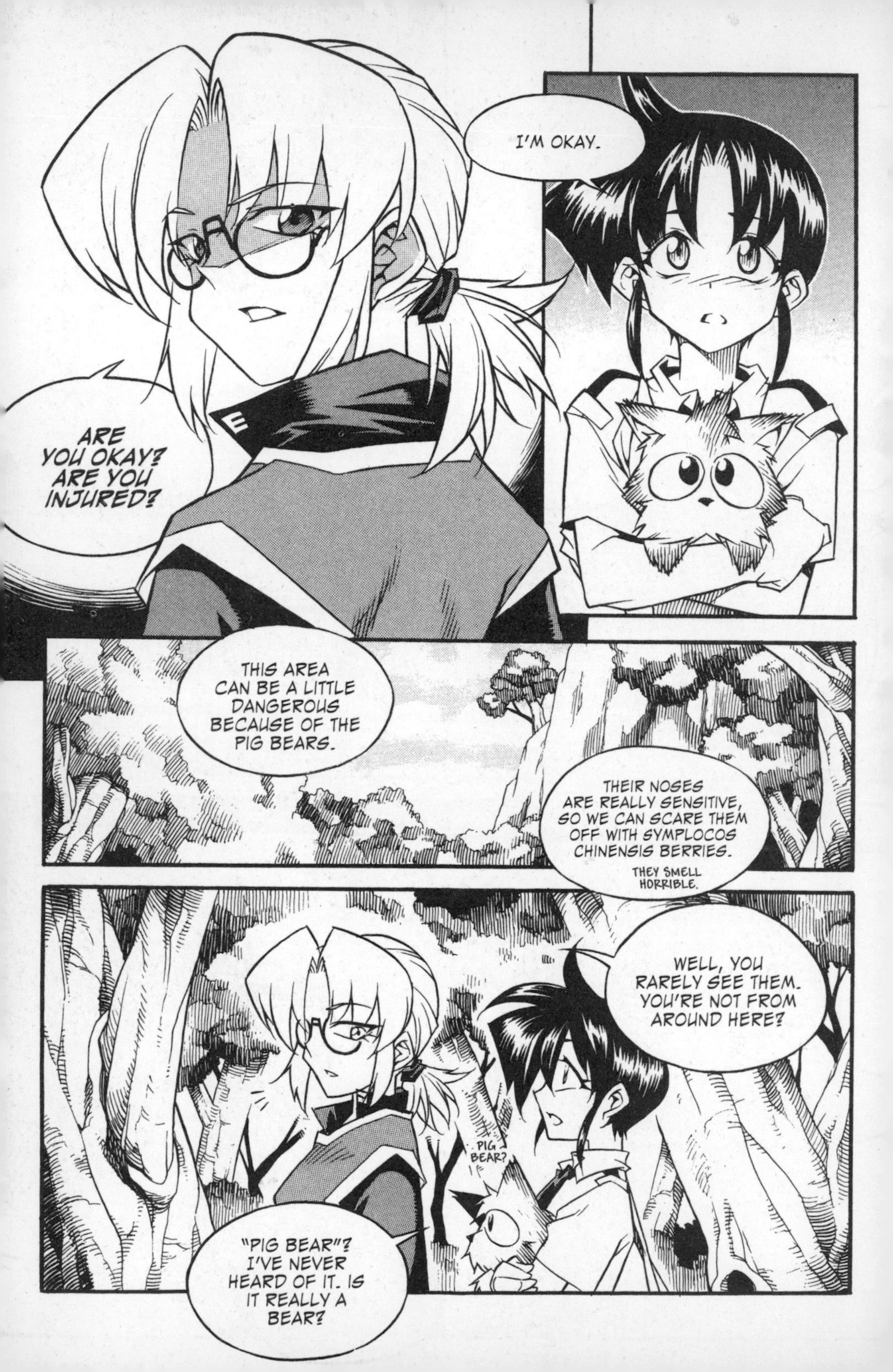
ARE YOU OKAY? ARE YOU INJURED?
I'M OKAY.
THIS AREA CAN BE A LITTLE DANGEROUS BECAUSE OF THE PIG BEARS.
THEIR NOSES ARE REALLY SENSITIVE, SO WE CAN SCARE THEM OFF WITH SYMPLOCOS CHINENSIS BERRIES.
THEY SMELL HORRIBLE.
"PIG BEAR"? I'VE NEVER HEARD OF IT. IS IT REALLY A BEAR?
PIG BEAR?
WELL, YOU RARELY SEE THEM. YOU'RE NOT FROM AROUND HERE?

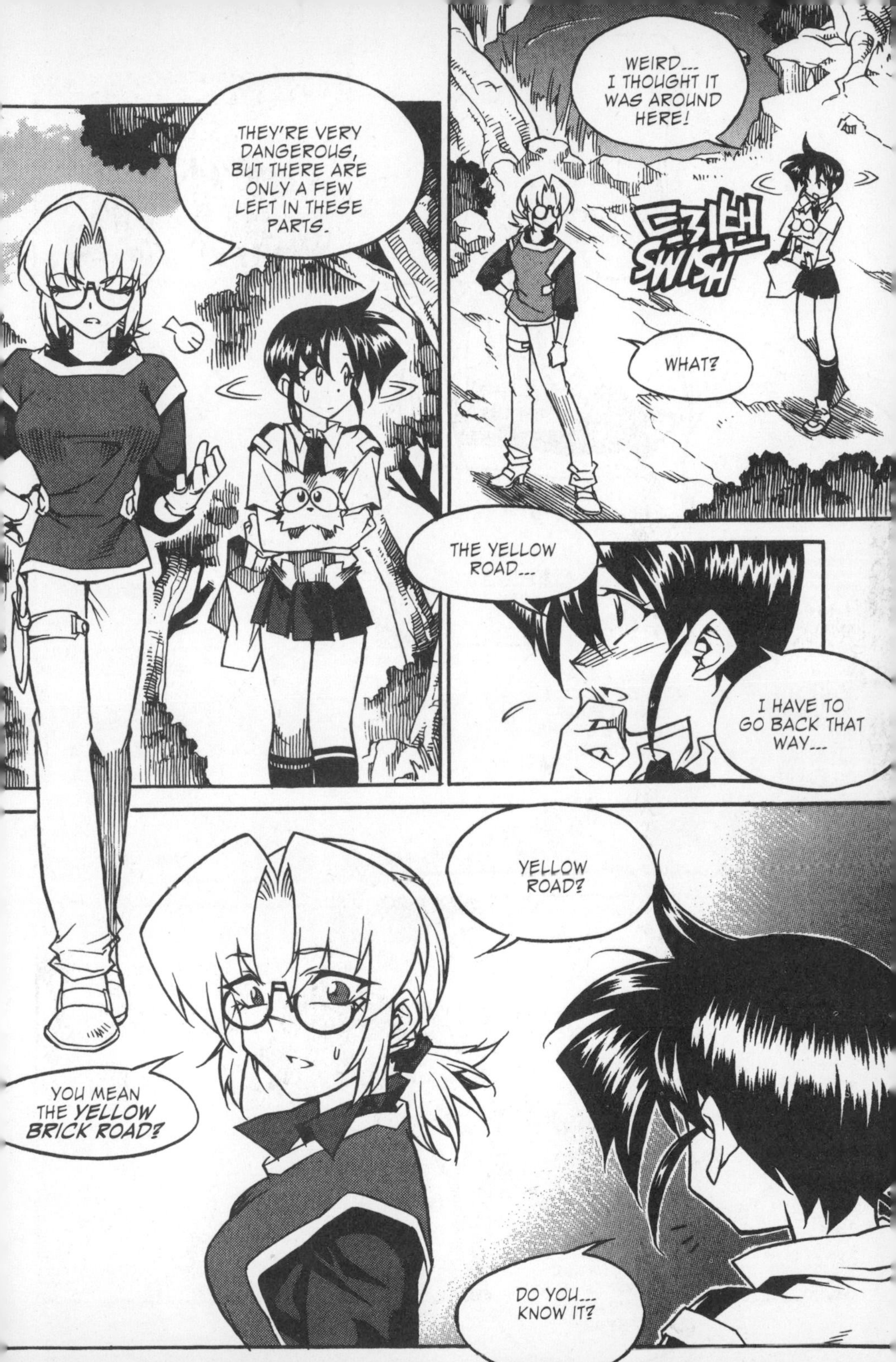
THEY'RE VERY DANGEROUS, BUT THERE ARE ONLY A FEW LEFT IN THESE PARTS.
WEIRD... I THOUGHT IT WAS AROUND HERE!
SWISH
WHAT?
THE YELLOW ROAD...
I HAVE TO GO BACK THAT WAY...
YELLOW ROAD?
YOU MEAN THE *YELLOW BRICK ROAD?*
DO YOU... KNOW IT?

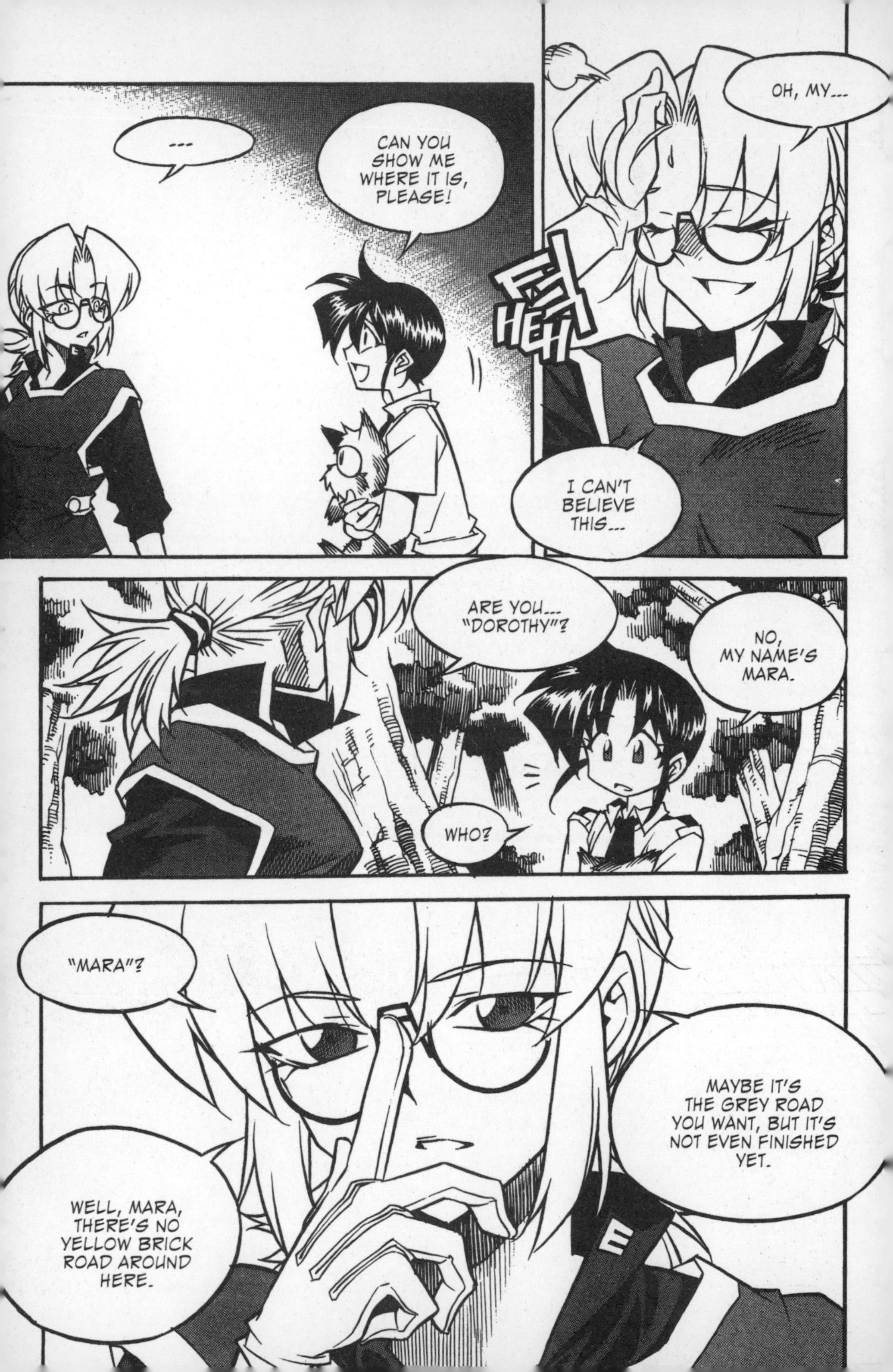
...
CAN YOU SHOW ME WHERE IT IS, PLEASE!
OH, MY...
HEH HEH
I CAN'T BELIEVE THIS...
ARE YOU... "DOROTHY"?
WHO?
NO, MY NAME'S MARA.
"MARA"?
WELL, MARA, THERE'S NO YELLOW BRICK ROAD AROUND HERE.
MAYBE IT'S THE GREY ROAD YOU WANT, BUT IT'S NOT EVEN FINISHED YET.

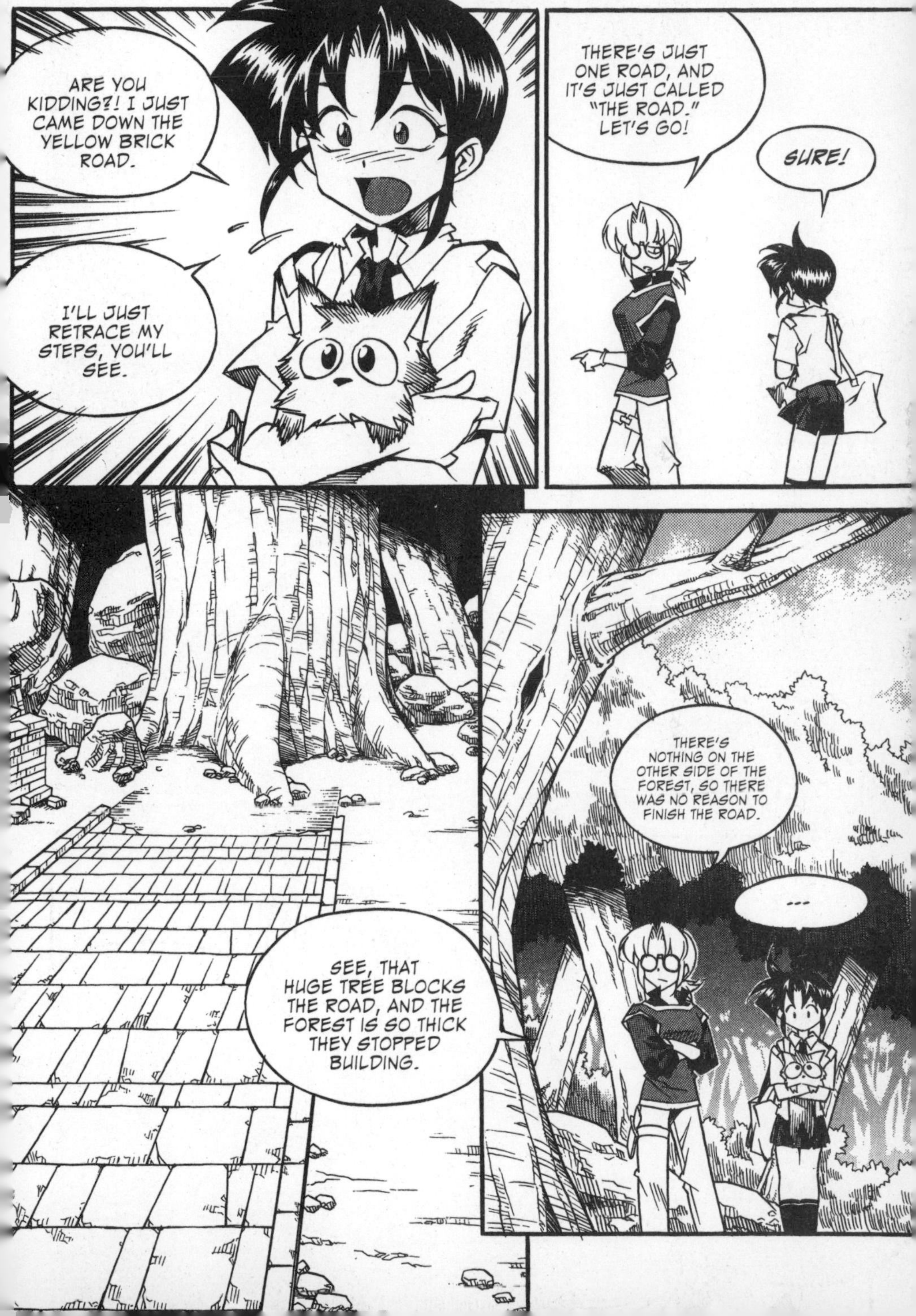
ARE YOU KIDDING?! I JUST CAME DOWN THE YELLOW BRICK ROAD.
I'LL JUST RETRACE MY STEPS, YOU'LL SEE.
THERE'S JUST ONE ROAD, AND IT'S JUST CALLED "THE ROAD." LET'S GO!
SURE!
SEE, THAT HUGE TREE BLOCKS THE ROAD, AND THE FOREST IS SO THICK THEY STOPPED BUILDING.
THERE'S NOTHING ON THE OTHER SIDE OF THE FOREST, SO THERE WAS NO REASON TO FINISH THE ROAD.
...

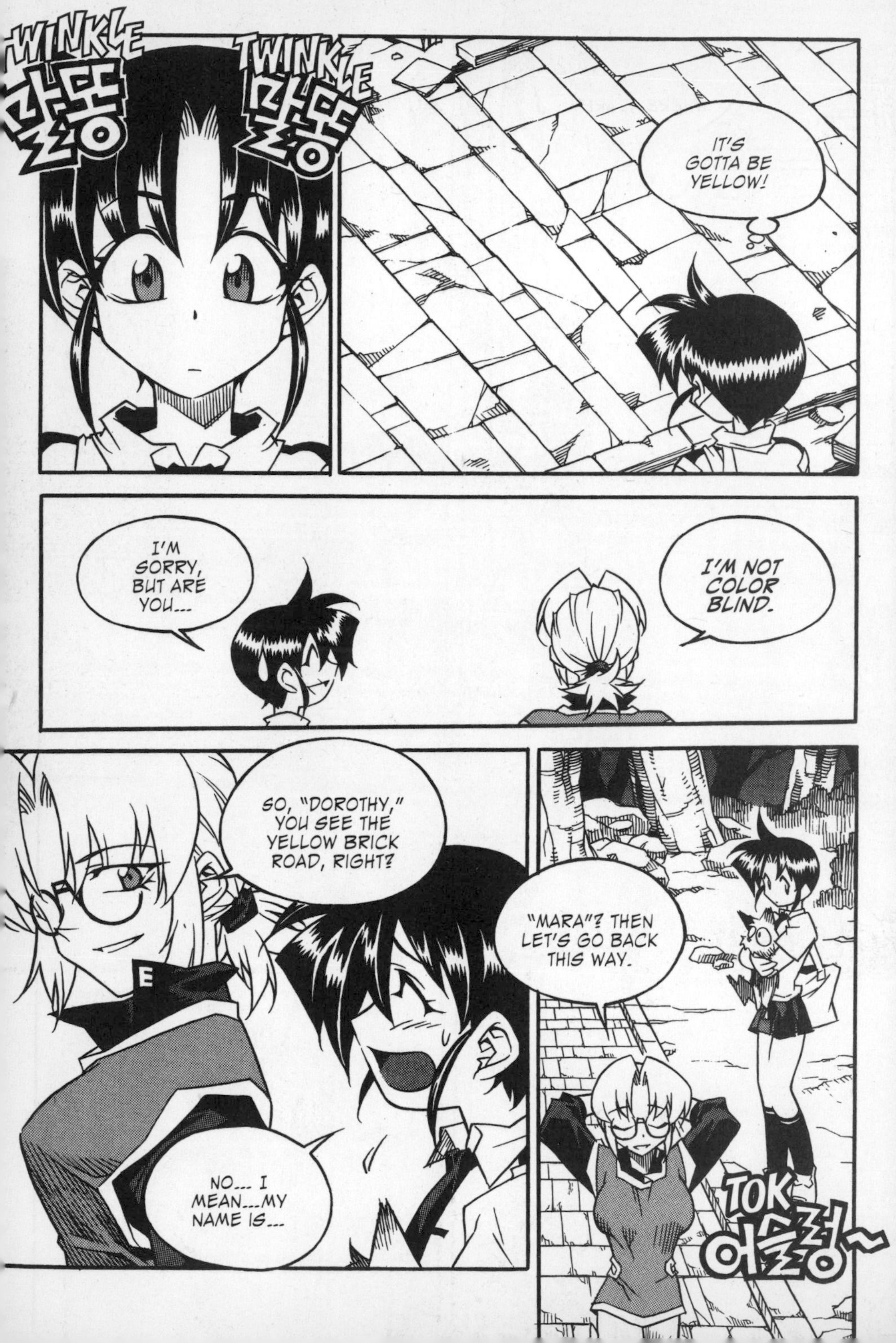
TWINKLE
반짝
TWINKLE
반짝
IT'S GOTTA BE YELLOW!
I'M SORRY, BUT ARE YOU...
I'M NOT COLOR BLIND.
SO, "DOROTHY," YOU SEE THE YELLOW BRICK ROAD, RIGHT?
NO... I MEAN...MY NAME IS...
"MARA"? THEN LET'S GO BACK THIS WAY.
TOK
어쩔~

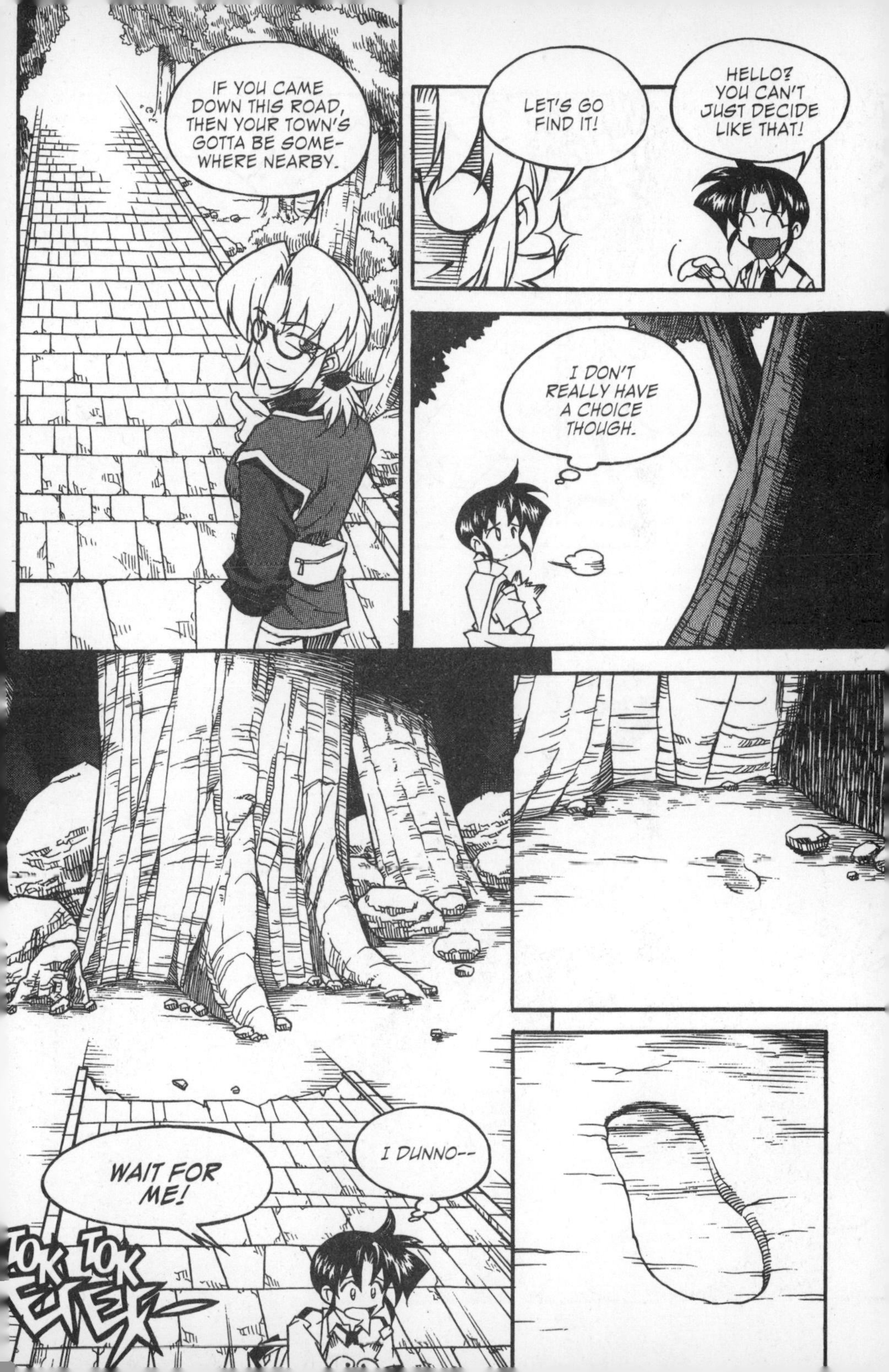
IF YOU CAME DOWN THIS ROAD, THEN YOUR TOWN'S GOTTA BE SOME-WHERE NEARBY.
LET'S GO FIND IT!
HELLO? YOU CAN'T JUST DECIDE LIKE THAT!
I DON'T REALLY HAVE A CHOICE THOUGH.
WAIT FOR ME!
I DUNNO--
TOK TOK

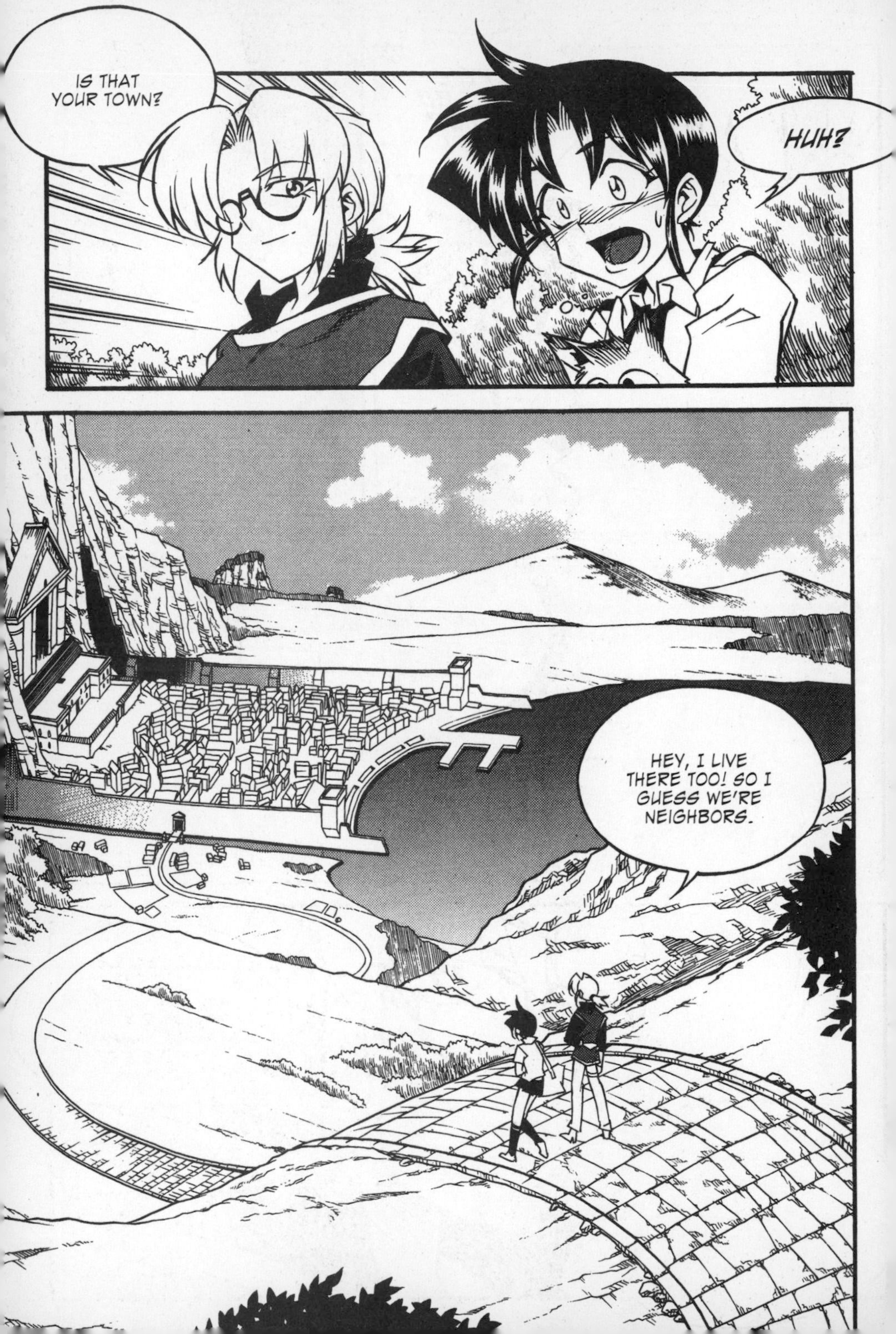
IS THAT YOUR TOWN?
HUH?
HEY, I LIVE THERE TOO! SO I GUESS WE'RE NEIGHBORS.

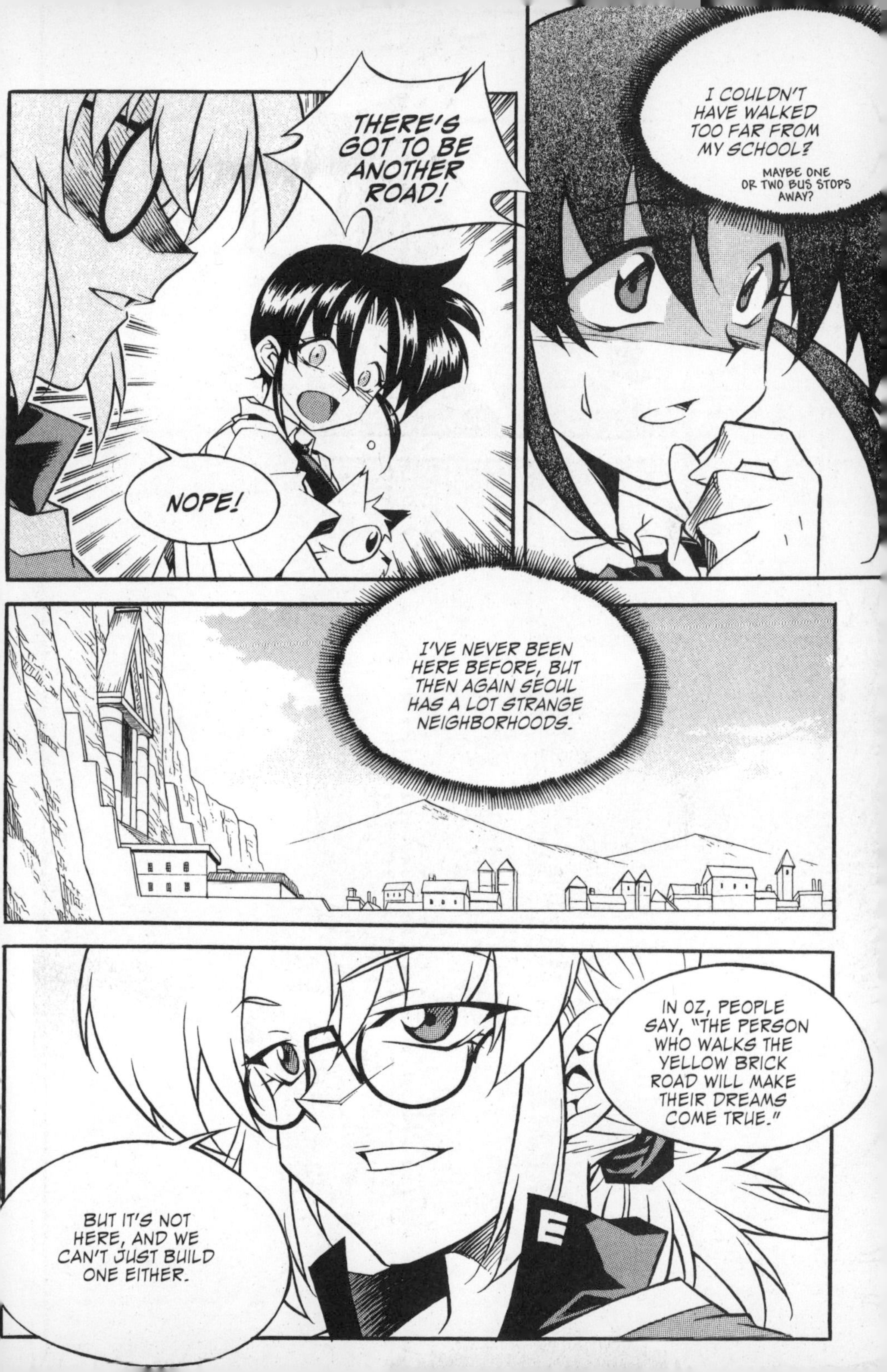
THERE'S GOT TO BE ANOTHER ROAD!
NOPE!
I COULDN'T HAVE WALKED TOO FAR FROM MY SCHOOL?
MAYBE ONE OR TWO BUS STOPS AWAY?
I'VE NEVER BEEN HERE BEFORE, BUT THEN AGAIN SEOUL HAS A LOT STRANGE NEIGHBORHOODS.
IN OZ, PEOPLE SAY, "THE PERSON WHO WALKS THE YELLOW BRICK ROAD WILL MAKE THEIR DREAMS COME TRUE."
BUT IT'S NOT HERE, AND WE CAN'T JUST BUILD ONE EITHER.

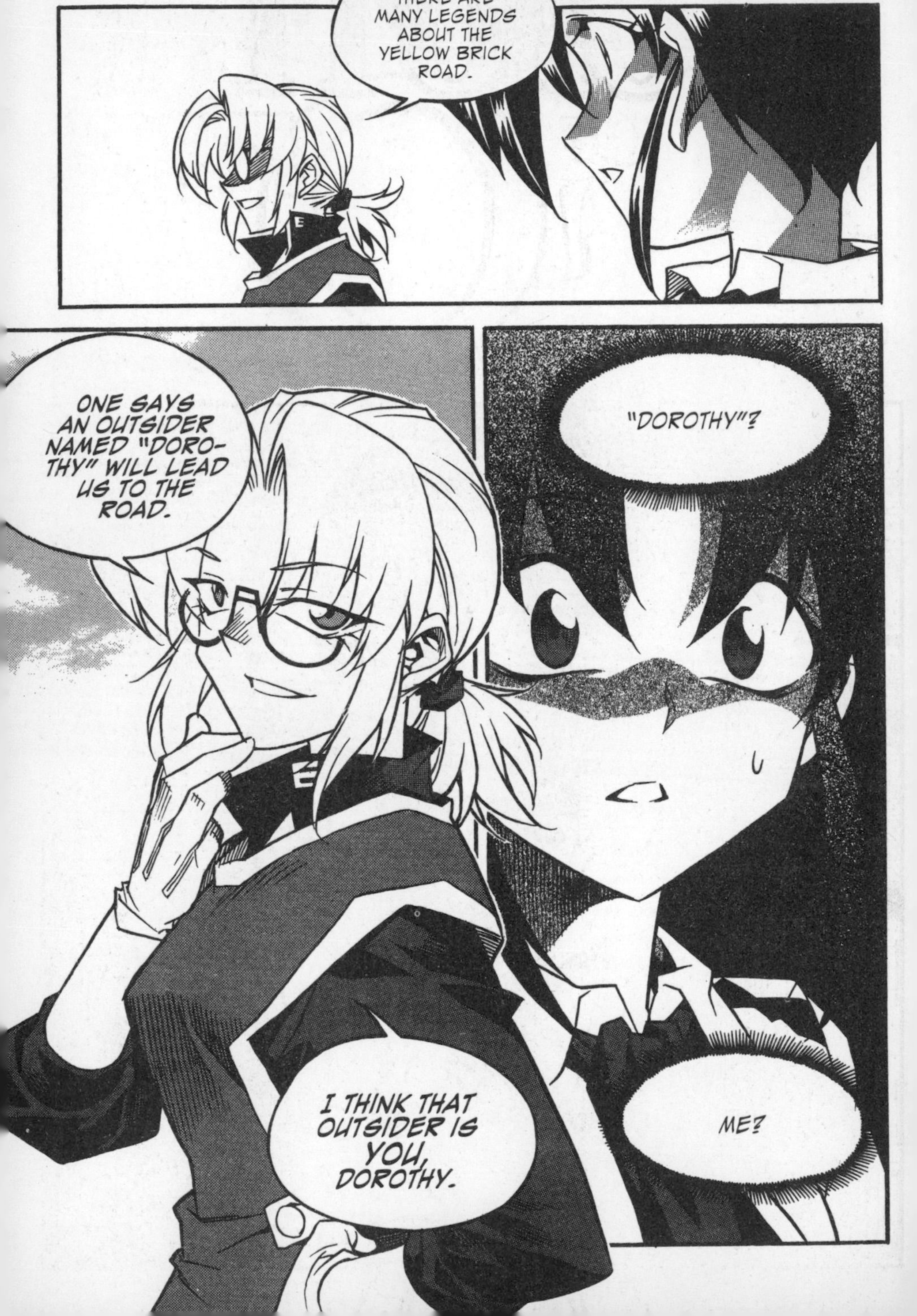
THERE ARE MANY LEGENDS ABOUT THE YELLOW BRICK ROAD.
ONE SAYS AN OUTSIDER NAMED "DORO-THY" WILL LEAD US TO THE ROAD.
"DOROTHY"?
I THINK THAT OUTSIDER IS YOU, DOROTHY.
ME?

DOROTHY OF OZ

Step 7 WHERE AM I?

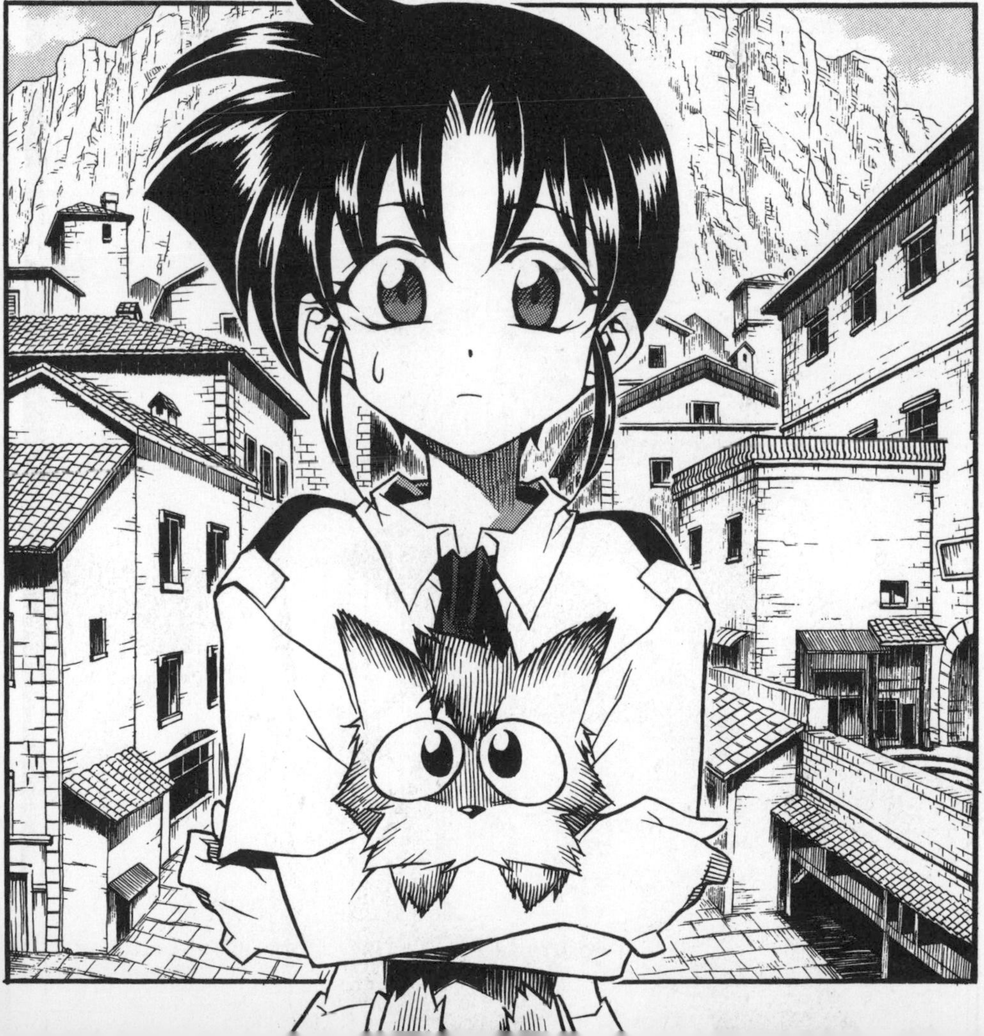

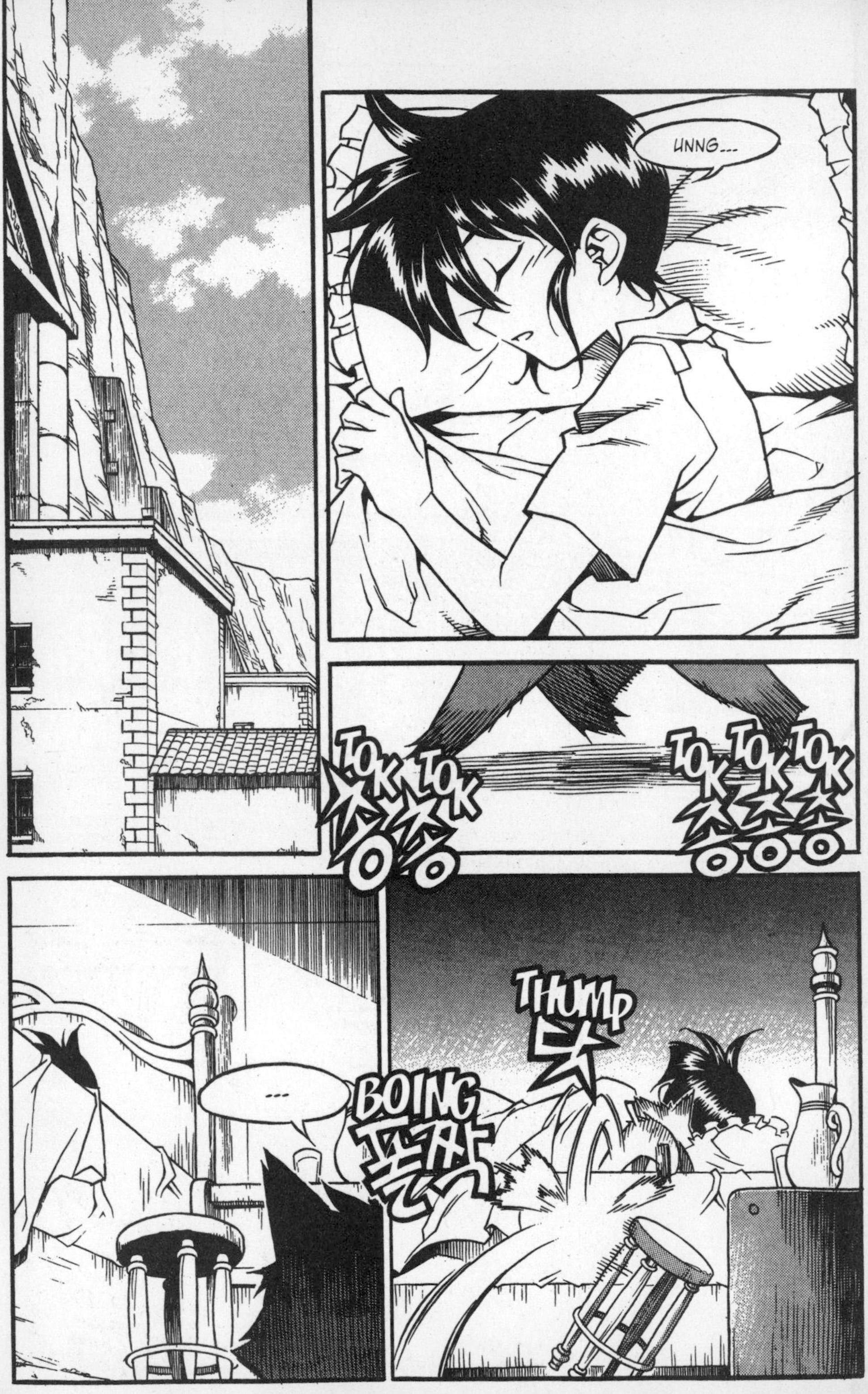
UNNG...
TOK TOK
TOK TOK TOK
...
THUMP
BOING

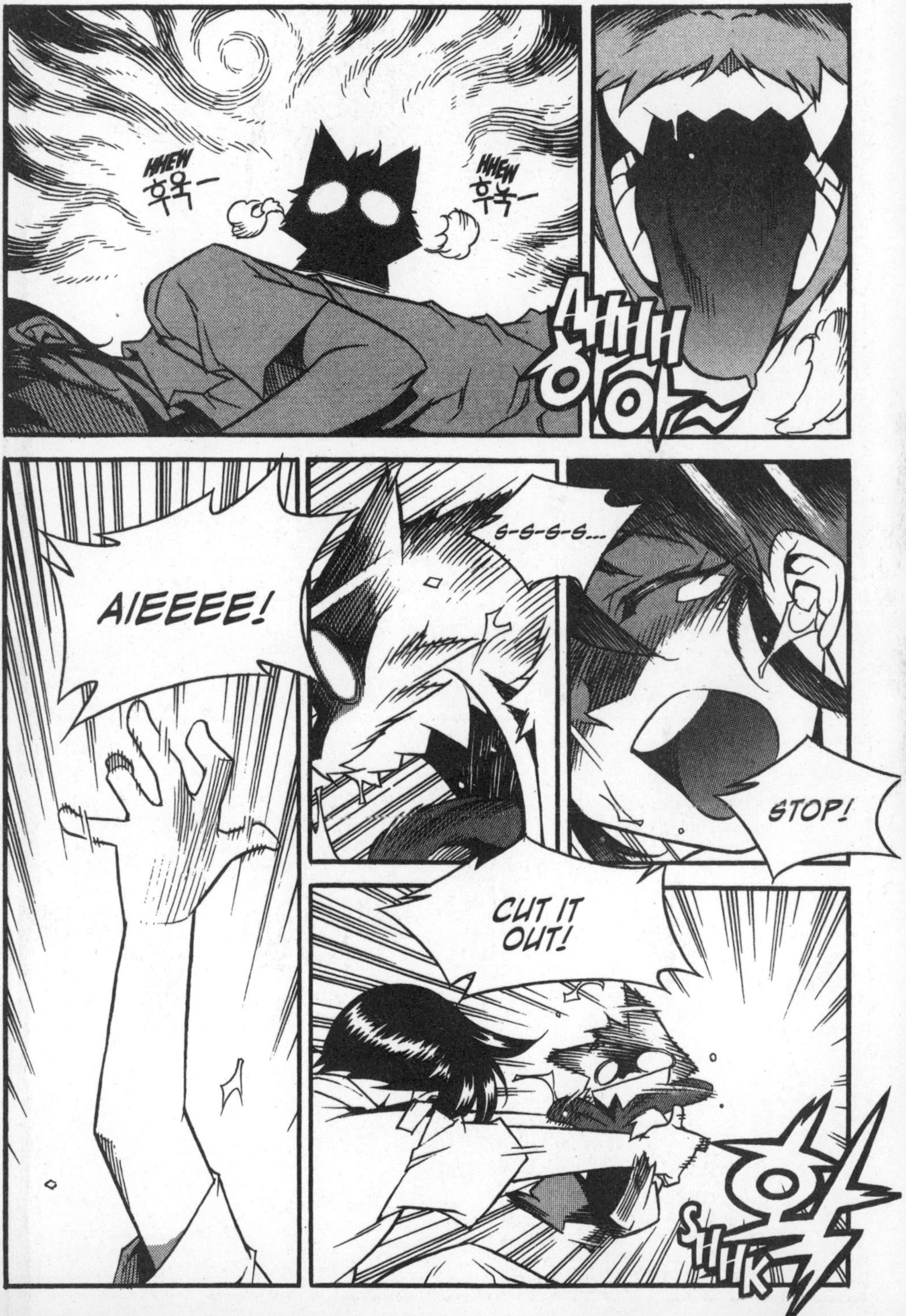

HHEW
후욱~
HHEW
후욱~
AHHH
하아~
AIEEEE!
S-S-S-S...
STOP!
CUT IT OUT!
SHHK

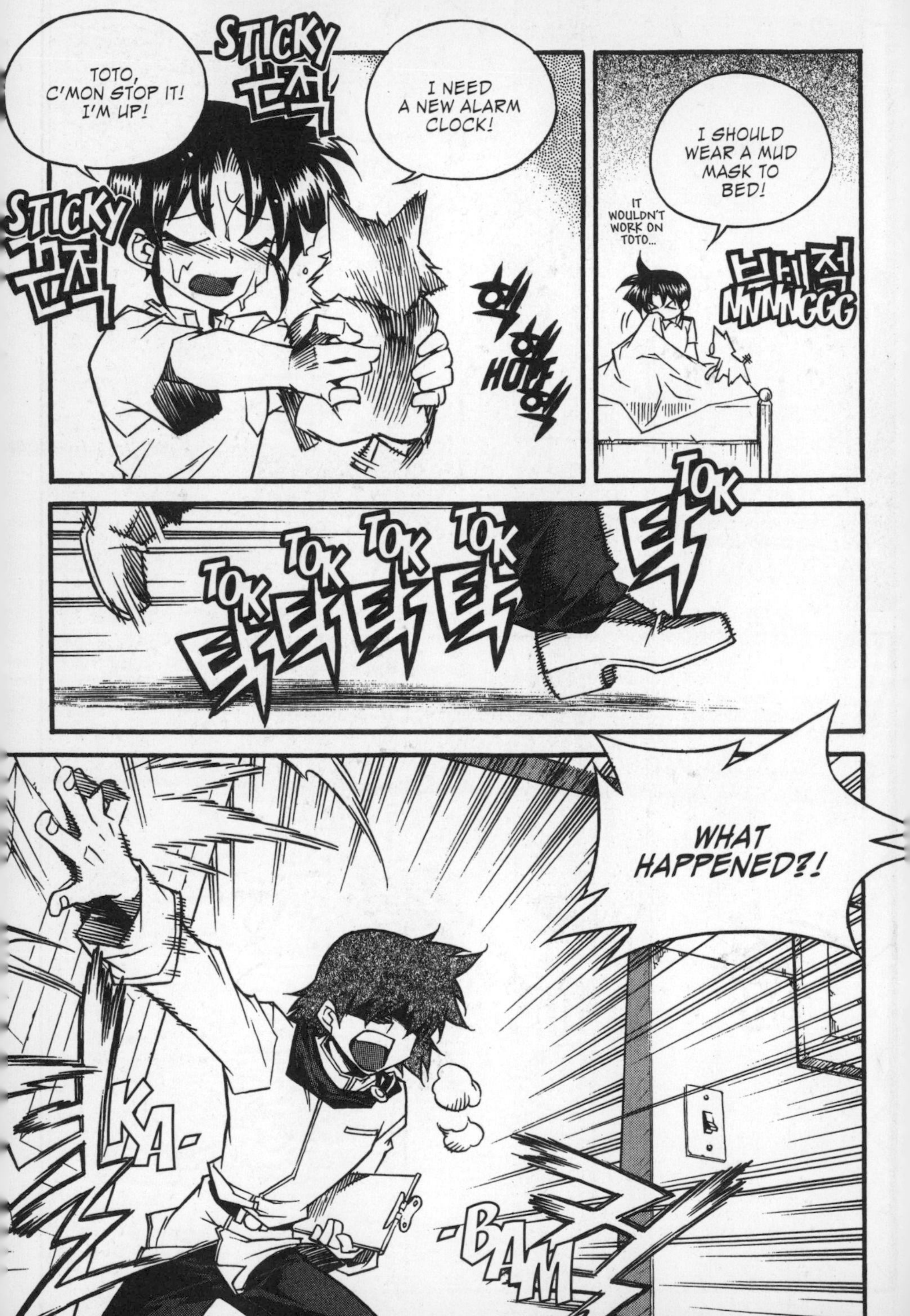
TOTO, C'MON STOP IT! I'M UP!
STICKY
끈적
STICKY
끈적
I NEED A NEW ALARM CLOCK!
HUFF
I SHOULD WEAR A MUD MASK TO BED!
IT WOULDN'T WORK ON TOTO...
MNNNGGG
TOK TOK TOK TOK TOK
탁탁탁탁탁
WHAT HAPPENED?!
KA-
-BAM

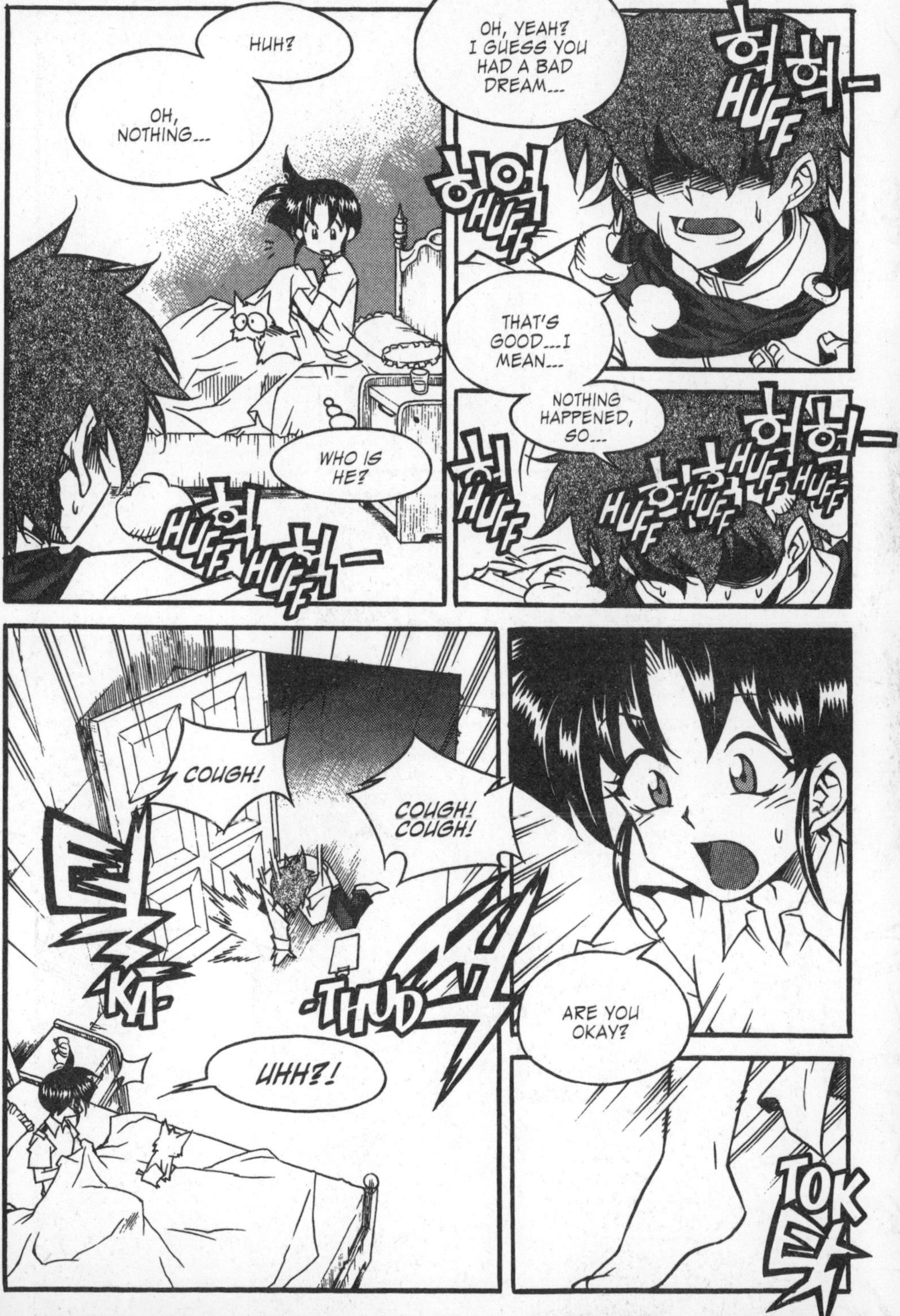
HUH?
OH, NOTHING...
WHO IS HE?
HUFF HUFF
허억 허억—
OH, YEAH? I GUESS YOU HAD A BAD DREAM...
허억— HUFF
허억 HUFF
THAT'S GOOD...I MEAN...
NOTHING HAPPENED, SO...
HUFF HUFF HUFF HUFF HUFF
COUGH!
COUGH! COUGH!
KA-
-THUD
UHH?!
ARE YOU OKAY?
TOK

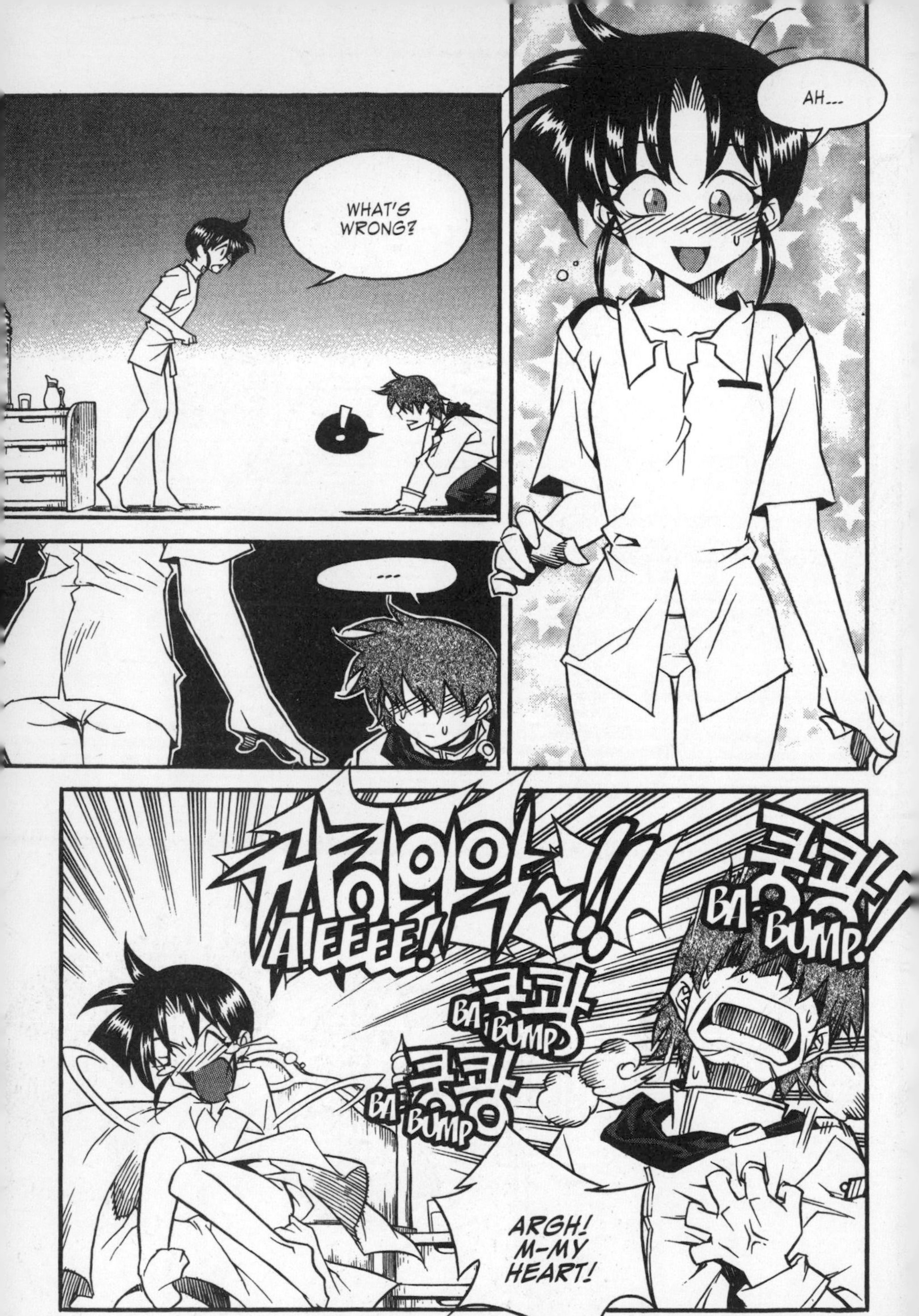
WHAT'S WRONG?
!
...
AH...
꺄아아아악~!!
AIEEEE!
쿵쾅!
BA-BUMP!
쿵쾅!
BA-BUMP
쿵쾅
BA-BUMP
ARGH! M-MY HEART!

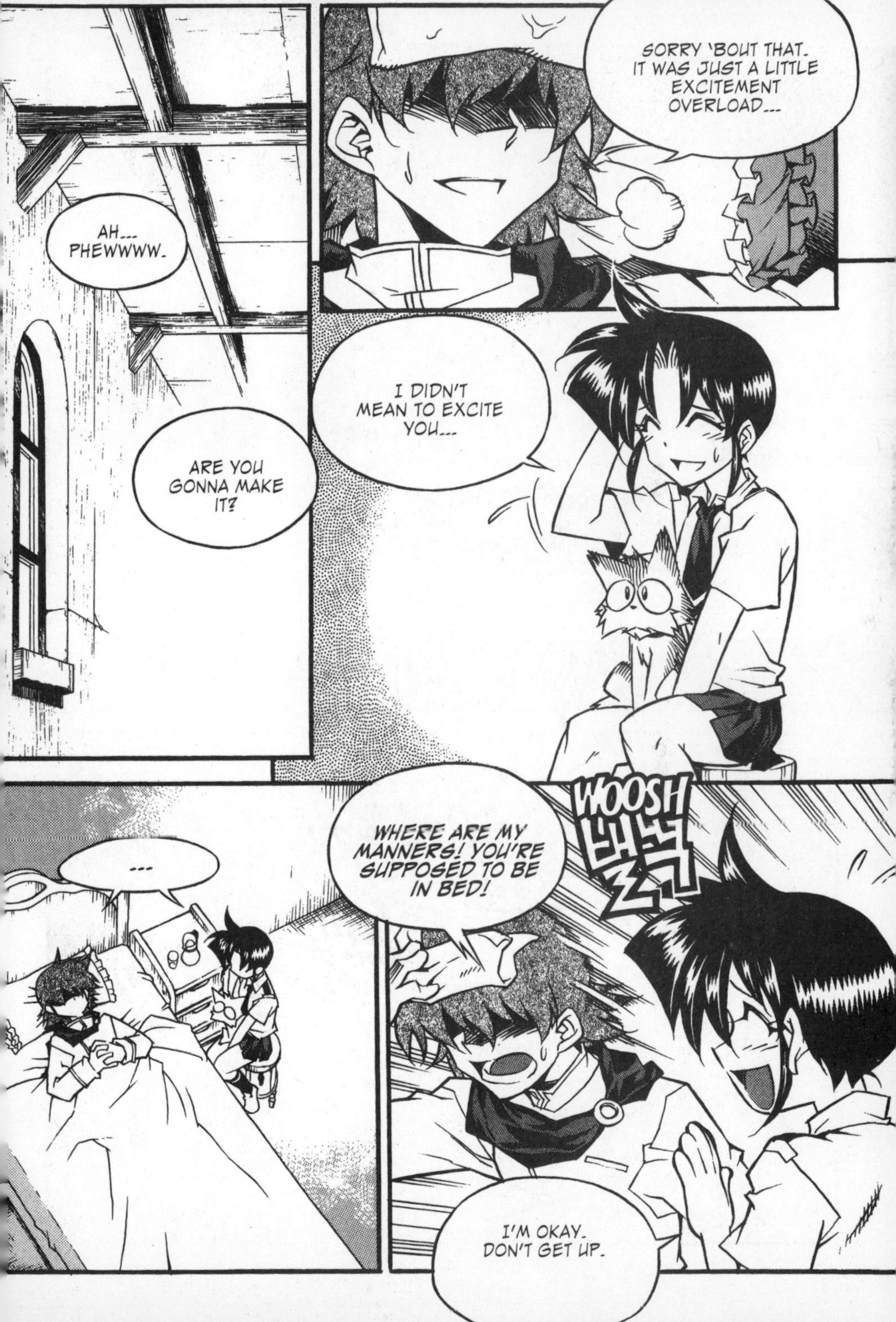
AH... PHEWWWW.
ARE YOU GONNA MAKE IT?
SORRY 'BOUT THAT. IT WAS JUST A LITTLE EXCITEMENT OVERLOAD...
I DIDN'T MEAN TO EXCITE YOU...
...
WOOSH
WHERE ARE MY MANNERS! YOU'RE SUPPOSED TO BE IN BED!
I'M OKAY. DON'T GET UP.

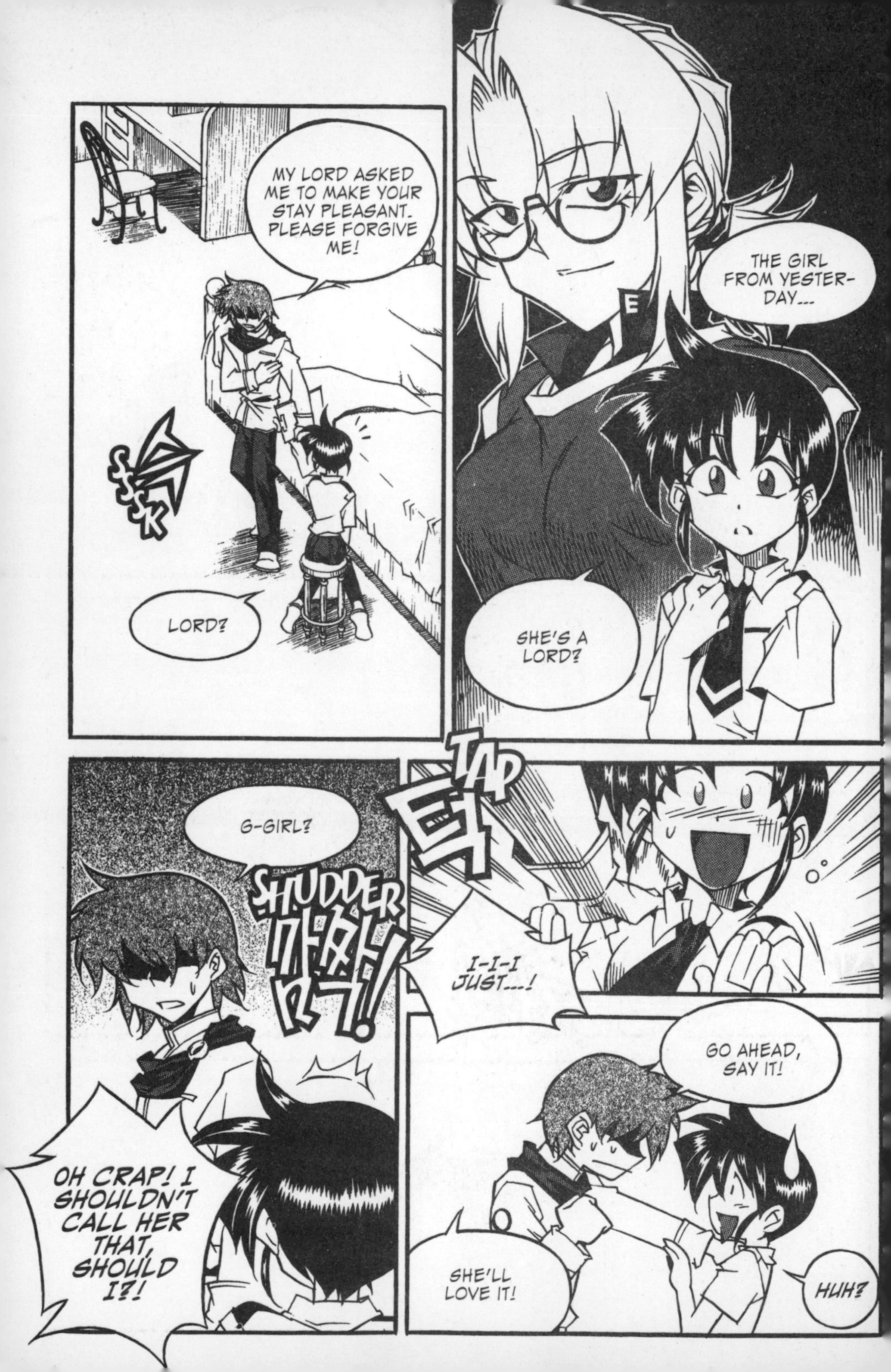
MY LORD ASKED ME TO MAKE YOUR STAY PLEASANT. PLEASE FORGIVE ME!
SSSK
LORD?
THE GIRL FROM YESTER-DAY...
SHE'S A LORD?
G-GIRL?
SHUDDER
OH CRAP! I SHOULDN'T CALL HER THAT, SHOULD I?!
TAP
I-I-I JUST...!
GO AHEAD, SAY IT!
SHE'LL LOVE IT!
HUH?

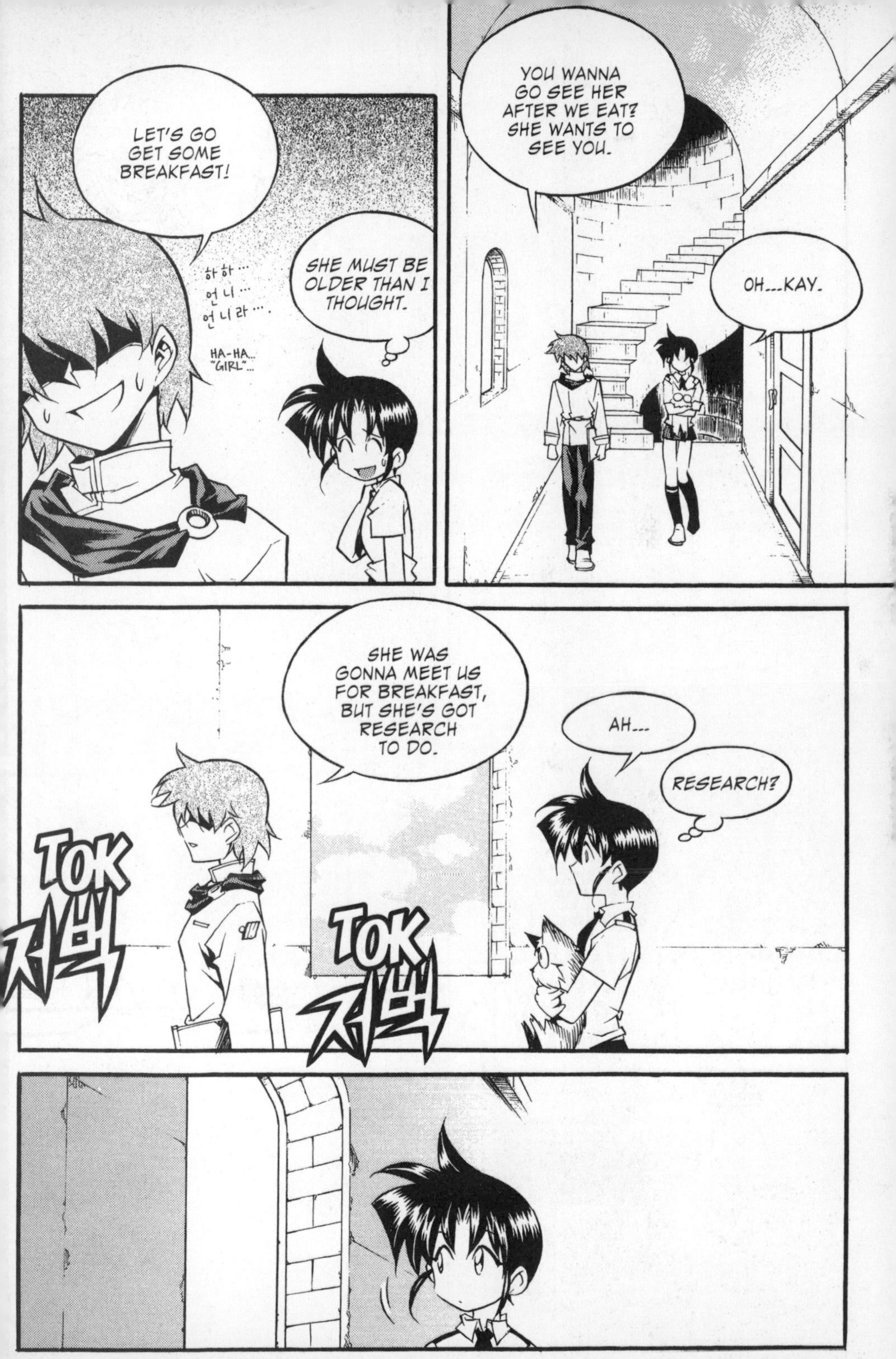
LET'S GO GET SOME BREAKFAST!
하하…
언니…
언니라…
HA-HA… "GIRL"…
SHE MUST BE OLDER THAN I THOUGHT.
YOU WANNA GO SEE HER AFTER WE EAT? SHE WANTS TO SEE YOU.
OH…KAY.
SHE WAS GONNA MEET US FOR BREAKFAST, BUT SHE'S GOT RESEARCH TO DO.
AH…
RESEARCH?
TOK
TOK

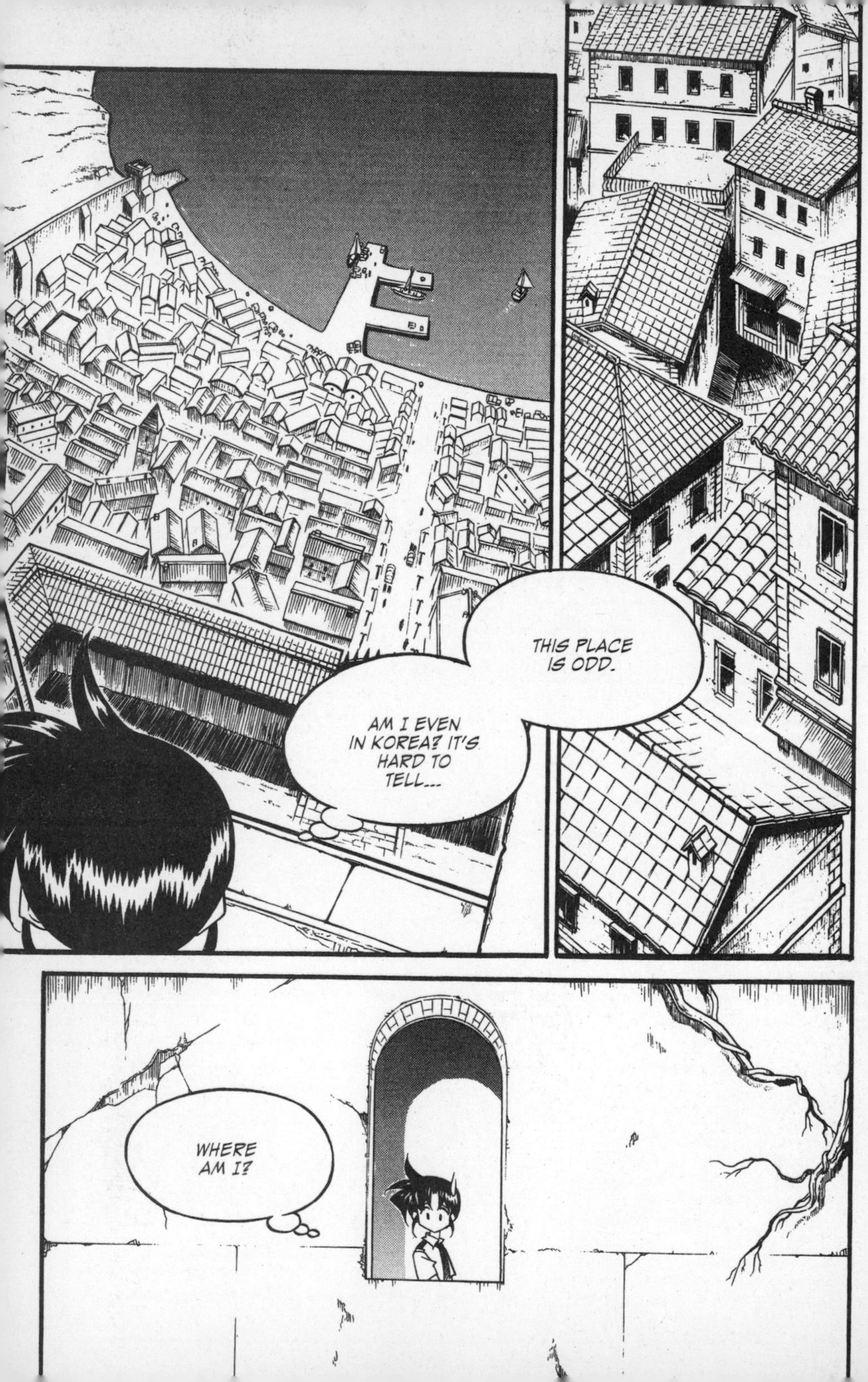
THIS PLACE IS ODD.
AM I EVEN IN KOREA? IT'S HARD TO TELL...
WHERE AM I?

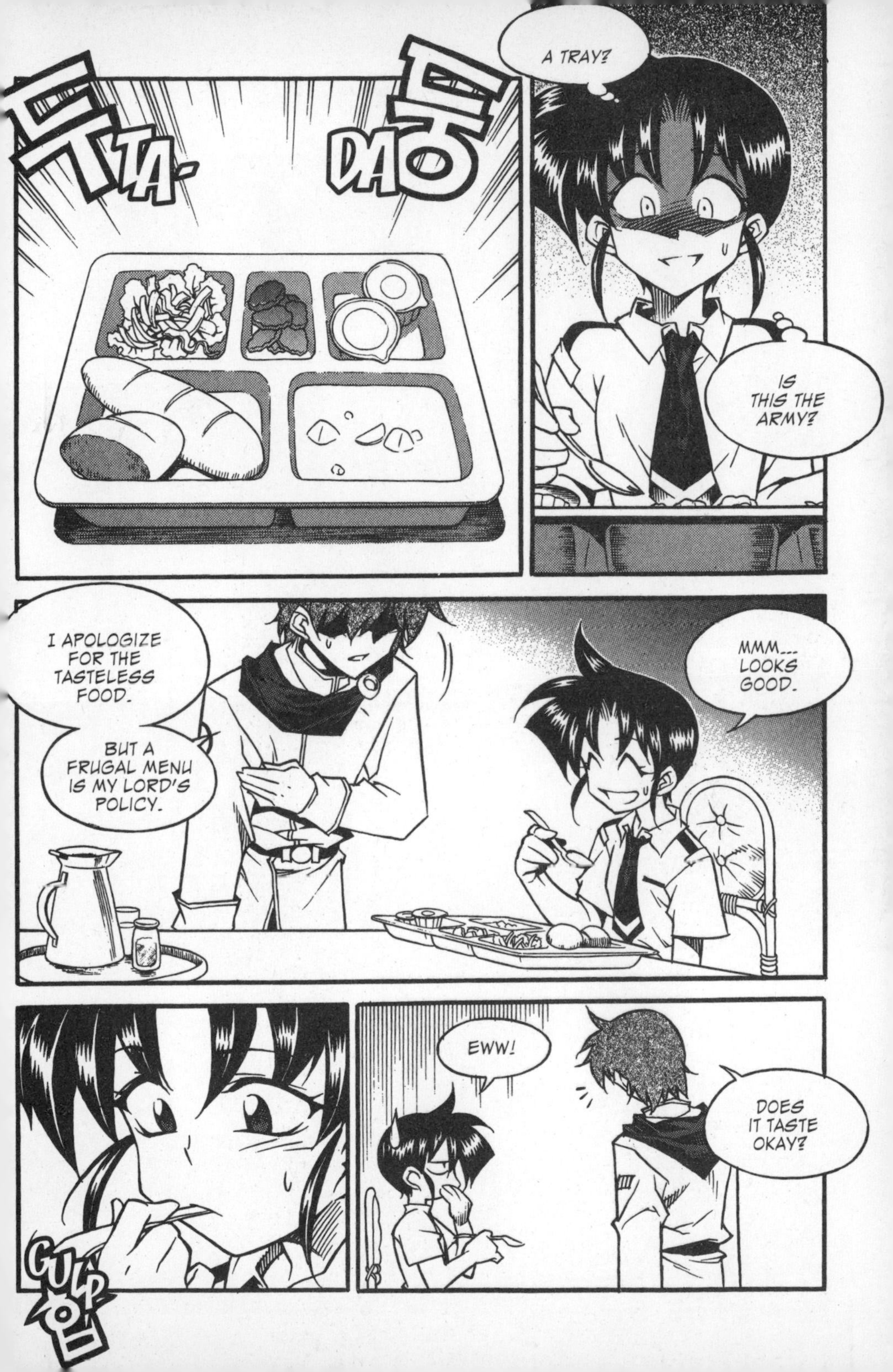

TA-
DA
A TRAY?
IS THIS THE ARMY?
I APOLOGIZE FOR THE TASTELESS FOOD.
BUT A FRUGAL MENU IS MY LORD'S POLICY.
MMM... LOOKS GOOD.
GULP
EWW!
DOES IT TASTE OKAY?

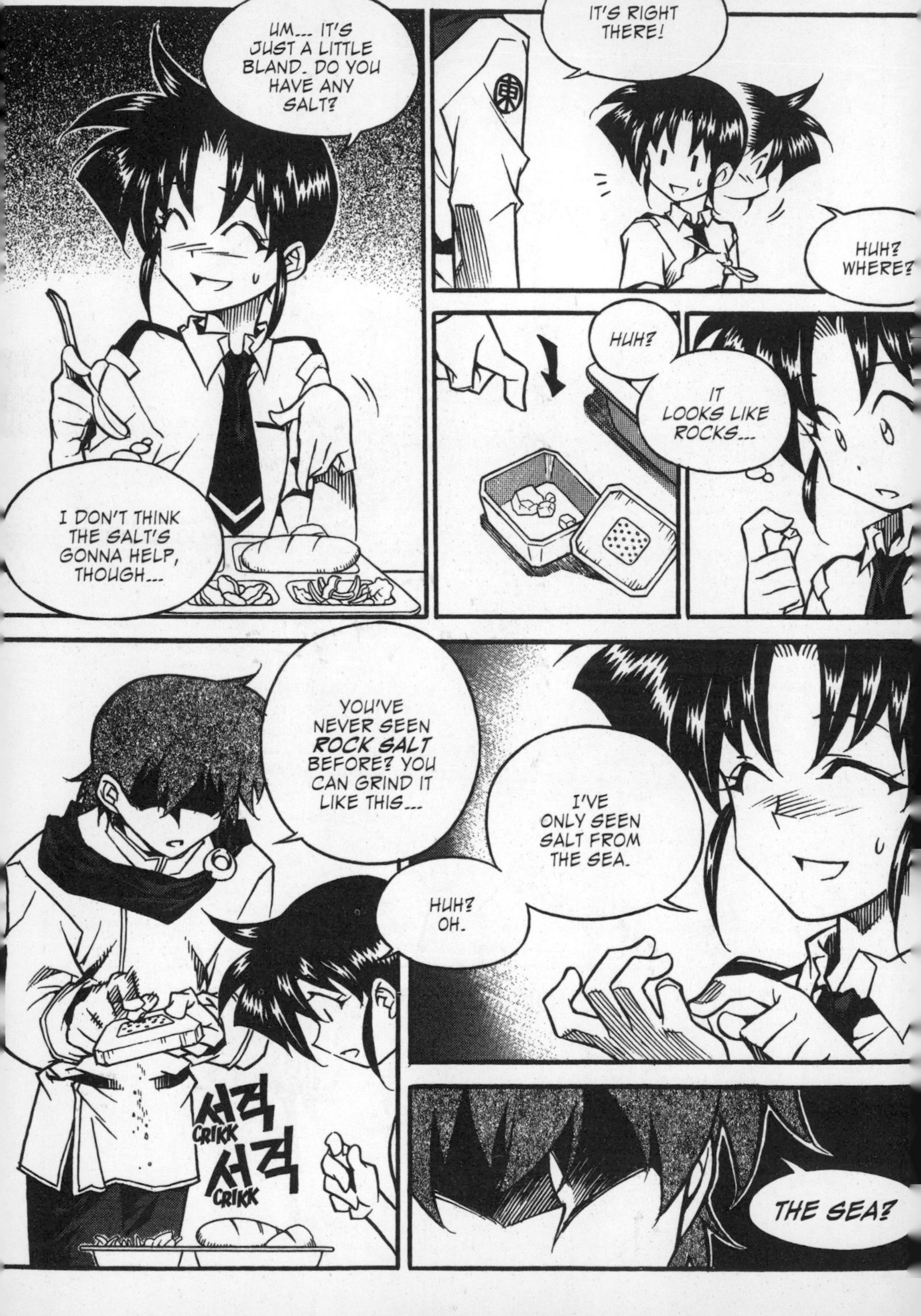
UM... IT'S JUST A LITTLE BLAND. DO YOU HAVE ANY SALT?
I DON'T THINK THE SALT'S GONNA HELP, THOUGH...
IT'S RIGHT THERE!
HUH? WHERE?
HUH?
IT LOOKS LIKE ROCKS...
YOU'VE NEVER SEEN ROCK SALT BEFORE? YOU CAN GRIND IT LIKE THIS...
HUH? OH.
서걱
CRIKK
서걱
CRIKK
I'VE ONLY SEEN SALT FROM THE SEA.
THE SEA?

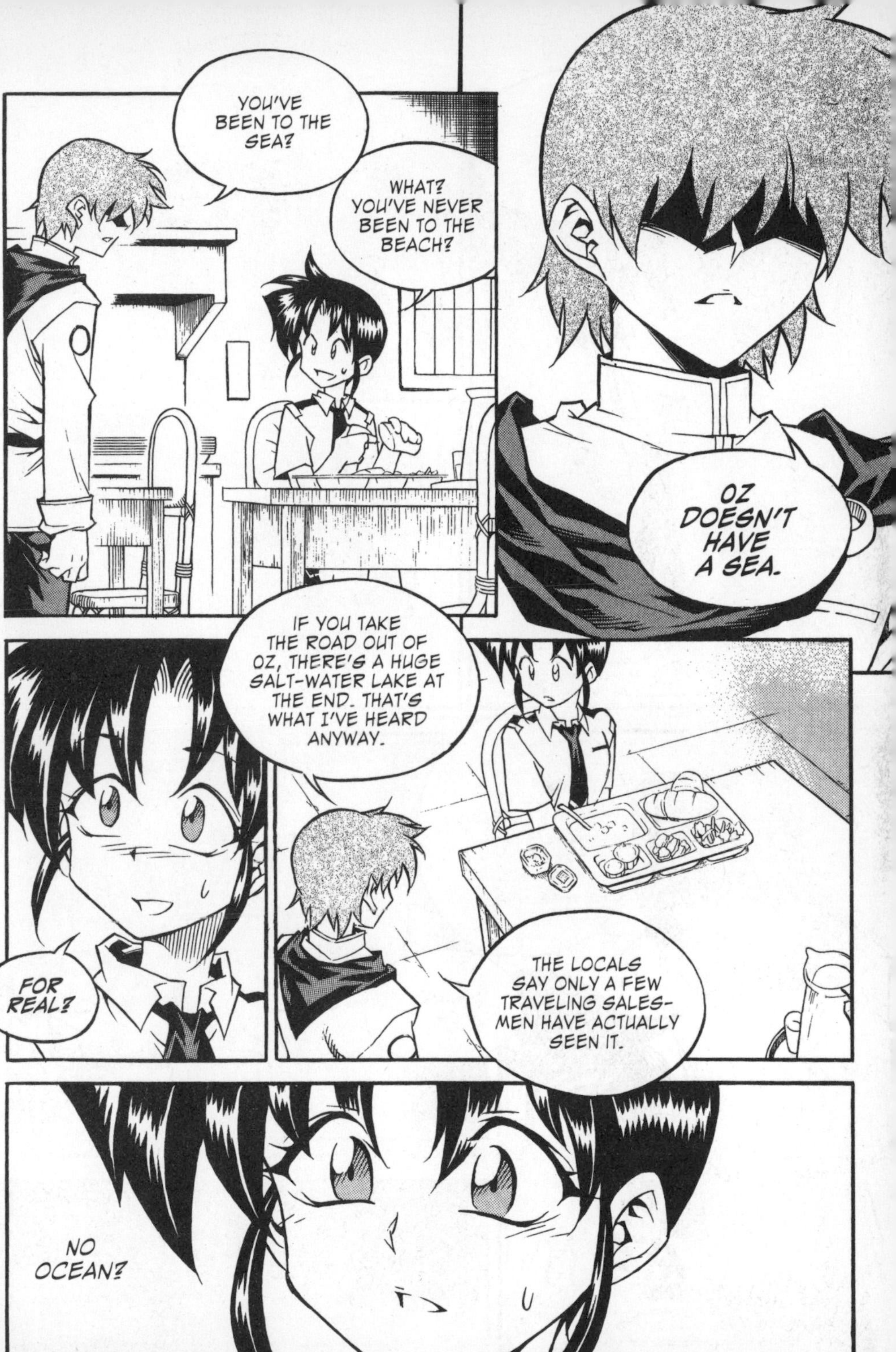
YOU'VE BEEN TO THE SEA?
WHAT? YOU'VE NEVER BEEN TO THE BEACH?
OZ DOESN'T HAVE A SEA.
FOR REAL?
IF YOU TAKE THE ROAD OUT OF OZ, THERE'S A HUGE SALT-WATER LAKE AT THE END. THAT'S WHAT I'VE HEARD ANYWAY.
THE LOCALS SAY ONLY A FEW TRAVELING SALES-MEN HAVE ACTUALLY SEEN IT.
NO OCEAN?

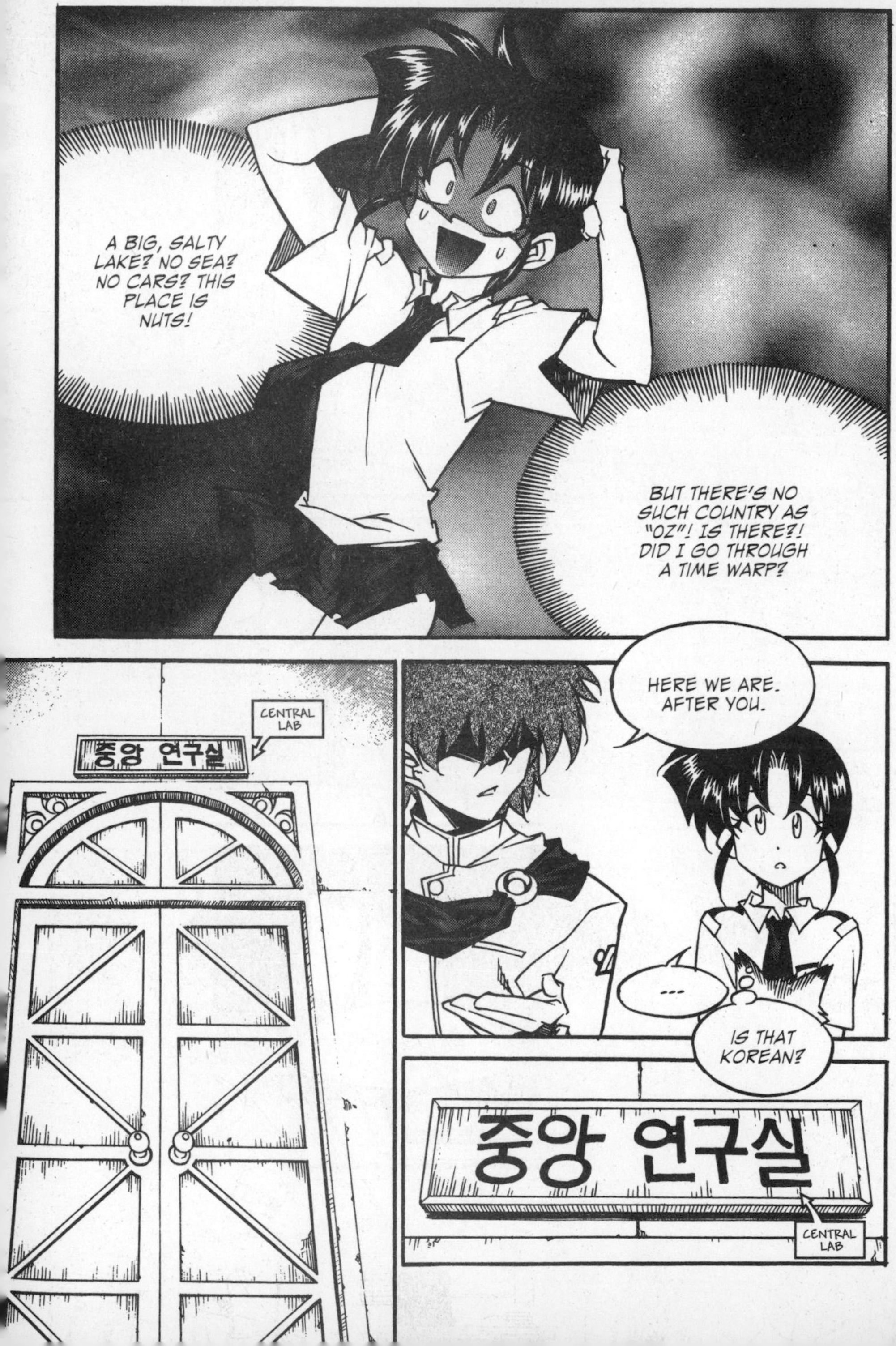
A BIG, SALTY LAKE? NO SEA? NO CARS? THIS PLACE IS NUTS!
BUT THERE'S NO SUCH COUNTRY AS "OZ"! IS THERE?! DID I GO THROUGH A TIME WARP?
CENTRAL LAB
중앙 연구실
HERE WE ARE. AFTER YOU.
...
IS THAT KOREAN?
중앙 연구실
CENTRAL LAB

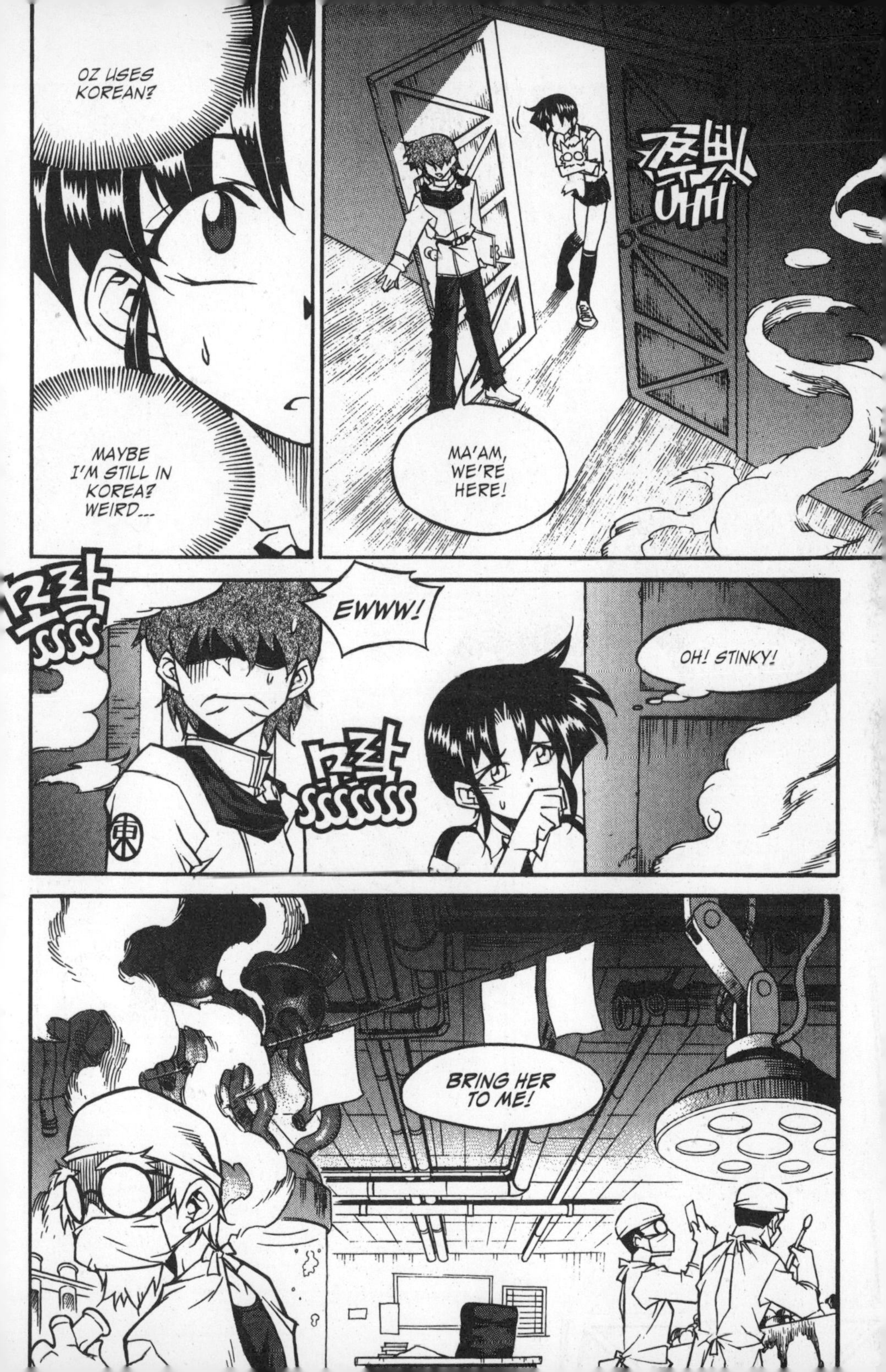
OZ USES KOREAN?
MAYBE I'M STILL IN KOREA? WEIRD...
UHH
MA'AM, WE'RE HERE!
EWWW!
OH! STINKY!
BRING HER TO ME!

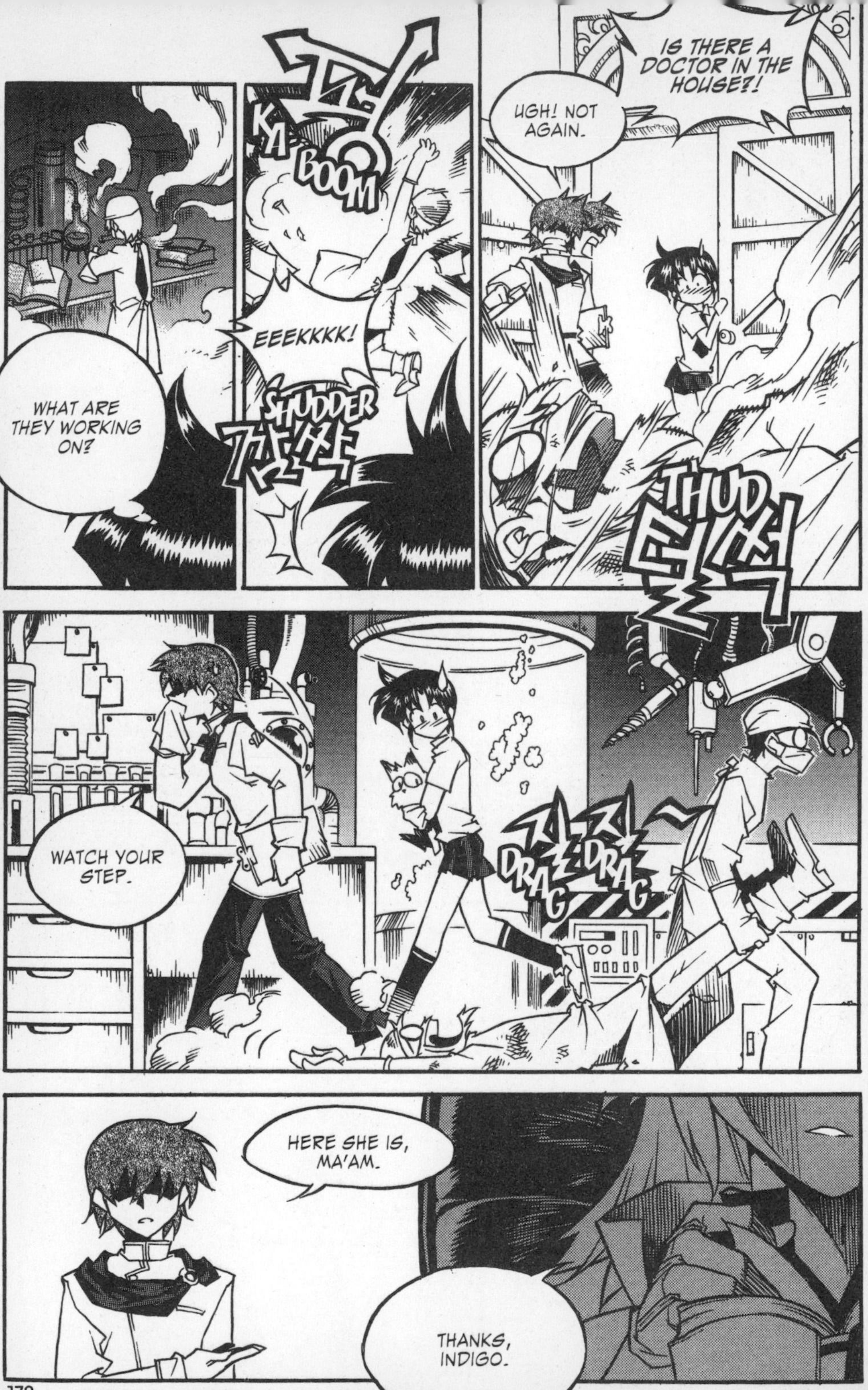
WHAT ARE THEY WORKING ON?
KA BOOM
EEEKKKK!
SHUDDER
IS THERE A DOCTOR IN THE HOUSE?!
UGH! NOT AGAIN.
THUD
WATCH YOUR STEP.
DRAG DRAG
HERE SHE IS, MA'AM.
THANKS, INDIGO.

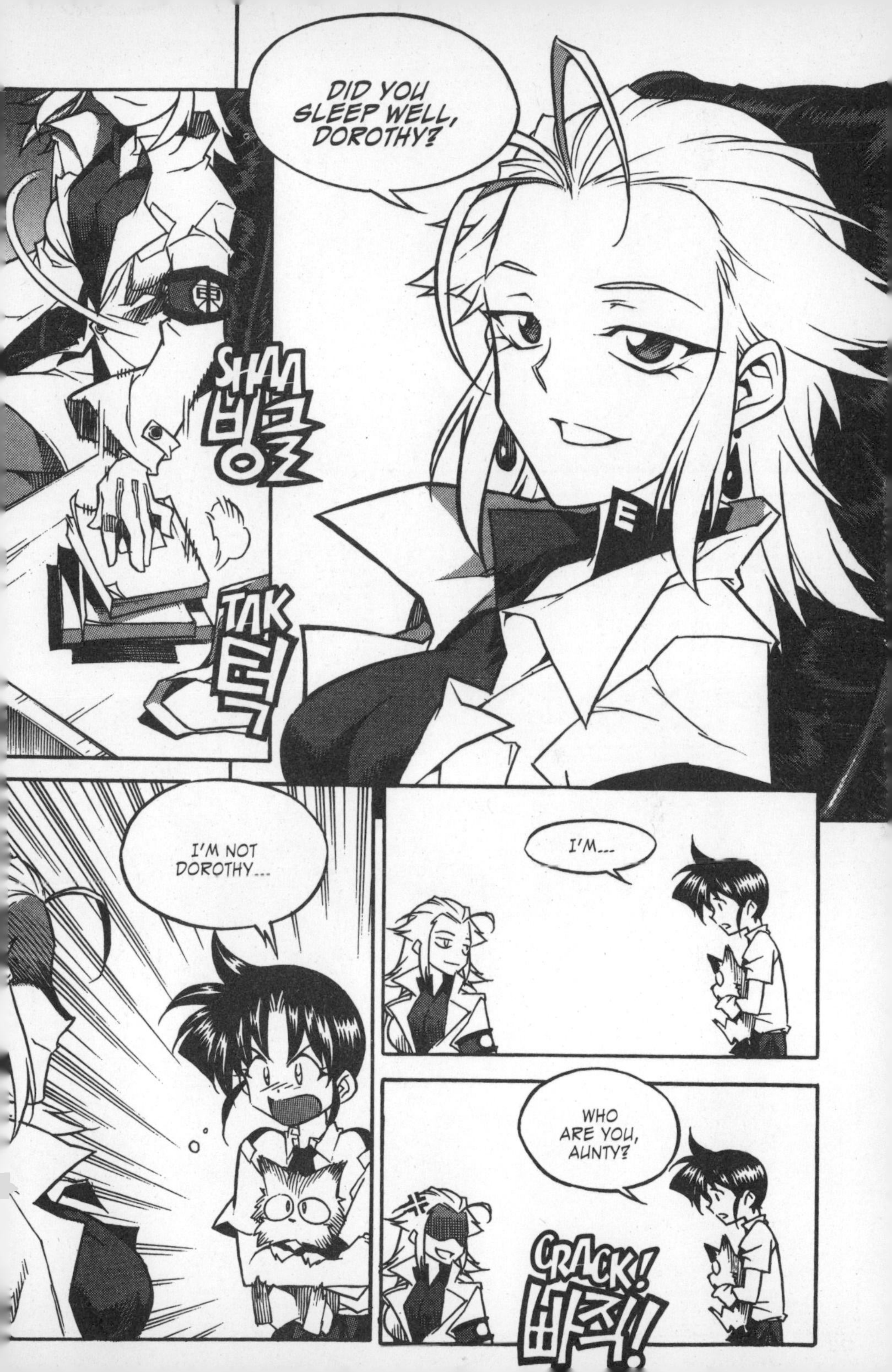
SHAA
TAK
DID YOU SLEEP WELL, DOROTHY?
I'M NOT DOROTHY...
I'M...
WHO ARE YOU, AUNTY?
CRACK!
빠직!

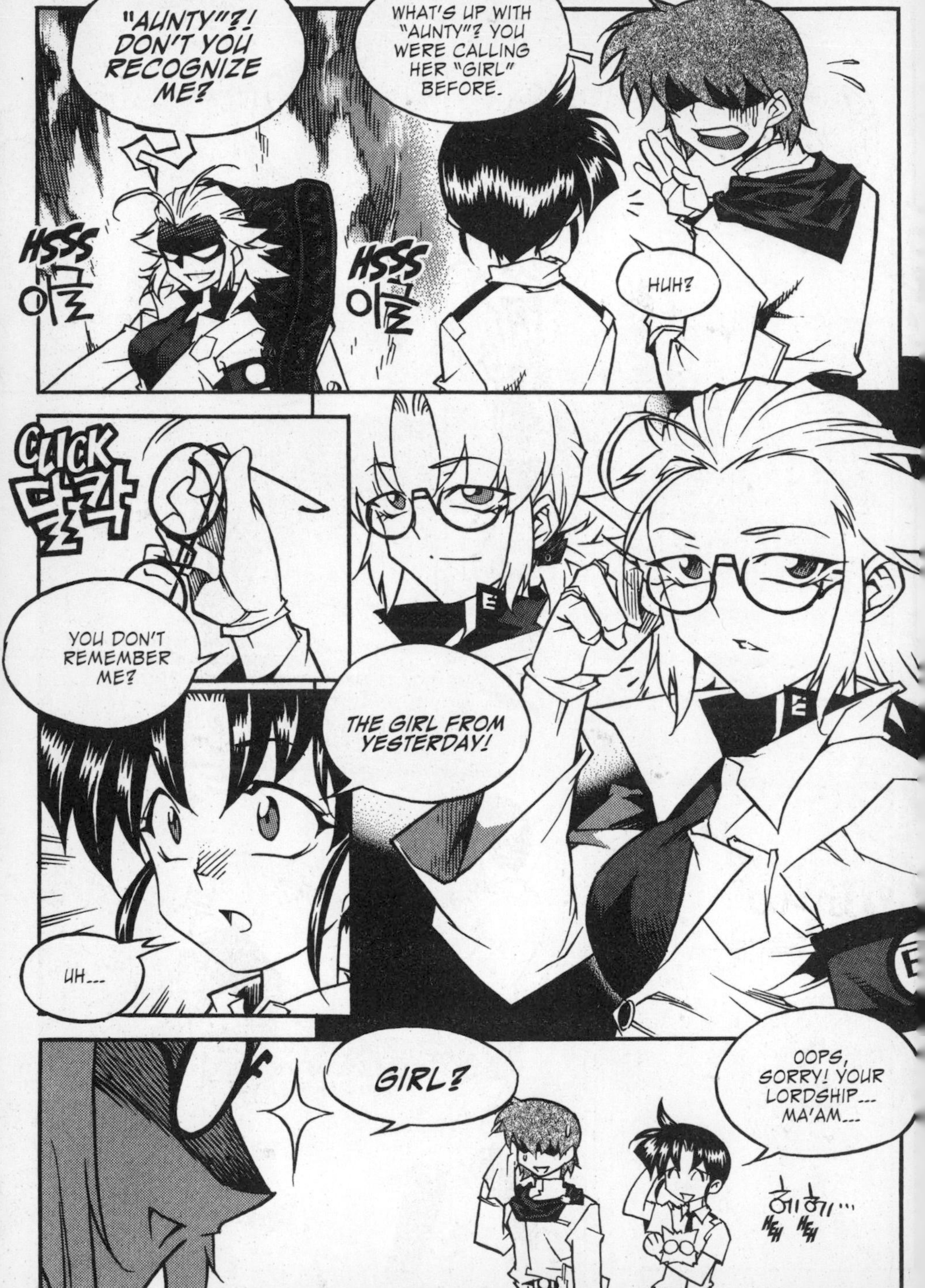
"AUNTY"?! DON'T YOU RECOGNIZE ME?
WHAT'S UP WITH "AUNTY"? YOU WERE CALLING HER "GIRL" BEFORE.
HSSS
아글
HSSS
아글
HUH?
CLICK
딸칵
YOU DON'T REMEMBER ME?
THE GIRL FROM YESTERDAY!
UH...
GIRL?
OOPS, SORRY! YOUR LORDSHIP... MA'AM...
헤헤...
HEH
HEH

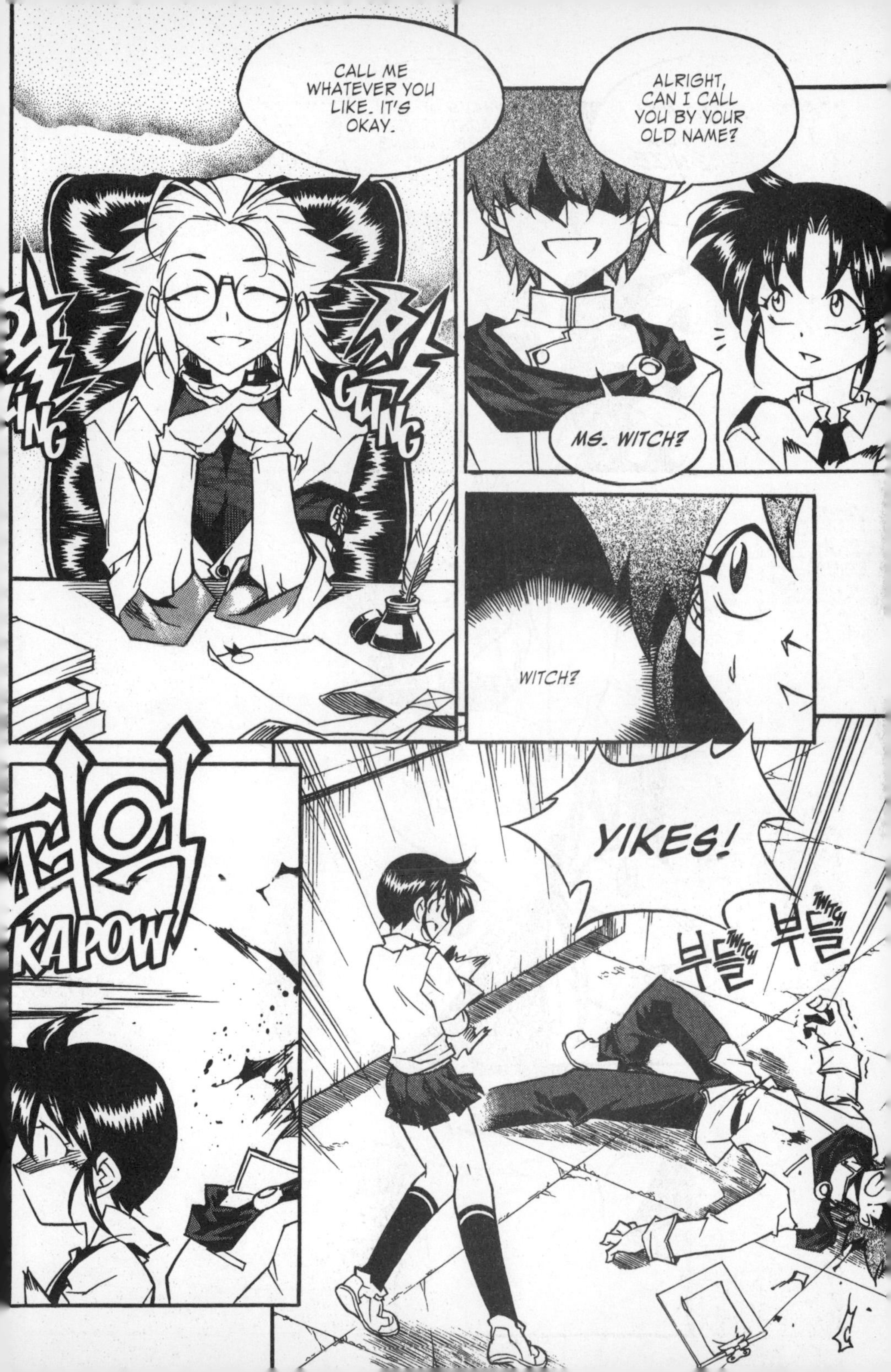
CALL ME WHATEVER YOU LIKE. IT'S OKAY.
LING
GLING
ALRIGHT, CAN I CALL YOU BY YOUR OLD NAME?
MS. WITCH?
WITCH?
KAPOW
YIKES!
부들 TWITCH
부들 TWITCH

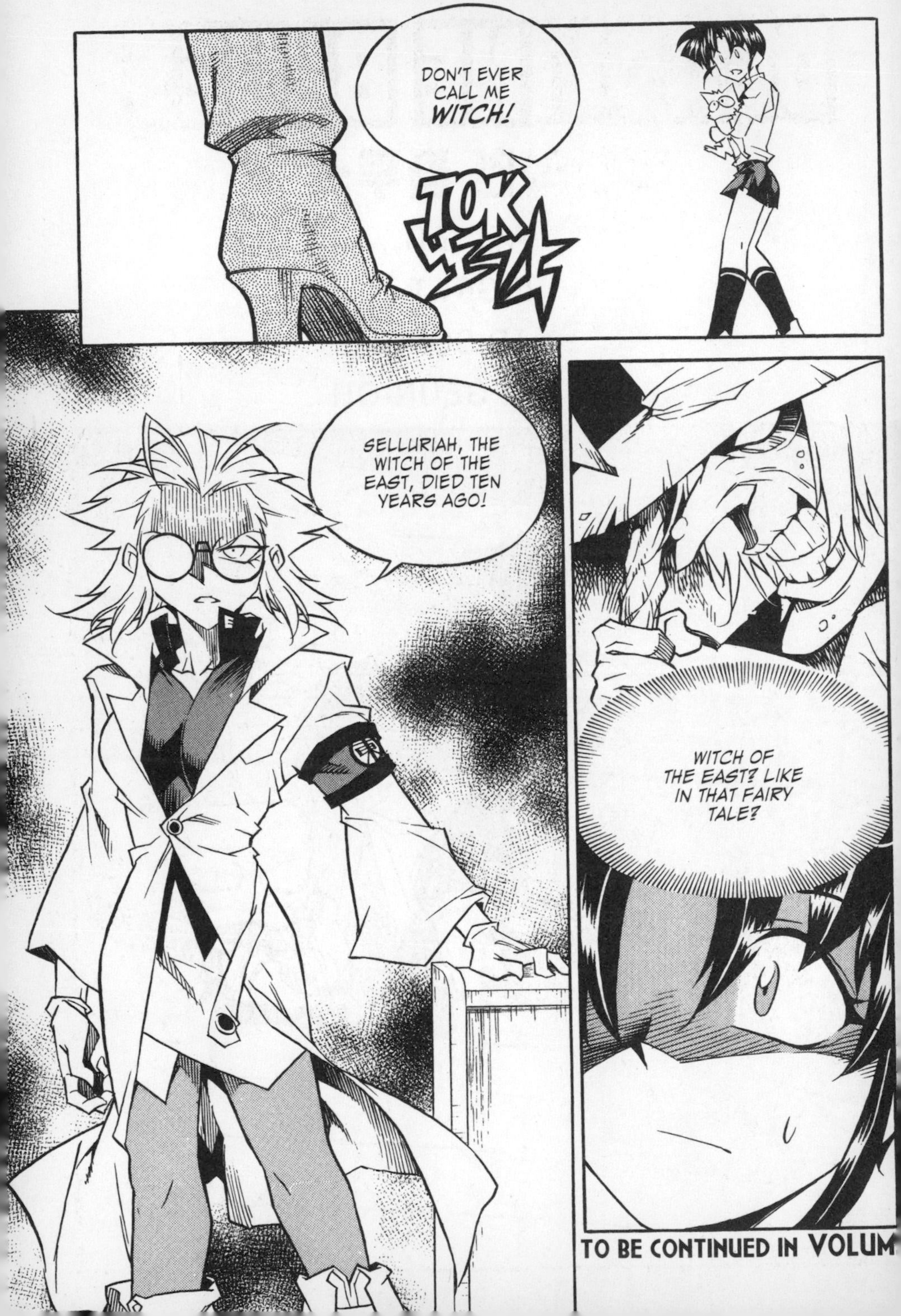
DON'T EVER CALL ME WITCH!
TOK
SELLURIAH, THE WITCH OF THE EAST, DIED TEN YEARS AGO!
WITCH OF THE EAST? LIKE IN THAT FAIRY TALE?
TO BE CONTINUED IN VOLUM

DEADLINE BLUES

데드라인 블루스

BATTLER

REGRET

DEAD SONG

HYBRID GEUN-OH

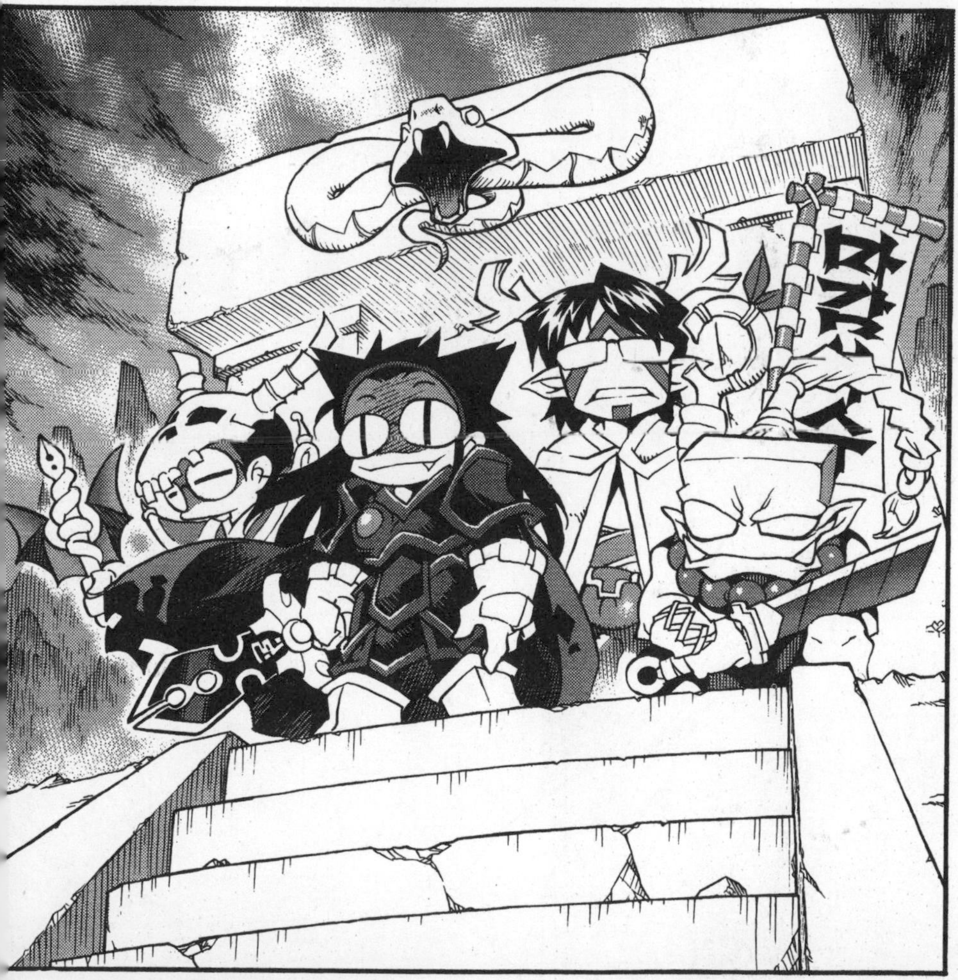

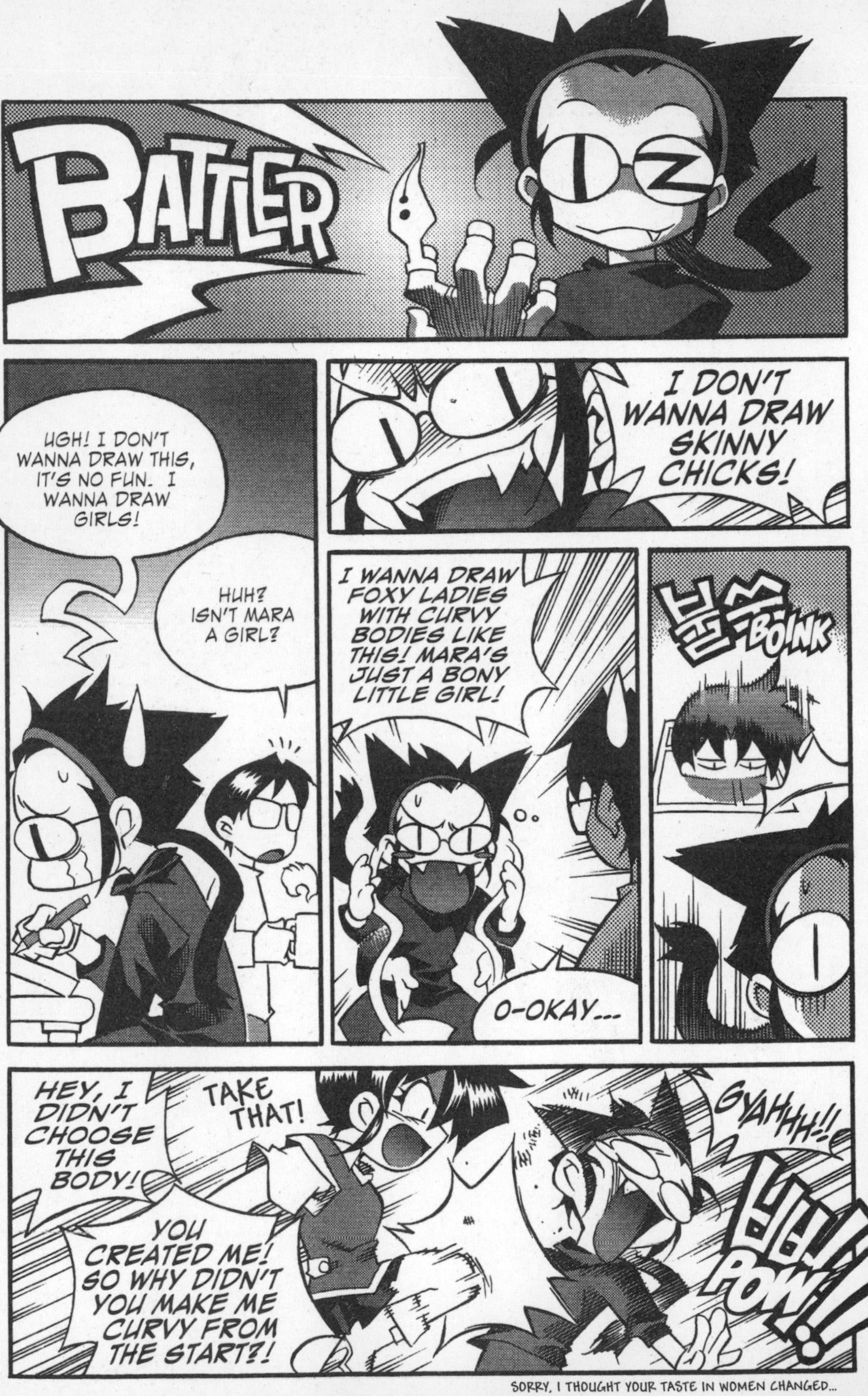
BATTLER
UGH! I DON'T WANNA DRAW THIS, IT'S NO FUN. I WANNA DRAW GIRLS!
HUH? ISN'T MARA A GIRL?
I DON'T WANNA DRAW SKINNY CHICKS!
I WANNA DRAW FOXY LADIES WITH CURVY BODIES LIKE THIS! MARA'S JUST A BONY LITTLE GIRL!
O-OKAY...
BOINK
HEY, I DIDN'T CHOOSE THIS BODY!
TAKE THAT!
YOU CREATED ME! SO WHY DIDN'T YOU MAKE ME CURVY FROM THE START?!
GYAHHH!!
POW!!!

SORRY, I THOUGHT YOUR TASTE IN WOMEN CHANGED...

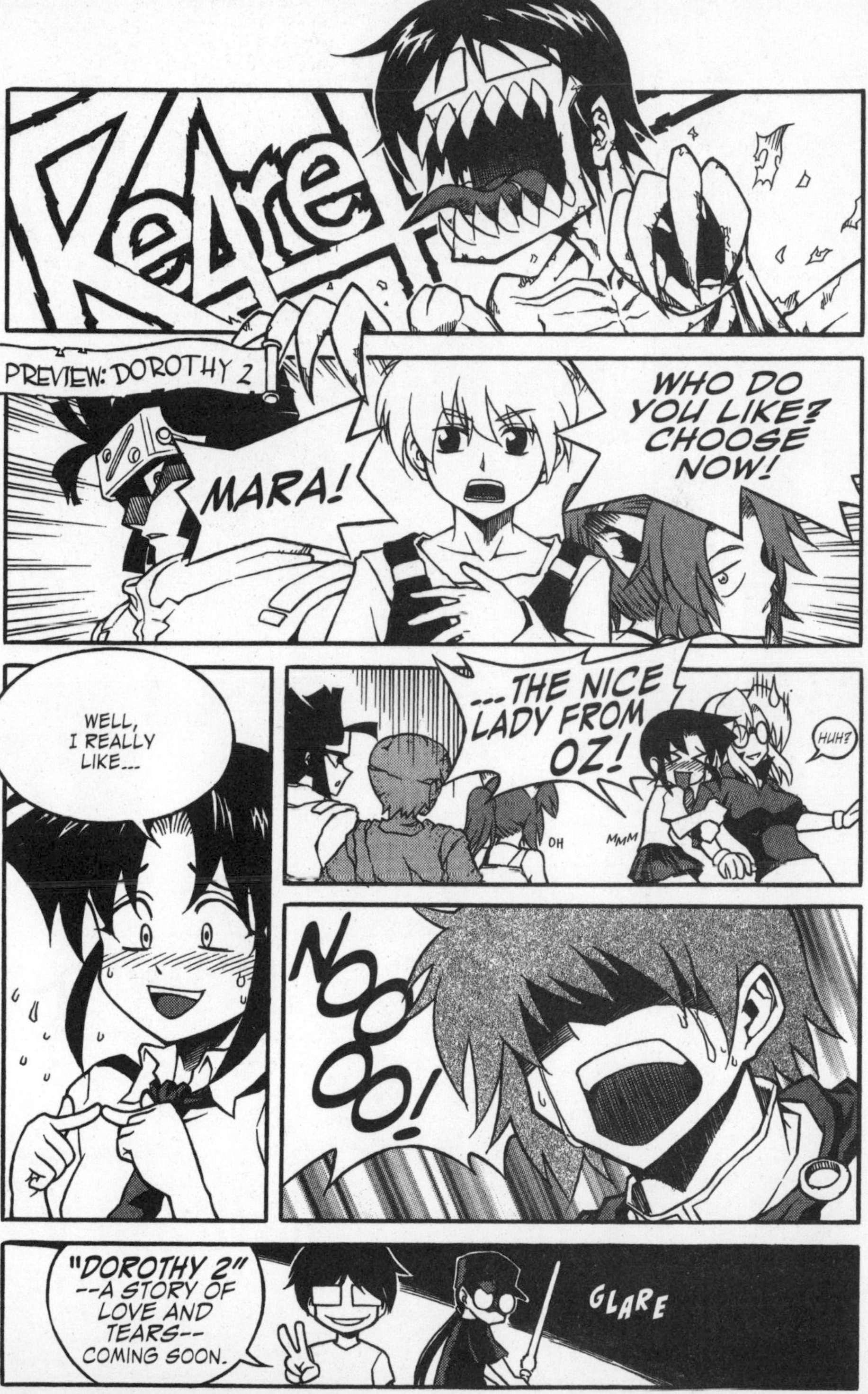

PREVIEW: DOROTHY 2
MARA!
WHO DO YOU LIKE? CHOOSE NOW!
WELL, I REALLY LIKE...
...THE NICE LADY FROM OZ!
HUH?
OH
MMM
NOOOO!
"DOROTHY 2" --A STORY OF LOVE AND TEARS-- COMING SOON.
GLARE

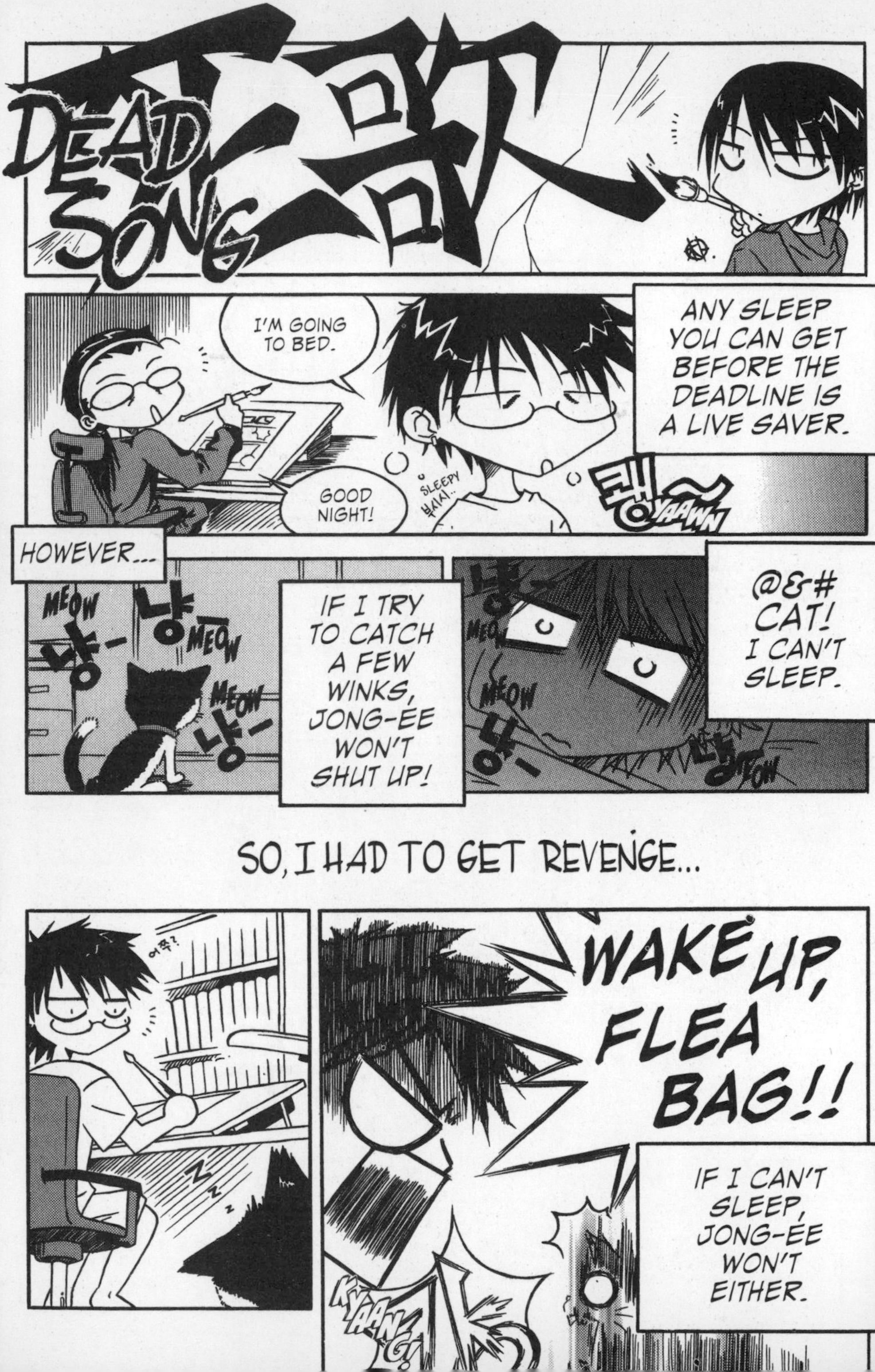
DEAD SONG
I'M GOING TO BED.
GOOD NIGHT!
SLEEPY
ANY SLEEP YOU CAN GET BEFORE THE DEADLINE IS A LIVE SAVER.
YAAWN
HOWEVER...
MEOW
냥-
MEOW
냥-
MEOW
냥-
IF I TRY TO CATCH A FEW WINKS, JONG-EE WON'T SHUT UP!
냥-
MEOW
MEOW
냥-
@&#
CAT!
I CAN'T SLEEP.
SO, I HAD TO GET REVENGE...
WAKE UP, FLEA BAG!!
IF I CAN'T SLEEP, JONG-EE WON'T EITHER.
KYAANG!

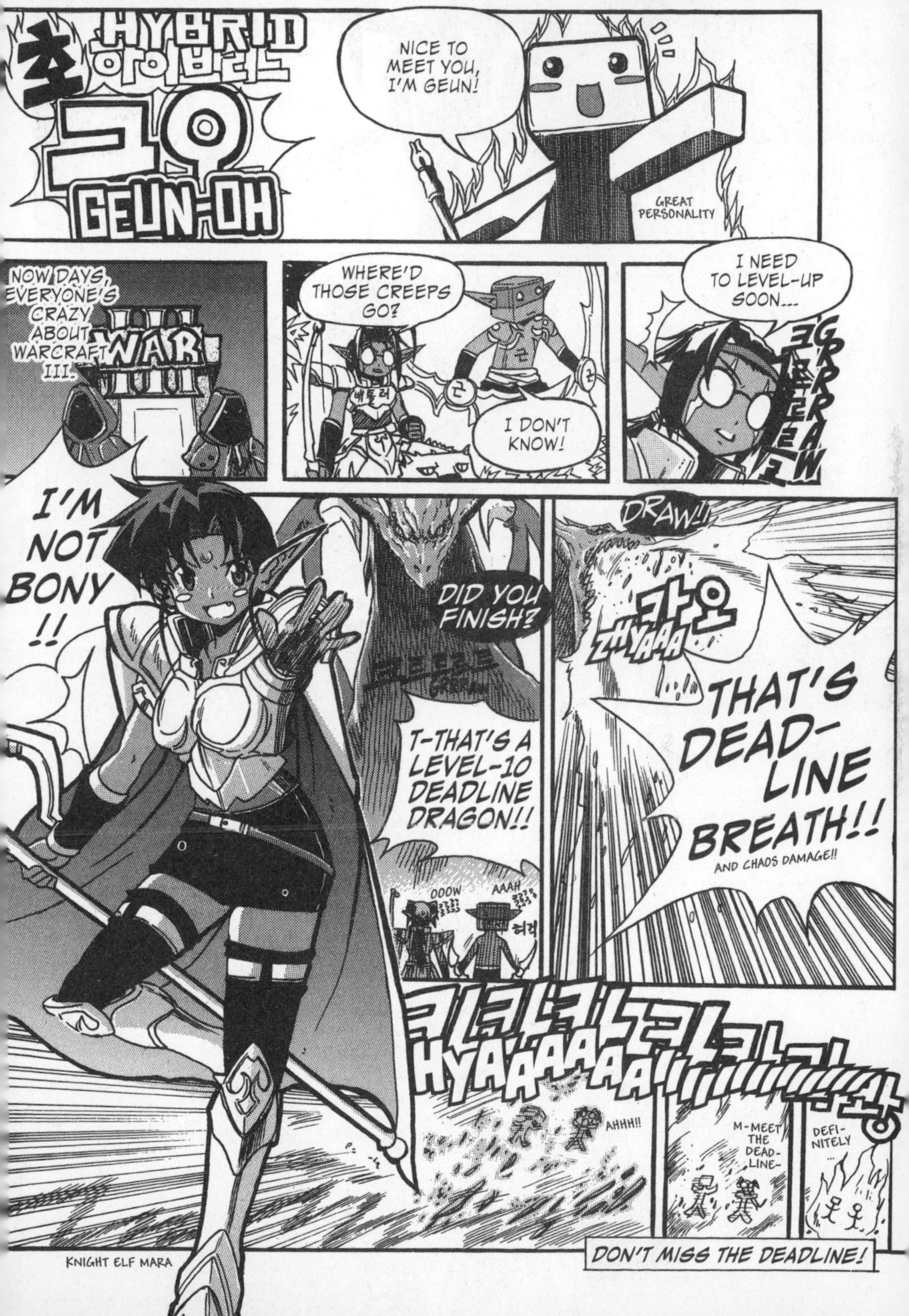
HYBRID
하이브리드
GEUN-OH
NICE TO MEET YOU, I'M GEUN!
GREAT PERSONALITY
NOW DAYS EVERYONE'S CRAZY ABOUT WARCRAFT III.
WAR III
WHERE'D THOSE CREEPS GO?
I DON'T KNOW!
I NEED TO LEVEL-UP SOON...
GRRRRAW
I'M NOT BONY !!
KNIGHT ELF MARA
DID YOU FINISH?
T-THAT'S A LEVEL-10 DEADLINE DRAGON!!
OOOW
AAAH
DRAW!!
카오
ZHYAAA
THAT'S DEAD-LINE BREATH!!
AND CHAOS DAMAGE!!
HYAAAAAAAIIIIIIIII
AHHH!!
M-MEET THE DEAD-LINE~
DEFI-NITELY ...
DON'T MISS THE DEADLINE!

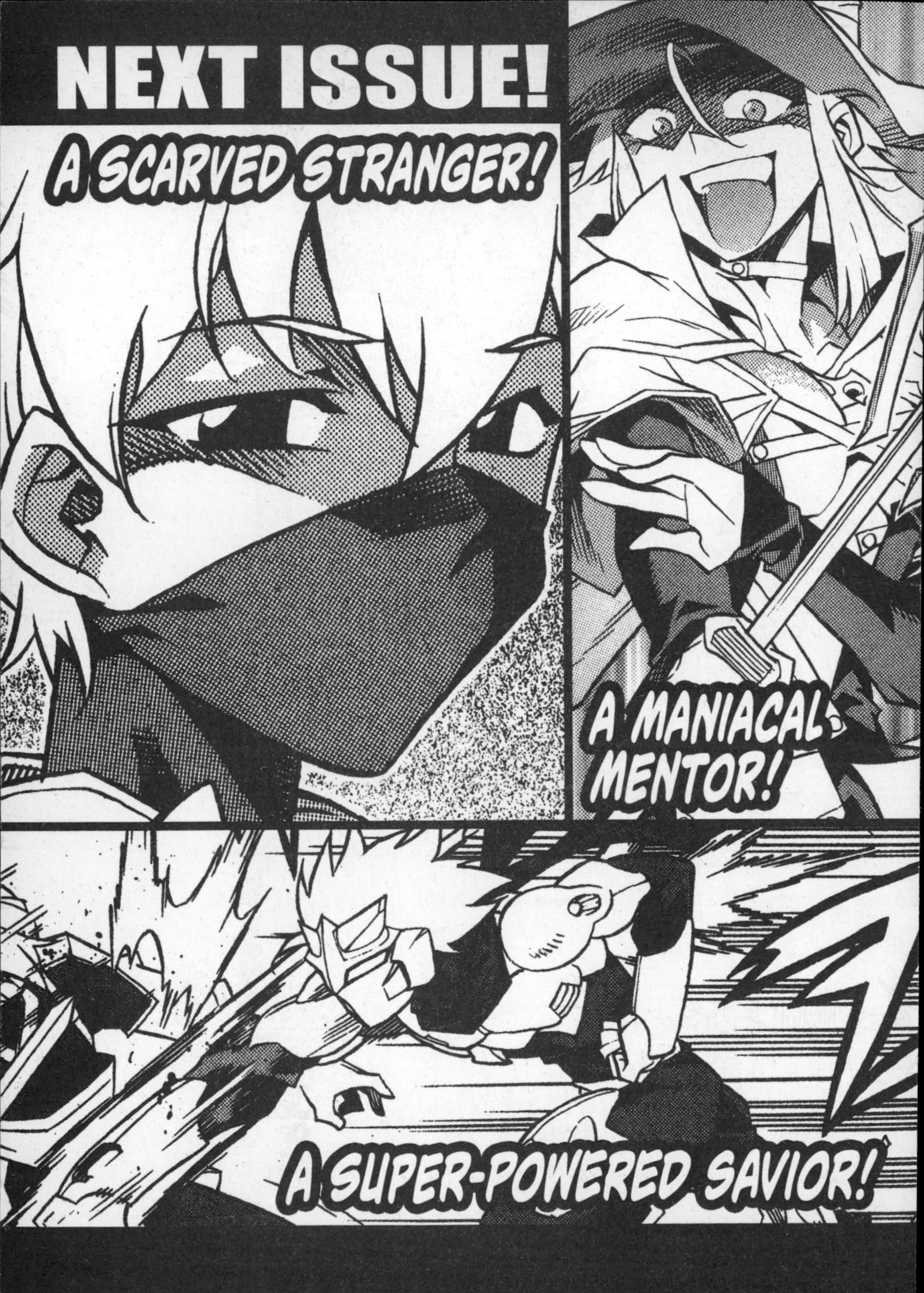
NEXT ISSUE!
A SCARVED STRANGER!
A MANIACAL MENTOR!
A SUPER-POWERED SAVIOR!

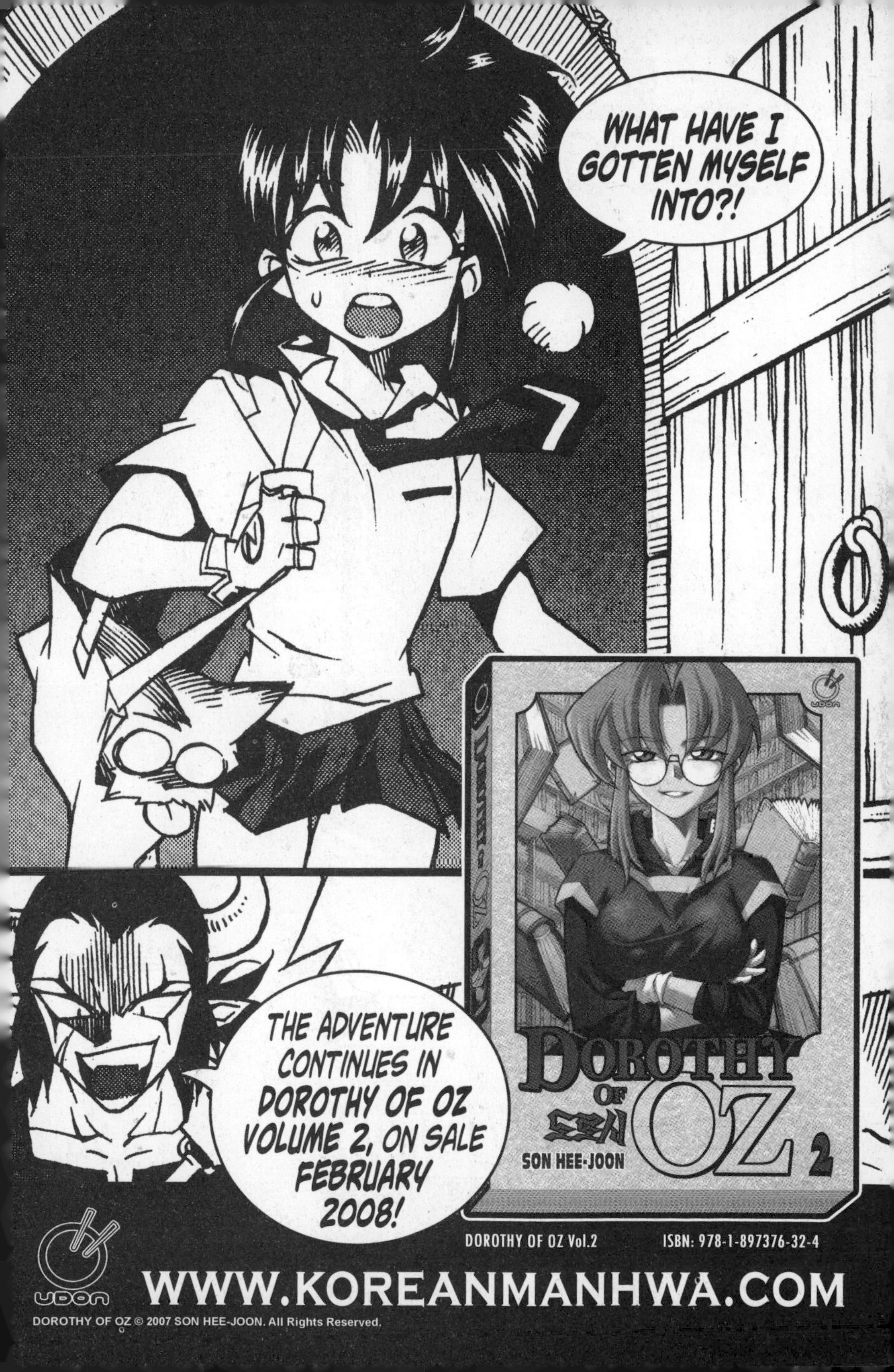
WHAT HAVE I GOTTEN MYSELF INTO?!
THE ADVENTURE CONTINUES IN DOROTHY OF OZ VOLUME 2, ON SALE FEBRUARY 2008!
DOROTHY OF OZ
SON HEE-JOON
2

ISBN: 978-1-897376-32-4

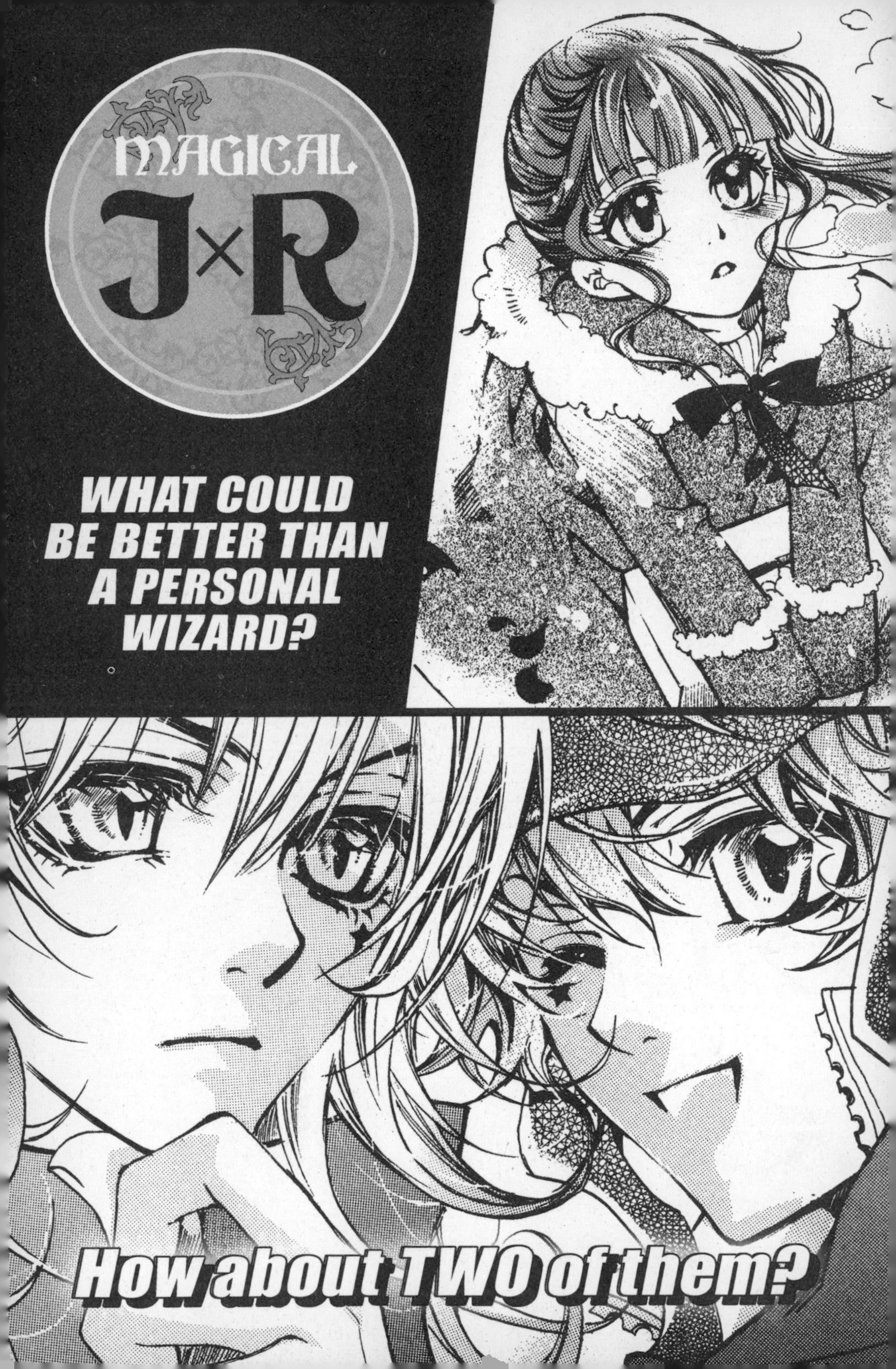
MAGICAL
J×R
WHAT COULD BE BETTER THAN A PERSONAL WIZARD?
How about TWO of them?

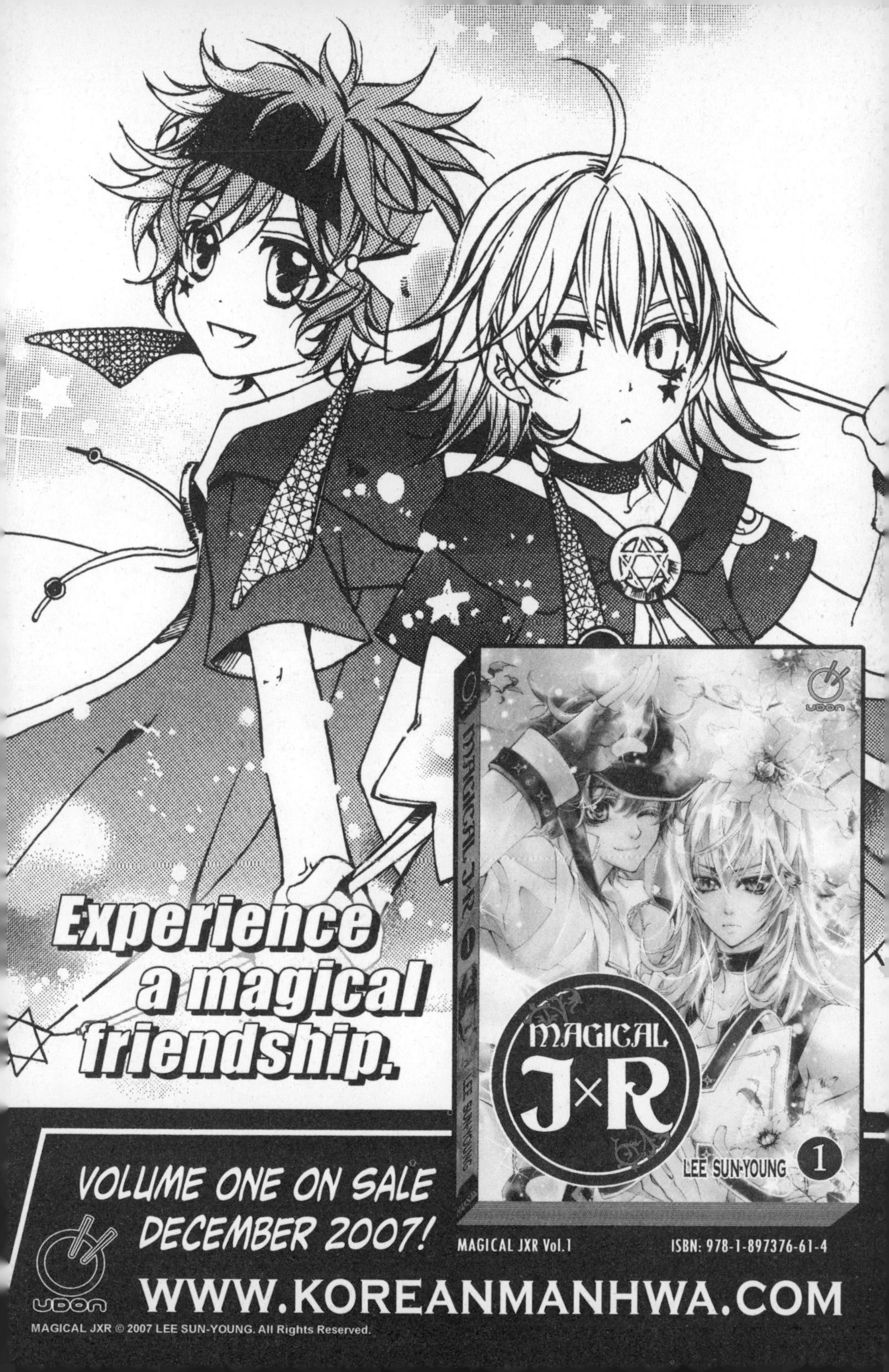

Experience
a magical
friendship.
MAGICAL
J×R
LEE SUN-YOUNG
1
VOLUME ONE ON SALE
DECEMBER 2007!
MAGICAL JXR Vol.1
ISBN: 978-1-897376-61-4
WWW.KOREANMANHWA.COM
MAGICAL JXR © 2007 LEE SUN-YOUNG. All Rights Reserved.

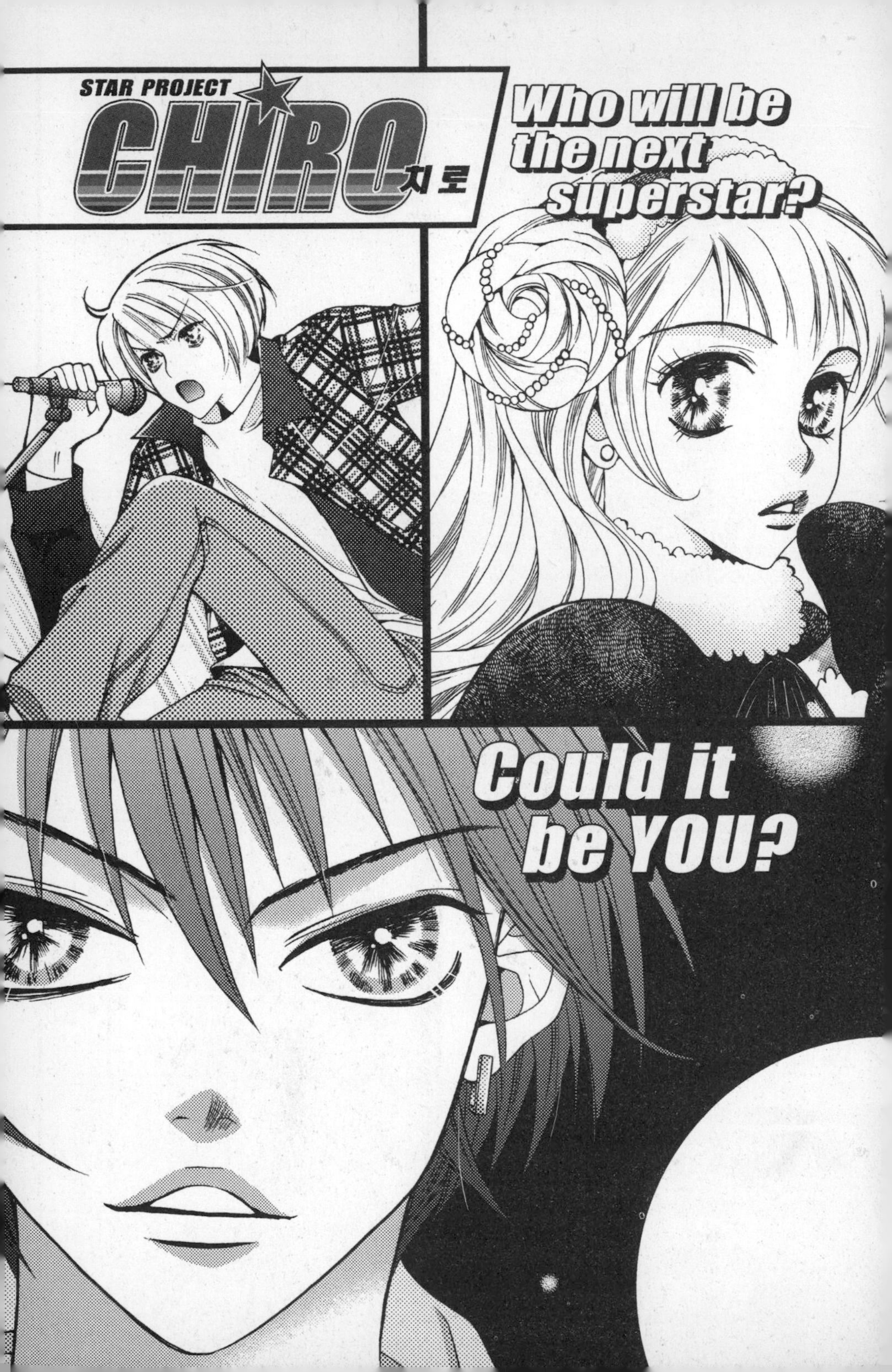
STAR PROJECT
CHIRO
치로
Who will be the next superstar?
Could it be YOU?

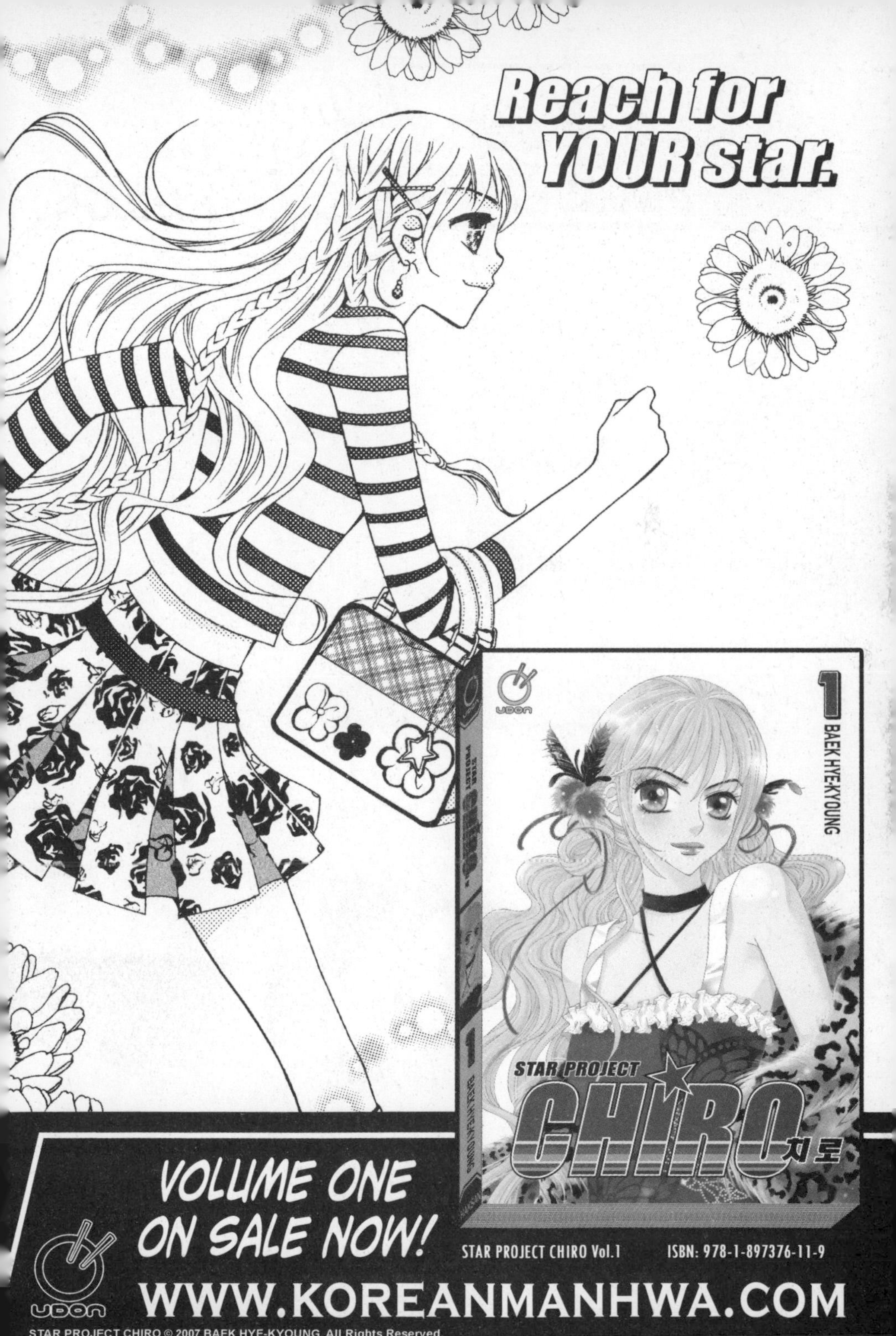
Reach for YOUR star.
UDON
1
BAEK HYE-KYOUNG
STAR PROJECT
CHIRO 치로
VOLUME ONE
ON SALE NOW!
STAR PROJECT CHIRO Vol.1
ISBN: 978-1-897376-11-9
UDON
WWW.KOREANMANHWA.COM
STAR PROJECT CHIRO © 2007 BAEK HYE-KYOUNG. All Rights Reserved.

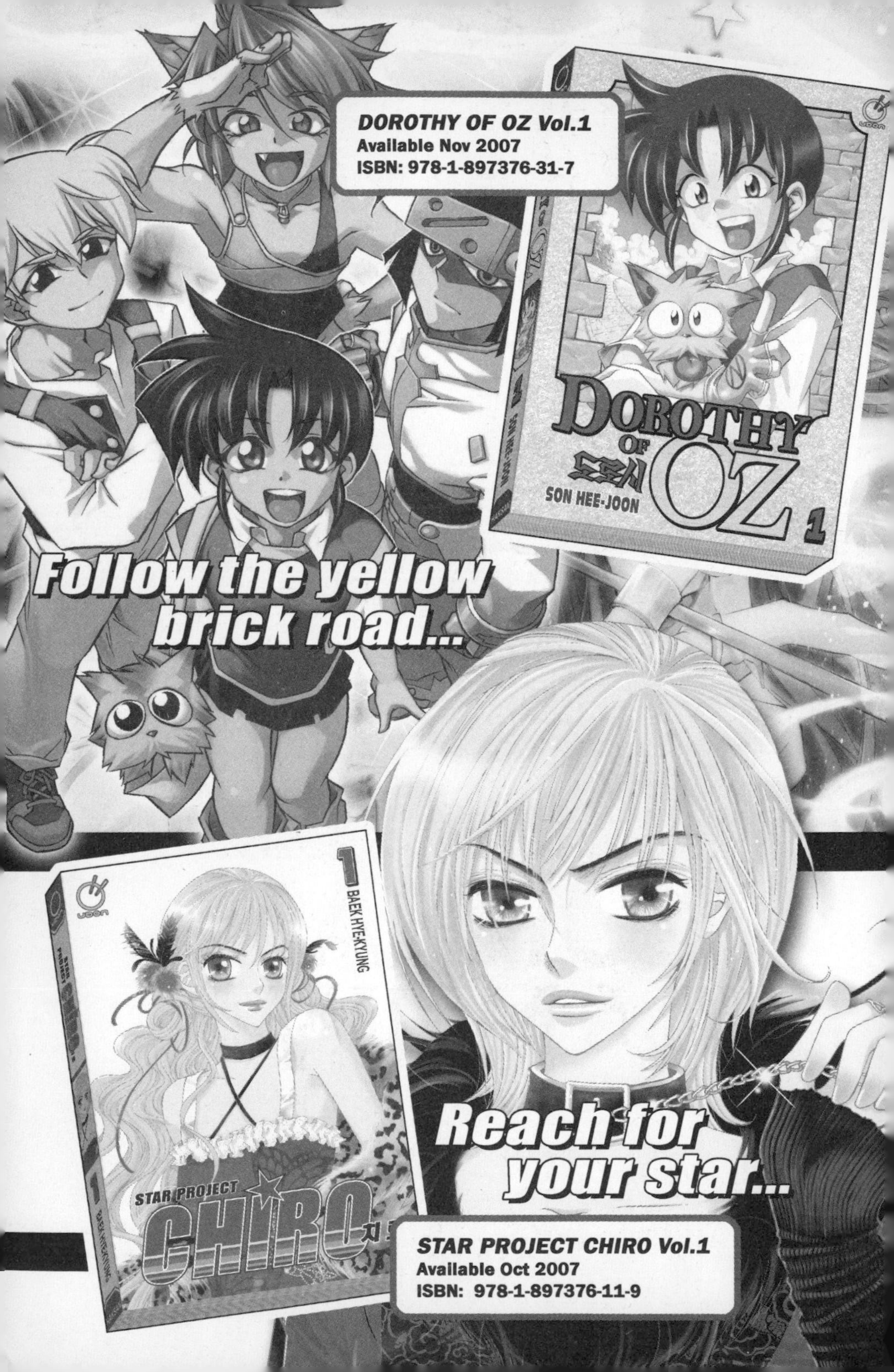
DOROTHY OF OZ Vol.1
Available Nov 2007
ISBN: 978-1-897376-31-7
DOROTHY OF OZ
도로시
SON HEE-JOON
1
Follow the yellow brick road...
1
BAEK HYE-KYUNG
STAR PROJECT CHIRO
Reach for your star...
STAR PROJECT CHIRO Vol.1
Available Oct 2007
ISBN: 978-1-897376-11-9

KOREAN MANHWA

Combine unique storytelling techniques and manga-influenced artwork with the rich and diverse culture of Korea and you'll end up with the latest craze in Asian comics – Korean Manhwa!

Learn more at our web site:

WWW.KOREANMANHWA.COM

DOROTHY OF OZ Volume 1

Story and Art : Son Hee-Joon

English Translations : Nahee Jung
English Adaptations : Kevin M. Kilgore

Editorial Consultant: J. Torres
Coordinating Editor: Hye-Young Im

Lettering : Marshall Dillon with Terri Delgado

Cover & Graphic Design :
Erik Ko with Matt Moylan

English Logo : Alex Chung

DOROTHY OF OZ #1
©2007 SON HEE-JOON.
All Rights Reserved. First published in Korea by Haksan Publishing Co., Ltd.
This translation rights arranged with Haksan Publishing Co., Ltd.
through Shinwon Agency Co. in Korea.

English launguage version produced and published by UDON Entertainment Corp.
P.O. Box 32662, P.O. Village Gate, Richmond Hill, Ontario, L4X 0A2, Canada.

www.udonentertainment.com

First Printing: October 2007   ISBN-13 : 978-1-897376-31-7   ISBN-10 : 1-897376-31-6
Printed in Canada